The Roman father, with his monopoly of property rights and power of life and death over his children, has been prominent in the formulation of the concept of patriarchy in European thought. However, the severe, authoritarian image, based on legal rules and legends, provides, according to Professor Saller, a misleading view of relations between the generations in Roman families. Starting from a demographic analysis, aided by computer simulation of the kinship universe, he shows how the family changed through a Roman's life course, leaving many children fatherless. Examination of the Roman language, *exempla* and symbolic behaviour of family relations reveals the mutuality of family obligation within the larger household in which children and slaves were differentiated by status marked by the whip. The concerned, loving father appears as a contrast to the exploitative master. An understanding of demography and cultural values, in turn, yields insights into the use of the sophisticated Roman legal institutions of inheritance, guardianship and dowry for the transmission of patrimony essential to the continuity of family status.

This book contains much of importance to scholars and students of ancient history and classics and also to those whose interests lie in the field of historical demography.

D1478196

Patriarchy, property and death in the Roman family

Cambridge Studies in Population, Economy and Society in Past Time 25

Series editors

PETER LASLETT, ROGER SCHOFIELD, and E. A. WRIGLEY

ESCR Cambridge Group for the History of Population and Social Structure

Recent work in social, economic and demographic history has revealed much that was previously obscure about societal stability and change in the past. It has also suggested that crossing the conventional boundaries between these branches of history can be very rewarding.

This series exemplifies the value of interdisciplinary work of this kind, and includes books on topics such as family, kinship and neighbourhood; welfare provision and social control; work and leisure; migration; urban growth; and legal structures and procedures, as well as more familiar matters. It demonstrates that, for example, anthropology and economics have become as close intellectual neighbours to history as have political philosophy or biography.

For a full list of titles in the series, please see end of book

Patriarchy, property and death in the Roman family

RICHARD P. SALLER

Professor of History and Classics,
University of Chicago

CAMBRIDGE
UNIVERSITY PRESS

Published by the Press Syndicate of the University of Cambridge
The Pitt Building, Trumpington Street, Cambridge, CB2 1RP
40 West 20th Street, New York, NY 10011-4211, USA
10 Stamford Road, Oakleigh, Melbourne 3166, Australia

First published 1994
Reprinted 1996
First paperback edition 1997

Printed in Great Britain by the University Press, Cambridge

A catalogue record for this book is available from the British Library

Library of Congress cataloguing in publication data
Saller, Richard P.
Patriarchy, property and death in the Roman family by Richard P. Saller.
p.   cm. – (Cambridge studies in population, economy, and society in past time: 25)
Includes bibliographical references and index.
ISBN 0 521 32603 6 (hardback)
1. Family – Rome.   2. Patriarchy – Rome.   3. Property – Rome.
I. Title.   II. Series
HQ511.S35   1994
306.85'0945'632–DC20   93-45700   CIP

ISBN 0 521 32603 6 hardback
ISBN 0 521 59978 4 paperback

UP

To my parents

Contents

ix

Tables

x

Preface

This book has taken shape gradually over the past decade, prompted initially by a sense that too little research had been done on the subject of the Roman family. Since the early 1980s a stream of valuable books and articles has appeared, many of them designed to bring the neglected people of the Roman empire, women and children, into the historical narrative. I have only a little to add to those works. Instead, I wish to return to the figure represented by (male) Roman authors as the center of the family and household, the *paterfamilias*, so familiar in his severe authority. The familiarity has bred neglect or the repetition of stereotypes. There is more to be said about Roman patriarchy, in my view, in order to appreciate the complexities of daily experience in the Roman household and to understand the nuances of paternal authority in Roman ideology.

Some of the basic themes of the following chapters have been presented in my articles, but none of the chapters is a reprint of those articles. I have substantially rewritten to take account of criticisms, to reformulate arguments, and to add new materials. Perhaps the most substantial change in my thinking from the earliest articles is an increased awareness of the need to distinguish between the normative order of Roman culture and the diffuse experiences and individual choices of daily social life. Failure to pursue that distinction, it seems to me, has left Roman historians arguing at cross-purposes about issues such as the "nuclear family," which was at once central to the normative order and in practice often disrupted by death or divorce. My aim is to present an account of the Roman family experience that encompasses the normative order (Part II), the demographic vagaries of the life course (Part I), and, within the circumstances thus created, the strategic choices made by Romans in the transmission of their property (Part III).

During a decade of research, I have accumulated more debts than I can remember. Through the years, my old teachers and friends in Cambridge have continued to provide support and guidance. Sir Moses Finley, who at first summarily dismissed the historical interest of the subject, generously read some early papers and gradually came to accept the Roman family as a useful field of research; I would like to believe that he would have been particularly interested in the conclusions of the chapters on whipping and guardianship, composed long after his death. John Crook and Peter Garnsey read many of the chapters and provided valuable suggestions: the influence of their ideas about law and society (though not their erudition) is evident in the following pages. I owe a particular debt of gratitude to my friend and colleague, Brent Shaw, whose collaboration over the years has stimulated my own work and broadened my perspective. David Johnston kindly gave me the benefit of his legal expertise by reading chapters 7–9 and saving me from at least some of the mistakes that a non-lawyer will inevitably make in discussing legal sources. I have also profited greatly from intellectual exchange with Bruce Frier, to whom I am grateful for permission to use his study of the Egyptian household census data in advance of publication.

An originally fortuitous connection with the Cambridge Group for the History of Population and Social Structure has ultimately had an immeasurable impact on the book. For a decade James Smith has generously incorporated a Roman model in his work on the microsimulation of historical kinship universes: the results can be found in the tables accompanying chapter 3, which are essential to a better understanding of the Roman life course. Jim Oeppen also provided valuable help in adapting the simulation to illuminate the Roman experience. Peter Laslett's keen personal interest and intellectual enthusiasm have pushed this project to completion.

Over the years I have presented much of the material to seminars and workshops around the world, and can only offer a general thanks to those who gave me comments and suggestions. My graduate students at Chicago (1984–93) and at Berkeley (1989) have helped me clarify my thinking through discussions in graduate seminars. Special thanks are due to my research assistants, Sara Gentili, Brian Messner, and Ilse Mueller, without whom the book would not yet be finished. In particular, I want to acknowledge Ilse Mueller's survey of the funerary inscriptions of *CIL* 6 compiled in Table 2.2.a, material which I omitted in my earlier study of men's age at marriage.

Several institutions have provided support over the years. The National Endowment for the Humanities and the Center for Advanced Studies in the Behavioral Sciences supported a leave in 1986–87. Trinity College, Cambridge, gave me the luxury of a term to write in marvellously hospitable surroundings in the autumn of 1991. The American Philosophical Society provided a grant to enable me to travel to Cambridge to work on the simulation. The University of Chicago and a Biomedical Research Support Grant, PHS 2 507 RR–07029–25, have made funds available to complete the research and to prepare the manuscript for publication. Finally, I am grateful to Linda Bree for her meticulous care in editing the typescript for publication.

Abbreviations

The abbreviations of titles of ancient works are the standard ones listed in the *Oxford Classical Dictionary*. Journal titles have been abbreviated in accordance with *L'Année Philologique*. The following abbreviations are used for standard reference works:

CIL   *Corpus Inscriptionum Latinarum*
FIRA *Fontes Iuris Romani Antejustiniani*. 3 vols. (1941–43)
ILS   *Inscriptiones Latinae Selectae*, ed. H. Dessau (1892–1916)
PIR   *Prosopographia Imperii Romani*
RE   Pauly-Wissowa-Kroll, *Real-Encyclopaedie der classischen Altertums-wissenschaft* (1894–)

1

Introduction: approaches to the history of the Roman family

The discipline of history began nearly two and a half millennia ago with the study of war and politics. Little more than two and a half decades old, the subfield of family history is still struggling to agree on the right questions and the appropriate level of generalization.[1] The family as a historical phenomenon can be both banal and symbolically charged. It can be banal in the sense that family life so thoroughly permeates our experience that a description of mothers, fathers and children may hold few surprises and little interest. Roman authors believed family formation and the organization of the household to be natural steps in social evolution, rather than a matter of culturally specific development susceptible to historical analysis (Cicero, *Off.* 1.54).

At the same time, as a nearly universal experience, family relations have been used as a politically charged barometer of moral and social wellbeing. This is true today, as sociologists attempt to measure the disintegration of the family and the popular media carry stories such as the *Chicago Tribune's* front-page series entitled "Killing our Children."[2] The moral preoccupation with the family can be found in ancient Rome as well. In accounts of the horrors of the civil wars of the last century before Christ, stories of the violation of family bonds were narrated to illustrate social breakdown, and stories of family loyalty were told in praise of individual virtue.[3] When Augustus enforced a new regime on the Romans, his legislation to improve society focussed primarily on matters of family and household – marriage, child-bearing, and slavery.[4] Despite these laws, laments of moral decay within the family echoed down through the generations, to be exploited by early Christian communities claiming a higher morality.

[1] Anderson 1980; Kertzer and Saller 1991: ch. 1.
[2] On July 19, 1993, the annual toll stood at thirty-five, of whom eighteen were the victims of abuse within their own homes. [3] Appian, *BCiv.* 4.13, *ILS* 8393
[4] Treggiari 1995

For the Roman historian, the central methodological challenge of family history is to rescue it from banality by asking significant questions answerable with the available evidence. The kinds of generalizations found in modern sociological discussions of the disintegration of families are mostly beyond the Roman historian's reach. In the nearly complete absence of quantitative evidence, much less a reliable time series of quantitative data, we are quite unable to identify trends in marriage, divorce, and child-bearing. The inconclusive debate over the frequency of divorce in imperial Rome shows how helpless we are with respect to such questions.[5] The sort of analysis done by Wrigley and Schofield suggesting economic influences on family formation over centuries of modern English history, in particular the relation between rates of marriage and real wages, is well beyond the reach of the ancient historian.[6] The Roman social historian must settle for painting with a broader brush.

This book aims to explore three general aspects of Roman family life which differentiate it from family life in the contemporary west. The three aspects, represented in the title, are "Patriarchy, property and death." The Roman family has been central to the elaboration of the image of primitive patriarchy. A recent sociological collection entitled *Fatherhood and Families in Cultural Context* begins its "Historical overview of concept of fathering" with the tale of the father Verginius' execution of his daughter to save her from violation and the absolute powers granted to fathers by Roman law.[7] Such stories convey a powerful image of patriarchy, but are the stuff of legendary caricature, not to be mistaken for sociological description. They do not make good social history, nor even good cultural history, without careful nuancing. I do not mean to deny that the Roman normative order endowed fathers with power and authority in the household, but the quality of that patriarchy is often exaggerated and misunderstood. The stark image of the severe, all-powerful father is a legal construct which too easily ignores the complexities of human relationships in everyday life. The hundreds of letters of Cicero, our most intimate evidence for the day-to-day experiences of Roman families, give no hint of the exercise of the absolute legal powers of the father. At the level of Roman cultural values, the paternal caricature has tended to distract historians from exploring how the Romans construed the father figure in a social context pervaded by slavery. Part II presents an analysis of how the Romans defined their family and household within the slave context, and then seeks to understand how the quality of family relationships was construed and affected in practice by the presence of slaves. Latin texts over four

---

[5] Compare the views of Treggiari 1991c and Bradley 1991: ch. 7.
[6] Wrigley and Schofield 1981: 421–25
[7] Tripp-Reimer and Wilson 1991: 1–2, citing Veyne 1987.

centuries reveal a strong polarity in Roman thought between the power of the master, enforced by the whip, and the dutiful affection of the father.

Roman families of all social strata sought their basic sustenance primarily from agriculture. Property transmitted within the family, more than anything else, determined a Roman's place in the social hierarchy. That feature Roman society shared with many others before industrialization. Rome's special interest lies in the sophisticated set of institutions and instruments that Roman law provided for the protection and transmission of property. On account of the flexibility permitted by these institutions and instruments, the historian will look in vain through the legal corpus for a clearly structured "system" of property transmission of the sort that family historians of other eras can identify, such as primogeniture or ultimogeniture. Part III examines how the possibilities created by the legal institutions of inheritance, guardianship, and dowry were manipulated by individuals within the particular Roman demographic, social, cultural, and economic context. My model in these chapters envisages individual Romans pursuing strategies through a wide array of legal instruments toward goals given meaning by shared values within a demographic context marked by high and unpredictable mortality.

Since the transmission of property within the family was associated with major events in the life course, an understanding of it must incorporate a knowledge of the patterns of the basic events of life. Death, marriage, and birth occurred in rhythms in the Roman world quite different from, and much less predictable than, those of contemporary experience. While classicists are aware of the difference in regard to infant mortality, their general sense of the changing shape of the family and kin circle through the usual life course is much less satisfactory. Part I reviews the evidence for the Roman patterns of death, marriage and birth, and then explores the implications for the family unit through a computer microsimulation. The results of the simulation will affect our views of the configuration of authority in Roman families and will help us to make sense of important features of Roman strategies in the transmission of property. In particular, the simulation shows how the combination of high mortality and late male marriage limited the application of paternal power, as most Romans lost their fathers before adulthood.

It may be worthwhile to add briefly what this book does not attempt to offer and why. It is not a general and comprehensive description of the Roman family, which is now available in S. Dixon's *The Roman Family*. My special interest is in the father and intergenerational relations, in part because the subject of women in the family and marriage has been well served in the past few years by other historians, and also because European social and political thought has given the Roman father a special prominence.[8]

In treating "the Roman family," the book is concerned with family life in regions of the Latin-speaking western empire affected by Roman culture during the classical era (c. 200 BC – AD 235). This focus inevitably biases the study toward the urban and elite populations that left written testimony to their family relations. It is not meant to be a judgment about the value of the history of the rural, working classes, but a pragmatic recognition of the limits of our sources. Where the evidence permits, I try to take the analysis to social strata below the elite. However, since so much of the local written evidence from the western provinces comes in standard Roman cultural formulae inscribed on stone and erected in towns, there is no point in pretending that the historian can adequately capture the regional variations in family practices in the vast unromanized areas away from the towns. The census data from Egypt lead us to expect differences in household formation between towns and countryside, but the nature of those differences cannot be described with the available evidence.[9]

The approach of this book diverges from some earlier influential studies, which advance diachronic theses about the development of family affection. My approach has only a small diachronic dimension and does not make affection the main subject. The synchronic analyses of the following chapters seek to describe the complex relations among demographic patterns, cultural definitions and values, and individual aims within a highly elaborated legal framework. There are few diachronic arguments because of the methodological difficulties in demonstrating changes in family senti-ments and practices. I believe that those difficulties are not always fully acknowledged by historians.[10] To trace change in social relations with confidence requires a series of comparable evidence over time. The uneven preservation of material from antiquity largely frustrates the historian's search for a time series of evidence of tolerable quality. Perhaps the best series is to be found in the law, but the relation of law to social practice and ideology is problematic and does not permit the historian easy deductions about the nature of family life. Moreover, the principal legal institutions and instruments discussed in the following chapters were already in place by the second century before Christ, when Roman society began to emerge into the light of history and Latin authors for the first time wrote works that have survived. The earliest authors show that the written will was already being used to divide family estates among heirs and legatees and to choose guardians, that marriage *sine manu* and divorce were already practiced, and

[8] See especially Treggiari 1991a, Dixon 1988, and Gardner 1986.
[9] Bagnall and Frier 1994: ch. 2.3.
[10] Bradley 1993 and Treggiari 1991b do express skepticism about change in family life.

that the residual agnatic rules regarding property were already giving way.[11]

Change from earliest times, there must have been, but the nature of that change is beyond our grasp. It is a methodological mistake, I believe, to take the stories of Livy, Dionysius, and Valerius Maximus about the virtuous early Romans as historical description rather than idealizing legend. Those legends tell us something of the ordering of values in the Augustan age, but nothing of family life in fifth and fourth-century BC Rome. By the period of our earliest surviving Latin literary works, the early second century BC, the conquests that placed Rome among the most powerful and richest states of the Mediterranean were already generations in the past, and moralizing authors like Cato were already complaining of decline. We have no contemporary written evidence for family relations from that pristine age before the decline. Historians may either imagine that an age of convergence of ideals and practice really existed in the prehistoric past, or believe that the virtuous age before the decline is a recurrent motif of moral rhetoric and should not be confused with the social realities of the prehistoric era. The latter strikes me as more plausible.[12]

I am deeply suspicious of the standard story of evolution from the severely authoritarian, extended family to the affectionate, simple family. This story overcomes the banality of describing family life by advancing an arresting thesis with a strong intuitive appeal, to judge by its application to various times and places. However, the evolutionary period before spouses, parents and children learned to love each other has been elusive, disappearing when the evidence for the period before the invention of family love is scrutinized.[13] Such is true of Rome.

Roman historians have advanced various hypotheses about the development of affection between spouses or between parents and children.[14] The difficulties with these hypotheses are suggested by the varied chronologies: did family affection develop in the second century BC or the first century BC or the first century of the imperial era? The latest chronology seems obviously to be excluded by Lucretius' poignant verses from the 50s BC about the common desire of men to return home to "the best of wives and children who race to snatch the first kiss and touch their hearts with silent sweetness" (3.894). The truth is that even the early chronology is impossible to sustain in any precise form, because the earliest surviving Latin literature already clearly represents family bonds as affectionate and

[11] Boyer 1950; Gardner 1986: 263; Dixon 1985a; Crook 1986a.
[12] It is interesting that already in the earliest surviving Latin literature, Plautus' characters are discussing whether there really has been a decline in family discipline or whether that sense is just a paternal illusion; see *Bacch.* 410 and *Pseud.* 437.
[13] See Pollock 1983 for a powerful critique of the evolutionary scheme of Stone 1977.
[14] Veyne 1978; Manson 1983; Dixon 1991.

pleasurable. Though Plautus may not apply the adjectives *dulcis* (sweet) and *suavis* (pleasant) to children in his plays, that argument from silence hardly proves the absence of parental affection, as has been claimed.[15] In Plautus' plays, fathers use diminutives to express affection toward their daughters (*Poen.* 26, 1105; *Rud.* 39), and children are referred to as "my pleasure" or "your chick" (*Poen.* 1292). As part of the background of the plot of the *Menaechmi* (334–36), Plautus tells of a father who died of heart-sickness after the disappearance of one of his seven-year-old sons. Terence's comic characters speak of sons as the "pleasure" of their parents (*delectatio, Heaut.* 987) and explicitly indicate that a small son (*parvolus*) is expected to give his parents "delight" (*oblectatio, Adelph.* 49). Whatever the realities of family relations in the second century BC, Romans could certainly imagine families motivated by affection.[16] The works of other literary genres of this early period are very fragmentary, but even the fragments provide evidence of parental affection: the early epic poet Ennius has Ilia, the legendary mother of Romulus and Remus, address her sister as the one "whom our father loved" (*amavit*) (*Annales* I.36, Skutsch). If there existed an era in Roman history devoid of parental affection, it simply cannot be documented.

The empirical case for the emergence of conjugal affection is similarly doubtful. In Roman comedies male characters marry female characters out of passion and affection. Older male characters, it is true, make disparaging jokes about their wives and the trials of married life, but such jokes hardly exclude conjugal affection, as contemporary experience shows. Against Foucault's widely repeated suggestion that marriage took on a novel importance in noble Romans' construction of their subjective identity in the imperial era, it should be pointed out that the father of Latin prose literature, Cato, regarded it as higher praise to be judged a good husband than a great senator.[17] I know of no comparably strong statement about the importance of marriage from an imperial senator. Given the lack of empirical support, the evolutionary story of Roman family life ought to go the way of other simplistic evolutionary interpretations applied to early Roman history, such as the religious evolution from animism to anthropomorphism.[18] These schemes, I would suggest, are more the product of deep-seated presuppositions about early society than of convincing evidence.

---

[15] Emphasized by Manson 1983 and repeated by Dixon 1991.

[16] For a fuller discussion of the value of comedy as historical evidence for Roman family life, see Saller 1993

[17] Plutarch, *Cato maior* 20.2. How this statement of principle affected Cato's family life is impossible to know, but this statement and the evidence of comedy demonstrates that family affection and devotion were not later discoveries of the Romans. Foucault's discussion (1986) about the inflection in subjectivity in favor of the marriage bond omits the evidence of Cato. For a critique of Foucault's position, see Cohen and Saller 1994.

[18] North 1989 deploys new archaeological evidence to challenge this once standard view.

The effort to write Roman family history in terms of trends in affection is, in my view, methodologically misconceived for at least two reasons. First, as Plautus' comedies or Cicero's letters show, family bonds were for the Romans a complex mixture of love and frustration, discipline and leniency, devotion and independence, as they have been in other times. The mixture of these qualities must have varied greatly from family to family within Roman society at any particular moment, with the result that it is unclear how a chronological trend over the generations could be established. The usual method has been to resort to selective quotation. For instance, L. DeMause in his influential *The History of Childhood* made the claim on the basis of selected quotations and examples that mankind has progressed from the pre-Christian age of child abuse to the enlightened modern era of affectionate attention to children's interest. Given the variety of family experiences in any age, a different choice of examples would be possible, and the developmental scheme could even be reversed by quoting ancient authors on paternal love and then the current series in the *Chicago Tribune*, "Killing our Children," for contemporary child abuse. The point is that the extremes of loving devotion and cruel abuse can be found in many societies, so that any defensible account of change will have to be written in terms of shifts in patterns within the extremes. But it is difficult to imagine what kinds of evidence the Roman historian could find to document broad behavioral *patterns* of family affection or abuse.

Second, the problem of evidence is exacerbated by the fact that affection is demonstrated through culturally constructed expressions whose meanings must be interpreted through the eyes of the historical actors (not the historian) and have been subject to revaluation. For instance, increasing divorce in Roman society (if it could be securely documented) could easily be interpreted by the historian as evidence of a weakening conjugal bond. Yet, as B. M. Rawson rightly points out, more frequent divorce could also be a positive sign, the result of higher expectations and more freedom to pursue emotional satisfaction in marriage.[19] At the extreme, it would seem that infanticide and exposure must be incontrovertible evidence of lack of affection toward newborns, yet P. D. A. Garnsey has pointed out that such practices could also be interpreted as the result of parental concern for the survival of the whole family in economic circumstances demanding "stern realism."[20] Plutarch went so far as to suggest that some poor men, judging poverty a worse fate than death, decided not to rear their children out of love for them (*Mor.* 497E). Given the changing meanings attached to family practices, it is unclear what indicator the historian could use to track changes in the level of family affection. More plausibly, the historian can identify

[19] Rawson 1986: 25.   [20] Garnsey 1991: 49–51.

revaluations of certain practices such as abortion and divorce. Within the classical period, I see no clear evidence for major revaluations, but rather ongoing philosophical debates concerning the value of marriage and child-rearing that preceded and continued after the classical era, with little noticeable effect on behavior.[21] Rather than pursuing an intellectual history through philosophical works, the following chapters aim to illuminate Roman norms and practices of family life through examination of broader demographic, social and cultural patterns, which probably underwent no major changes in the classical era.

[21] Cohen and Saller 1994.

PART I

Roman life course and kinship: biology and culture

The Antonine senator Fronto wrote a moving account of his anguish over the deaths in infancy of his first five offspring and of his first grandson – an experience that would be so rare in the contemporary developed world that it would raise suspicions of criminal wrongdoing.[1] High infant mortality is only one aspect of the very different patterns of births and deaths that separate our own family experiences from those of antiquity. Those demographic patterns are fundamental to an understanding of Roman family relations, and yet are problematic to study. Demography is a discipline based on quantitative data. For the Roman historian, the obstacle to demographic study is the lack of reliable statistics from antiquity and the nearly complete lack of samples of data from which meaningful statistics may be constructed. At the level of family and household, we have records neither of births, marriages, and deaths – the basis of reconstitution studies – nor of household census data for the empire outside Egypt. The absence of solid data may suggest the impossibility of worthwhile demographic studies to many classicists, accustomed to constructing arguments from fixed texts, though of course the fixity of the classical text is sometimes an illusion.[2]

Against any attempt at demographic understanding, the skeptical classical scholar will point out that comparative evidence from other societies cannot supply the data that we do not possess for ancient Rome. The argument against filling in the blanks from comparative material is certainly valid for

---

[1] *De nepote amisso* 2.1–2. Much has been written about the emotional impact of this sensational aspect of ancient mortality patterns (on which see the recent sensitive discussion of Golden 1988).

[2] I am in sympathy with the position of Parkin 1992: ch. 2, except that I think it an exaggeration to say that "demography as a mathematical science deals in facts, not impressions" in contrast to demography of the ancient world (p. 69). Modern demographers use models to analyze data which are problematic, though not nearly as problematic as data from antiquity.

the types of history usually pursued by classical historians. In writing a narrative of singular military and political events, the historian cannot hope that comparative evidence will lead to the discovery of previously unknown behavior. This line of argument, however, is not transferable to the study of the demography of the family, which rests on a few life course events. Birth and death are biological events, albeit interpreted through culture. Marriage is a cultural construct, but was more or less universal in the ancient Mediterranean world. Monogamy in Roman marriage simplifies the possible range of behavior. Thus, in approaching the demography of the Roman family, we are dealing with a limited set of variables, and those variables are heavily constrained by human biology. Consequently, it is possible to think in terms of the range of the probable in regard to mortality, age at marriage, and fertility in a way that is impossible in matters of politics, the wider social organization, or culture. Further, it makes sense to ask how the variables interact, given different probable values for them.

The following chapter will discuss each of the fundamental events of the life course – mortality, age at marriage, and fertility – in an attempt to establish the range of the probable. Then, the next chapter will be devoted to understanding how the probable distributions for each event over the life course interact to produce families and kinship universes of certain sizes and shapes through an individual's life. For instance, how did certain mortality rates and ages at marriage for men and women affect the likelihood that at a given age a Roman would have a mother or father alive? Even though the variables are few, the interactions are complex and best assessed through a computer microsimulation.

The computer microsimulation will be explained in detail in chapter 3, but perhaps a few preliminary words of defense should be offered here to allay the suspicions of classicists likely to view modelling and simulation as little more than a computer fantasy game. This defense is necessary for a humanist, and perhaps especially a classical, audience. In my experience, colleagues in the sciences require no apologetic, because they take for granted computer modelling as a tool to further our understanding of the real world. Models for the purpose of simplification are essential to understanding phenomena comprising individual events so numerous that they cannot be accounted for – indeed, have no significance – when taken individually.

The simulation is not intended to produce an exact replica of the Roman experience, but to reveal the consequences of interactions among variables with assumed values – consequences that are not obvious even in much better documented societies of the early modern era. Thus, to assess the results, the proper question to pose is not whether the numbers generated by the simulation are precisely accurate: they are not, although the appendix to chapter 3 shows that the central features of the model population are similar to those of the household census data from Roman Egypt analyzed by Frier. Rather, the proper question is: would alteration of the input parameters (rates of mortality and fertility, and ages at marriage) within the range of the probable change the results enough to vitiate the particular conclusions being drawn. The value of the microsimulation depends upon formulating questions that can be meaningfully answered in terms of rough proportions rather than exact numbers. The aim in using the computer model is to move beyond unspoken assumptions derived from our own family experience of the twentieth century, with our dramatically longer life expectancy and lower fertility rates. The impact of the demographic transition in the nineteenth and twentieth centuries on the balance between young and old, and the shape of families and kinship universes, can hardly be overstated.[3]

To anticipate another objection to this approach, I should stress that I am not a biological determinist or a quantitative reductionist. The study of the family experience should not be reduced to biology or numbers (Parts II and III focus on social norms and cultural values), and even biological reproduction before the age of modern medical technology was not immune to cultural influences such as customary ages at marriage. Nevertheless, it would be naive to ignore the fact that families were formed and property transmitted in the Roman world in the context of biological events patterned in substantially different ways from modern experience. Common-sense informed only by ancient texts is not adequate to appreciate the consequences of those very different patterns. Within a context of demographic patterns, social practices and legal institutions may take on new and unexpected meanings and significance, which will be explored in Parts II and III.

---

[3] Laslett 1989. If we define as "dependant" on account of age those under fifteen years of age and those over sixty-five, the proportion of the population that is dependant is probably much the same today as it was in antiquity (between 35 percent and 40 percent), but the ratio of those under fifteen to those over sixty-five has changed dramatically from roughly 7:1 in antiquity to 1:1 in contemporary developed societies. (See Table XIII in Coale, Demeny, and Vaughan 1983: 31).

2

Roman patterns of death, marriage and birth

As a pre-transition society, Rome undoubtedly had far higher birth and death rates than those of the industrialized world today: more than 35 births and deaths per 1,000 per year, as compared with less than 10 births and deaths per 1,000 today. The aim of this chapter is to review and evaluate the problematic evidence and arguments for mortality and fertility rates and ages at marriage in the Roman population, and thus to justify the choices for the values of the parameters used in the microsimulation.

Mortality

The mortality experience of a population can be expressed in various ways.[1] Most directly, the mortality rate can be summarized as the number of deaths per thousand per year – a statistic of interest to the historian studying broad trends in the population as a whole. For the historian concerned with the individual and family experience, it is more useful to think in terms of mortality rates at given ages, from which average life expectancy (e) may be derived. Average life expectancy is the average number of years those of a particular age will live and is calculated by adding together the additional years of life of those of a given age and then dividing by the number of individuals in that age group. It is important to keep in mind that average life expectancy is not the typical, or modal, experience. In a population with an average life expectancy at birth of twenty-five ($e_0 = 25$), the most common age at death will be under one year and relatively few will die at age twenty-five.

General agreement among students of Roman demography has emerged in favor of an average life expectancy at birth for the Romans in the range

---

[1] Parkin 1992: 92–111.

of twenty to thirty years.[2] This is a rather crude estimate, glossing over the variations over time, space, class, and gender that undoubtedly existed. Is it possible to discover empirical evidence to fix the average life expectancy of Romans more precisely within this general range and to document differences between segments of the population? This question has generated a debate between those who may be called empiricists (most notably, Frier) and others who may be labelled skeptics (Hopkins and, most recently, Parkin).[3] The debate continues, and while no final conclusions are in prospect, the debate has moved to a far higher level of sophistication than is to be found in Burn's much cited article of forty years ago, "*Hic breve vivitur*: a study of the expectation of life in the Roman empire."[4]

In principle, we would very much like to have reliable empirical evidence to justify assumptions about life expectancy in classical antiquity. Frier in a series of important papers has explored various types of ancient evidence in an effort to produce empirically based life tables for the Roman empire. Because his studies possess the demographic awareness to avoid the pitfalls of some earlier analyses, they form the starting point of the current discussion. In summarizing the debate, I make no attempt at an exhaustive treatment of all the arguments, such as that presented by Parkin.[5]

Ulpian's life table. Over the decades scholars' attention has turned again and again to *Digest* 35.2.68 as a source of demographic information about imperial Rome. This excerpt from Aemilius Macer gives a formula for expectation of life, ascribed to Ulpian. The formula runs as follows: those up to twenty years of age are assigned a life expectancy of an additional thirty years; those between twenty and twenty-four, an additional twenty-eight years; between twenty-five and twenty-nine, an additional twenty-five years; between thirty and thirty-four, an additional twenty-two years; between thirty-five and thirty-nine, an additional twenty years; between forty and forty-nine, the difference between the actual age and sixty, minus one year; between fifty and fifty-four, an additional nine years, between fifty-five and fifty-nine, an additional seven years; any age sixty or older, an additional five years. Frier argues that this formula was developed to calculate the value of life annuities and usufruct so that the beneficiary could be taxed at a rate of five percent of the total value.[6] It replaced a cruder formula, which assigned a life expectancy of thirty years to everyone up to the age of thirty and then subtracted one year for each year over thirty, until a sixty-year-old beneficiary was assigned no additional life expectancy (a

---

[2] Hopkins 1966; Brunt 1971; Frier 1982, 1983; Duncan-Jones 1990: 93–105; Parkin 1992: 84. Of course, the consensus does not prove that the generalization is right, but those who know the comparative evidence for pre-modern societies do not believe that this generalization can be far wrong, for reasons to be discussed below.
[3] See references in n. 2.   [4] Burn 1953.   [5] Parkin 1992.   [6] Frier 1982.

grim prediction, perhaps, but one that saved the elderly beneficiary from paying the inheritance tax). Frier asserts that imperial functionaries used empirical data to construct Ulpian's new formula for the purpose of achieving greater verisimilitude. If the functionaries possessed the appropriate statistical techniques and data, then the formula would be a more reliable guide to life expectancy than any of the surviving problematic evidence (see below). Frier suggests that the formula best corresponds to a model life table with an average expectation at birth in the low twenties.

Frier's argument has been criticized on various grounds, some mutually contradictory. Hopkins, following Greenwood, remains doubtful "that Romans thought analytically about population statistics. In my opinion, the coincidence of Ulpian's interpolations with a modern life table is both approximate and adventitious."[7] Parkin has elaborated the case against believing that Roman functionaries had the requisite statistical data and techniques, and has insisted that any explanation of Ulpian's formula must start from its administrative purpose, which remains uncertain and surely did not demand demographic verisimilitude.[8] For instance, whatever their awareness of the demographic accuracy of the assignment to those over sixty of five years' expectation of life rather than no years, the imperial tax collectors must have realized that Ulpian's formula would make some additional legacies subject to the inheritance tax, thus generating more revenue.[9]

Duncan-Jones has pointed out that the correspondence between Ulpian's formula and Frier's model life table is not particularly close, and that if the expectation of life given by Ulpian is compared with an appropriate set of life tables (Coale–Demeny Model South), an unrealistically low average life expectancy for the whole population (under twenty years at birth) is implied.[10] Duncan-Jones suggests three possible explanations: (1) Ulpian's formula applied to only a segment of the population with an especially dismal life expectancy, ex-slaves who received annuities from former masters; (2) Ulpian's formula was not based on accurate demographic observation; (3) the Roman population, and more recent populations on

---

[7] Hopkins 1987: 121; Greenwood 1940.   [8] Parkin 1992: 27–41.
[9] If neither the heir nor the beneficiary of the legacy was close kin, then both would have had to pay the *vicesima* and the tax revenue would not have changed under the different formulae. But, as often, where the primary heirs were close kin of the testator and hence exempt from the *vicesima hereditatium*, the change of formula would have altered the income to the state.
[10] Duncan-Jones 1990: 96–100. In his review of the book Frier rightly argues that the Princeton Regional Life Tables are models and not meant to represent particular geographical areas. Therefore, there is no justification for using Model South tables; it is better to use the general-purpose tables of Model West. Having made this point, Frier then inexplicably remarks: "Granted the location of Canusium, Model South is likely to be the correct model life table, but certainty is impossible" (1992: 289).

which life tables are based, have had such different experiences that the former cannot be interpreted in terms of the latter. The first of these hypotheses opens the way to a differential demography, which Duncan-Jones pursues with a suggestion that the servile population experienced far higher mortality rates than the elite (see below).

Frier has responded to some of the criticisms, but has also conceded that his earlier argument is problematic.[11] To my mind, the schematism of Ulpian's formula makes it impossible to believe that it was constructed by functionaries who had the three necessary ingredients for a realistic life table: the aim of verisimilitude, the data, and the statistical techniques. For example, the reduction in the new formula of one year of expectation of life for each year lived between ages forty and forty-nine implies a constant expectation of life to age sixty for the entire cohort. If, as Frier suggests, the functionaries were calculating medians, this would further imply that no one died between forty and forty-nine, and then half of those in their fifties died by age sixty. This would appear patently impossible to anyone of any demographic sophistication. Frier recognizes the difficulty and suggests that the explanation of the distortion lies in the habit of age-exaggeration.[12] Such exaggeration could conceivably explain the underrepresentation of mortality of those in their forties, but it cannot account for the overrepresentation of those in their fifties, also implied by the formula. Moreover, to accept this explanation, it would be necessary to believe that the imperial functionaries had the quantitative sophistication to construct a life table from empirical data, and yet were blind to blatant age-exaggeration or unwilling to deal with the distortion. If they were blind to the obvious difficulty, their statistical capabilities cannot have been great; if they chose not to deal with it, then their chief aim cannot have been verisimilitude. Once either alternative is conceded, the value of the formula as demographic evidence is seriously undermined.

Funerary inscriptions. If we cannot depend on the emperor's freedmen to have gathered the data for mortality and analyzed them for us, then we must search for a source of raw data from antiquity that we can analyze for ourselves. Most conspicuous are the thousands and thousands of inscribed funerary commemorations giving the age of the deceased. Attempts have been made to survey those ages at death in order to discover patterns of mortality. The central problem with any such attempt is that those commemorated with an age at death are not a representative sample of all deceased. More than twenty-five years ago Hopkins levelled a devastating

---

[11] Frier 1992.

[12] Contrary to Frier's hypothesis that age-exaggeration among those over fifty-five years old accounts for the peculiarities of the formula, the formula actually significantly *underestimates* the life expectancy of those between fifty-five and sixty-five.

attack on the use of tombstones to produce mortality statistics, and he has recently reasserted his view that "we are dealing with the statistics of commemoration, and not with the statistics of mortality."[13] That is to say, there were cultural preferences, varying by region, for commemorating certain age groups. Not only was the act of erecting an epitaph influenced by cultural norms and by the differing availability of kin to commemorate through the life course, but also the propensity to include age at death in the inscription was culturally conditioned. For instance, among dedications to deceased men from the city of Rome, those from father to son are four times more likely to give an age at death than those from son to father. Obviously, any life table derived from such data will drastically overestimate the mortality of youths in comparison with the mortality of mature men.[14]

In an effort to circumvent the problem of specification of age, Frier looked for a corpus of epitaphs in which age at death is universally given. He found such a group in the region of Cirta in North Africa and argued that the similarity in the distribution of ages at death of five to fifty-year-olds in Cirta and in Mauritius (1942–46) demonstrated the demographic plausibility of the former. He then suggested that in the absence of patent commemorative bias these epitaphs can be taken as representative of the mortality experience in this region of North Africa.[15] Hopkins has replied that the plausibility evaporates when the statistics are disaggregated; in addition, if a demographically plausible sample can be found, it is impossible to know whether the plausibility is a result of true representativeness or of a concatenation of biases, hence without demographic significance.[16] In the end, the sources of commemorative bias are too numerous and too difficult to discern to allow the historian to control for them sufficiently to construct a reliable life table.

Recently, Duncan-Jones has argued against the use of any source which depends on Romans' very imperfect knowledge of their own age and has turned attention to a different type of epigraphic source for life expectancy, the album of Canusium listing members of the town council.[17] The album lists sixty-eight living members who are ex-magistrates. Duncan-Jones reasons that, if we assume that sixty-eight was the number of survivors of

---

[13] Hopkins 1987: 124.

[14] This skewing, which is more pronounced in some regions than in others, leaves me doubtful about the method of Shaw 1991: 66–90, which infers the cultural valuation of an age group from the numbers of deceased with certain given ages. In order to accept his argument about "valuation" of individuals of certain ages, one would have to believe that all those who received a commemoration omitting an age at death were unvalued or undervalued, or that similar proportions across age groups and regions omitted the age at death so that comparisons would be meaningful. The latter premise is demonstrably untrue, and I do not believe that the many funerary monuments dedicated to fathers but without an age at death should be interpreted as a sign of undervaluation of older men.

[15] Frier 1982.   [16] Hopkins 1987: 123–25.   [17] Duncan-Jones 1990: 101–3.

those who had held one of the two quaestorships at age twenty-five, then the average life expectancy at age twenty-five for the group can be calculated. The sixty-eight survivors imply "that expectation of life at twenty-five (e_{25}) is thirty-four years. The closest fit in the Princeton Tables (South) is with Level 6, where expectation of life at birth is 31.7 years."[18] According to Duncan-Jones, this approach is preferable because it does not rely on age-reporting,[19] but he acknowledges factors that could undermine the conclusion: (1) the holding of the quaestorship at ages other than twenty-five; (2) the adlection of influential men in mid-cursus; (3) a singular event that fortuitously affected this particular group of men. On the basis of this evidence and Ulpian's formula, Duncan-Jones ventures to suggest a large gap in mortality rates between the fortunate few, with an average life expectancy at birth somewhat more than thirty years, and the miserable slave population, with a shockingly low life expectancy at birth of less than twenty years.

This line of argument is vulnerable to uncertainties arising from the small size of the population: small changes in the numbers would significantly alter the estimate of life expectancy. As Parkin points out, if the four men listed as *adlecti inter quinquennalicios* did not hold the quaestorship (a possibility allowed by Duncan-Jones), then the number of surviving ex-quaestors declines to sixty-four, the average life expectancy at twenty-five drops to thirty-two years, and e_0 declines to twenty-seven years (if Model South tables are used).[20] Duncan-Jones also realizes that his own argument depends on the regularity of municipal careers – a reasonable assumption, he suggests, to judge by the common formula "O(mnibus) H(onoribus) F(unctus)" in municipal career inscriptions from the later Principate.[21] The orderly holding of the quaestorship, the aedileship and the duumvirate may well have been the ideal, but a glance at the Italian municipal career inscriptions in *Inscriptiones Latinae Selectae* points to the possibility of enough deviation seriously to distort the calculations: there are careers without a quaestorship, iterated quaestorships, underage quaestors, and magistracies out of order (which would mean that the holder would not be at the standard age).[22] Indeed, given the limited circle of curial families in small

---

[18] Duncan-Jones 1990: 94.

[19] In fact, even this approach requires that the local elite of Canusium know and accurately represent their age when standing for the quaestorship.

[20] Parkin 1992: 137–38. Frier 1992: 289, points out that the use of Model West tables rather than Model South would yield a somewhat higher estimate of life expectancy.

[21] Duncan-Jones 1990: 94.

[22] The iterated quaestorship (*ILS* 5365) probably was exceptional; however, career inscriptions listing a series of higher magistracies without a quaestorship are not unusual (*ILS* 3742, 6659, 6662, 6665, 6744, 6745, 6747). These seven cases may be compared with the seventeen Italian cases in *ILS* listing the three municipal magistracies in the standard order. In addition, a similar number of career inscriptions formulaically claim to have held

towns, it would be extraordinary if there had been a regular supply of two and only two twenty-five-year-old men available every year for the quaestorship: early, late, skipped, and repeated magistracies must have recurred to adjust the supply of men to the number of positions.[23]

In sum, I accept the negative conclusions of Hopkins and Parkin that none of the epigraphic evidence is of sufficient quality to fix Roman life expectancy within the probable range or to differentiate among segments of the population.

Skeletal evidence. The hope of progress in the subject of ancient mortality may seem to lie with skeletal evidence. Excavations will provide a continual flow of new evidence, and skeletons do not present some of the problems of epitaphs, in particular, distortion of the age at death by the deceased or commemorator. Frier analyzed the findings from a late imperial Pannonian graveyard excavated at Keszthely-Dobogó.[24] The sample from the burial site includes 120 skeletons, 99 of which were aged at 5 years or older. The distribution by age of those 99, according to Frier, corresponds to a population with an average life expectancy at birth of just over 20 years, close to the experience suggested by Ulpian's formula and the epigraphic data from Cirta.

Unfortunately, the archaeological data based on skeletons are vulnerable to some of the same criticisms as epitaphs, and additional criticisms as well. Burial, like commemoration, was an act subject to cultural influences.[25] All dead may need to be disposed of, but not necessarily in a single cemetery. Consequently, the skeletons of the Pannonian graveyard may not be representative of the population living in the area in the late fourth century of the Christian era. The clearest indication, once again, is the underrepresentation of children under five. Moreover, it is impossible to know whether this population was stable and stationary, necessary assumptions to derive life expectancy from model life tables. A sample as small as the graveyard at Keszthely-Dobogó could be seriously affected by the in- or out-migration of a few families.

---

all offices (but not necessarily *suo anno* [at the minimum age] or in the standard order or each office only once). Although neither *ILS* nor *CIL* can be assumed to present a representative sample of all municipal magistrates, the proportion of irregular careers (well over 10 percent in *ILS*) is enough to cast doubt on the argument and cannot be set aside as a "minor area of imprecision" (Duncan-Jones 1990: 96). If 10 percent of the sixty-eight listed on the album of Canusium skipped the quaestorship, the method used by Duncan-Jones would yield an average life expectancy at birth in the middle twenties – much closer to that assumed for the general population. The imprecision is serious enough that this method yields results no more exact than the general range of probable life expectancies suggested by Hopkins and others.

[23] Hopkins' similar argument for the Roman senate is not so vulnerable to this criticism because the senate was ten times larger and drew on a wider pool of candidates.
[24] Frier 1983.   [25] Morris 1992: ch. 1.

In addition, Parkin and Morris have recently underlined the technical difficulties associated with skeletal evidence. Adult male skeletons are disproportionately likely to survive intact so that they can be aged by the archaeologist, while children's skeletons are more likely to disintegrate. But it is for children's skeletons that archaeologists have the most accurate criteria for determining age. Often based on less than complete remains, estimates of age do not always have the scientific certitude that they may appear to have. Parkin's Table 3 shows that different archaeologists often enough assign to the same skeleton different sexes and ages differing by twenty years or more.[26] In view of these problems, Parkin's pessimism about archaeology providing solutions to demographic questions seems justified.

Egyptian household census data. The census returns from Roman Egypt listing household members and their ages offer the best evidence for the age-distribution of a population of the empire.[27] The census sought to account for the whole population, avoiding some of the biases of selection; the ages given do not appear to be obviously distorted; and through the regular censuses every fourteen years there was some administrative control on reporting.[28] Using a fresh reading of the papyri by Bagnall, Frier has presented a thorough and sophisticated analysis of the census fragments. The age-distribution of living women best corresponds to a slightly growing population with an average life expectancy at birth of about twenty-two and a half years (Coale–Demeny Level 2 West).[29] The distribution of males is more problematic: the shifting sex ratio over the life course (in favor of males under ten and over forty, in favor of females between ten and thirty-nine) suggests that the census records are missing some young men in their teens, twenties, and thirties, perhaps as a result of temporary migration away from home in search of a job.[30]

Although the body of census data was not influenced by biases of commemorative selection, it is problematic in other respects. Obviously, it is not a scientific sample of the Egyptian population; indeed, it is not a sample of a single population at all, since the fragments come from different censuses taken in different places over generations. Yet I am unable to identify any clear indications of major distortions as a result. Duncan-Jones has argued that the census data are unreliable because the recorded ages are self-reported by Egyptians who were as likely to be ignorant of their age as inhabitants of other regions of the empire.[31] Certainly, some of the Egyptian evidence reveals ignorance of age; on the other hand, there are no claims to

[26] Parkin 1992: 142; Morris 1992: 72–90.   [27] Parkin 1992: 19.
[28] Bagnall and Frier 1994: chs. 1–2.
[29] Bagnall and Frier 1994: ch. 4, esp. Table 4.3.
[30] Bagnall and Frier 1994: ch. 5. The problem of sex ratios is illustrated by Parkin 1992: 141 (Table 1) and is cautiously assessed by Frier.   [31] Duncan-Jones 1990: 102–3.

the incredibly high ages found in other types of Roman evidence elsewhere.[32]

At this point, Frier appears to be right in his assertion that "the Egyptian census returns provide what is undoubtedly the best surviving evidence for Roman demography."[33] The question is not whether the data are without problems, but whether they are so problematic as to vitiate all conclusions. Such skepticism does not seem warranted. This is not to say that the finding of female average life expectancy of twenty-two and a half years at birth should be used as a precise result applicable across the empire and across the centuries. Rather, the study of Bagnall and Frier gives empirical support to the broad generalization that in the Roman world average life expectancy at birth was under thirty years. In addition, a comparison of Frier's analysis of the Egyptian census data with the results of the microsimulation (see the appendix to chapter 3) provides reassurance that the central features of the model population generated by the computer are not an unrealistic representation of the Roman experience.

Conclusion. All of the empirical data for mortality from the Roman world are problematic to one degree or another. That in itself is not a damning criticism, since demographers working with census data collected by modern bureaucracies must be constantly aware of anomalies and distortions, and must look for ways to correct raw data in order to arrive at a meaningful set of statistics. The Roman data are far more problematic, to be sure, than census data from contemporary, developed countries (though not more problematic than some collected in underdeveloped nations).[34] Frier's recent studies of various types of data are not without difficulties and uncertainties, and so, taken individually, are not compelling. On the other hand, none of his studies, nor any other recent, serious demographic work on the Roman empire, gives the slightest reason to doubt the standard view of an average life expectancy at birth between twenty and thirty years. There is good reason to think that Duncan-Jones' slightly higher estimate for the decurions of Canusium may be too high, though some difference in mortality rates by class is not intrinsically improbable, though unlikely to be substantial.[35]

If the imperfect data give no reason to doubt the "uncontroversial

---

[32] Bagnall and Frier 1994: ch. 2.

[33] Frier 1992: 290, a view subscribed to by Parkin 1992: 19.

[34] Newell 1988: 24 gives 316 as Whipple's Index for age-rounding in Bangladesh in a census of 1974, a more pronounced rounding than found in some sets of Roman data. See Frier 1992: 288.

[35] See n. 22 above: the largest observable source of distortion, the omission of the quaestorship in municipal careers, would result in an overestimate of life expectancy. For comparative evidence against the assumption of a large difference in life expectancy between classes, see Livi-Bacci 1991: 64.

working assumption about Roman life-expectancy at birth ... within a range between twenty and thirty years,"[36] it can also be said that the information about Roman living conditions gives little reason for a more optimistic estimate, whether one is inclined to stress substandard nutrition or contagious disease as the fundamental cause of high mortality.[37] In a powerful study, Scobie draws a lurid picture of the "squalid condition" of urban life throughout the empire.[38] In a steeply hierarchical society with huge concentrations of wealth and widespread poverty, the imperial and local governments made no attempt to provide a welfare net to insure minimal food, clothing and shelter for the empire's inhabitants. Emperors did occasionally intervene to alleviate food shortages in various parts of the empire. They also managed the grain supply for the privileged residents of Rome, and in the second century provided *alimenta* (a subsistence payment) to some Italian children. But none of this was enough to relieve the chronic malnutrition of the impoverished masses.[39] Infants of the rich and poor were especially vulnerable to deadly gastrointestinal illnesses, and the best-intentioned medical advice directed to the wealthy about nursing the newborn and weaning the infant would not have reduced infant mortality rates and may have increased them.[40]

Roman engineering accomplishments produced some improvement in public hygiene. Aqueducts supplied Rome and other cities with fresh water, and sewers carried away some of the urban refuse. Yet Scobie has shown why the effects of these public works should not be overestimated. A crucial aspect of public hygiene to prevent the spread of disease is the removal of human waste, which carries disease. Scobie points out that latrines in houses were generally not hooked up to sewers for the very good reason that without traps gases and worse would have backed up from the sewers into the house; moreover, the latrines in houses were often next to the kitchens, providing convenient opportunity for contamination of food by insects and rodents.[41]

The impact of a fresh water supply on mortality rates is impossible to assess from the ancient evidence. To make an informed judgment, it is helpful to turn to the experience of urban areas of nineteenth-century England, where "improvements in diet and public sanitation ... (for example, a purer water supply) had little effect on infant mortality, while the crowded

---

[36] Duncan-Jones 1990: 103.
[37] See Livi-Bacci 1991 for a stress on contagious disease and Fogel 1991 for a stress on nutrition and other factors.   [38] Scobie 1986: 399.   [39] Garnsey 1988.
[40] Garnsey 1991: 62–65. Livi-Bacci 1991: 76 cites studies showing that the discrediting of Soranus' advice against feeding the newborn colostrum (milk secreted for a few days after birth, with a high protein and antibody content) *c.* AD 1700 may have "contributed to a notable decline in mortality (nought to 28 days)."   [41] Scobie 1986.

conditions of urban life tended to increase the risk of early infection."[42]
More broadly, the comparative evidence suggests that in the mid-nineteenth
century, before the advent of medical technology effective in the control of
disease, mortality remained "density-dependent."[43] The relatively high
level of urbanization in the early empire reinforces our expectation of high
mortality rates. The deadly effects of dense urbanization are documented in
a new study of seasonal patterns of mortality in the city of Rome in the late
imperial era. In a forthcoming study Shaw finds that the level of mortality,
as evidenced by the date of death registered on tombstones, was more than
50 percent higher in the late summer months than in the healthier months
of winter and spring. The strong seasonality of death is characteristic of
demographic regimes with high mortality due to infectious diseases, which
have been largely suppressed in modern, developed countries. The general
living conditions are the reason why, for all the strenuous debate between
those I have labelled "empiricists" and the "skeptics," in fact they are in
agreement that average life expectancy at birth in the Roman empire was
roughly twenty-five years.

Model life tables. Because mortality and fertility are rooted in human
biology, the distribution of those events by age is not random. In her
uniformitarian theory of human paleodemography, now widely accepted by
demographers, N. Howell argues that the shapes of mortality curves of
different populations, though different, fall into the same essential pattern:
mortality rates are relatively high among newborns, then decline through
the weeks and months after birth as the infant survives the period of highest
vulnerability to disease; mortality rates reach a low point around age ten,
then increase gradually again until the later forties, when they begin to
increase significantly.[44] Although the actual rates at a given age may differ
greatly from one population to another, the lopsided "V" shape of the
mortality curve does not change. Thus, it is highly probable that the Roman
population experienced high mortality distributed by age in a pattern
roughly similar to that of other human populations. This provides the
justification for using model life tables, developed from data from better
documented populations.[45] In their standard work, *Regional Model Life
Tables and Stable Populations* (2nd edition, 1983), Coale and Demeny present
a set of model life tables, beginning with an average life expectancy at birth
of a bare 20 years (labelled Level 1). Tables are presented for progressively

[42] Wrigley 1969: 170.
[43] Wrigley 1969: 175; with regard to infant mortality, Livi-Bacci 1991: 78 suggests that
"the wide divergence in infant mortality in urban areas between different social strata was
attributable above all to environmental factors, such as the density of living conditions
and the easier transmission of infections."   [44] Howell 1976.
[45] Parkin 1992: ch. 2 for a more detailed discussion of the appropriate use of model life
tables.

higher levels of life expectancy at intervals of 2.5 years (so Level 2 for $e_0 =$ 22.5 years, Level 3 for $e_0 = 25$ years, and so on). At each level, four tables with different mortality distributions by age are offered and given regional labels (North, South, East, West). The Model Life Table allows the historian to understand the implications of a demographically realistic mortality distribution – that is, the decline in numbers of a birth cohort as it ages, the resulting changes in average life expectancy, and so on. Because I am not confident that the data from the Roman empire are good enough to justify reliance on any particular life table and because there must have been variation by time and location, I have adopted a different strategy. In what follows, I use Coale–Demeny Model Life Table Level 3 West: Level 3 West not because it is certain to represent *the* Roman experience, but because it provides a general-purpose table that is unlikely to be grossly misleading. With an average life expectancy at birth of twenty-five years, Level 3 falls into the middle of the range of the probable; the region West tables are intended for use where data are not available to make nuanced choices among the regional models.[46] It is a strategy to avoid the need for unattainable precision.

Most of the arguments derived from demography in the following chapters are based on the high rate of mortality and low life expectancy presented by Model Life Table Level 3 West. To assess the effect of a somewhat more optimistic estimate of Roman life expectancy, I will also present Model Life Table Level 6 West ($e_0 = 32.5$) as a kind of upper boundary of the probable range (or the worst case for my arguments, if not for the Romans). If, as Frier's analyses suggest, average life expectancy at birth was actually lower than twenty-five years, at least in Egypt, then my claims (for instance, about the large number of orphans in the population) would be strengthened.

By way of brief explanation of the columns, Age (x) gives exact age, so that age (o) represents the day of birth and age (1) represents the first birthday. The column headed q(x) gives the probability of dying before the next exact age in the table. The column l(x) represents a notional birth cohort which at birth is conventionally set at 100,000 and decreases from one age to the next in accordance with q(x). The column headed e(x) gives the resulting average life expectancy at age (x). Thus, for a Level 3 West Female model population, 30.556 percent of the newborns die by age 1, leaving 69,444 out of an initial cohort of 100,000. The female newborns have an average life expectancy of 25 years, which rises to an additional 34.846 years for the 69 percent fortunate enough to survive to their first birthday. Between ages 1 and 5, 21.582 percent of those survivors die,

---

[46] Coale, Demeny, and Vaughan 1983: 25.

Table 2.1: Model Life Tables Levels 3, 6, 24 West Female

	LEVEL 3 Female				LEVEL 6 Female				LEVEL 24 Female		
Age (x)	q(x)	l(x)	e(x)	Age (x)	q(x)	l(x)	e(x)	Age (x)	q(x)	l(x)	e(x)
0	.30556	100000	25.000	0	.23438	100000	32.500	0	.00905	100000	77.500
1	.21582	69444	34.846	1	.16130	76562	41.342	1	.00104	99095	77.207
5	.06061	54456	40.062	5	.04569	64213	45.031	5	.00063	98992	73.286
10	.04738	51156	37.502	10	.03570	61279	42.079	10	.00053	98930	68.331
15	.06153	48732	34.237	15	.04673	59091	38.541	15	.00092	98877	63.366
20	.07660	45734	31.312	20	.05845	56330	35.303	20	.00135	98786	58.422
25	.08565	42231	28.693	25	.06551	53037	32.333	25	.00177	98652	53.497
30	.09654	38614	26.138	30	.07393	49563	29.417	30	.00236	98478	48.588
35	.10541	34886	23.653	35	.08112	45899	26.558	35	.00353	98245	43.697
40	.11227	31208	21.134	40	.08725	42175	23.673	40	.00583	97898	38.842
45	.11967	27705	18.477	45	.09462	38496	20.688	45	.01051	97327	34.055
50	.15285	24389	15.636	50	.12200	34853	17.578	50	.01713	96304	29.389
55	.19116	20661	12.988	55	.15472	30601	14.659	55	.02822	94654	24.856
60	.27149	16712	10.443	60	.22153	25867	11.866	60	.04680	91983	20.502
65	.34835	12175	8.366	65	.29119	20137	9.503	65	.08510	87678	16.381
70	.47131	7934	6.448	70	.40306	14273	7.339	70	.15148	80216	12.663
75	.60808	4194	4.878	75	.53518	8520	5.540	75	.26073	68065	9.460
80	.73485	1644	3.567	80	.67735	3960	4.039	80	.40074	50318	6.914
85	.86502	436	2.544	85	.82408	1278	2.866	85	.57879	30154	4.862
90	.95126	59	1.784	90	.93072	225	1.994	90	.76776	12701	3.297
95	1.00000	3	1.234	95	1.00000	16	1.364	95	.91501	2950	2.163

leaving 54,456 of the initial 100,000 at age 5, with an average life expectancy of an additional 40.062 years. A glance at the table shows that in this model population, nearly half of the newborns die in childhood before age 10. For those who survive the childhood diseases, life expectancy goes up, and slightly less than one-half of the 10-year-olds live to age 50, a little less than one-third survive to 60, and less than one-sixth to age 70. At age 20 the average life expectancy is an additional 31 years; at age 30, an additional 26 years.

How much difference does it make to use the more optimistic assessment of life expectancy in the model life table for Level 6 Female $e_0 = 32.5$)? In this model infant mortality takes away 23 percent in their first year and 39 percent by age 10. Of the survivors to age 10, 57 percent live to age 50, 42 percent to age 60, and 23 percent to age 70. The average life expectancy at 20 is an additional 35 years; and at age 30, another 29 years. The differences between this model and Level 3 are noticeable, but their magnitude is small when compared with the table for Level 24, representing contemporary experience in the developed world. In the late twentieth century, the first months are still the most vulnerable of childhood, but the mortality rate is about 1 percent, instead of 30 percent (Level 3) or 23 percent (Level 6). Of those who survive to age 10 today, more than 75 percent can expect to reach age 70, in contrast to 16 percent (Level 3) or 23 percent (Level 6). At Level 24 the average life expectancy for females at age 20 is an additional 58 years (31 years at Level 3, 35 years at Level 6). The fact that the differences between Level 3 and Level 6, within the range of the probable, are relatively minor in comparison with Level 24 is the reason why it is possible to draw meaningful social implications from Roman demography, even though there is uncertainty about whether Model Life Table Level 1 or 6, South or West, best fits the Roman experience.

Ages at First Marriage

Of the basic demographic variables, the timing of marriage was most subject to control by individual decision and cultural norms. It is also the variable for which the Roman evidence is soundest, though not unproblematic. Age at first marriage is an important issue for demographers because it establishes the length of time in marriage for legitimate fertility. For social historians, women's and men's ages at marriage are important because they influence the shape of family and household. Hajnal's classic papers on basic family forms drew distinctions based on the timing of marriage: early male and female marriage characterized the eastern type, late male and female marriage the western type, and late male/early female the Mediterranean type.[47]

In a fundamental paper, Hopkins sought to identify the age at which Roman women typically married. His data came from funerary inscriptions giving both the age at death and the length of the marriage. Hopkins showed that the women of these epitaphs married very young: half were married by age sixteen. Hopkins further argued that this conclusion was consistent with the literary and legal evidence. The law set the minimum age for marriage at twelve for women and fourteen for men, and permitted pre-pubertal marriage.[48]

As Hopkins recognized, the literary and legal evidence was mainly concerned with a narrow elite. The funerary inscriptions giving length of marriage were erected by a wider circle, but were limited in number (only a few hundred from around the empire for men and women) and were disproportionately concentrated in the area of Rome and in the freed class. Just as there was a commemorative bias in favor of registering ages at death for youths, so also there may have been a bias toward registering the length of unusually long or early marriages of freedmen, who would have had special motives to publicize the legitimacy of their conjugal bond.[49]

In order to widen the geographical and social distribution of the data, I have adopted a different method to study the age at marriage.[50] From the tens of thousands of funerary inscriptions I have sorted out all those for males over age ten which give age at death and the relationship of the commemorator, who dedicated the memorial. The result is a body of data more than ten times larger than that used by Hopkins and Harkness. Shaw, following my method, produced a similar study for women.[51] His presentation differed in certain respects from mine: he counted only dedications from parents and spouses, and graphed them year by year. In what follows, I have relied on his results, but have displayed them in a format similar to the one for men in order to facilitate comparison.

For Rome and each region the data have been grouped and tabulated by age at death and relationship of the commemorator. The aim is to reveal age-specific commemorative patterns to answer the question: at what age

[47] Hajnal 1965, 1983.
[48] Hopkins 1965, developing the epigraphic study of Harkness 1896.
[49] The case of Petronia Iusta, whose status at birth was disputed by her mother's former master, illustrates why freedmen might have been eager to document the legitimacy of their marriage and hence the free birth of their children (see Weaver 1991). The iconography of family groups on the tombs of freedmen (Kleiner 1977) shows that they were especially eager to leave monuments to their family bonds as a marker of their free citizen status.
[50] Saller 1987a. The following pages build on my earlier study and answer criticisms of it.
[51] Shaw 1987a. My thanks to Professor Shaw for his help in providing me with the data for his study.

did the responsibility for the memorial shift from the natal family (parents, and also siblings) to the conjugal family (wife and children)? The patterns offer a partial insight into the living kin closest to the commemorated at the time of death. Tables are given for each region that yielded enough epitaphs with the two requisite pieces of information to make a study meaningful. This study illuminates only those areas in which funerary commemorations in the standard Roman formulae are found in sufficient numbers. In general, the illumination falls on urbanized areas and leaves the countryside undocumented.[52] Some of the less urbanized areas of northwestern Europe have produced too few epitaphs for statistical study. Other regions, such as certain areas of North Africa, have yielded plenty of inscriptions, but without the vital indication of commemorator. In addition, I have given a table (2.2.i) indicating the proportion in each group that would be expected to have a father or mother alive to commemorate based on Model Life Table 3 West (explained in chapter 3). After examining each table in turn, we may ask whether the data suggest early, late, or intermediate age at first marriage for men and women, and then address the difficulties of interpretation.

City of Rome (Table 2.2.a). The epigraphic record for the capital city is far denser than for other regions or provinces, yet the patterns of commemoration by age and relationship correspond closely to most of the others.[53] For men, parents are the most common commemorators of boys and youths up to age twenty-five – indeed, almost exactly in the proportion that we would expect at least one parent to have been alive and able to commemorate, to judge from Table 2.2.i; the minority of youths without parents in these age groups were usually commemorated by a sibling or more distant relative. Parents decline noticeably as dedicators to men dying between ages twenty-five and twenty-nine (57 percent), and then largely disappear from epitaphs for men in their early thirties (15 percent). A very few wives appear for men in their late teens (3 percent), a few more for men in their early twenties (11 percent), and then wives appear as a significant

---

[52] Bagnall and Frier 1994: ch. 6 documents differences in marriage patterns in Roman Egypt between metropolis and village. I would expect differences between town and country also in the western empire, but am completely unable to document them. Any chronological changes in marriage patterns that may have occurred are also beyond our documentation, because the funerary inscriptions used in this study are not dated. We can only say that they come from the first three centuries after Christ, and that most were probably erected in the second or early third centuries.

[53] I rely here on data gathered by my research assistant, Ilse Mueller. She will publish her own study of this material, addressing many issues passed over here. In my initial study, I avoided the city of Rome on account of my expectation that the heavy proportion of ex-slaves in the epigraphic record would result in atypical patterns of marriage, but in fact the Roman pattern is quite similar to those found in northern Italy, southern Gaul, and elsewhere. The fact that the far richer Roman data produce similar patterns lends credibility to the patterns based on fewer data found outside Rome.

Tables 2.2.a–i: *Distribution of epitaphs for men and women by age and by relation of commemorator*

a. City of Rome

Men
Relationship of commemorator

		Parent	Sibling	Wife	Child[a]	Kin[b]	Total
Age of	10–14	185 (92)	11 (5)	—	—	6 (3)	202
deceased	15–19	203 (87)	23 (10)	6 (3)	1 (–)	—	233
	20–24	118 (75)	22 (14)	17 (11)	—	—	157
	25–29	60 (57)	13 (12)	32 (30)	1 (1)	—	106
	30–34	13 (15)	8 (9)	62 (73)	1 (1)	1 (1)	85
	35–39	9 (13)	9 (13)	51 (73)	—	1 (1)	70
	40–49	6 (6)	7 (7)	78 (76)	10 (10)	1 (1)	102
	50+	1 (1)	7 (4)	107 (68)	42 (27)	—	157
	Total	595	100	353	55	9	1112

Women
Relationship of commemorator

		Parent	Husband	Total
Age of	10–14	51 (98)	1 (2)	52
deceased	15–19	47 (69)	21 (31)	68
	20–24	22 (39)	35 (61)	57
	25–29	8 (29)	24 (71)	32
	30–34	1 (3)	32 (97)	33
	Total	129	113	242

b. Northern Peninsular Italy

Men
Relationship of commemorator

		Parent	Sibling	Wife	Child[a]	Kin[b]	Total
Age of	10–14	12 (92)[c]	—	—	—	1 (8)	13
deceased	15–19	21 (95)	1 (5)	—	—	—	22
	20–24	6 (60)	2 (20)	1 (10)	—	1 (10)	10
	25–29	7 (78)	—	2 (22)	—	—	9
	30–34	2 (29)	1 (14)	4 (57)	—	—	7
	35–39	3 (43)	1 (14)	3 (43)	—	—	7
	40–49	1 (12)	—	7 (88)	—	—	8
	50+	—	1 (9)	7 (64)	3 (27)	—	11
	Total	52	6	24	3	2	87

Women
Relationship of commemorator

		Parent	Husband	Total
Age of	10–14	14 (87)	2 (13)	16
deceased	15–19	23 (79)	6 (21)	29
	20–24	8 (33)	16 (67)	24
	25–29	4 (29)	10 (71)	14
	30–34	1 (6)	15 (94)	16
	Total	50	49	99

Tables 2.2.a–i (*cont.*)

c. Southern Italy

Men
Relationship of commemorator

		Parent	Sibling	Wife	Child[a]	Kin[b]	Total
Age of	10–14	16 (94)[c]	—	—	—	1 (6)	17
deceased	15–19	21 (91)	—	—	—	2 (9)	23
	20–24	23 (100)	—	—	—	—	23
	25–22	16 (100)	—	—	—	—	16
	30–34	5 (56)	—	3 (33)	—	1 (11)	9
	35–39	2 (29)	1 (14)	4 (57)	—	—	7
	40–49	—	—	9 (100)	—	—	9
	50+	—	—	11 (69)	5 (31)	—	16
	Total	83	1	27	5	4	120

Women
Relationship of commemorator

		Parent	Husband	Total
Age of	10–14	12 (100)	0 (—)	12
deceased	15–19	22 (73)	8 (27)	30
	20–24	15 (79)	4 (21)	19
	25–29	7 (47)	8 (53)	15
	30–34	0 (—)	7 (100)	7
	Total	56	27	83

d. Gaul: Narbonensis and Aquitania for men; Narbonensis only for women

Men
Relationship of commemorator

		Parent	Sibling	Wife	Child[a]	Kin[b]	Total
Age of	10–14	8 (67)[c]	1 (8)	—	—	3 (25)	12
deceased	15–19	19 (95)	—	—	—	1 (5)	20
	20–24	15 (79)	1 (5)	—	—	3 (16)	19
	25–29	7 (58)	—	4 (33)	—	—	11
	30–34	1 (25)	—	3 (75)	—	—	4
	35–39	1 (17)	1 (17)	3 (50)	1 (17)	—	6
	40–49	—	—	10 (83)	1 (8)	1 (8)	12
	50+	—	1 (12)	2 (25)	5 (62)	—	8
	Total	51	4	22	7	8	92

Women
Relationship of commemorator

		Parent	Husband	Total
Age of	10–14	9 (90)	1 (10)	10
deceased	15–19	16 (84)	3 (16)	19
	20–24	12 (46)	14 (54)	26
	25–29	4 (29)	10 (71)	14
	30–34	4 (50)	4 (50)	8
	Total	45	32	77

Tables 2.2.a–i *(cont.)*

e. Danubian provinces

		Men Relationship of commemorator					
		Parent	Sibling	Wife	Child[a]	Kin[b]	Total
Age of	10–14	19 (90)[c]	—	—	—	2 (10)	21
deceased	15–19	22 (79)	1 (4)	—	—	5 (18)	28
	20–24	19 (76)	5 (20)	—	—	1 (4)	25
	25–29	11 (46)	5 (21)	7 (29)	1 (4)	—	24
	30–34	9 (36)	5 (20)	10 (40)	—	1 (4)	25
	35–39	2 (12)	2 (12)	10 (63)	2 (12)	—	16
	40–49	4 (13)	1 (3)	17 (55)	9 (29)	—	31
	50+	1 (1)	2 (3)	33 (47)	30 (43)	4 (6)	70
	Total	87	21	77	42	13	240

		Women Relationship of commemorator		
		Parent	Husband	Total
Age of	10–14	15 (100)	0 (—)	15
deceased	15–19	19 (79)	5 (21)	24
	20–24	11 (41)	16 (59)	27
	25–29	8 (29)	20 (71)	28
	30–34	10 (30)	23 (70)	33
	Total	63	64	127

f. Africa: Theveste region

		Men Relationship of commemorator					
		Parent	Sibling	Wife	Child[a]	Kin[b]	Total
Age of	10–14	4 (100)[c]	—	—	—	—	4
deceased	15–19	3 (60)	—	—	—	2 (40)	5
	20–24	3 (75)	1 (25)	—	—	—	4
	25–29	6 (75)	2 (25)	—	—	—	8
	30–34	4 (50)	2 (25)	1 (12)	1 (12)	—	8
	35–39	3 (60)	1 (20)	1 (20)	—	—	5
	40–49	1 (8)	2 (15)	5 (38)	5 (38)	—	13
	50+	—	3 (4)	17 (24)	50 (70)	1 (1)	71
	Total	24	11	24	56	3	118

		Women Relationship of commemorator		
		Parent	Husband	Total
Age of	10–14	9 (100)	0 (—)	9
deceased	15–19	18 (72)	7 (28)	25
	20–24	11 (48)	12 (52)	23
	25–29	2 (18)	9 (82)	11
	30–34	2 (7)	26 (93)	28
	Total	42	54	96

Tables 2.2.a–i (*cont.*)

g. Africa: Mauretania Caesariensis

Men

		Parent	Sibling	Wife	Child[a]	Kin[b]	Total
Age of	10–14	2 (100)[c]	—	—	—	—	2
deceased	15–19	9 (90)	1 (10)	—	—	—	10
	20–24	6 (86)	1 (14)	—	—	—	7
	25–29	3 (37)	3 (37)	2 (25)	—	—	8
	30–34	—	—	1 (100)	—	—	1
	35–39	1 (25)	1 (25)	2 (50)	—	—	4
	40–49	3 (16)	3 (16)	11 (58)	2 (11)	—	19
	50+	1 (3)	4 (11)	17 (46)	14 (38)	1 (3)	37
	Total	25	13	33	16	1	88

Women

Relationship of commemorator

		Parent	Husband	Total
Age of	10–14	9 (100)	0 (—)	9
deceased	15–19	9 (69)	4 (31)	13
	20–24	3 (21)	11 (79)	14
	25–29	4 (20)	16 (80)	20
	30–34	0 (—)	10 (100)	10
	Total	25	41	66

h. Spain: Lusitania and Baetica

Men

Relationship of commemorator

		Parent	Sibling	Wife	Child[a]	Kin[b]	Total
Age of	10–14	3 (75)[c]	—	—	—	1 (25)	4
deceased	15–19	16 (80)	3 (15)	—	—	1 (5)	20
	20–24	15 (75)	2 (10)	1 (5)	—	2 (10)	20
	25–29	9 (60)	2 (13)	4 (27)	—	—	15
	30–34	5 (42)	4 (33)	3 (25)	—	—	12
	35–39	6 (50)	2 (17)	2 (17)	1 (8)	1 (8)	12
	40–49	4 (18)	2 (9)	11 (50)	3 (14)	2 (9)	22
	50+	—	1 (3)	14 (42)	18 (55)	—	33
	Total	58	16	35	22	7	138

Women

Relationship of commemorator

		Parent	Husband	Total
Age of	10–14	8 (100)	0 (0)	8
deceased	15–19	19 (90)	2 (10)	21
	20–24	16 (70)	7 (30)	23
	25–29	13 (54)	11 (46)	24
	30–34	7 (28)	18 (72)	25
	Total	63	38	101

Tables 2.2.a–i *(cont.)*

i. Microsimulation model: proportion with living kin at time of death (derived from Table 3.1.b)

		Parent	Sibling	Wife	Child
Age of	10–14	92%	83%	—	—
deceased	15–19	86%	81%	—	—
	20–24	76%	79%	1%	—
	25–29	64%	77%	30%	15%
	30–34	52%	75%	76%	50%
	35–39	38%	72%	95%	74%
	40–49	20%	66%	97%	78%

Notes:
  [a] In cases where a wife and children provided a joint commemoration the dedication was counted in the wife column, so that the column headed "child" generally represents independent commemorations from children.
  [b] "Kin" here includes only relatives outside the immediate family.
  [c] The figures in parentheses give the percentage of all dedications within the age bracket.

presence as commemorators for men in their late twenties and a large majority only for men over thirty. Thus, the commemorative shift from parents to spouses appears in the table between the late twenties and the early thirties.

Parents also predominate in the commemoration of women in their early teens (98 percent) and late teens (69 percent), but give way to husbands in epitaphs for women in their early twenties.[54] Husbands barely appear for young teenage girls, constitute a substantial minority for older teenage girls, and then are a clear majority for women over twenty. The commemorative shift for women occurs from the late teens to early twenties.

Northern Peninsular Italy (Table 2.2.b). Here the data are not numerous for men (n = 87) or women (n = 99), but they are concentrated in the age range of interest for a study of age at marriage. Parents predominate as commemorators for deceased men in their teens and twenties. Although there is some fluctuation, parents appear in roughly the proportion that they would be expected to have been alive for men through age twenty-nine, with mothers (60 percent) becoming especially noticeable for men in their later twenties as the older fathers died. Among the deceased under twenty-

---

[54] It must be remembered that the percentages for commemorators of women are based on the total of parent- and husband-dedications only, whereas the percentages for men are based on the number of dedications from all kin. This explains why the proportion of young teenage girls commemorated by parents (98 percent) is so much higher than the comparable figure for young teenage boys.

five years without parent commemorators, siblings or more distant kin take up the obligation. Only one young man under twenty-five received a dedication from a wife (as against six from parents, two from siblings and one from a more distant kinsman). Wives appear as a significant proportion only for men over twenty-five, and become the most numerous commemorators for men over thirty. Thus, the shift in commemoration from parents to wives comes for deceased men between ages twenty-five and thirty-four.

Like men, women in northern Italy dying in their teens were very likely to be commemorated by parents; for women over twenty, parents form a decreasing minority. There is some evidence here for marriage of girls in their early and later teens, as husbands appear as dedicators, but far less often than parents. For women over age twenty, husbands become a marked and increasing majority of dedicators. The decisive shift from parents to spouses occurs from the late teens to the early twenties.

Southern Italy (Table 2.2.c). This area yields a comparable number of useful dedications, with more to men and fewer to women than northern Italy. Parents dominate commemoration to men through their twenties, then gradually decline in proportion for men in their thirties, and disappear for men older than forty. No wife appears as a dedicator to men in their teens or twenties; for men in their early thirties wives form a significant minority, then a majority for men over thirty-five. In this population the commemorative shift comes very late, in the middle thirties.

For southern Italian girls in their early teens only parents commemorate; they remain a majority for women in their late teens (73 percent) and early twenties (79 percent), then they gradually decline as commemorators of deceased in their late twenties (47 percent) and disappear for older women. Husbands begin to appear for women in their late teens and early twenties, and predominate only for women in their late twenties and older. As with men, the shift from parents to spouses comes quite late and only gradually (a phenomenon to be discussed below).

Gaul (Table 2.2.d). The patterns in the tables for Gallia Narbonensis (and Aquitania for men) resemble those for northern Italy. Parents dominate the commemorations for men up to age twenty-five, with a few siblings and other kin occasionally taking up the duty. The proportion of parent-commemorators noticeably declines for men in their late twenties (58 percent) and then drops off sharply for men in their thirties. Dedications from wives appear only for men over twenty-five years – as a significant minority for men in their late twenties and then as the largest group for men in their thirties and forties. The commemorative shift from parents to spouses is marked and occurs from the late twenties to the early thirties.

The great majority of dedications to women in their early and late teens in this region comes from parents, who form a minority for those over age twenty. Husbands are attested for teenage girls, but only as a small minority both for early teens (10 percent) and later teens (16 percent). The significant shift appears for women dying in their early twenties, the majority of whom received dedications from husbands.

Danubian provinces (Table 2.2.e). This large area yields a more numerous sample, also more evenly distributed over the age cohorts. Here again, parents are much the most common dedicators for boys and youths under twenty-five years; a scattering of siblings and other kin are also found for the proportion that would be expected to have been without a living parent. The proportion of parent-commemorations declines substantially for men in their late twenties, but they remain the single largest group. Parents then decline further to a distinct minority for men in their early thirties (36 percent). Wives are absent as commemorators for men through their early twenties, then appear as a significant minority (29 percent) for men in their later twenties, and become the best represented group for men in their thirties and older. The balance between parents and spouses shifts from the late twenties to early thirties.

For women in their teens parents are the predominant commemorators, then substantially decline for women in their early twenties as husbands take over the duty. Husbands are not in evidence for young teenage girls, appear as a minority (21 percent) for older teenage girls, and assume the principal responsibility for women over twenty. As in Rome, northern Italy and southern Gaul, the shift from parents to spouses occurs between the late teens and early twenties.

Africa: Theveste region (Table 2.2.f). This area of North Africa offers more data than much of the rest of Roman Africa, but not as useful a group of inscriptions as those from other provinces. The data are numerous enough but, in the case of men, heavily skewed toward older ages.[55] Consequently, the dedications in the crucial categories up to age twenty-nine are few, and the conclusions correspondingly tentative. Parents are the primary commemorators for men dying in their teens, twenties, and even thirties. Wives begin to appear for men in their thirties, but only as a small minority; they are better represented for men in their forties, yet still a minority. Children, rather than wives, were the principal commemorators for men over fifty. This distinctive pattern throws into relief the essential similarities of the patterns from other regions: in the Theveste region wives were not the preferred commemorators at any stage in life, as they were elsewhere.

Epitaphs for women of the Theveste region, following the pattern found elsewhere, do not present the same anomalies. Parents predominate as

---

[55] Shaw 1991 discusses the preferences for certain age groups.

commemorators for teenage women, then give way to husbands for women over twenty years. There is no evidence of husbands for women in their early teens; husbands begin to appear for women in their late teens (27 percent), become a majority for women in their early twenties (52 percent), and dominate the dedications to older women. The commemorative shift is discernible, as elsewhere, around the age of twenty.

Africa: Mauretania Caesariensis (Table 2.2.g). The data from Mauretania Caesariensis present the same difficulties as the Theveste evidence — a heavy skewing in favor of older men. Of the nineteen dedications for men under twenty-five years, seventeen come from parents. For men over age twenty-five, parents are in the minority as wives begin to appear, but in small numbers. There is a shift in commemoration from parents to wives in the late twenties and early thirties, but it would be unwise to rely on the single dedication to a man in his early thirties as a firm guide to the timing of marriage.

The pattern for women, again, looks more like those found elsewhere around the empire. Parents, not husbands, supply the dedications for young teenage women; they continue to dominate in dedications for older teenagers (69 percent), as husbands begin to appear (31 percent). Husbands (79 percent) significantly outnumber parents (21 percent) for women aged twenty to twenty-four. There is a marked shift in the commemorative pattern at the usual point around twenty years of age.

Spain: Lusitania and Baetica (Table 2.2.h). A distinctive pattern emerges from the large body of data for Spain. Parents are the most numerous commemorators for boys and youths up to age twenty-five, then decline as a proportion for men in their late twenties and thirties. The decline is gradual, at roughly the rate that both parents would be expected to have died. Fathers participated in most of the parental commemorations for those up to twenty-five, but then, as they died, mothers, who were generally younger (see below), lived on and assumed the obligation on their own. As a result, parental commemorations do not decline to a distinct minority in the table until the rows for the forty–forty-nine and fifty-plus year-old cohorts. A wife is found as a commemorator for one man under age twenty-five (5 percent); wives then appear as a significant minority for men in their later twenties and thirties, but, owing to the preference for mothers to commemorate, wives become the largest group only for men in their forties. In this table, then, the commemorative shift is not as sharp as elsewhere.

The dedications to women also follow this distinctively Spanish pattern, with parents only gradually being replaced by spouses. No husband commemorates a young teenage woman; then the ratio of parent-commemorators to husband-commemorators slowly shifts from 9.5:1 for late teens, to 2.3:1 for women in their early twenties, to nearly 1:1 for those in their late twenties, to 1:2.6 as husbands ultimately become the primary commemorators for women in their early thirties.

Interpretation. We would like to be able to use the epigraphic data to plot a curve of the proportion of men and women ever married in each age cohort.[56] The data, however, are not full or exact enough for such a precise treatment, as Romans rounded and exaggerated their ages, or simply did not list an age at certain times of life (see below). Since the data are only approximate, it is best to use them to test only general hypotheses about the median ages at first marriage for men and women to discover whether they were early, late or intermediate. Of course, early, intermediate, and late are relative terms, to be defined with reference to other populations. For women, I will define an early marriage pattern as one in which women begin to marry in their early or middle teens, with half married by their late teens and most married in their early twenties. An intermediate pattern will have women beginning to marry in their late teens, with half married in their early twenties. In a late pattern the median age for marriage will fall in the mid to late twenties, as found in some early modern English populations with mean age at marriage over twenty-five years in some communities.[57]

Men differ from women in the timing of their biological reproductive capacity: they are able to reproduce later in life, and in most populations they first marry at a later age.[58] Therefore, the definitions of the early, middle and late patterns are somewhat different for men. I will define an early marriage pattern for males as one in which they begin to marry in significant numbers in their later teens, with half married by age twenty. An intermediate marriage pattern will have half of the men married by age twenty-five. In the late pattern, men begin to marry in significant numbers in their mid or late twenties, with a median age at first marriage around thirty and many postponing marriage until after thirty.

Which of these patterns for women and men are most easily reconciled with the distribution of commemorators by age in the tables? With respect to women, no one has argued for the type of late marriage found in northwestern Europe in the early modern period, nor do the tables support such a hypothesis. In Rome, northern Italy, Gallia Narbonensis, the Danubian and Theveste regions, husbands are already a significant presence in commemorations for women in their late teens, and a majority for women in their early twenties. Spain and southern Italy are exceptions to this distribution: these areas exhibit no marked shift from parents to husbands,

---

[56] As Frier has done for Roman Egypt in Bagnall and Frier 1994: figs. 6.1 and 6.2.
[57] Wrightson and Levine 1979: 47, give some examples. On longer term changes in mean ages at first marriage in England, see Wrigley and Schofield 1981: 255.
[58] Newell 1988: 96.

because parents seem to have been the culturally preferred commemorators, disappearing at a gradual rate that can be best explained by their death (a feature also found in dedications to men of these areas). In southern Italy and Spain, it is possible that women married later, but probably their husbands were less well represented on account of the preference for parents.

A hypothesis of very early female marriage was advocated by Hopkins, who placed the median age at marriage at sixteen years.[59] This hypothesis is difficult to reconcile with the distribution of the broader corpus of commemorations. In southern Italy, the Danubian region, Spain, the Theveste region, and Mauretania, *no* girl dying between ten and fourteen years of age received a dedication from a husband; in Rome, only one of fifty-two; in Gallia Narbonensis, one of ten; and in northern Italy, two of sixteen. It is difficult to explain why, if a significant proportion of twelve, thirteen, and fourteen-year-olds were married, their husbands would be so rare in these data, to an extent that goes well beyond mere under-representation. The marriage of early teenage girls was certainly not considered outrageous or distasteful by the Romans, but husbands appear as a significant minority of dedicators for women only in their later teens and older, and then in most populations form a majority for women dying in their early twenties. The fact that women from age twenty are most often commemorated as wives weighs against the intermediate hypothesis and in favor of an early pattern, but for most populations not as early as Hopkins suggested.[60] Hopkins' literary and legal evidence was written by the elite, and it is entirely likely that senatorial and other elite girls married at younger ages than the wider population with the epigraphic habit.[61] The best estimate of median age at first marriage for non-senatorial women, then, is twenty years, give or take a couple of years.

For men a similar shift from parental to conjugal commemoration is observable, but a decade later in life. The early marriage pattern for men would seem to be excluded by the nearly complete absence of wives' dedications to men under twenty. Some of the inscriptions listed by Harkness giving length of marriage do point to a few cases of male teenage marriage, but such marriages must have been highly exceptional, and perhaps were specified for that reason. The intermediate pattern, with half of the men married by age twenty-five, also appears improbable, since in most regions no wife is recorded as a commemorator for a male twenty to twenty-four years old. In northern Italy and in Spain, we do find one wife commemorating (10 percent and 5 percent of the commemorators, respectively). In all regions except southern Italy and Theveste, wives

[59] Hopkins 1965.
[60] Shaw 1987a: fig. 2, table 10 shows the predominance of husbands as commemorators of women twenty and older.   [61] In addition to Hopkins 1965, see Syme 1987.

appear in significant numbers for men in their late twenties, and become the most numerous commemorators for men in their thirties in Gaul, northern Italy, the Danubian region and Mauretania. The shift in commemoration around thirty supports the late hypothesis. In Spain, southern Italy and the Theveste region, a decisive shift to wife-commemorators appears either very late in life or not at all, because of the continuing presence of parents. Interpretation of these data must be less secure, but nothing in these tables points positively to the early or intermediate hypothesis. The exceptions, again, are senatorial men, who were given incentives by the Augustan laws to marry somewhat younger, in their early twenties. Aside from the incentives, it is not unusual for aristocrats to have marriages arranged at younger ages, to judge by comparative evidence.[62]

Objections and caveats. Inference of age at marriage from funerary dedications is neither straightforward nor unproblematic, but I believe the criticisms and doubts can be met. The question is not whether precision can be achieved, but whether the imprecisions and uncertainties are so great as to lend plausibility to a pattern other than early female/late male marriage.

An initial objection is that the epitaphs do not record age at marriage but age at death, which occurred some time after marriage in cases where a spouse dedicates. Thus, the age in the epitaph would always be higher than age at marriage.[63] My method, however, does not ask about the specific age at marriage, but what proportion of the women or men dying at a given age are recorded as having a spouse. The fact that a significant proportion of men in their late twenties were commemorated by a wife, but not men in their early twenties, suggests that men began to marry in substantial numbers in the interval. The alternative demographic explanation – that a large proportion of men were married in their early twenties, but only their unmarried peers died – is patently implausible.

Alternative cultural explanations of the commemorative shift have been suggested. One could imagine a cultural preference for parents as commemorators over spouses after marriage: such a preference would mean that the appearance of spouses as commemorators of second choice was a function of the preceding deaths of fathers and mothers of the deceased rather than a function of the timing of marriage. This explanation may be tested by examination of the rate at which the proportion of parent-commemorations declines for offspring dying in their teens, twenties, and

---

[62]   Hughes 1975: 22; Stone 1977: 50.
[63]   This methodological problem is in principle the same as the one solved by demographers using census data, which do not give length of marriage but only what proportion of men and women at given ages are married at the time of the census. For a more precise and sophisticated mathematical analysis of the problem than the epitaphs will permit, see Hajnal 1953, and Bagnall and Frier 1994: ch. 6.

thirties.[64] Table 2.2.i, derived from the microsimulation model in chapter 3, shows the kinship universe that men dying at a particular age would have had. A comparison of the column giving the proportion at a given age having at least one living parent with the proportion actually commemorated by a parent in the city of Rome shows a strikingly close correlation up to age twenty-four.[65] The correlation suggests that, if parents were living, they nearly always commemorated deceased sons up to that age. Over the age of twenty-five, however, the proportion of men actually commemorated by parents declines much faster than can be explained by the parents' death, according to Model Life Tables. Even high mortality cannot explain the rapid disappearance of parent-commemorators from the late teens to the early twenties for women, and from the late twenties to the early thirties for men. It is demographically implausible that half of the late teenage women with a parent alive no longer had a living parent only five years later. Furthermore, if parents' death were the explanation for their disappearance from commemorations, the shift in favor of spouses should appear for sons and daughters at the same ages, but that is not the case: the shift to spouse commemoration occurs ten years earlier in the life course for women. As noticed before, the commemorative patterns in Spain and southern Italy differ from the rest in the gradual decline of parental dedications; for these regions the life-long preference for parents as dedicators presents a special obstacle to interpretation to be discussed below.

The tables for most regions reveal a point in the life course at which spouses come to be generally preferred over parents to fulfill the obligation of commemoration. It has been claimed that the timing of the shift to spouses does not correspond to the time of marriage, but to some later point in life after conjugal affection had time to develop.[66] There are several answers to this criticism. First, one could imagine that the conjugal bond would strengthen with the birth of a child after a year or two of marriage, but my argument about ages at marriage would not be significantly affected by the supposition of a year or two of lag time between marriage and acceptance of the duty of commemoration. To suppose a longer lag time seems to me to be problematic: is it plausible that husbands and wives married for four or five years with children still had so tenuous a bond as to exclude spouses from dedications almost completely? This is the scenario we would have to accept in order to believe that a large proportion of women in their early teens and men in their early twenties were married.

---

[64] Since in all regions except Theveste, mothers participate in commemoration both with their husbands and alone, the question is whether the spouse appears as a secondary commemorator after the death of both parents.

[65] I use the table for the city of Rome here because the sample is much larger than for other areas.   [66] Evans 1991: 205, n. 53.

Moreover, if there were some indeterminate lag time, the marked commemorative shift between age cohorts in most areas becomes difficult to explain, unless we suppose that men and women regularly remained attached to their parents for five years and only five years after marriage. Finally, as previously pointed out, it is telling that wives are nearly invisible as commemorators of men under twenty-five, not only by comparison with parents, but also by comparison with siblings and more distant kin.[67] Clearly, siblings and other kin were not the preferred commemorators at any stage of life, so their appearance in dedications for twenty–twenty-four year-olds without parents, in greater numbers than wives, suggests that most of the deceased were not married.

Whereas the relationships listed on the dedications may be presumed to be generally (though not always) correct, the given ages present various difficulties and biases. The first is age-heaping – that is, the tendency to give an age ending in -X or -V. Age-heaping is detectable in the data used to construct the tables, but does not vitiate the argument. Misrepresentation of age is greatest for men of advanced years, who are of no concern here. Some age-heaping for deceased in their teens and twenties would not drastically affect the results. Only if spouses regularly overstated the age of the deceased by more than several years could we reconcile the commemorative pattern with significantly lower typical ages at first marriage.

Beyond misrepresentation of age, the differential propensity to include age at death poses an obstacle to interpretation. Put in its most extreme form, if parents customarily included the age of their son or daughter at death and spouses did not, the ratio of parent- to spouse-commemorations giving ages would not represent the ratio of all parent- to spouse-commemorations, and hence would not be a reliable guide to marriage. A look at the numbers of dedications shows that parents in most regions were indeed more likely to include age at death of their offspring than were spouses. The total number of dedications tends to decline as age increases, not because the deaths are fewer or even because the dedications are fewer, but because age is given in fewer dedications for older age cohorts dominated by spouse commemorations. But the differential propensity is not extreme; spouses obviously *do* include age at death often enough that the general absence of spouse-commemorations at certain ages is meaningful. We cannot deduce the precise proportion of men or women in an age cohort who are married from the ratio of parent-commemorations to spouse-commemorations, but the near or complete absence of spouse-

[67] Saller 1987a: 25.

commemoration in a cohort does warrant the conclusion that marriage was not typical in that cohort.[68]

The clear exceptions to the pattern of a marked shift are southern Italy and Spain, where, as noted above, continued parent commemoration makes it difficult to deduce the timing of marriage. For men in Spain, an alternative approach is to exclude parents as the preferred commemorators and to compare the number of dedications from wives with those from siblings and more distant kin. For men under twenty-five years the one wife is a distinct minority even among secondary commemorators; wives become more numerous for men twenty-five and older. The epitaphs from southern Italy do not allow such a comparison: we can only say that if men were married at a younger age in this region than in others, their wives have left no trace in the epigraphic record. For women of the two regions, there is no hint of very early marriage. Husbands begin to appear, as in most other regions, for women in their late teens, but the pace of the shift to husbands thereafter probably does not mirror the proportion married, since husbands become a majority of commemorators only for women older than thirty.

To summarize, cultural preferences for certain types of commemorators and for registering certain ages, as well as age-heaping, blur to some degree funerary commemoration as a marker of the life course transition to marriage. But these distortions are not so pronounced in most populations as to eradicate the connection between the timing of marriage and of the commemorative shift from parents to spouses. That shift in most regions is marked from one five-year age cohort to the next, and leads to the conclusion that Romans of the inscription-erecting class exhibited the same "Mediterranean" pattern found in more recent eras – that is, late male and early female marriage. For purposes of further argument, I will use as the mean age at first marriage for women twenty years and for men thirty years. These numbers are not meant to be exact, but approximations that the evidence supports as against, say, fifteen years for women and twenty-five years for men. In addition, a distinction will be made between the broader inscription-erecting class characterized by these means and the senatorial elite who tended to marry five years or so younger.

Fertility

No empirical evidence exists to document fertility rates in the western empire. Clearly, the Romans would have had a "high pressure" regime with

---

[68] Parkin's doubt (1992: 124–25) that the dedications "always reflect differences in marital status" attributes an exactness to these conclusions that was never claimed and is unnecessary. The question is not whether the differences are always reflected – they are certainly not – , but whether they are broadly and imperfectly reflected in a way to make judgment between the three general hypotheses possible.

a high birth rate to go along with the high death rate.[69] Over the centuries of the empire births must have been on average more or less in balance with deaths, because even a modest rate of constant growth or decline – even as little as 0.5 percent per year – would have cumulatively produced over the centuries drastic changes in total population of the sort that no historian would be willing to defend. Thus, it is reasonable to posit a stationary population (no growth or decline) for purposes of modelling the kinship universe.[70]

To maintain a stationary population in an environment with an average life expectancy at birth of twenty-five years would have required each woman who lived through her reproductive years to bear an average of five children.[71] Two aspects of this statement deserve emphasis. It refers to children ever born, not the actual size of the living family at any point in time, which would have been reduced by severe infant mortality. Second, the statement gives an average, which encompasses a great variety of family sizes.[72] If completed family size greatly varied in the Roman empire, that implies that fertility was spread over decades for some couples – all the more so for men who remarried much younger women late in life. It is this divergence from contemporary experience and the complexity of the interaction of high fertility, high mortality and early female/late male marriage that require computer simulation to appreciate the implications for the kinship universe through the life course.

[69] Parkin 1992: 92.
[70] I should perhaps stress that the assumption of a stationary population might be far enough wrong to make a difference in a study of the total population of the empire, but not in a study modelling the kinship universe of individuals. For instance, the assumption of mild growth in population of 0.3 percent per year, rather than no growth, would alter the proportions having living kin in table 3.1.b by no more than 2–3 percent in nearly all cases.
[71] Frier 1982 stresses the high fertility needed to compensate for the high mortality. Parkin 1992: 160 gives a convenient graph to show the GRR necessary for certain growth rates at certain life expectancies. The GRR or Gross Reproduction Rate is the average number of daughters a woman who lives through her reproductive years bears. The GRR necessary to produce a stationary population at $e_o = 25$ (Model West) is 2.55, which yields an average of 5.1 children for women who live to fifty. See Parkin 1992: 86–88, for definitions and explanation.
[72] To the late twentieth-century westerner, one of the most striking tables in Wrigley's *Population and History* gives the distribution of family sizes in Great Britain from the late nineteenth to the early twentieth centuries: in the 1870s there were roughly similar probabilities of having no children or three children or eight children or more than eleven children; by 1925 the distribution is concentrated so that the sizes of 80 percent of families fall into the 0–3 children range so familiar to us. Wrigley 1969: 198.

3

Simulation of Roman family and kinship

The Romans considered the bonds of family and kinship to be biologically based but not biologically determined. It is the biological basis that opens the possibility of simulating the kinship universe with the aid of a computer. Roman authors saw the beginnings of kinship bonds and of the wider society in the biological reproduction of the married man and woman.[1] Roman law, to be sure, offered citizens a flexibility in restructuring their kinship bonds that was remarkable by later European standards: not only were divorce and remarriage easy in the classical period, but adoption permitted change of filiation.[2] Nevertheless, adoption was apparently not so common as to vitiate a model of the kinship universe based on biological reproduction.[3]

Anthropologists have stressed that, within the universe of those linked by reproduction or marriage, not only do particular cultures systematically stress certain bonds over others, but individuals make choices about which relationships to maintain and cultivate out of the kinship system as culturally

---

[1] Cicero, *Off.* 1.54. [2] Corbier 1991a.
[3] Hopkins 1983: 74, on the low rate of adoption during the Republic. Salomies 1992 concludes that it is very difficult to identify adoptions from nomenclature during the Principate. Veyne 1987: 9 has presented a radically cultural view of Roman kinship, suggesting that membership in a family was a result not of biological reproduction, but of ritual acceptance of the newborn (*tollere*) by the *paterfamilias*. This half-truth has been widely repeated. The element of truth is that exposure of a newborn was accepted as a de facto means of breaking the family tie. But from a legal point of view the claim is false. As Watson 1967: 81, points out, "a Digest text from the Empire ... puts it beyond doubt that *patria potestas* was created by birth, not by the act of picking up the child" (i.e., *tollere*). That *Digest* passage (40.4.29, Scaevola) shows that the offspring of *matrimonium iustum* acquired a claim on his father's estate by birth, with or without *tollere*. More generally, many juristic interpretations rest on the timing of conception and birth (e.g., the claim of the posthumous offspring on the estate). Overall, while Roman culture did not take a rigidly biological approach to defining bonds of kinship, the biological basis of juristic thinking about kinship bonds was strong enough to make biological reproduction a reasonable simplifying assumption or starting point for the analysis of many issues.

defined from the biological kinship universe. Generally, choice becomes more evident among more distant kin. The significance of cultural and individual choices in defining kinship roles is beyond question, but to understand the choices and the definition of kinship roles it is important to have a sense of the kinship universe that flowed from marriage at certain ages and from the biological events of birth and death. For example, Roman law suggests that paternal uncles had a special culturally defined role; the social significance of that role, however, depended in part on whether Romans at certain stages of life had a living paternal uncle to fulfill the role.

We would like to have empirical evidence to show the changing shape of the kinship universe for Romans through their life course. Such evidence simply does not exist, even in the household census returns from Roman Egypt.[4] Indeed, evidence of that quality and detail does not exist for much better documented societies of recent centuries.[5] The terms of early modern English wills, for example, may list certain relatives, but they do not provide the historian with a complete inventory of living relatives.[6] Therefore, computer simulations have considerable value for family historians with much fuller data. For the Roman historian, the simulation offers an invaluable opportunity to understand the implications of what we know of the Roman life course.

Several simulations designed to generate kinship universes have been developed for use by historians. I have relied on CAMSIM developed by James Smith, who has generously produced the Roman simulations. CAMSIM is now in its third version: the technical refinements made over the past few years explain the minor differences between the tables presented in this chapter and those in my earlier article.[7] The differences serve as a firm reminder that we are dealing not with hard, exact numbers, but with approximate proportions. Considered in the latter terms, what follows is consistent with the earlier publication.

How does the simulation work? The basic idea is that the simulation generates a model population by simulating the basic events of birth, death and marriage, month by month, in accordance with the age-specific probabilities of those events as established by the demographic parameters. Smith has provided a detailed description of the simulation, which I summarize.[8]

This is a microsimulation rather than a macrosimulation. That is, it does not start from a whole population, but posits a limited set of individuals (egos) of one or the other sex, which provides the starting point from which

---

[4] For a comparison of the central averages in the demography of Roman Egypt and in the computer simulation, see the appendix at the end of the chapter.   [5] Laslett 1988.
[6] Wrightson and Levine 1979: 92–94.   [7] Saller 1987a.
[8] Smith and Oeppen 1993.

to generate a model population. A set of 5,000 egos has been found to be large enough to generate stable estimates in the tables.[9] Each of the 5,000 is simulated independently, and a stable population is assumed.[10] The simulation involves taking each ego through the life course, month by month, from birth, to marriage, through the fertile period, to death. The demographic parameters fed into the computer – average life expectancy at birth, the distribution of age at first marriage, the distribution of fertility – define the probability of a given life event occurring in a given month.[11]

Parameters. Model life tables were used to fix the probability of death at a given age. Chapter 2 provides the argument to justify the use of Coale–Demeny Level 3 West Female ($e_0 = 25$) as the best all-purpose estimate of Roman mortality rates, and Level 6 West ($e_0 = 32.5$) as the probable upper limit of average life expectancy at birth. Tables of kin from the simulations on both assumptions are presented to allow the reader to see how much variation results from different educated assumptions about mortality rates.

In the simulations, age at first marriage is modelled on the basis of the conclusions drawn from the funerary inscriptions. For the "ordinary" population the average age at first marriage was set at twenty years for women and thirty years for men. First marriages were distributed around these averages from ages fifteen to forty for women and from ages twenty-four to forty for men, in accordance with Coale's marriage model.[12] In addition to the set of tables for the "ordinary," inscription-erecting population, a set is offered for the "senatorial" population to show the consequences of marrying at younger ages (see chapter 2). These simulations are based on mean ages at first marriage of fifteen for women and twenty-five for men with women's first marriages distributed from ages

---

[9] That is, random differences from one run to the next do not change the overall proportion given in the tables.

[10] Smith has now developed the program to model populations that are not stable, but that added refinement makes little difference to the Roman historian who cannot document changing mortality patterns.

[11] A random number generator in the program decides the individual outcome on the basis of the probability.

[12] Coale and McNeill 1972. The inscriptions allow us to estimate the mean age at first marriage, but give neither clear minimum and maximum ages at first marriage, nor firm distributions. For minimum ages at first marriage in the ordinary population, we used the ages at which spouses begin to appear in commemorations in noticeable numbers. In order to distribute the marriage ages around the means, we used the distribution of marriage ages around the mean in early modern England. Comparison with the Egyptian household census data, recently analyzed by Bagnall and Frier (1994), suggests the possibility that this assumption may distribute marriages around the mean too tightly, but the great majority of those data fit the assumptions of the simulation, especially if brother–sister marriages in Egypt, which tended to occur at younger ages, are excluded.

twelve to thirty-three and men's first marriages distributed from ages twenty to forty.

The simulation assumes that ego after the death of a spouse will remarry up to the age of fifty in the case of women and sixty in the case of men. This assumption is based on the Augustan marriage legislation and is obviously a simplification. The simulation does not attempt to model divorce, because the rate of divorce cannot be documented and, unlike mortality or fertility, has no natural constraints. As a result, the first row for husband or wife in the tables giving proportion with living kin is not useful for egos at older ages (see appendix). Furthermore, we have not been able to present a kinship model including step-siblings. These limitations are unimportant for certain questions about the kin universe and important for others. The model probably overestimates the number of full siblings, just as it underestimates half-siblings and step-siblings.[13]

Modelling fertility is a difficult and complex matter. The ultimate constraint is that the model must yield a birth rate which will produce a nearly stationary population. In the simulation, each female after marriage is assigned an interval of time to the birth of her first child based on comparative evidence. Females then give birth to subsequent children in accordance with the probabilities assigned by Parity Progression Ratios.[14] The simulation varies the intervals between births from female to female in order to reflect the fact that some women were more fecund than others. In addition, the simulation applies an age-specific sterility schedule drawn from modern study so that as females age, an increasing proportion of them become biologically sterile.

Although a simplification, the microsimulation is in fact highly sophisticated, taking into account more parameters and biological patterns than would be possible by individual calculations. Using the parameters, the microsimulation generates kin sets, as each ego progresses through life, bearing children, each of whom in turn is simulated in accordance with the probabilities of dying, marrying, and giving birth month by month. This method produces a set of descending kin. Ascending generations are produced by assigning ego as a birth of a mother and father whose life

---

[13] The significance of the limitation will depend in part on Roman definitions of the roles of half-siblings and step-siblings, which are not well documented. A passage from Cicero's *Pro Cluentio* 21 hints at a blurring of the distinction between full and half-siblings: a uterine half-brother is called simply *frater* and is instituted heir, despite the lack of agnatic connection (see Moreau 1986). On the other hand, step-siblings could be perceived as competitors for the estate.

[14] The Parity Progression Ratios (PPRs) provide a sequence of numbers giving the probabilities that a woman who has had a certain number of children will have one more. The probability of another child declines with each child. The PPRs were adjusted in the simulation to produce a stationary population.

courses are then simulated. Through the simulation of the parents' lives, a set of lateral kin (siblings) is generated for ego. By simulating additional ascending generations, a wider set of collateral relatives is produced.

After the computer has created a population of tens of thousands of these lives, that population can be analyzed to show the shape of the kin universe as egos move through the life course. CAMSIM produces three standard types of table by age of ego and category of kin: (a) the mean number of living kin in a given category for ego at a given age; (b) the proportion of egos at a given age who have at least one living kin in a given category; (c) the average age of living kin in a given category.[15] At the end of this chapter these three types of table are presented for females and males of three different model populations: "ordinary" marriage ages with Level 3 West ($e_0 = 25$) mortality (Tables 3.1), "senatorial" marriage ages with Level 3 West ($e_0 = 25$) mortality (Tables 3.2), and "senatorial" marriage ages with Level 6 West ($e_0 = 32.5$) mortality (Tables 3.3). As an illustration, for "ordinary" females with an average life expectancy at birth of twenty-five years, Table 3.1.a tells us that at age ten they would have an average of 2.2 living siblings; Table 3.1.b indicates that 83 percent of them have at least one living sibling; and Table 3.1.c suggests that the average age of those siblings is 10.3 years. In addition to these standard tables, the simulated population can be analyzed with reference to other questions formulated in specifically Roman terms (see for example Table 8.1 analyzing male kin available for guardianship).

Once again, I want to emphasize that the microsimulation is meant not to generate precisely accurate numbers, but to give the historian a general idea of how demographic parameters interact to produce kin.[16] Consequently, in using the tables, the reader should think in terms of broad proportions rather than exact percentages. Of course, the results of the simulation are vulnerable to the criticism summed up in colloquial terms as "garbage in – garbage out." In evaluating that criticism, it is essential not to lose sight of the central issue, which is not whether the simulation exactly replicates the Roman experience. It does not, and in any case there was no single Roman experience of mortality, fertility, and marriage, but different experiences of varying probablities. Any demographic model, to be useful, must simplify that variation. The right question is whether the simplifications and assumptions are likely to be so far wrong as to vitiate the conclusion being drawn. That question can be answered only with reference to specific arguments and conclusions. In general, it can be said that the comparison in the appendix between the results of the analysis of the Egyptian household

[15] Notice in the third type of table that the average age of the kin does not increase as much as ego's age because, as ego grows older, older kin are more likely to die and so drop out of the calculation of the average. [16] Parkin 1992: 68.

Table 3.1.a: Female, "ordinary," Level 3 West: mean number of living kin

Kin	EXACT AGE OF EGO (YEARS)														
	0	5	10	15	20	25	30	35	40	45	50	55	60	65	70
Husband	.	.	.	0.0	0.6	0.9	1.0	1.0	1.0	0.9	0.9	0.9	0.7	0.5	0.3
Parent	2.0	1.8	1.6	1.3	1.1	0.9	0.7	0.5	0.3	0.2	0.1	0.0	0.0	0.0	0.0
Father	1.0	0.9	0.8	0.6	0.5	0.4	0.2	0.2	0.1	0.0	0.0	0.0	0.0	.	.
Mother	1.0	0.9	0.8	0.7	0.6	0.5	0.4	0.3	0.2	0.2	0.1	0.0	0.0	0.0	0.0
Sibling	1.3	2.1	2.2	2.1	2.0	1.8	1.7	1.5	1.4	1.2	1.0	0.8	0.7	0.5	0.3
Brother	0.6	1.0	1.1	1.0	1.0	0.9	0.8	0.7	0.7	0.6	0.5	0.4	0.3	0.2	0.1
Sister	0.7	1.1	1.1	1.1	1.0	0.9	0.9	0.8	0.7	0.6	0.5	0.5	0.4	0.3	0.2
Child	.	.	.	.	0.3	1.3	1.9	2.2	2.3	2.3	2.1	2.0	1.8	1.6	1.4
Son	.	.	.	.	0.2	0.6	1.0	1.1	1.2	1.2	1.1	1.0	0.9	0.8	0.7
Daughter	.	.	.	.	0.1	0.7	1.0	1.1	1.2	1.1	1.1	1.0	0.9	0.8	0.7
Grandparent	1.3	1.0	0.7	0.4	0.2	0.1	0.1	0.0	0.0	0.0	.	.	.	.	.
Grandfather	0.5	0.3	0.2	0.1	0.0	0.1	0.0	0.0	.	.	.	.	.	.	.
Grandmother	0.8	0.7	0.5	0.3	0.2	0.1	0.0	0.0	.	0.0	.	.	.	.	.
Maternal grandfather	0.3	0.2	0.1	0.1	0.0	0.0	0.0	0.0	.	.	.	.	.	.	.
Paternal grandfather	0.1	0.1	0.0	0.0	0.0	0.0	0.0	0.0	.	.	.	.	.	.	.
Maternal grandmother	0.5	0.4	0.3	0.2	0.1	0.1	0.0	0.0	0.0	0.0	.	.	.	.	.
Paternal grandmother	0.3	0.2	0.2	0.1	0.0	0.0	0.0	0.0	.	.	.	.	.	.	.
Grandchild	.	.	.	.	.	.	.	.	0.1	0.4	1.1	2.0	2.8	3.3	3.6
Grandson	.	.	.	.	.	.	.	.	0.0	0.2	0.6	1.0	1.4	1.7	1.8
Granddaughter	.	.	.	.	.	.	.	.	0.0	0.2	0.6	1.0	1.4	1.7	1.8
Aunt/uncle	3.2	2.8	2.5	2.2	1.9	1.5	1.2	0.9	0.6	0.4	0.2	0.1	0.0	0.0	0.0
Aunt	1.6	1.4	1.3	1.1	1.0	0.8	0.7	0.5	0.3	0.2	0.1	0.1	0.0	0.0	0.0
Uncle	1.6	1.4	1.2	1.1	0.9	0.7	0.6	0.4	0.3	0.2	0.1	0.0	0.0	0.0	0.0
Maternal aunt	0.9	0.8	0.7	0.7	0.6	0.5	0.4	0.3	0.2	0.2	0.1	0.1	0.0	0.0	0.0
Paternal aunt	0.7	0.6	0.5	0.5	0.4	0.3	0.2	0.2	0.1	0.1	0.0	0.0	0.0	0.0	0.0
Maternal uncle	0.9	0.8	0.7	0.6	0.5	0.4	0.3	0.3	0.2	0.1	0.1	0.0	0.0	0.0	0.0
Paternal uncle	0.7	0.6	0.5	0.5	0.4	0.3	0.2	0.1	0.1	0.0	0.0	0.0	0.0	0.0	0.0
Nephew/niece	0.0	0.0	0.0	0.2	0.6	1.3	2.2	2.8	3.3	3.3	3.2	3.0	2.8	2.5	2.2
Nephew	0.0	0.0	0.0	0.1	0.3	0.7	1.1	1.4	1.6	1.6	1.6	1.5	1.4	1.2	1.1
Niece	0.0	0.0	0.0	0.1	0.3	0.7	1.1	1.5	1.7	1.7	1.6	1.5	1.4	1.3	1.1

Note: . indicates no occurrences in simulation; 0.0 indicates less than 0.1
Demographic analysis of 'ordinary', Level 3 West population: Gross Reproduction Rate: 2.44; Net Reproduction Rate: 1.00; Mean Age at Maternity: 26.48

Table 3.1.b: *Female, "ordinary," Level 3 West: proportion having living kin*

Kin	0	5	10	15	20	25	30	35	40	45	50	55	60	65	70
							EXACT AGE OF EGO (YEARS)								
Husband	.	.	.	0.00	0.59	0.92	0.96	0.95	0.95	0.95	0.94	0.93	0.71	0.51	0.33
Parent	1.00	0.99	0.95	0.89	0.81	0.70	0.58	0.45	0.30	0.19	0.10	0.05	0.02	0.00	0.00
Father	1.00	0.87	0.76	0.62	0.49	0.37	0.25	0.15	0.08	0.04	0.01	0.00	0.00	.	0.00
Mother	1.00	0.90	0.81	0.71	0.62	0.53	0.44	0.35	0.24	0.16	0.09	0.04	0.02	0.00	0.00
Sibling	0.62	0.85	0.83	0.82	0.81	0.79	0.76	0.73	0.69	0.65	0.60	0.54	0.47	0.37	0.27
Brother	0.43	0.62	0.62	0.61	0.58	0.56	0.53	0.50	0.46	0.41	0.36	0.31	0.25	0.18	0.13
Sister	0.43	0.63	0.63	0.62	0.60	0.58	0.56	0.52	0.48	0.44	0.40	0.35	0.30	0.23	0.17
Child	.	.	.	.	0.26	0.73	0.83	0.85	0.85	0.84	0.82	0.80	0.78	0.75	0.70
Son	.	.	.	.	0.14	0.47	0.60	0.64	0.65	0.64	0.62	0.59	0.56	0.52	0.47
Daughter	.	.	.	.	0.14	0.49	0.61	0.65	0.66	0.65	0.63	0.60	0.57	0.53	0.49
Grandparent	0.80	0.67	0.52	0.36	0.22	0.12	0.05	0.02	0.00	0.00					
Grandfather	0.42	0.29	0.18	0.10	0.05	0.02	0.01	0.00	.	.					
Grandmother	0.68	0.56	0.43	0.30	0.18	0.10	0.05	0.02	0.00	0.00					
Maternal grandfather	0.33	0.23	0.15	0.08	0.04	0.02	0.01	0.00	.	.					
Paternal grandfather	0.15	0.09	0.04	0.02	0.01	0.00	0.00	.	.	0.00					
Maternal grandmother	0.52	0.42	0.33	0.23	0.15	0.09	0.04	0.02	0.00	.					
Paternal grandmother	0.33	0.24	0.16	0.09	0.04	0.02	0.01	0.00	.	0.00					
Grandchild	.	.	.	.	.	.	.	.	0.04	0.25	0.45	0.60	0.69	0.73	0.74
Grandson	.	.	.	.	.	.	.	.	0.03	0.16	0.33	0.47	0.58	0.62	0.64
Granddaughter	.	.	.	.	.	.	.	.	0.02	0.16	0.33	0.48	0.57	0.63	0.64
Aunt/uncle	0.94	0.92	0.89	0.86	0.81	0.75	0.66	0.55	0.42	0.30	0.18	0.09	0.04	0.01	0.01
Aunt	0.77	0.74	0.70	0.65	0.60	0.54	0.46	0.37	0.28	0.19	0.11	0.06	0.03	0.01	0.00
Uncle	0.77	0.73	0.68	0.63	0.56	0.49	0.42	0.32	0.22	0.14	0.08	0.04	0.02	0.01	0.00
Maternal aunt	0.56	0.53	0.50	0.47	0.43	0.38	0.32	0.27	0.20	0.15	0.09	0.05	0.02	0.01	0.00
Paternal aunt	0.48	0.44	0.40	0.35	0.31	0.26	0.20	0.15	0.10	0.05	0.02	0.01	0.00	0.00	0.00
Maternal uncle	0.55	0.51	0.48	0.44	0.39	0.33	0.28	0.22	0.16	0.10	0.06	0.03	0.01	0.00	0.00
Paternal uncle	0.49	0.44	0.40	0.35	0.30	0.24	0.19	0.13	0.08	0.04	0.02	0.01	0.00	0.00	0.00
Nephew/niece	0.00	0.01	0.03	0.10	0.27	0.46	0.59	0.68	0.70	0.71	0.71	0.70	0.69	0.68	0.66
Nephew	0.00	0.00	0.02	0.07	0.19	0.35	0.48	0.57	0.60	0.61	0.60	0.59	0.57	0.55	0.52
Niece	0.00	0.00	0.02	0.07	0.19	0.34	0.48	0.57	0.60	0.60	0.59	0.58	0.57	0.55	0.52

Note: . indicates no occurrences in simulation; 0.00 indicates less than 0.01

Table 3.1.c: Female, "ordinary," Level 3 West: mean age of living kin

EXACT AGE OF EGO (YEARS)

Kin	0	5	10	15	20	25	30	35	40	45	50	55	60	65	70
Husband	.	.	.	28.8	32.6	36.0	39.5	42.9	46.4	48.7	50.3	51.5	55.1	58.1	60.4
Parent	31.6	36.4	41.1	45.7	50.2	54.6	58.8	62.8	66.8	70.6	74.2	78.1	82.1	.	.
Father	36.3	41.1	45.8	50.4	55.0	59.6	64.1	68.3	72.8	76.8	80.9	85.1	88.8	85.4	87.9
Mother	26.9	31.8	36.7	41.5	46.4	51.1	55.8	60.4	64.7	69.2	73.6	77.7	82.0	85.4	87.9
Sibling	4.3	6.1	10.1	14.8	19.7	24.6	29.5	34.4	39.3	44.2	49.0	53.8	58.6	62.9	67.2
Brother	4.1	6.0	10.0	14.6	19.5	24.4	29.3	34.2	39.1	43.9	48.8	53.6	58.4	62.7	67.2
Sister	4.4	6.2	10.2	14.9	19.8	24.7	29.7	34.6	39.5	44.4	49.2	54.0	58.7	63.1	67.1
Child	.	.	.	.	0.9	2.7	5.4	8.8	12.7	16.9	21.6	26.5	31.5	36.3	41.1
Son	.	.	.	.	0.9	2.7	5.4	8.8	12.6	16.8	21.6	26.5	31.3	36.2	40.9
Daughter	.	.	.	.	0.9	2.7	5.5	8.9	12.7	16.9	21.7	26.6	31.6	36.5	41.4
Grandparent	57.2	60.8	64.2	67.5	70.9	73.7	76.5	80.2	82.6	86.1	.	.	.	.	.
Grandfather	61.7	65.3	68.6	72.1	76.1	79.3	82.8	83.9	.	.	.	.	.	.	.
Grandmother	54.7	58.7	62.5	66.1	69.6	72.7	75.8	80.1	82.6	86.1	.	.	.	.	.
Maternal grandfather	59.4	63.1	67.0	70.6	75.0	78.7	82.6	83.9							
Paternal grandfather	66.9	71.0	74.0	77.8	81.6	84.2	86.0								
Maternal grandmother	51.6	56.0	60.2	64.1	68.0	71.4	75.1	79.9	82.6	86.1					
Paternal grandmother	59.5	63.6	67.5	71.0	75.0	78.8	81.4	87.3	82.6	86.1					
Grandchild									1.1	2.1	3.7	5.4	7.5	10.2	13.4
Grandson									1.2	2.1	3.7	5.5	7.5	10.2	13.5
Granddaughter									0.9	2.2	3.7	5.3	7.5	10.1	13.3
Aunt/uncle	29.6	34.3	39.0	43.7	48.2	52.6	56.8	60.6	64.2	67.9	71.0	74.0	76.6	77.9	80.5
Aunt	29.4	34.1	38.9	43.6	48.1	52.6	56.8	60.6	64.2	67.7	70.9	73.9	76.2	77.5	78.9
Uncle	29.8	34.5	39.2	43.7	48.2	52.6	56.8	60.5	64.1	68.1	71.2	74.2	77.2	78.5	82.3
Maternal aunt	25.4	30.2	35.2	40.0	44.7	49.3	53.8	58.0	62.0	66.0	69.4	73.0	75.5	77.5	78.4
Paternal aunt	34.5	39.3	44.0	48.6	53.3	57.9	61.9	65.7	69.3	72.8	76.5	78.4	81.1	77.8	82.8
Maternal uncle	25.8	30.6	35.4	40.1	44.8	49.4	53.8	58.0	62.0	66.3	69.9	72.8	76.0	77.8	81.7
Paternal uncle	34.7	39.4	44.1	48.5	53.0	57.3	61.4	65.0	68.6	72.3	75.7	78.7	81.4	81.5	83.8
Nephew/niece	1.3	2.0	2.6	2.9	3.5	4.7	6.3	8.6	11.4	15.1	19.4	24.1	28.9	33.6	38.4
Nephew	1.7	2.4	2.7	2.9	3.4	4.7	6.3	8.6	11.4	15.0	19.3	23.9	28.6	33.4	38.1
Niece	0.6	1.6	2.4	2.8	3.6	4.7	6.4	8.6	11.5	15.2	19.6	24.3	29.1	33.9	38.7

Note: . indicates no occurrences in simulation; 0.0 indicates less than 0.1

Table 3.1.d: *Male, "ordinary," Level 3 West: mean number of living kin*

Kin	EXACT AGE OF EGO (YEARS)														
	0	5	10	15	20	25	30	35	40	45	50	55	60	65	70
Wife	.	.	.	.	.	0.0	0.6	0.9	1.0	1.0	1.0	1.0	0.9	0.7	0.5
Parent	2.0	1.8	1.6	1.4	1.2	0.9	0.7	0.5	0.3	0.2	0.1	0.0	0.0	0.0	.
Father	1.0	0.9	0.7	0.6	0.5	0.4	0.2	0.2	0.1	0.0	0.0	0.0	0.0	.	.
Mother	1.0	0.9	0.8	0.7	0.6	0.6	0.5	0.4	0.3	0.2	0.1	0.0	0.0	0.0	.
Sibling	1.2	1.9	2.0	2.0	1.8	1.7	1.6	1.4	1.3	1.1	0.9	0.8	0.6	0.5	0.3
Brother	0.6	1.0	1.0	1.0	0.9	0.9	0.8	0.7	0.6	0.5	0.5	0.4	0.3	0.2	0.1
Sister	0.6	1.0	1.0	1.0	0.9	0.8	0.8	0.7	0.6	0.6	0.5	0.4	0.3	0.2	0.2
Child	.	.	.	.	.	0.0	0.3	1.4	2.1	2.4	2.5	2.6	2.6	2.5	2.3
Son	.	.	.	.	.	0.0	0.2	0.7	1.0	1.2	1.3	1.3	1.3	1.2	1.1
Daughter	.	.	.	.	.	0.0	0.1	0.7	1.0	1.2	1.2	1.3	1.3	1.2	1.1
Grandparent	1.4	1.1	0.7	0.5	0.3	0.1	0.1	0.0	0.0	0.0	.	.	.	.	.
Grandfather	0.5	0.3	0.2	0.1	0.0	0.0	0.0	0.0	0.0	.	.	.	.	.	.
Grandmother	0.9	0.7	0.5	0.3	0.2	0.1	0.1	0.0	0.0	0.0	.	.	.	.	.
Maternal grandfather	0.3	0.2	0.2	0.1	0.0	0.0	0.0	0.0	0.0	.	.	.	.	.	.
Paternal grandfather	0.2	0.1	0.1	0.0	0.0	0.0	0.0	.	.	.	.	.	.	.	.
Maternal grandmother	0.5	0.4	0.4	0.2	0.2	0.1	0.0	0.0	0.0	.	.	.	.	.	.
Paternal grandmother	0.4	0.3	0.2	0.1	0.0	0.0	0.0	.	.	.	.	.	.	.	.
Grandchild	.	.	.	.	.	.	.	.	.	0.0	0.1	0.5	1.2	2.1	3.1
Grandson	.	.	.	.	.	.	.	.	.	0.0	0.0	0.2	0.6	1.0	1.6
Granddaughter	.	.	.	.	.	.	.	.	.	0.0	0.0	0.2	0.6	1.1	1.6
Aunt/uncle	3.1	2.8	2.5	2.1	1.8	1.5	1.2	0.9	0.6	0.4	0.2	0.1	0.0	0.0	0.0
Aunt	1.5	1.4	1.2	1.1	0.9	0.8	0.6	0.5	0.3	0.2	0.1	0.1	0.0	0.0	0.0
Uncle	1.5	1.4	1.2	1.1	0.9	0.7	0.6	0.4	0.3	0.2	0.1	0.1	0.0	0.0	.
Maternal aunt	0.8	0.7	0.7	0.6	0.5	0.5	0.4	0.3	0.2	0.2	0.1	0.1	0.0	0.0	0.0
Paternal aunt	0.7	0.7	0.6	0.5	0.4	0.3	0.3	0.2	0.1	0.1	0.0	0.0	0.0	0.0	.
Maternal uncle	0.8	0.7	0.7	0.6	0.5	0.4	0.3	0.3	0.2	0.1	0.1	0.0	0.0	0.0	0.0
Paternal uncle	0.7	0.6	0.5	0.5	0.3	0.3	0.2	0.1	0.1	0.0	0.0	0.0	0.0	0.0	.
Nephew/niece	.	0.0	0.0	0.2	0.6	1.2	2.0	2.7	3.2	3.4	3.4	3.2	3.0	2.8	2.5
Nephew	.	0.0	0.0	0.1	0.3	0.6	1.0	1.4	1.6	1.7	1.7	1.6	1.5	1.4	1.3
Niece	.	0.0	0.0	0.1	0.3	0.6	1.0	1.4	1.6	1.7	1.7	1.6	1.5	1.4	1.3

Note: . indicates no occurrences in simulation; 0.0 indicates less than 0.1

Table 3.1.e: Male, "ordinary," Level 3 West: proportion having living kin

Kin	EXACT AGE OF EGO (YEARS)														
	0	5	10	15	20	25	30	35	40	45	50	55	60	65	70
Wife						0.00	0.59	0.93	0.97	0.98	0.96	0.96	0.86	0.74	0.62
Parent	1.00	0.99	0.95	0.89	0.82	0.73	0.61	0.47	0.32	0.21	0.11	0.05	0.02	0.00	0.00
Father	1.00	0.88	0.75	0.63	0.51	0.39	0.28	0.17	0.09	0.04	0.01	0.00	0.00	0.00	·
Mother	1.00	0.91	0.81	0.72	0.65	0.56	0.46	0.37	0.26	0.17	0.10	0.05	0.02	0.00	·
Sibling	0.61	0.85	0.84	0.83	0.81	0.79	0.77	0.73	0.69	0.64	0.59	0.53	0.45	0.36	0.25
Brother	0.42	0.63	0.63	0.62	0.59	0.57	0.54	0.50	0.46	0.41	0.36	0.32	0.26	0.19	0.13
Sister	0.42	0.62	0.62	0.60	0.58	0.55	0.52	0.48	0.45	0.41	0.38	0.33	0.28	0.22	0.15
Child						0.00	0.27	0.77	0.86	0.88	0.88	0.88	0.86	0.85	0.82
Son						0.00	0.16	0.51	0.65	0.67	0.69	0.69	0.68	0.65	0.62
Daughter						0.00	0.13	0.51	0.63	0.67	0.68	0.68	0.67	0.66	0.63
Grandparent	0.82	0.70	0.56	0.39	0.24	0.13	0.06	0.02	0.01						
Grandfather	0.45	0.31	0.20	0.10	0.04	0.01									
Grandmother	0.71	0.59	0.46	0.32	0.21	0.11	0.06	0.02	0.01						
Maternal grandfather	0.34	0.24	0.15	0.08	0.04	0.01	0.00								
Paternal grandfather	0.17	0.10	0.05	0.02	0.00	0.00	0.00								
Maternal grandmother	0.54	0.45	0.35	0.25	0.17	0.10	0.05	0.02	0.01						
Paternal grandmother	0.37	0.28	0.18	0.10	0.05	0.02	0.01	0.00	0.01						
Grandchild										0.00	0.06	0.27	0.48	0.66	0.75
Grandson										0.00	0.03	0.17	0.34	0.51	0.64
Granddaughter										0.00	0.04	0.17	0.36	0.53	0.63
Aunt/uncle	0.94	0.93	0.90	0.86	0.82	0.75	0.67	0.55	0.41	0.29	0.17	0.09	0.04	0.02	0.00
Aunt	0.77	0.73	0.69	0.64	0.59	0.53	0.45	0.35	0.27	0.19	0.11	0.05	0.02	0.01	0.00
Uncle	0.77	0.74	0.70	0.64	0.58	0.50	0.42	0.33	0.22	0.15	0.08	0.04	0.01	0.01	0.00
Maternal aunt	0.53	0.50	0.47	0.43	0.40	0.35	0.30	0.25	0.19	0.14	0.08	0.04	0.02	0.01	·
Paternal aunt	0.50	0.47	0.43	0.38	0.33	0.28	0.21	0.15	0.10	0.06	0.03	0.01	0.00	0.00	·
Maternal uncle	0.54	0.51	0.48	0.44	0.39	0.34	0.29	0.23	0.16	0.11	0.07	0.03	0.01	0.01	·
Paternal uncle	0.49	0.45	0.41	0.36	0.30	0.25	0.19	0.13	0.08	0.04	0.02	0.01	0.00	0.00	·
Nephew/niece	·	0.00	0.02	0.10	0.25	0.45	0.60	0.69	0.72	0.73	0.73	0.72	0.71	0.70	0.68
Nephew	·	0.00	0.01	0.06	0.17	0.32	0.47	0.57	0.61	0.63	0.62	0.61	0.59	0.57	0.54
Niece	·	0.00	0.01	0.06	0.17	0.33	0.47	0.57	0.61	0.62	0.62	0.61	0.58	0.56	0.54

Note: . indicates no occurrences in simulation; 0.00 indicates less than 0.01

Table 3.1.f: Male, "ordinary," Level 3 West: mean age of living kin

Kin	EXACT AGE OF EGO (YEARS)														
	0	5	10	15	20	25	30	35	40	45	50	55	60	65	70
Wife							21.7	25.1	29.1	33.1	36.6	39.2	44.0	48.7	53.2
Parent	30.8	35.7	40.4	45.1	49.7	54.2	58.7	62.7	66.6	70.5	74.3	78.3	82.5	86.0	88.9
Father	35.0	39.9	44.7	49.6	54.3	59.0	63.8	68.3	72.7	77.3	81.6	86.7	89.4	91.6	.
Mother	26.6	31.5	36.4	41.2	46.1	50.8	55.6	60.2	64.5	68.9	73.3	77.9	82.1	85.5	88.9
Sibling	4.3	6.2	10.0	14.7	19.6	24.6	29.5	34.4	39.3	44.2	49.1	53.8	58.4	62.8	66.9
Brother	4.4	6.2	10.2	14.8	19.7	24.7	29.5	34.5	39.4	44.2	49.0	53.8	58.3	62.6	66.8
Sister	4.2	6.1	9.9	14.6	19.5	24.5	29.4	34.3	39.2	44.2	49.1	53.9	58.5	62.9	66.9
Child							0.9	2.7	5.4	8.8	12.4	15.9	19.5	23.8	28.4
Son							0.9	2.7	5.4	8.8	12.4	16.0	19.5	23.7	28.4
Daughter							0.9	2.7	5.4	8.8	12.4	15.9	19.5	23.9	28.4
Grandparent	57.1	60.8	64.4	67.6	70.4	73.6	76.7	80.5	82.6	87.3	92.4				
Grandfather	61.5	65.6	69.4	73.0	75.9	79.7	82.6	93.8							
Grandmother	54.5	58.6	62.5	66.0	69.4	72.9	76.2	80.3	82.6	87.3	92.4				
Maternal grandfather	59.0	63.2	67.3	71.1	74.8	78.9	82.6	93.8							
Paternal grandfather	66.6	71.2	75.4	79.7	84.3	87.6									
Maternal grandmother	51.3	55.6	60.0	63.8	67.9	71.7	75.4	79.7	82.6	87.3	92.4				
Paternal grandmother	59.2	63.4	67.4	71.5	75.0	78.9	82.8	88.8							
Grandchild										0.6	1.0	2.3	3.7	5.3	7.2
Grandson										0.6	0.9	2.3	3.8	5.4	7.2
Granddaughter											1.0	2.3	3.7	5.3	7.2
Aunt/uncle	29.4	34.2	38.9	43.6	48.1	52.5	56.7	60.5	64.2	67.6	70.8	73.8	76.7	79.0	80.7
Aunt	29.6	34.4	39.2	43.9	48.4	52.8	56.9	60.7	64.3	67.7	70.7	73.6	76.2	78.2	79.7
Uncle	29.3	34.0	38.7	43.3	47.8	52.2	56.4	60.3	64.0	67.6	71.0	74.3	77.5	80.2	81.7
Maternal aunt	25.7	30.5	35.3	40.1	44.9	49.4	53.9	58.0	62.0	65.7	69.0	72.1	74.9	77.5	79.7
Paternal aunt	34.0	38.9	43.7	48.4	52.9	57.4	61.4	65.4	69.1	72.7	76.2	80.7	84.5	88.6	
Maternal uncle	25.3	30.1	34.8	39.6	44.3	48.9	53.5	57.8	61.9	66.1	69.8	73.3	77.2	79.3	
Paternal uncle	33.9	38.7	43.4	48.1	52.6	57.1	61.3	64.9	68.5	71.7	75.1	78.4	79.0	88.0	81.7
Nephew/niece	0.9	2.1	2.2	2.4	3.3	4.5	6.2	8.2	10.9	14.2	18.1	22.2	26.5	31.0	35.5
Nephew	0.9	2.8	2.5	2.5	3.4	4.6	6.2	8.3	11.0	14.3	18.1	22.2	26.5	30.9	35.4
Niece		1.1	1.9	2.3	3.1	4.4	6.1	8.1	10.9	14.2	18.1	22.1	26.5	31.1	35.7

Note: . indicates no occurrences in simulation; 0.0 indicates less than 0.1

Table 3.2.a: Female, "senatorial," Level 3 West: mean number of living kin

Kin	EXACT AGE OF EGO (YEARS)														
	0	5	10	15	20	25	30	35	40	45	50	55	60	65	70
Husband	·	·	·	0.6	1.0	1.0	1.0	1.0	1.0	0.9	0.9	0.9	0.7	0.5	0.3
Parent	2.0	1.8	1.6	1.4	1.2	1.0	0.8	0.6	0.4	0.3	0.2	0.1	0.0	0.0	0.0
Father	1.0	0.9	0.8	0.7	0.5	0.4	0.3	0.2	0.1	0.1	0.0	0.0	0.0	0.0	0.0
Mother	1.0	0.9	0.8	0.8	0.7	0.6	0.5	0.4	0.3	0.2	0.1	0.1	0.0	·	0.0
Sibling	1.2	1.9	2.0	1.9	1.8	1.7	1.5	1.4	1.3	1.1	0.9	0.8	0.6	0.4	0.3
Brother	0.6	0.9	1.0	1.0	0.9	0.8	0.8	0.7	0.6	0.5	0.5	0.4	0.3	0.2	0.1
Sister	0.6	1.0	1.0	1.0	0.9	0.8	0.8	0.7	0.6	0.6	0.5	0.4	0.3	0.2	0.2
Child	·	·	·	·	1.2	1.8	2.0	2.1	2.1	2.1	1.9	1.8	1.6	1.4	1.2
Son					0.6	0.9	1.0	1.1	1.1	1.0	1.0	0.9	0.8	0.7	0.6
Daughter					0.6	0.9	1.0	1.1	1.1	1.0	1.0	0.9	0.8	0.7	0.6
Grandparent	1.8	1.5	1.1	0.8	0.6	0.4	0.2	0.1	0.0	0.0	0.0	·	·	·	·
Grandfather	0.8	0.6	0.4	0.2	0.1	0.1	0.0	0.0	0.0	0.0	0.0				
Grandmother	1.1	0.9	0.7	0.6	0.4	0.3	0.2	0.1	0.0	0.0	0.0				
Maternal grandfather	0.5	0.4	0.3	0.2	0.1	0.1	0.0	0.0	0.0	·	0.0				
Paternal grandfather	0.3	0.2	0.1	0.1	0.0	0.0	0.0	0.0	0.0	·					
Maternal grandmother	0.6	0.5	0.5	0.4	0.3	0.2	0.1	0.1	0.0	0.0	0.0				
Paternal grandmother	0.5	0.4	0.3	0.2	0.1	0.1	0.0	0.0	0.0	0.0					
Grandchild	·	·	·	·	·	·	·	0.2	0.8	1.6	2.5	3.1	3.5	3.6	3.5
Grandson								0.1	0.4	0.8	1.2	1.5	1.7	1.8	1.7
Granddaughter								0.1	0.4	0.8	1.3	1.6	1.8	1.8	1.8
Aunt/uncle	3.2	2.9	2.6	2.3	2.0	1.7	1.4	1.1	0.8	0.5	0.3	0.2	0.1	0.0	0.0
Aunt	1.6	1.4	1.3	1.2	1.0	0.9	0.7	0.6	0.4	0.3	0.2	0.1	0.1	0.0	0.0
Uncle	1.6	1.5	1.3	1.1	1.0	0.8	0.7	0.5	0.4	0.2	0.1	0.1	0.0	0.0	0.0
Maternal aunt	0.9	0.8	0.7	0.7	0.6	0.5	0.4	0.4	0.3	0.2	0.1	0.1	0.0	0.0	0.0
Paternal aunt	0.7	0.7	0.6	0.5	0.4	0.4	0.3	0.2	0.1	0.1	0.0	0.1	0.1	0.0	0.0
Maternal uncle	0.9	0.8	0.7	0.7	0.6	0.5	0.4	0.3	0.2	0.2	0.1	0.1	0.0	0.0	0.0
Paternal uncle	0.7	0.7	0.6	0.5	0.4	0.3	0.2	0.2	0.1	0.1	0.0	0.0	0.0	0.0	0.0
Nephew/niece	0.0	0.0	0.1	0.5	1.1	1.9	2.6	3.1	3.2	3.2	3.0	2.8	2.5	2.3	2.0
Nephew	0.0	0.0	0.1	0.2	0.5	1.0	1.3	1.5	1.6	1.6	1.5	1.4	1.3	1.1	1.0
Niece	0.0	0.0	0.1	0.3	0.6	0.9	1.3	1.5	1.6	1.6	1.5	1.4	1.3	1.1	1.0

Note: · indicates no occurrences in simulation; 0.0 indicates less than 0.1

Demographic analysis of "senatorial", Level 3 West population: Gross Reproduction Rate: 2.29; Net Reproduction Rate: 1.00; Mean Age at Maternity: 22.45

Table 3.2.b: Female, "senatorial," Level 3 West: proportion having living kin

Kin	EXACT AGE OF EGO (YEARS)														
	0	5	10	15	20	25	30	35	40	45	50	55	60	65	70
Husband				0.60	0.97	0.97	0.96	0.96	0.95	0.95	0.94	0.92	0.70	0.51	0.35
Parent	1.00	0.99	0.96	0.92	0.84	0.75	0.65	0.52	0.40	0.27	0.16	0.09	0.04	0.01	0.00
Father	1.00	0.89	0.78	0.67	0.54	0.41	0.31	0.21	0.12	0.07	0.03	0.01	0.00	.	.
Mother	1.00	0.93	0.85	0.75	0.67	0.58	0.50	0.41	0.32	0.23	0.14	0.08	0.03	0.01	0.00
Sibling	0.60	0.82	0.80	0.79	0.77	0.75	0.73	0.70	0.66	0.62	0.56	0.51	0.42	0.34	0.24
Brother	0.41	0.59	0.60	0.58	0.56	0.54	0.51	0.48	0.45	0.41	0.35	0.30	0.23	0.18	0.12
Sister	0.41	0.60	0.60	0.58	0.56	0.53	0.50	0.47	0.44	0.40	0.36	0.32	0.27	0.21	0.14
Child					0.73	0.81	0.82	0.82	0.81	0.81	0.79	0.76	0.73	0.70	0.66
Son					0.47	0.58	0.61	0.62	0.62	0.61	0.58	0.54	0.51	0.47	0.42
Daughter					0.46	0.58	0.61	0.62	0.62	0.61	0.59	0.55	0.52	0.48	0.45
Grandparent	0.89	0.82	0.71	0.58	0.45	0.32	0.18	0.09	0.04	0.01	0.00	.	.	.	.
Grandfather	0.62	0.48	0.33	0.22	0.14	0.07	0.03	0.01	0.00	0.00	0.00	.	.	.	.
Grandmother	0.78	0.70	0.60	0.48	0.38	0.27	0.16	0.08	0.03	0.01	0.00	.	.	.	.
Maternal grandfather	0.48	0.37	0.26	0.17	0.11	0.06	0.03	0.01	0.00	0.00	0.00	.	.	.	.
Paternal grandfather	0.28	0.18	0.11	0.07	0.03	0.01	0.00	.	.	.	.	.	.	.	.
Maternal grandmother	0.61	0.53	0.45	0.36	0.29	0.21	0.13	0.07	0.03	0.01	0.00	.	.	.	.
Paternal grandmother	0.45	0.38	0.29	0.20	0.14	0.08	0.04	0.01	0.00	0.00	.	.	.	.	.
Grandchild	.	.	.	.	.	.	.	0.16	0.38	0.56	0.66	0.71	0.72	0.73	0.73
Grandson	.	.	.	.	.	.	.	0.09	0.25	0.41	0.53	0.59	0.62	0.62	0.62
Granddaughter	.	.	.	.	.	.	.	0.09	0.28	0.43	0.54	0.61	0.62	0.63	0.63
Aunt/uncle	0.93	0.91	0.89	0.86	0.82	0.77	0.70	0.61	0.51	0.38	0.26	0.16	0.08	0.03	0.01
Aunt	0.76	0.74	0.70	0.67	0.62	0.56	0.50	0.42	0.33	0.24	0.16	0.10	0.05	0.02	0.01
Uncle	0.77	0.74	0.70	0.65	0.60	0.54	0.45	0.37	0.29	0.20	0.13	0.07	0.03	0.01	0.00
Maternal aunt	0.55	0.52	0.49	0.46	0.42	0.38	0.34	0.28	0.23	0.18	0.13	0.08	0.04	0.02	0.01
Paternal aunt	0.49	0.46	0.42	0.38	0.34	0.30	0.24	0.19	0.13	0.08	0.04	0.02	0.01	0.00	0.00
Maternal uncle	0.55	0.52	0.49	0.46	0.42	0.37	0.31	0.26	0.20	0.15	0.10	0.06	0.02	0.01	0.00
Paternal uncle	0.50	0.46	0.42	0.36	0.31	0.27	0.20	0.15	0.11	0.07	0.04	0.02	0.00	0.00	0.00
Nephew/niece	0.00	0.01	0.06	0.23	0.41	0.57	0.65	0.69	0.69	0.68	0.68	0.67	0.65	0.63	0.61
Nephew	0.00	0.01	0.04	0.15	0.30	0.45	0.54	0.58	0.60	0.59	0.57	0.56	0.54	0.51	0.48
Niece	0.00	0.01	0.04	0.16	0.30	0.44	0.53	0.58	0.59	0.58	0.57	0.55	0.53	0.50	0.47

Note: . indicates no occurrences in simulation; 0.00 indicates less than 0.01

Table 3.2.c: Female, "senatorial," Level 3 West: mean age of living kin

Kin	EXACT AGE OF EGO (YEARS)														
	0	5	10	15	20	25	30	35	40	45	50	55	60	65	70
Husband	.	.	.	27.0	31.2	35.5	39.0	42.5	45.4	47.6	49.2	50.1	53.3	55.9	57.8
Parent	27.8	32.5	37.2	41.9	46.5	50.8	55.1	59.1	63.2	67.3	71.1	75.1	79.2	82.9	87.5
Father	32.6	37.3	42.0	46.7	51.3	55.7	60.2	64.6	68.9	73.4	77.7	81.7	87.5	.	.
Mother	23.0	27.9	32.8	37.7	42.6	47.3	51.9	56.3	61.0	65.6	69.9	74.5	78.8	82.9	87.5
Sibling	4.2	6.1	10.1	14.8	19.7	24.6	29.5	34.4	39.3	44.1	49.1	53.8	58.4	63.0	67.1
Brother	4.2	6.1	10.0	14.8	19.6	24.5	29.3	34.3	39.2	43.9	48.8	53.6	58.3	62.8	67.0
Sister	4.2	6.1	10.1	14.8	19.7	24.7	29.6	34.6	39.5	44.3	49.3	54.0	58.6	63.1	67.3
Child	.	.	.	.	2.0	5.0	8.6	12.3	16.3	20.5	25.2	30.1	34.9	39.7	44.5
Son	.	.	.	.	2.0	5.0	8.6	12.4	16.3	20.6	25.4	30.2	35.0	39.7	44.5
Daughter	.	.	.	.	2.0	5.0	8.5	12.2	16.2	20.4	25.0	29.9	34.8	39.6	44.4
Grandparent	50.6	54.6	58.2	61.8	65.3	68.6	71.8	75.0	78.5	81.3	87.7	.	.	.	.
Grandfather	54.9	58.9	62.6	66.1	69.8	73.5	76.9	79.5	82.5	86.3	89.0	.	.	.	.
Grandmother	47.5	51.9	55.9	59.9	63.8	67.4	70.9	74.5	78.0	80.8	87.0	.	.	.	.
Maternal grandfather	52.1	56.4	60.4	64.2	68.2	72.4	76.1	79.5	82.5	86.3	89.0	.	.	.	.
Paternal grandfather	59.8	63.9	67.7	71.3	75.6	79.0	82.7	.	.	.	.	.	.	.	.
Maternal grandmother	43.9	48.5	52.9	57.3	61.5	65.6	69.4	73.5	77.4	80.6	87.0	.	.	.	.
Paternal grandmother	52.3	56.8	60.7	64.6	68.9	72.5	76.3	80.2	84.6	86.8	.	.	.	.	.
Grandchild	.	.	.	.	.	.	.	1.1	2.8	4.6	6.5	9.1	12.1	15.7	19.6
Grandson	.	.	.	.	.	.	.	1.1	2.8	4.5	6.4	9.0	12.0	15.7	19.6
Granddaughter	.	.	.	.	.	.	.	1.1	2.8	4.7	6.6	9.2	12.2	15.7	19.6
Aunt/uncle	25.8	30.5	35.2	39.9	44.5	48.9	53.1	57.3	61.1	64.8	68.2	71.6	74.0	76.7	80.7
Aunt	26.0	30.7	35.4	40.2	44.9	49.4	53.5	57.6	61.3	65.0	68.3	71.5	74.1	77.0	82.1
Uncle	25.7	30.3	34.9	39.5	44.1	48.5	52.6	56.9	60.8	64.7	68.1	71.7	73.8	76.2	76.5
Maternal aunt	21.9	26.7	31.5	36.4	41.2	45.8	50.4	54.8	58.9	63.0	66.8	70.3	73.2	76.2	81.9
Paternal aunt	30.8	35.6	40.3	45.2	49.7	54.1	58.3	62.2	66.0	69.7	72.9	76.0	79.1	81.5	83.0
Maternal uncle	21.5	26.2	30.9	35.7	40.6	45.2	49.7	54.2	58.5	62.7	66.6	70.8	73.7	76.1	75.7
Paternal uncle	30.6	35.4	40.1	44.7	49.2	53.5	57.4	61.9	65.8	69.4	72.0	75.1	73.9	77.2	83.9
Nephew/niece	2.2	2.1	2.5	2.8	4.2	5.7	8.0	10.7	14.1	18.1	22.6	27.2	32.0	36.7	41.4
Nephew	4.8	1.9	2.4	2.9	4.1	5.6	7.9	10.7	14.2	18.2	22.7	27.3	32.0	36.7	41.4
Niece	1.4	2.3	2.6	2.8	4.2	5.9	8.0	10.7	14.1	18.0	22.5	27.1	31.9	36.7	41.3

Note: . indicates no occurrences in simulation; 0.0 indicates less than 0.1

Table 3.2.d: *Male, "senatorial," Level 3 West: mean number of living kin*

Kin	EXACT AGE OF EGO (YEARS)														
	0	5	10	15	20	25	30	35	40	45	50	55	60	65	70
Wife	·	·	·	·	·	0.6	0.9	1.0	1.0	1.0	1.0	1.0	0.9	0.7	0.6
Parent	2.0	1.8	1.6	1.4	1.2	1.0	0.8	0.6	0.4	0.3	0.2	0.1	0.0	0.0	0.0
Father	1.0	0.9	0.8	0.7	0.5	0.4	0.3	0.2	0.1	0.1	0.0	0.0	0.0	·	·
Mother	1.0	0.9	0.8	0.8	0.7	0.6	0.5	0.4	0.3	0.2	0.1	0.1	0.0	0.0	0.0
Sibling	1.2	1.9	2.0	1.9	1.8	1.6	1.5	1.3	1.2	1.0	0.9	0.7	0.6	0.4	0.3
Brother	0.6	0.9	1.0	0.9	0.9	0.8	0.8	0.7	0.6	0.5	0.4	0.4	0.3	0.2	0.1
Sister	0.6	1.0	1.0	0.9	0.9	0.8	0.7	0.7	0.6	0.5	0.4	0.4	0.3	0.2	0.2
Child	·	·	·	·	·	0.3	1.2	1.7	1.9	1.9	1.8	1.7	1.5	1.4	1.2
Son	·	·	·	·	·	0.2	0.6	0.9	0.9	0.9	0.9	0.8	0.8	0.7	0.6
Daughter	·	·	·	·	·	0.1	0.6	0.9	1.0	0.9	0.9	0.8	0.8	0.7	0.6
Grandparent	1.8	1.4	1.1	0.8	0.5	0.3	0.2	0.1	0.0	0.0	0.0	·	·	·	·
Grandfather	0.7	0.5	0.4	0.2	0.1	0.1	0.0	0.0	0.0	0.0	·	·	·	·	·
Grandmother	1.0	0.9	0.7	0.5	0.4	0.2	0.1	0.1	0.0	0.0	0.0	·	·	·	·
Maternal grandfather	0.5	0.3	0.2	0.2	0.1	0.1	0.0	0.0	0.0	0.0	·	·	·	·	·
Paternal grandfather	0.3	0.2	0.1	0.1	0.0	0.0	0.0	0.0	·	·	·	·	·	·	·
Maternal grandmother	0.6	0.5	0.4	0.3	0.2	0.2	0.1	0.1	0.0	0.0	0.0	·	·	·	·
Paternal grandmother	0.4	0.4	0.3	0.2	0.1	0.1	0.0	0.0	0.0	0.0	·	·	·	·	·
Grandchild	·	·	·	·	·	·	·	·	0.0	0.3	1.0	1.8	2.5	2.9	3.1
Grandson	·	·	·	·	·	·	·	·	0.0	0.2	0.5	0.9	1.2	1.4	1.5
Granddaughter	·	·	·	·	·	·	·	·	0.0	0.2	0.5	0.9	1.2	1.5	1.6
Aunt/uncle	3.1	2.8	2.5	2.2	1.9	1.6	1.3	1.0	0.7	0.5	0.3	0.2	0.1	0.0	0.0
Aunt	1.5	1.4	1.3	1.1	1.0	0.9	0.7	0.6	0.4	0.3	0.2	0.1	0.0	0.0	0.0
Uncle	1.6	1.4	1.2	1.1	0.9	0.8	0.6	0.5	0.3	0.2	0.1	0.1	0.0	0.0	0.0
Maternal aunt	0.8	0.8	0.7	0.6	0.6	0.5	0.4	0.3	0.3	0.2	0.1	0.1	0.0	0.0	0.0
Paternal aunt	0.7	0.6	0.6	0.5	0.4	0.3	0.3	0.2	0.1	0.1	0.0	0.0	0.0	0.0	·
Maternal uncle	0.8	0.8	0.7	0.6	0.5	0.5	0.4	0.3	0.2	0.1	0.1	0.1	0.0	0.0	0.0
Paternal uncle	0.7	0.6	0.6	0.5	0.4	0.3	0.2	0.2	0.1	0.1	0.0	0.0	0.0	0.0	·
Nephew/niece	0.0	0.0	0.1	0.5	1.1	1.9	2.6	3.0	3.1	3.1	2.9	2.7	2.5	2.2	1.9
Nephew	0.0	0.0	0.1	0.3	0.6	0.9	1.3	1.5	1.6	1.5	1.5	1.4	1.2	1.1	1.0
Niece	0.0	0.0	0.1	0.3	0.6	1.0	1.3	1.5	1.6	1.5	1.5	1.3	1.2	1.1	1.0

Note: . indicates no occurrences in simulation; 0.0 indicates less than 0.1

Table 3.2.e: Male, "senatorial," Level 3 West: proportion having living kin

Kin	EXACT AGE OF EGO (YEARS)														
	0	5	10	15	20	25	30	35	40	45	50	55	60	65	70
Wife	.	.	.	.	.	0.59	0.93	0.97	0.97	0.97	0.97	0.96	0.85	0.72	0.58
Parent	1.00	0.99	0.96	0.91	0.85	0.76	0.65	0.53	0.40	0.27	0.17	0.09	0.04	0.01	0.00
Father	1.00	0.90	0.78	0.66	0.54	0.43	0.32	0.22	0.13	0.07	0.03	0.01	0.00	.	.
Mother	1.00	0.91	0.83	0.75	0.66	0.58	0.49	0.41	0.31	0.22	0.15	0.08	0.04	0.01	0.00
Sibling	0.60	0.83	0.81	0.80	0.78	0.76	0.73	0.69	0.66	0.61	0.56	0.49	0.42	0.34	0.23
Brother	0.40	0.59	0.60	0.59	0.57	0.54	0.51	0.48	0.44	0.40	0.35	0.30	0.24	0.18	0.11
Sister	0.41	0.60	0.60	0.58	0.56	0.53	0.50	0.46	0.43	0.39	0.35	0.30	0.25	0.20	0.14
Child	.	.	.	.	.	0.26	0.69	0.77	0.78	0.78	0.76	0.73	0.71	0.68	0.65
Son	.	.	.	.	.	0.14	0.44	0.56	0.58	0.58	0.56	0.53	0.50	0.47	0.43
Daughter	.	.	.	.	.	0.14	0.46	0.56	0.58	0.58	0.56	0.53	0.51	0.48	0.45
Grandparent	0.89	0.81	0.70	0.55	0.41	0.27	0.15	0.08	0.03	0.01	0.00	.	.	.	.
Grandfather	0.60	0.47	0.33	0.22	0.13	0.07	0.02	0.01	0.00	0.00	.	.	.	.	.
Grandmother	0.76	0.68	0.58	0.45	0.34	0.23	0.13	0.07	0.03	0.01	0.00	.	.	.	.
Maternal grandfather	0.46	0.35	0.25	0.17	0.10	0.05	0.02	0.01	0.00	0.00	.	.	.	.	.
Paternal grandfather	0.27	0.19	0.11	0.06	0.03	0.01	0.00	0.00	.	.	.	.	.	.	.
Maternal grandmother	0.59	0.51	0.42	0.33	0.25	0.18	0.11	0.06	0.03	0.01	0.00	.	.	.	.
Paternal grandmother	0.43	0.35	0.28	0.20	0.12	0.07	0.03	0.01	0.00	0.00	.	.	.	.	.
Grandchild	.	.	.	.	.	.	.	.	0.02	0.20	0.41	0.58	0.65	0.68	0.67
Grandson	.	.	.	.	.	.	.	.	0.01	0.12	0.30	0.45	0.53	0.57	0.58
Granddaughter	.	.	.	.	.	.	.	.	0.01	0.13	0.30	0.45	0.53	0.57	0.59
Aunt/uncle	0.93	0.91	0.88	0.84	0.80	0.75	0.68	0.59	0.48	0.36	0.24	0.13	0.07	0.03	0.01
Aunt	0.75	0.72	0.68	0.64	0.59	0.54	0.47	0.40	0.32	0.23	0.15	0.09	0.05	0.02	0.01
Uncle	0.77	0.73	0.68	0.64	0.59	0.52	0.44	0.35	0.27	0.19	0.12	0.06	0.03	0.01	0.00
Maternal aunt	0.53	0.51	0.48	0.44	0.41	0.37	0.33	0.28	0.23	0.17	0.12	0.07	0.04	0.02	0.01
Paternal aunt	0.48	0.44	0.40	0.37	0.32	0.28	0.22	0.17	0.12	0.08	0.04	0.02	0.01	0.00	.
Maternal uncle	0.54	0.51	0.48	0.44	0.40	0.35	0.30	0.24	0.19	0.14	0.09	0.05	0.02	0.01	0.00
Paternal uncle	0.50	0.46	0.41	0.37	0.32	0.27	0.21	0.15	0.10	0.06	0.03	0.02	0.00	0.00	0.00
Nephew/niece	0.01	0.02	0.07	0.24	0.43	0.58	0.67	0.70	0.71	0.70	0.70	0.69	0.68	0.66	0.63
Nephew	0.00	0.01	0.05	0.16	0.31	0.45	0.54	0.59	0.60	0.59	0.58	0.57	0.54	0.52	0.48
Niece	0.00	0.01	0.05	0.16	0.31	0.46	0.55	0.60	0.61	0.60	0.58	0.57	0.55	0.52	0.49

Note: . indicates no occurrences in simulation; 0.00 indicates less than 0.01

Table 3.2.f: Male, "senatorial," Level 3 West: mean age of living kin

Kin	EXACT AGE OF EGO (YEARS)														
	0	5	10	15	20	25	30	35	40	45	50	55	60	65	70
Wife						17.8	21.3	25.6	30.0	34.1	38.2	41.7	46.3	50.5	54.4
Parent	28.0	32.8	37.5	42.1	46.7	51.1	55.3	59.5	63.6	67.5	71.1	75.0	78.5	82.2	87.3
Father	32.7	37.5	42.3	46.9	51.4	56.0	60.5	64.8	69.5	73.7	77.6	82.4	88.2	82.2	.
Mother	23.2	28.1	33.1	37.9	42.8	47.5	51.9	56.6	61.2	65.7	69.8	74.1	78.3	82.2	87.3
Sibling	4.3	6.3	10.2	14.9	19.8	24.7	29.6	34.5	39.3	44.2	49.0	53.6	58.2	62.7	67.0
Brother	4.3	6.2	10.1	14.8	19.6	24.6	29.4	34.4	39.2	44.0	48.8	53.5	58.1	62.6	66.9
Sister	4.4	6.3	10.4	15.0	19.9	24.8	29.7	34.6	39.4	44.4	49.2	53.7	58.3	62.8	67.1
Child						0.9	2.8	5.7	9.4	13.9	18.7	23.7	28.6	33.5	38.4
Son						0.9	2.8	5.6	9.4	13.8	18.6	23.6	28.4	33.3	38.3
Daughter						0.9	2.8	5.7	9.5	13.9	18.8	23.8	28.7	33.7	38.5
Grandparent	50.8	54.7	58.4	62.1	65.5	68.8	72.1	75.4	79.2	83.4	87.3	.	.	.	.
Grandfather	55.0	59.0	62.7	66.6	70.1	73.7	77.0	80.5	84.2	90.0	.	.	.	.	.
Grandmother	47.7	52.0	56.3	60.1	63.9	67.5	71.2	74.8	78.9	83.2	87.3	.	.	.	.
Maternal grandfather	52.2	56.4	60.5	64.6	68.8	72.5	76.1	79.6	84.2	90.0	.	.	.	.	.
Paternal grandfather	59.8	63.7	67.6	71.7	74.6	78.7	82.3	87.1	.	.	.	.	.	.	.
Maternal grandmother	44.4	48.8	53.3	57.3	61.6	65.6	69.7	73.7	78.3	83.0	87.3	.	.	.	.
Paternal grandmother	52.3	56.6	60.7	64.8	68.7	72.6	77.0	80.6	84.6	87.7	.	.	.	.	.
Grandchild									0.5	1.7	3.3	5.0	7.3	10.2	13.6
Grandson									0.5	1.7	3.3	5.0	7.2	10.2	13.6
Granddaughter									0.4	1.7	3.3	5.1	7.3	10.2	13.6
Aunt/uncle	26.1	30.9	35.5	40.2	44.8	49.2	53.4	57.5	61.2	64.7	68.3	71.4	74.4	77.7	81.4
Aunt	26.1	30.9	35.7	40.4	45.0	49.5	53.7	57.7	61.4	65.0	68.5	71.5	74.9	78.2	82.5
Uncle	26.2	30.8	35.4	39.9	44.6	48.9	53.0	57.2	60.9	64.3	68.0	71.2	73.6	77.0	79.8
Maternal aunt	22.0	26.9	31.8	36.6	41.4	45.8	50.4	54.7	58.9	62.7	66.6	70.3	74.2	77.9	82.5
Paternal aunt	30.8	35.7	40.5	45.2	49.8	54.5	58.9	62.9	66.7	70.5	74.4	77.7	80.0	83.1	.
Maternal uncle	22.2	26.9	31.6	36.4	41.1	45.6	50.0	54.5	58.5	62.4	66.5	69.9	72.8	76.1	79.7
Paternal uncle	30.8	35.4	40.1	44.6	49.1	53.5	57.6	61.7	65.7	68.9	72.5	75.5	79.6	84.4	80.7
Nephew/niece	1.7	2.6	2.8	3.2	4.5	6.1	8.2	10.9	14.4	18.5	23.0	27.7	32.5	37.3	41.9
Nephew	1.8	2.7	2.9	3.3	4.6	6.2	8.3	11.0	14.5	18.6	23.1	27.8	32.6	37.3	41.8
Niece	1.5	2.6	2.7	3.2	4.4	6.0	8.1	10.8	14.4	18.3	22.8	27.6	32.3	37.2	42.0

Note: . indicates no occurrences in simulation; 0.0 indicates less than 0.1

Table 3.3.a: Female, "senatorial," Level 6 West: mean number of living kin

Kin						EXACT AGE OF EGO (YEARS)									
	0	5	10	15	20	25	30	35	40	45	50	55	60	65	70
Husband	.	.	.	0.6	1.0	1.0	1.0	1.0	1.0	1.0	1.0	0.9	0.7	0.6	0.4
Parent	2.0	1.8	1.7	1.5	1.4	1.2	1.0	0.8	0.6	0.4	0.3	0.2	0.1	0.0	0.0
Father	1.0	0.9	0.8	0.7	0.6	0.5	0.4	0.3	0.2	0.1	0.1	0.0	0.0	0.0	0.0
Mother	1.0	0.9	0.9	0.8	0.7	0.7	0.6	0.5	0.4	0.3	0.2	0.1	0.1	0.0	0.0
Sibling	1.1	1.8	1.9	1.9	1.8	1.7	1.6	1.5	1.3	1.2	1.1	0.9	0.8	0.6	0.4
Brother	0.5	0.9	0.9	0.9	0.9	0.8	0.8	0.7	0.7	0.6	0.5	0.5	0.4	0.3	0.2
Sister	0.5	0.9	0.9	0.9	0.9	0.8	0.8	0.7	0.7	0.6	0.5	0.5	0.4	0.3	0.2
Child	.	.	.	.	1.3	1.9	2.0	2.1	2.1	2.1	1.9	1.8	1.7	1.5	1.3
Son	.	.	.	.	0.7	0.9	1.0	1.0	1.0	1.0	1.0	0.9	0.8	0.7	0.6
Daughter	.	.	.	.	0.7	0.9	1.0	1.0	1.0	1.0	1.0	0.9	0.8	0.8	0.7
Grandparent	2.2	1.9	1.5	1.1	0.8	0.6	0.3	0.2	0.1	0.0	0.0	0.0	0.0	.	.
Grandfather	1.0	0.8	0.6	0.4	0.3	0.1	0.1	0.0	0.0	0.0	0.0	0.0	.	.	.
Grandmother	1.2	1.1	0.9	0.7	0.6	0.4	0.3	0.2	0.1	0.0	0.0	0.0	0.0	.	.
Maternal grandfather	0.6	0.5	0.4	0.3	0.2	0.1	0.1	0.0	0.0	0.0	0.0	0.0	·	·	·
Paternal grandfather	0.4	0.3	0.2	0.1	0.1	0.0	0.0	0.0	0.0	0.0	·	·	·	·	·
Maternal grandmother	0.7	0.6	0.6	0.5	0.4	0.3	0.2	0.1	0.1	0.0	·	0.0	0.0	·	·
Paternal grandmother	0.5	0.5	0.4	0.3	0.2	0.1	0.1	0.0	0.0	0.0	0.0	0.0	·	·	·
Grandchild							·	0.3	1.1	1.9	2.7	3.3	3.6	3.6	3.6
Grandson							·	0.1	0.5	1.0	1.4	1.6	1.8	1.8	1.8
Granddaughter							·	0.1	0.5	1.0	1.4	1.7	1.8	1.8	1.8
Aunt/uncle	3.3	3.0	2.8	2.6	2.3	2.0	1.7	1.4	1.1	0.8	0.5	0.3	0.2	0.1	0.0
Aunt	1.6	1.5	1.4	1.3	1.1	1.0	0.9	0.7	0.6	0.4	0.3	0.2	0.1	0.0	0.0
Uncle	1.7	1.5	1.4	1.3	1.1	1.0	0.8	0.7	0.5	0.4	0.2	0.1	0.1	0.0	0.0
Maternal aunt	0.9	0.8	0.8	0.7	0.6	0.6	0.5	0.4	0.4	0.3	0.2	0.1	0.1	0.0	0.0
Paternal aunt	0.8	0.7	0.6	0.6	0.5	0.4	0.4	0.3	0.2	0.1	0.1	0.0	0.0	0.0	0.0
Maternal uncle	0.9	0.8	0.8	0.7	0.7	0.6	0.5	0.4	0.3	0.3	0.2	0.1	0.1	0.0	0.0
Paternal uncle	0.8	0.7	0.6	0.6	0.5	0.4	0.3	0.2	0.2	0.1	0.1	0.0	0.0	0.0	0.0
Nephew/niece	0.0	0.0	0.1	0.4	1.1	1.9	2.6	3.0	3.2	3.1	3.0	2.8	2.6	2.4	2.1
Nephew	0.0	0.0	0.0	0.2	0.5	0.9	1.2	1.5	1.6	1.5	1.5	1.4	1.3	1.2	1.0
Niece	0.0	0.0	0.0	0.2	0.6	1.0	1.3	1.5	1.6	1.6	1.5	1.4	1.3	1.2	1.1

Note: . indicates no occurrences in simulation; 0.0 indicates less than 0.1

Demographic analysis of "senatorial," Level 6 West population: Gross Reproduction Rate: 1.84; Net Reproduction Rate: 1.01; Mean Age at Maternity: 21.78

Table 3.3.b: Female, "senatorial," Level 6 West: proportion having living kin

Kin	EXACT AGE OF EGO (YEARS)														
	0	5	10	15	20	25	30	35	40	45	50	55	60	65	70
Husband	.	.	.	0.62	0.97	0.98	0.97	0.97	0.96	0.95	0.95	0.95	0.75	0.55	0.38
Parent	1.00	0.99	0.97	0.94	0.89	0.82	0.74	0.65	0.53	0.40	0.27	0.15	0.07	0.03	0.01
Father	1.00	0.91	0.82	0.72	0.62	0.51	0.41	0.30	0.20	0.12	0.06	0.03	0.01	0.00	0.00
Mother	1.00	0.94	0.87	0.80	0.73	0.66	0.59	0.51	0.42	0.32	0.22	0.13	0.06	0.03	0.01
Sibling	0.59	0.82	0.81	0.80	0.79	0.77	0.75	0.72	0.70	0.66	0.62	0.57	0.51	0.42	0.32
Brother	0.38	0.59	0.59	0.58	0.56	0.54	0.53	0.50	0.47	0.43	0.39	0.34	0.29	0.23	0.16
Sister	0.39	0.58	0.58	0.56	0.55	0.53	0.51	0.49	0.47	0.44	0.40	0.36	0.32	0.26	0.20
Child	.	.	.	.	0.78	0.83	0.83	0.84	0.84	0.83	0.82	0.80	0.77	0.74	0.70
Son	.	.	.	.	0.50	0.60	0.62	0.62	0.63	0.61	0.59	0.56	0.53	0.50	0.45
Daughter	.	.	.	.	0.50	0.61	0.62	0.62	0.62	0.61	0.59	0.57	0.54	0.51	0.47
Grandparent	0.96	0.91	0.83	0.73	0.60	0.45	0.29	0.17	0.08	0.04	0.01	0.00	0.00	.	.
Grandfather	0.74	0.63	0.49	0.36	0.24	0.14	0.06	0.03	0.01	0.00	0.00	.	.	.	.
Grandmother	0.86	0.80	0.72	0.61	0.50	0.38	0.26	0.15	0.08	0.03	0.01	0.00	0.00	.	.
Maternal grandfather	0.59	0.48	0.38	0.28	0.19	0.12	0.06	0.02	0.01	0.00	0.00	.	.	.	.
Paternal grandfather	0.38	0.28	0.19	0.11	0.06	0.03	0.01	0.00	0.00	.	.	.	.	.	.
Maternal grandmother	0.70	0.63	0.55	0.47	0.39	0.29	0.21	0.13	0.07	0.03	0.01	0.00	0.00	.	.
Paternal grandmother	0.54	0.46	0.36	0.27	0.20	0.13	0.06	0.03	0.01	0.00	0.00	.	.	.	.
Grandchild	.	.	.	.	.	.	.	0.21	0.47	0.63	0.71	0.75	0.76	0.76	0.76
Grandson	.	.	.	.	.	.	.	0.12	0.33	0.50	0.59	0.64	0.66	0.66	0.65
Granddaughter	.	.	.	.	.	.	.	0.12	0.34	0.49	0.59	0.64	0.66	0.66	0.66
Aunt/uncle	0.95	0.93	0.92	0.90	0.87	0.83	0.78	0.71	0.61	0.50	0.37	0.24	0.14	0.06	0.03
Aunt	0.78	0.75	0.72	0.70	0.66	0.62	0.57	0.50	0.42	0.33	0.23	0.15	0.09	0.04	0.02
Uncle	0.79	0.76	0.73	0.70	0.65	0.60	0.53	0.45	0.37	0.28	0.20	0.12	0.06	0.03	0.01
Maternal aunt	0.56	0.54	0.51	0.48	0.45	0.42	0.39	0.34	0.30	0.24	0.18	0.12	0.07	0.04	0.02
Paternal aunt	0.51	0.48	0.45	0.42	0.38	0.34	0.29	0.23	0.18	0.12	0.07	0.03	0.02	0.01	0.00
Maternal uncle	0.57	0.55	0.52	0.49	0.46	0.42	0.37	0.32	0.27	0.21	0.15	0.10	0.05	0.02	0.01
Paternal uncle	0.51	0.48	0.44	0.40	0.35	0.31	0.26	0.20	0.14	0.09	0.05	0.03	0.01	0.00	0.00
Nephew/niece	0.00	0.01	0.05	0.22	0.43	0.58	0.67	0.71	0.71	0.71	0.70	0.69	0.68	0.67	0.65
Nephew	0.00	0.00	0.03	0.14	0.30	0.44	0.54	0.58	0.59	0.59	0.58	0.57	0.55	0.52	0.49
Niece	0.00	0.01	0.04	0.15	0.32	0.46	0.56	0.60	0.60	0.60	0.59	0.58	0.56	0.54	0.52

Note: . indicates no occurrences in simulation; 0.00 indicates less than 0.01

Table 3.3.c: Female, "senatorial," Level 6 West: mean age of living kin

Kin	EXACT AGE OF EGO (YEARS)														
	0	5	10	15	20	25	30	35	40	45	50	55	60	65	70
Husband	.	.	.	27.3	31.6	35.8	39.8	43.4	46.7	49.1	50.7	52.0	55.6	58.4	60.5
Parent	27.1	31.8	36.6	41.2	45.8	50.2	54.6	59.0	63.0	67.2	71.3	75.3	78.8	83.1	88.3
Father	32.1	36.9	41.6	46.2	50.8	55.3	59.9	64.5	68.8	73.1	77.7	82.3	84.7	88.9	93.9
Mother	22.0	27.0	31.9	36.8	41.6	46.4	51.0	55.7	60.3	64.9	69.6	73.9	78.2	83.0	88.0
Sibling	3.9	5.9	10.1	14.7	19.5	24.4	29.3	34.3	39.2	44.1	48.9	53.8	58.5	63.1	67.4
Brother	3.8	5.8	10.1	14.7	19.5	24.3	29.2	34.1	39.0	43.9	48.6	53.5	58.3	62.9	67.3
Sister	3.9	5.9	10.1	14.8	19.6	24.5	29.4	34.4	39.4	44.4	49.2	54.1	58.7	63.3	67.5
Child					2.2	5.5	9.4	13.6	17.7	21.9	26.6	31.5	36.4	41.2	46.1
Son					2.2	5.5	9.5	13.6	17.7	21.9	26.6	31.6	36.4	41.3	46.0
Daughter					2.1	5.4	9.4	13.5	17.6	21.8	26.6	31.5	36.3	41.2	46.1
Grandparent	50.2	54.3	58.1	61.8	65.3	68.9	71.9	75.4	78.7	82.4	87.1	88.8	94.6		
Grandfather	54.6	58.7	62.7	66.5	70.0	73.6	76.9	80.5	85.6	89.0	91.4				
Grandmother	46.8	51.1	55.3	59.3	63.3	67.2	70.7	74.6	78.0	81.8	87.0	88.8	94.6		
Maternal grandfather	51.4	55.7	59.8	64.1	68.2	72.3	76.1	80.0	85.1	89.0	91.4				
Paternal grandfather	59.8	64.1	68.2	72.2	75.9	79.6	83.0	87.2	91.7						
Maternal grandmother	42.9	47.4	52.0	56.3	60.6	64.8	68.9	73.1	77.1	81.3	86.4	88.8	94.6		
Paternal grandmother	51.9	56.3	60.4	64.5	68.8	72.9	76.8	80.7	85.2	88.3	94.1				
Grandchild								1.2	3.1	5.0	7.4	10.3	13.7	17.5	21.5
Grandson								1.2	3.1	5.1	7.4	10.3	13.7	17.4	21.5
Granddaughter								1.2	3.1	5.0	7.4	10.2	13.7	17.5	21.5
Aunt/uncle	25.8	30.6	35.3	40.0	44.6	49.2	53.6	57.7	61.7	65.6	69.2	72.5	76.0	79.0	80.9
Aunt	25.9	30.7	35.5	40.3	44.9	49.5	53.8	58.0	62.1	65.8	69.3	72.7	76.2	79.0	80.4
Uncle	25.8	30.5	35.1	39.8	44.4	48.9	53.3	57.5	61.3	65.2	69.0	72.3	75.7	78.8	82.0
Maternal aunt	21.3	26.2	31.0	35.9	40.8	45.5	50.3	54.9	59.3	63.4	67.3	71.4	75.0	78.5	80.2
Paternal aunt	31.1	36.0	40.8	45.6	49.9	54.5	58.8	62.9	67.2	71.1	75.0	78.0	82.2	82.9	84.1
Maternal uncle	21.4	26.2	31.0	35.8	40.5	45.2	49.8	54.3	58.6	63.0	67.2	70.9	74.6	78.6	81.6
Paternal uncle	30.9	35.7	40.3	45.1	49.7	54.3	58.7	62.9	66.9	70.7	74.6	77.5	81.9	81.1	85.1
Nephew/niece	3.2	3.0	3.0	2.9	4.2	5.9	8.2	11.0	14.7	18.9	23.5	28.3	33.1	37.9	42.6
Nephew	4.0	4.3	3.0	2.9	4.1	5.9	8.1	10.9	14.6	18.7	23.3	28.0	32.8	37.6	42.2
Niece	2.2	2.2	3.0	2.9	4.2	6.0	8.2	11.2	14.9	19.2	23.8	28.6	33.4	38.3	43.1

Note: . indicates no occurrences in simulation; 0.0 indicates less than 0.1

Table 3.3.d: Male, "senatorial," Level 6 West: mean number of living kin

Kin	EXACT AGE OF EGO (YEARS)														
	0	5	10	15	20	25	30	35	40	45	50	55	60	65	70
Wife	·	·	·	·	0.0	0.6	0.9	1.0	1.0	1.0	1.0	1.0	0.9	0.8	0.6
Parent	2.0	1.8	1.7	1.5	1.4	1.2	1.0	0.8	0.6	0.4	0.3	0.1	0.1	0.0	0.0
Father	1.0	0.9	0.8	0.7	0.6	0.5	0.4	0.3	0.2	0.1	0.1	0.0	0.0	0.0	·
Mother	1.0	0.9	0.9	0.8	0.7	0.7	0.6	0.5	0.4	0.3	0.2	0.1	0.1	0.0	0.0
Sibling	1.1	1.8	1.9	1.8	1.8	1.7	1.6	1.5	1.3	1.2	1.1	0.9	0.8	0.6	0.4
Brother	0.5	0.9	0.9	0.9	0.9	0.8	0.8	0.7	0.7	0.6	0.5	0.4	0.4	0.3	0.2
Sister	0.6	0.9	0.9	0.9	0.9	0.8	0.8	0.7	0.7	0.6	0.6	0.5	0.4	0.3	0.2
Child	·	·	·	·	·	0.3	1.3	1.8	1.9	1.9	1.8	1.7	1.6	1.4	1.3
Son	·	·	·	·	·	0.2	0.7	0.9	0.9	0.9	0.9	0.8	0.8	0.7	0.7
Daughter	·	·	·	·	·	0.2	0.7	0.9	0.9	0.9	0.9	0.8	0.8	0.7	0.7
Grandparent	2.2	1.8	1.5	1.1	0.8	0.5	0.3	0.2	0.1	0.0	0.0	0.0	·	·	·
Grandfather	0.9	0.7	0.5	0.4	0.2	0.1	0.1	0.0	0.0	0.0	0.0	0.0	·	·	·
Grandmother	1.2	1.1	0.9	0.7	0.6	0.4	0.3	0.2	0.1	0.0	0.0	0.0	·	·	·
Maternal grandfather	0.6	0.5	0.4	0.3	0.2	0.1	0.1	0.0	0.0	0.0	0.0	0.0	·	·	·
Paternal grandfather	0.4	0.3	0.2	0.1	0.1	0.0	0.0	0.0	0.0	0.0	·	·	·	·	·
Maternal grandmother	0.7	0.6	0.5	0.5	0.4	0.3	0.2	0.1	0.1	0.0	0.0	0.0	·	·	·
Paternal grandmother	0.5	0.5	0.4	0.3	0.2	0.1	0.1	0.0	0.0	0.0	0.0	0.0	·	·	·
Grandchild	·	·	·	·	·	·	·	·	0.0	0.4	1.1	1.9	2.6	3.0	3.2
Grandson	·	·	·	·	·	·	·	·	0.0	0.2	0.6	1.0	1.3	1.6	1.6
Granddaughter	·	·	·	·	·	·	·	·	0.0	0.2	0.6	1.0	1.3	1.5	1.6
Aunt/uncle	3.3	3.1	2.8	2.6	2.3	2.0	1.7	1.4	1.1	0.8	0.5	0.3	0.2	0.1	0.0
Aunt	1.6	1.5	1.4	1.3	1.2	1.1	0.9	0.7	0.6	0.4	0.3	0.2	0.1	0.0	0.0
Uncle	1.6	1.5	1.4	1.3	1.1	1.0	0.8	0.6	0.5	0.3	0.2	0.1	0.1	0.0	0.0
Maternal aunt	0.9	0.8	0.8	0.7	0.7	0.6	0.5	0.5	0.4	0.3	0.2	0.1	0.1	0.0	0.0
Paternal aunt	0.8	0.7	0.7	0.6	0.5	0.5	0.4	0.3	0.2	0.1	0.1	0.0	0.0	0.0	0.0
Maternal uncle	0.9	0.8	0.8	0.7	0.6	0.6	0.5	0.4	0.3	0.2	0.2	0.1	0.1	0.0	0.0
Paternal uncle	0.8	0.7	0.6	0.6	0.5	0.4	0.3	0.2	0.2	0.1	0.1	0.0	0.0	0.0	0.0
Nephew/niece	0.0	0.0	0.1	0.5	1.1	1.9	2.6	3.0	3.1	3.1	3.0	2.8	2.6	2.3	2.1
Nephew	0.0	0.0	0.1	0.2	0.6	1.0	1.3	1.5	1.6	1.6	1.5	1.4	1.3	1.2	1.0
Niece	0.0	0.0	0.1	0.2	0.6	1.0	1.3	1.5	1.6	1.5	1.5	1.4	1.3	1.2	1.1

Note: . indicates no occurrences in simulation; 0.0 indicates less than 0.1

Table 3.3.e: Male, "senatorial," Level 6 West: proportion having living kin

Kin	0	5	10	15	20	25	30	35	40	45	50	55	60	65	70
Wife	.	.	.	.	0.00	0.59	0.94	0.98	0.98	0.97	0.98	0.97	0.87	0.76	0.64
Parent	1.00	0.99	0.97	0.94	0.90	0.83	0.75	0.65	0.52	0.39	0.25	0.14	0.07	0.03	0.01
Father	1.00	0.90	0.82	0.72	0.62	0.51	0.40	0.30	0.20	0.11	0.05	0.02	0.01	0.00	.
Mother	1.00	0.94	0.88	0.81	0.74	0.67	0.59	0.51	0.41	0.31	0.21	0.13	0.06	0.02	0.01
Sibling	0.57	0.83	0.81	0.80	0.78	0.77	0.75	0.72	0.69	0.65	0.62	0.56	0.50	0.42	0.32
Brother	0.38	0.59	0.59	0.58	0.56	0.54	0.52	0.49	0.46	0.43	0.39	0.34	0.29	0.23	0.16
Sister	0.38	0.59	0.58	0.57	0.56	0.54	0.51	0.49	0.46	0.43	0.41	0.36	0.32	0.26	0.20
Child	.	.	.	.	.	0.27	0.73	0.81	0.81	0.80	0.79	0.77	0.75	0.72	0.69
Son	.	.	.	.	.	0.15	0.49	0.58	0.59	0.58	0.57	0.55	0.52	0.50	0.47
Daughter	.	.	.	.	.	0.15	0.48	0.57	0.58	0.58	0.56	0.53	0.51	0.49	0.46
Grandparent	0.95	0.90	0.82	0.72	0.58	0.44	0.29	0.17	0.08	0.03	0.01	0.00	.	.	.
Grandfather	0.72	0.60	0.47	0.34	0.21	0.13	0.06	0.02	0.01	0.00	0.00	.	.	.	.
Grandmother	0.85	0.79	0.71	0.60	0.49	0.37	0.25	0.15	0.07	0.03	0.01	0.00	.	.	.
Maternal grandfather	0.57	0.47	0.36	0.26	0.17	0.10	0.05	0.02	0.01	0.00	0.00	.	.	.	.
Paternal grandfather	0.35	0.26	0.18	0.10	0.05	0.03	0.01	0.00	0.01	0.00	0.00	.	.	.	.
Maternal grandmother	0.70	0.62	0.54	0.45	0.37	0.28	0.20	0.12	0.06	0.03	0.01	0.00	.	.	.
Paternal grandmother	0.54	0.46	0.37	0.28	0.20	0.12	0.06	0.03	0.01	0.00	0.00	0.00	.	.	.
Grandchild	.	.	.	.	.	.	.	.	0.02	0.26	0.47	0.62	0.69	0.72	0.72
Grandson	.	.	.	.	.	.	.	.	0.01	0.16	0.33	0.48	0.56	0.60	0.60
Granddaughter	.	.	.	.	.	.	.	.	0.01	0.17	0.34	0.49	0.57	0.61	0.61
Aunt/uncle	0.94	0.93	0.92	0.89	0.86	0.82	0.77	0.70	0.61	0.50	0.37	0.24	0.14	0.06	0.02
Aunt	0.78	0.76	0.74	0.70	0.67	0.62	0.57	0.50	0.43	0.34	0.24	0.16	0.09	0.04	0.01
Uncle	0.77	0.75	0.72	0.69	0.64	0.59	0.53	0.44	0.35	0.27	0.19	0.11	0.06	0.03	0.01
Maternal aunt	0.55	0.53	0.51	0.49	0.46	0.43	0.39	0.35	0.30	0.24	0.18	0.12	0.07	0.03	0.01
Paternal aunt	0.51	0.49	0.46	0.42	0.39	0.35	0.29	0.24	0.18	0.12	0.08	0.04	0.01	0.01	0.00
Maternal uncle	0.56	0.53	0.51	0.48	0.45	0.41	0.37	0.31	0.25	0.19	0.14	0.09	0.05	0.02	0.01
Paternal uncle	0.51	0.48	0.44	0.41	0.36	0.32	0.26	0.20	0.14	0.09	0.05	0.03	0.01	0.00	0.00
Nephew/niece	0.00	0.01	0.05	0.22	0.43	0.59	0.68	0.71	0.71	0.71	0.70	0.69	0.68	0.67	0.65
Nephew	0.00	0.01	0.03	0.15	0.31	0.46	0.56	0.60	0.60	0.59	0.58	0.57	0.55	0.53	0.51
Niece	0.00	0.01	0.03	0.15	0.32	0.46	0.56	0.59	0.60	0.60	0.59	0.57	0.56	0.54	0.52

Note: . indicates no occurrences in simulation; 0.00 indicates less than 0.01

Table 3.3.f: Male, "senatorial," Level 6 West: mean age of living kin

Kin	EXACT AGE OF EGO (YEARS)														
	0	5	10	15	20	25	30	35	40	45	50	55	60	65	70
Wife					19.8	17.9	21.5	25.9	30.5	34.7	38.6	42.4	47.0	51.5	55.8
Parent	27.2	32.0	36.7	41.4	45.9	50.5	54.8	59.2	63.4	67.3	71.2	75.3	79.5	83.8	87.5
Father	32.2	37.0	41.7	46.3	51.0	55.6	60.1	64.5	68.9	73.4	77.6	81.9	86.1	92.1	.
Mother	22.2	27.1	32.0	37.0	41.7	46.6	51.3	56.1	60.7	65.2	69.7	74.2	78.8	83.3	87.5
Sibling	4.0	6.0	10.2	14.9	19.8	24.7	29.7	34.6	39.6	44.5	49.4	54.2	58.8	63.5	67.9
Brother	3.9	5.9	10.1	14.8	19.7	24.6	29.6	34.5	39.5	44.4	49.3	54.0	58.7	63.4	67.8
Sister	4.0	6.1	10.3	15.0	19.9	24.8	29.8	34.7	39.7	44.6	49.5	54.3	58.9	63.7	68.0
Child						1.0	3.0	6.2	10.3	14.9	19.8	24.7	29.7	34.6	39.5
Son						1.0	3.1	6.2	10.3	14.9	19.8	24.7	29.7	34.6	39.5
Daughter						1.0	3.0	6.2	10.3	14.9	19.7	24.7	29.7	34.6	39.5
Grandparent	50.2	54.3	58.2	61.8	65.2	68.8	71.9	75.1	78.5	81.6	86.4				
Grandfather	54.7	58.8	62.7	66.3	69.9	73.7	77.2	80.6	84.5	87.8	93.7	90.5			
Grandmother	46.9	51.3	55.5	59.5	63.4	67.3	70.6	74.3	78.1	81.5	86.1	90.5			
Maternal grandfather	51.5	56.0	60.0	64.1	68.3	72.4	76.4	80.2	84.5	87.8	93.7				
Paternal grandfather	59.8	63.9	68.0	71.8	75.5	79.3	83.2	89.4							
Maternal grandmother	43.1	47.7	52.1	56.4	60.7	65.1	68.9	72.9	77.0	81.0	85.8	90.5			
Paternal grandmother	51.9	56.2	60.3	64.5	68.5	72.4	76.3	80.1	85.0	88.2	93.5				
Grandchild									0.7	1.9	3.7	5.6	8.1	11.1	14.9
Grandson									0.7	1.9	3.7	5.6	8.0	11.1	14.8
Granddaughter									0.7	1.9	3.7	5.7	8.2	11.2	14.9
Aunt/uncle	25.9	30.6	35.3	40.1	44.6	49.1	53.5	57.7	61.7	65.5	69.1	72.6	76.0	79.2	80.7
Aunt	25.7	30.5	35.3	40.0	44.7	49.2	53.7	57.9	61.9	65.7	69.3	72.9	76.4	79.6	81.5
Uncle	26.0	30.7	35.4	40.1	44.6	49.0	53.3	57.4	61.4	65.1	68.7	72.1	75.5	78.6	79.6
Maternal aunt	21.3	26.1	31.0	35.8	40.7	45.5	50.2	54.8	59.2	63.3	67.4	71.5	75.6	78.5	81.3
Paternal aunt	30.7	35.5	40.3	45.1	49.6	54.2	58.6	62.9	66.8	70.9	74.4	78.3	81.6	86.5	84.7
Maternal uncle	21.6	26.3	31.1	35.8	40.6	45.1	49.8	54.3	58.6	62.7	66.8	70.8	74.4	77.9	79.5
Paternal uncle	30.9	35.7	40.4	45.2	49.7	54.2	58.4	62.6	66.5	70.4	73.7	77.1	80.9	84.0	80.8
Nephew/niece	4.8	3.4	3.3	3.0	4.3	6.1	8.4	11.3	15.1	19.4	24.0	28.7	33.6	38.4	43.1
Nephew	6.7	3.4	2.8	2.8	4.2	6.0	8.4	11.3	15.0	19.3	23.8	28.6	33.4	38.2	42.9
Niece	4.3	3.4	3.7	3.2	4.3	6.2	8.5	11.4	15.2	19.5	24.1	28.9	33.8	38.6	43.3

Note: . indicates no occurrences in simulation; 0.0 indicates less than 0.1

census data and of the simulated population shows that the simulation is a realistic representation of the ancient Mediterranean experience and that the census data are coherent and demographically plausible.

One of the notable advantages of the computer simulation over empirical census data is that we are able to vary the parameters in order to study the consequences for the kin universe. The tables presented above permit the reader to assess the impact on the kin universe of younger ("senatorial") as against older ("ordinary") ages at first marriage, or lower ($e_0 = 25$) as against higher ($e_0 = 32.5$) life expectancy. To take a specific example, a comparison of the tables of proportion with living kin suggests that the proportion with a living father (of central interest in later chapters) varies more with differences in average age at first marriage for men than with differences in average life expectancy at birth. (That is, a decrease of five years in average age at marriage increases the proportion of twenty-year-olds with a living father by 6 percent, whereas an increase in average life expectancy at birth of seven and a half years increases the proportion of twenty-year-olds with a father by only 4 percent.) In view of the greater impact of age at marriage on such questions, we may take comfort in the fact that the empirical base for that parameter is the firmest. Most important, the tables show that the different assumptions for ages at marriage or life expectancy that could be defended as probable do not substantially alter the broad conclusions about social relations drawn in the following chapters.

The tables offer a wealth of information, much of which cannot be exploited in the following chapters. For instance, S. Pomeroy has written about the relationship between Roman women and their male kin.[17] The tables add another dimension to her discussion by showing how a woman's circle of living kinsmen changed through her life course. Despite the simplifications and limitations, the microsimulation will enable historians of the Roman family to understand, as never before, issues in terms of the complexities of the life course.

Comparison of the microsimulation output and the household census data from Roman Egypt

Although the Egyptian population of the census returns was unique in some respects – most obviously, in its propensity for brother–sister marriage – there is no reason to assume that the other basic demographic characteristics were significantly different from the rest of the Roman empire. A comparison of the Egyptian census data, as analyzed by Bagnall and Frier, and the output from the microsimulation for a Roman population may serve three purposes. (1) Comparison of the input parameters (mortality rates and ages at

[17] Pomeroy 1976.

marriage) with the empirical findings for Egypt will indicate whether the former are realistic for an ancient Mediterranean population; (2) comparison of the analysis of the simulation output with the analysis of the Egyptian data will provide a measure of the plausibility of the output; (3) in the reverse direction, the simulation may help the historian to judge whether the census returns offer a coherent set of data. The last of these is of value, because the census returns do not constitute a scientific sample, but are the result of unknown biases in the original procedure of collection and of accidents of survival. In addition, the data set is small enough to have required "smoothing." Given the imperfections of the data, models such as life tables and the simulation provide useful tests of the demographic quality of the census returns.

Table 3.4 presents some of the averages of input parameters and outputs from the simulation, and the corresponding numbers from the analysis of the Egyptian census returns.[18] From the simulation models, I have selected for comparison the "ordinary" population with mortality rates drawn from Coale–Demeny Level 3 West, because I believe this model to have the most general applicability to the Roman empire.

Mortality. In using Level 3 West ($e_0 = 25$), the simulation assumes somewhat less extreme mortality rates than Bagnall and Frier suggest for Egypt. They believe the empirical data for females to correspond best to the model population Level 2 West ($e_0 = 22.5$) with a mild annual growth of +0.2 percent. The difference between the simulation and the census data is not large: in fact, Bagnall and Frier point out that the margin of error in the analysis of the census data is such that the data could also fit the Level 3 West model with no growth, which are the conditions assumed in the simulation.[19]

Marriage. The mean ages of females at first marriage in the Egyptian population and in the simulation are very close (19.5 and 19.8 years, respectively). Whereas the simulation assumes that females begin to marry at age fifteen, the census returns show Egyptian girls beginning to marry somewhat younger. As Bagnall and Frier point out, the marriages at very young ages tend to be between brothers and sisters. In fact, three of the four married females under age fifteen were married to their brothers. If they are excluded, the age distribution of females at first marriage in Egypt and in the simulation are nearly identical.

The distribution of men's ages at first marriage is more problematic. An average cannot be reliably calculated for Egyptian men, because of the census' undercounting of men in their twenties. Of those in their twenties who were registered, slightly fewer than half were married. If the

[18] My thanks to Professor Frier for his willingness to share his analyses.
[19] Bagnall and Frier 1994: ch. 4.2, with table 4.3.

Table 3.4: *Comparision of microsimulation output and the household census data from Roman Egypt.*

	Roman Egypt	Simulation 0–3
e_0 (female)	22.5	25
Ages at first marriage		
female mean	19.5	19.8
female minimum	13	15
male median	25	29.2
male minimum	19	24
Annual growth rate	0.2%	0.0%
Gross Reproduction Rate	2.917	2.44
Mean age at maternity	27.1	26.3
Median age at paternity	c. 36	35.4

unregistered males are added in and assumed to be unmarried,[20] then the median age at first marriage would be around thirty years. Only in the cohort of thirty–thirty-four year-old males do a clear majority appear as married. This pattern is broadly similar to that found in the funerary commemorations of many western regions, where wives become the most prominent commemorators for men over age thirty. Although the median age at first marriage for males in the simulation may not differ much from that in Egypt, the Egyptian data do point to a wider dispersion than modelled in the simulation, which sets the minimum age at twenty-four years and the maximum at forty years. Egyptian men are found marrying at ages younger than twenty-four (in many cases, husband-brothers) and older than forty.

One of the clearest discrepancies between the Egyptian population and the simulation concerns remarriage. The simulation assumes that males up to age sixty and females up to age fifty remarry upon the death of the spouse. The Egyptian data, however, reveal that women often did not remarry after divorce or widowhood, with the result that about half of the women in their later thirties were no longer married. Clearly, the assumption of universal female remarriage in the simulation is inaccurate, but there is no empirical evidence from the west to correct it. Thus, the row for spouses in the tables giving proportion with living kin should be taken with a grain of salt – the result of an oversimplification in the absence of data.

Fertility. The propensity of women not to remarry was one means of limiting fertility.[21] Although the simulation does not limit fertility in this way, it does so through the Parity Progression Ratios, which imply that a

[20] Bagnall and Frier 1994: ch. 5.2 plausibly suggest that these men were not captured by the census because they had not yet established a household and had temporarily migrated in search of jobs.   [21] Bagnall and Frier 1994: ch. 7.2.

declining proportion of women bear another child as they grow older. Because we have no empirical evidence for the fertility parameters in the simulation, the comparison with Egypt is particularly important. As a result of the lower life expectancy and the higher growth rate assumed for Egypt, Bagnall and Frier propose a significantly higher Gross Reproduction Rate for Egypt than the simulation generates. However, the average ages at the birth of children for mothers and fathers attested in the Egyptian census returns and those resulting from the simulation are quite close. The average age at maternity in Egypt is calculated to be 27.1 years, whereas in the simulated population it is 26.3 years. The Egyptian data are not good enough for a reliable calculation of mean age at paternity, but the median is around thirty-six years. In the simulated population the mean age at paternity is 37.6 years and the median is 35.4. These numbers suggest that, despite its simplifications in the distribution of men's marriage ages and in the frequency of remarriage, the simulation has produced a population that is realistic in its pattern of child-bearing and its spacing between generations. The last point will be important to the arguments of later chapters. Furthermore, there is no reason to believe that certain important features of the Egyptian demographic experience were dissimilar from those of other populations in the empire. As the best empirical data, the Egyptian household census returns deserve wide attention.

PART II

Roman family and culture: definitions and norms

Basic demographic events influenced the shape of Roman families through the life course, but did not define the boundaries of the family and relations within it. Within a regime of high mortality and limited private property, significant cultural differences may be found from one society to another: one example would be Roman exogamous marriage in contrast to the endogamy characteristic of some eastern Mediterranean cultures. Despite J. Goody's effort to depict the pre-Christian, Eurasian plough cultures, including Rome, as broadly similar in the practice of close kin marriage, and to ground that practice in common economic exigencies, the empirical evidence supports Plutarch's perception of a basic cultural difference between the exogamous Romans and the endogamous Greeks.[1] The distinction dates back as far as the historical texts and is probably beyond the reach of historical explanation.

Against any position tinged with economic or demographic determinism, other historians have adopted radically cultural interpretations, claiming the irrelevance of biological reproduction to the construction of the family. It has been suggested that the Roman family was purely a ritual construct to which newborns were admitted by being ceremoniously "raised up" from the ground by the father. The implication is that there is nothing "natural" about the family, and little constraint of any kind in its construction. The Roman texts, however, do not support this interpretation. Family membership was not defined solely by ritual. The Roman jurists were extremely

---

[1] Goody 1990: 397: "it is central to my argument that certain aspects of the system of marriage and property rights that characterize the main stream of societies in East as in West Asia, both anciently and in the recent past, are closer to the European and further from the African pattern than has been commonly supposed. In some other respects, in particular the ban on close marriage, adoption and other strategies of heirship, later European marriage patterns diverge significantly from earlier European and most Asian ones." For a broader critique of Goody's historical interpretation of classical antiquity, see Saller 1991b.

attentive to the fine points of biological reproduction in their efforts to define family membership and rights to property.[2] In a sense, this concern for reproductive biology is a cultural feature of Roman society, but it does not make the family an arbitrary ritual construct.

In my view, an intermediate position on the importance of culture is most defensible: Roman society and culture were important to the conceptualization of the family unit and its relations, but in more subtle, less sensational ways than constitution of the family through ritual acts. Roman society was characterized by a steep hierarchy and fundamental distinctions of status between the honorable citizen and the rightless slave. Within the rank of citizen, fine divisions of rank and status marked off one Roman from another. These status distinctions had a formative influence on the Roman conceptualization and use of the house, and on relations within the household. In towns across the empire, the politically powerful advertised their position in the community by their physical house, which daily provided the stage for assertion of status and influence. In Roman society a position of power was defined in terms of heading a large house rather than in terms of a position in a clan or other kin group. Propertied Romans lived in their houses in relations marked by a fundamental distinction between family members whose bodies were protected by their honor and those of lower status who had no honor to protect them from abuse. The slaves, omnipresent in wealthier houses, were characterized by their vulnerability to sexual violation and the whip, against which they had no legitimate recourse.

Chapter 4 seeks to understand how the Romans defined the words for family, *familia* and *domus*. The semantic range and the use of these words provide insights into how the Romans believed status was achieved and transmitted within the family. An examination of the use of *domus* will suggest how the Romans perceived this basic unit of society to be organized and delimited at a normative level.

Chapter 5 analyzes the central values and powers that structured family relations within the household. The key terms most commonly associated with the Roman family are *pietas* and *patria potestas*. What configuration of authority and obligation did these quintessentially Roman concepts legitimize in family relations? I present a revisionist interpretation here, arguing that it is a gross oversimplification to represent Roman fathers as endowed with unlimited power, obeyed by children under unlimited obligation underwritten by the duty of *pietas*. This may have been the way that the Greeks as conquered foreigners understood Roman legends, but it is not the way that the Romans themselves understood family bonds.

[2] See above, ch. 3, n. 3.

Roman culture drew a clear distinction between the father's relationship with his children, characterized by mutual obligation and concern, and the master's exploitative power over his slaves.

That distinction was most overtly symbolized by the application of the whip, powerfully associated with slavery in Roman culture. Chapter 6 examines how the act of whipping was construed by the Romans as a symbol of subjection, and how that symbolism, so evident in public life, came into play in Roman thinking about the appropriate means of socialization of children.

4

Familia and *domus*: defining and representing the Roman family and household

The subject of "family" may seem self-explanatory, but different cultures have defined the "family" and its boundaries in various fashions. This chapter seeks to elucidate the Roman understanding of family through a close examination of the basic Latin vocabulary and how this fundamental social unit was represented in certain important contexts. An analysis of the semantic ranges of *familia* and *domus* will enable us to explore some of the implications of Roman characterizations and representations of their families and households.

Understanding the Roman conception of the family is a delicate task, encountering the problematic relation between words and patterns of social behavior. There is no easy, one-to-one correspondence between vocabulary and social entities, and it is well to recognize from the outset the futility of attempting to define or to characterize *the* Roman family. Certain definitions were appropriate to, and clarified by, particular contexts. In other contexts the meaning of the word was left ambiguous, sometimes deliberately so. Moreover, the Romans represented their family bonds and household groups in visual art, ritual, and symbolic behavior in varying but related ways. Finally, if the Romans conceived of family and household variously according to context, each Roman had to construct his or her own family and household out of the kin and resources available, with the consequence that in the real world family and household came in innumerable shapes and sizes.

In view of the definitional messiness of *familia* and *domus*, and, even more, of the real living unit, it is pointless to endeavor to identify *the* form of *the* Roman family.[1] Yet it is worthwhile to delineate the range of context-specific meanings of *familia* and *domus* and the emphases within the Roman

---

[1] This chapter draws materials from earlier articles, especially "*Familia, domus*, and the Roman conception of the family" (1984), but uses those materials in a somewhat different way. This chapter is less concerned with the form of the typical family of the Romans in

74

social context. The standard lexicons give general definitions that may seem to make the Roman family experience easily translatable. But detailed examination will show subtle differences between *familia* and "family," rooted in the very different social contexts. J.-L. Flandrin has illuminated changes in European family life over the past five centuries through the shift in the primary definitions of family. In the sixteenth and seventeenth centuries it was used to signify (1) persons related by blood or marriage (kin in a wide sense), or (2) a lineage or house (i.e., those descended from the same stock or blood), or (3) all those living under the same roof, including servants and other non-relatives. As Flandrin has shown, dictionaries of the period did not define family as "father, mother, and children," a primary definition today. That has emerged as a standard definition only in the past two centuries and is, in Flandrin's view, to be connected with the development of the father–mother–children triad as the typical household unit among the educated classes as servants were excluded.[2] For the social historian, then, more is at stake than semantics.

Familia

The *Oxford Latin Dictionary* gives the following definitions for *familia*:

1. All persons subject to the control of one man, whether relations, freedmen or slaves, a household. b. PATER, MATER, FILIUS, FILIA [-familias]. 2. The slaves of a household. 3. A group of servants domiciled in one place. 4. A body of persons closely associated by blood or affinity, family. 5. A school (of philosophy, etc.). 6. (leg.) Estate (consisting of the household and household property).

In its essential elements, this definition follows that of Ulpian in the *Digest* (50.16.195.1–4), but misses some significant nuances. Ulpian began by distinguishing between *familia* as *res* (the final entry in the *OLD*) and *familia* as *personae*. It is rightly noted that *familia* as property or estate is a legal usage, rarely found in classical literature except in legal discussions. Ulpian pointed to the archaic flavor of this meaning in quoting as an example from the XII Tables "adgnatus proximus familiam habeto" ("let the nearest agnate have the *familia*").

Ulpian then proceeded to enumerate a variety of meanings of *familia* used in respect of *personae*. The first is the strict legal sense of all *personae* in the *potestas* of the *paterfamilias*, either by nature or by law, including the *materfamilias*, sons, daughters, adopted children, grandsons, and grand-

---

practice and more concerned with the characteristically Roman configuration of definitions and representations of family and household.

2   Flandrin 1979: 4–10. Flandrin's work has come in for criticism, but his point about definition has been accepted: see Anderson 1980: ch. 3, esp. 41. On the distinction between lineage and other types of descent groups, see Goody 1983: App. 1.

daughters. This definition (I.b in the *OLD*) is the one that most closely approximates our primary meaning of "family" as father, mother, and children, but is in fact different in quite important respects. Again, its significance lay more in the legal realm than in the social: those *in potestate* (the *sui heredes* [own heirs] of a *paterfamilias* entitled to an equal share of the estate on intestacy) were included, but not the wife who in a marriage *sine manu* continued to belong to her father's *familia*.[3] Furthermore, as Ulpian pointed out, even an underage, orphaned boy (*pupillus*) could be a *paterfamilias* under this definition, since he held *dominium in domo* (power in the house), though the *familia* had no mother or children. This definition of *familia*, tied to the law of property, continued to have notable economic and social consequences, but it was essentially archaic to the extent that it did not coincide with the way Romans of the classical period regularly used the word outside the legal context.

This definition of *familia* underlines the ambiguous relationship of the *mater* to the *familia*. So long as *manus* marriages were usual and the woman entered the *potestas* of her husband, she became a member of her children's and her husband's *familia*.[4] But when marriage *sine manu* became common and the wife was no longer in her husband's *potestas*, a conflict arose between legal definition and the reality that the wife was a vital member of the household, the basic unit of reproduction. The ambiguity of the woman's position is reflected in the fact that in non-legal usage *familia* was occasionally taken to include the wife. For instance, in the *Pro Caelio* (33) Cicero could speak of Clodia as marrying *in familiam clarissimam* (the Metelli) and at the same time as being in the *familia Claudia*. Passages of this sort, which appear to violate the legal definition based on *potestas*, are quite rare in Latin literature. More often, the wife was treated as part of her father's *familia*. So Livia did not enter the *familia Iulia* upon her marriage to Octavian, but by adoption on Augustus' death.[5] Instead of *familia* the Romans more often used *domus* to indicate the living unit including the wife.

In common parlance, according to Ulpian, *familia* encompassed a wider group, since siblings did not cease to refer to themselves as a *familia* when their father died and each became *sui iuris* (in his/her own power) with his or her own property. Thus all *agnati* were called a *familia*, that is, the kin originating from the same house, and related by blood through males. On the

---

[3] *Dig.* 50.16.196, Gaius. Consequently Herlihy's characterization of the Roman family as a social unit (1983: 116–30) based on the definition of *familia* is inaccurate.

[4] It is on this basis that Labeo gives his etymology of *soror* as someone who leaves the *familia* (A. Gellius *NA* 13.10.3). For the development from *manus* to *sine manu* marriage see Watson 1967: 29–31. On the possibility of the woman marrying a member of her *familia*, see Saller and Shaw 1984b: 432–34.

[5] Tacitus *Ann.* 6.51. Similar examples include *Ann.* 12.1 and 15.22; Seneca *Cons. ad Marciam* 16.3.

agnatic principle children were in the same *familia* as their father's brother, his children, and their father's sister, but not the sister's children or their mother's siblings. As Gaius stated, "it is plain that *liberi feminarum* are not in the woman's *familia*, since those born to them succeed to the *familiam patris*."[6] *TLL* and the standard Latin–English dictionaries do not seem to have taken the jurists' reference to *agnati* seriously, and include agnate and cognate relatives without distinction in the definition of *familia*. Yet a survey of Latin literature produces only a very few, exceptional passages in which cognate kin are included in the *familia*, and more where they are by implication excluded.

Among the exceptions Apuleius in his *Metamorphoses* (5.28) included Cupid in the *familia* of Venus, but it would be unwise to try to specify and draw conclusions from precise relationships in the divine realm (presumably not subject to Roman family law). In a second, earthly example, Fronto wrote to his son-in-law Aufidius Victorinus, legate of Germany early in Marcus Aurelius' reign, that with the favor of the gods *nostra familia* would be increased *liberis ac nepotibus* (by children and grandchildren, *Ad amicos* 1.12). Fronto here pushed the word *familia* beyond its usual agnatic sense, in the hope that Gratia, his only surviving child, would provide grandchildren for him. As it happened, Fronto's name was perpetuated through his daughter's child, as *CIL* 11.6334 dedicated to his great-grandson M. Aufidius Fronto reveals. A third passage to include cognates in the *familia* comes from Suetonius. Tiberius, he wrote, "was incorporated into" (*insertus est*) the *Liviorum familia* by virtue of the fact that his maternal grandfather was adopted into it (*Tib.* 3).[7] Suetonius expressed Tiberius' kinship affiliations somewhat carelessly: the adoption of a maternal grandfather was legally irrelevant to Tiberius' membership in a *familia*. Tacitus indicated correctly the position of Tiberius: "his father was Nero and on each side his ancestry was of the Claudian *gens*, and soon he transferred into the Julian *familia*."[8] In other words, his mother's and

---

[6] *Dig.* 50.16.196. In the age of Justinian *familia* was broadened to include cognates (e.g., *gener* and *nurus*), as *CJ* 6.38.5.pr.1 explicitly states, but there is no comparable statement in the classical jurists. (In *Dig.* 38.8.1.4 the *adoptatus* is said to have *iura cognationis in familia naturalis patris*, which is not to say that he is part of it.) The fact that all three exceptions to the agnate rule are second-century may suggest some change of meaning in that period.

[7] In *Claud.* 39.2 the phrase *familiae insertus* clearly means acquiring membership in the *familia*.

[8] *Ann.* 6.51: "pater ei Nero et utrimque origo gentis Claudiae, quamquam mater in Liviam et mox Iuliam familiam adoptionibus transierit." Since Tacitus is usually precise, his treatment of the embarrassed *preces Marci Hortali* before Tiberius and the Senate for money to maintain the status of his four sons (*Ann.* 2.37–38) is especially puzzling. Like others, I assumed from the prominence of the later Republican orator, Q. Hortensius, in the plea that the embarrassed young senator was Marcus Hortensius Hortalus and that he was pleading for the preservation of the *familia* and *domus Hortensia* (1984: 346). Corbier

maternal grandfather's adoptions did not affect Tiberius' membership in the Claudian *gens*.

A survey of other uses of *familia* proves that Tacitus, not Suetonius, was in tune with ordinary usage in this case. When King Deiotarus of western Galatia was prosecuted by his daughter's son, Cicero spoke of the latter as a member of his father's *familia* as distinct from that of the king, his maternal grandfather (*Deiot.* 30). Similarly, in Cicero's attacks on Piso earlier in his career he tried to avoid insulting Piso's *familia* (their cognomen Frugi being evidence of their inborn virtue) and suggested that the iniquitous streak in his character derived from his *maternum genus*. Consequently, Piso's behavior was a stain on his *cognatio*, rather than on his *paternum genus*.[9] Cicero appears to draw a similar distinction in the *Pro Cluentio* (16) when he argues that the appalling activities of Cluentius' mother were a *dedecus* (disgrace) on both his *familia* and his *cognatio*. Valerius Maximus' story about Astyages, written about a century later, requires the reader to separate *familia* from cognate relatives: Astyages ordered his daughter's son Cyrus exposed "lest the honor of rule be transferred into his familia" (*ne in eius familiam regni decus transferretur*, 1.7.ext.5). As with the Deiotarus example, the family here is not Roman, but Roman family concepts are used in telling the story, in which the grandson by a daughter is not counted as a part of the *familia*.[10]

Even Suetonius, in the one other relevant passage in his work, seems to place only agnatic relatives in the *familia*. Otho's *familia*, said to be *vetus et honorata atque ex principibus Etruriae* (ancient and honored and from the leading men of Etruria), is contrasted with the humble birth of his grandfather's mother (*Otho* 1.1). Altogether, then, there is no good evidence that Romans commonly considered cognate relatives to be part of their *familia*.

In many passages referring to *familia* the context does not make it obvious whether the author intended his readers to understand *agnati* or the still larger lineage group including ancestors. Ulpian's last definition in the

(1991b) has shown from epigraphic evidence, however, that the embarrassed figure must have been Marcius Hortalus (the difference between Marcius and Marcus being disguised in the genitive), a descendant of the great orator and his last wife Marcia. The change of *nomen* must be explained by adoption of the impoverished senator or his father into Marcia's illustrious *familia*. It may be, as Corbier suggests, that *clarissima familia* in *Ann.* 2.37 is used in the strict agnatic sense and refers to the Marcii, though, if that was Tacitus' intention, his reference to this *familia* (nowhere clearly named in the passage) immediately after reference to the orator Hortensius is highly misleading. Or it may be that here is another exception to the generally agnatic connotation of *familia*, encouraged by the fact that this Marcius Hortalus may have preserved the memory of his grandfather's *nomen* in a *cognomen* Hortensinus, as Corbier suggests.   [9] *Sest.* 21, *Pis.* 53.
[10] It should be stressed that these are the passages in which cognates are treated as being outside the *familia*. Many dozens of others could be adduced to illustrate the fact that agnates are part of the *familia* – in contrast to the meagre three in which cognates are included.

above passage is "all *personae* born of the blood of the same ultimate ancestor." This is the most common sense of *familia* as used by Cicero and the prose authors of the Principate with reference to kinship. Since no one knows his or her "ultimate ancestors," *familia* could be more or less inclusive, sometimes taken be equivalent to *gens* or clan and other times more narrowly. Occasionally the distinction between *familia* and *gens* is made explicitly, as in Festus' statement that *gens Aemilia appellatur quae ex multis familiis conficitur* (the Aemilian clan is so called, which is made up of many families).[11] Of course, *gens* membership was usually associated with a common *nomen* and *familia* with a *cognomen*. Just as often *familia* is used as a synonym for *gens*, as in references to the *familia Aemilia* or *familia Fabia*.[12] In most cases, however, the context does not indicate to the reader how broad a descent group the author is referring to with the word *familia*. This is surely because the author is not trying to convey precise genealogical information so much as a general impression of quality of birth for which the *gens—familia* distinction was not necessarily important. In his speeches Cicero several times appealed to the triplet of *genus, nomen*, and *familia*. When, for example, reference is made in Cicero's *Pro Scauro* (111) to the *dignitas* of Scaurus' *genus, familia*, and *nomen, familia* obviously has the meaning of a descent group, but exactly what group and how *familia* differs, if at all, from *genus* and *nomen* are questions that cannot be answered, nor is Cicero likely to have expected his audience to worry over the fine distinctions.[13] As a group the three words brought to mind agnatic lineage and its prestige in a broad sense.

As in the early modern period, lineage as marked by *nomen* was claimed by the Roman elite to have an existence and prestige all its own.[14] In his defense of the patrician L. Valerius Flaccus before a wealthy jury, Cicero appealed for the preservation of not only the person of his client but also his *nomen clarissimum*. Wealthy aristocrats adopted adult sons in their wills on condition that as heirs they assume the testator's *nomen*.[15] The underlying

---

[11] Pauli Festus p. 94. Similar examples appear in Valerius Maximus 1.1.17 and Suetonius *Iul.* 6.1, *Ner.* 1.1, *Galba* 3.1.

[12] Tacitus *Ann.* 6.27; Valerius Maximus 4.1.5, where *gens* and *familia* are used interchangeably in the same passage, as they are in 5.2.ext.4, 5.6.4, and Livy 6.40.3. Already noted by Mommsen 1887: 3.16, n.2.

[13] The triplet also appears in *Verr.* 2.2.51, *Mur.* 12, and *Lig.* 20. On the manipulation of kinship reckoning, see Klapisch-Zuber 1991: 208–228.

[14] The analogy between the Roman and early modern periods cannot be taken too far. To judge by patterns of Roman testation, discussed below in chapter 7, Roman aristocrats placed comparatively more stress on *nomen* and less on blood than their early modern counterparts.

[15] Pliny *Ep.* 8.18 gives the example of Domitius Afer, who adopted two sons, Lucanus and Tullus, of a man whom he had destroyed. The will had been made long before Afer's death and before his hostile action against the father of Lucanus and Tullus.

premise is the notion that continuity of the *familia* and its name is, in itself, of some importance. Consequently, Seneca (*Ben.* 3.33.4) could describe a son as a *beneficium* (favor) to his father on the ground that the son would provide *domus ac familiae perpetuitas* (the continuation of house and family). The honor of the *familia* had an existence apart from its individual members. Valerius Maximus (9.7.2) reported that the censor of 131 BC Metellus would not accept a census registration from someone claiming to be the son of the deceased Tiberius Gracchus, saying that Gracchus' sons had died, "and it is not right that ignoble rabble be inserted into a most illustrious *familia*" (*neque oportere clarissimae familiae ignotas sordes inseri*).[16] Metellus felt in duty bound to protect the honor of Gracchus' *familia* even though Tiberius and his sons were dead. The feeling that a *familia* could be polluted appears again later in Tacitus' comment (*Ann.* 4.7) that the planned marriage of Claudius' son to Sejanus' daughter and the possibility that Sejanus would share grandsons *cum familia Drusorum* would represent a stain on the *nobilitas familiae*. During the Republic the significance of *familia* and *nomen* was part of the more general contest over how closed politics were to be. Not every Roman shared the censor Metellus' concern about the honor of the *familia*: indeed, the *populus* stoned him for his effort on behalf of the Gracchi. Only a narrow circle of aristocrats can have known enough about their male ancestors to attach great importance to their agnatic descent group.

Domus

Domus, like *familia*, covered a broad semantic range, but, unfortunately, the *Digest* title *De significatione verborum* does not offer a systematic set of definitions. *Domus* was used with regard to household and kinship to mean (1) the physical house; (2) the household including family and slaves; (3) the broad kinship group including agnates and cognates, ancestors and descendants; and (4) the patrimony.

(1) The physical house. Ernout attempted to show that *domus* was not commonly used for the physical house (*aedes*) so much as for the domain in which the *dominus* exercised his control (along the lines of our house/home distinction).[17] In very many passages, especially where *domus* is used adverbially ("to return *domum*," or "to be *domi*"), it is impossible to know whether authors intended one or the other of Ernout's meanings. There are, however, enough passages in which *domus* can mean only the physical

---

[16] According to Pliny (*HN* 35.7), the same sentiment prompted Valerius Messala to write his *De familia*.

[17] Ernout 1932: 304. It is unclear on what grounds Benveniste (1973: 243) claims that "*domus* always signifies 'house' in the sense of 'family'", but the assertion is clearly wrong.

building to show that such usage was quite normal.[18] For instance, during and immediately after his exile Cicero repeatedly expressed concern about recovering his *domus*. When he spoke of the senate ordering it to be rebuilt, he was clearly referring to the physical structure and not to the household over which he exercised *dominium*.[19]

Yet Ernout was right to sense that the physical structure did not in itself necessarily constitute a *domus*. Wealthy Romans often owned more than one residence, prompting the jurists to worry over how to interpret laws specifying some action at the *domus*. For example, a wife was supposed to send notification of the birth of a child to her husband or his father at his *domus*, which was defined in law as the place "where they established the *lar* for the marriage" (*ubi larem matrimonio collocarent*, Dig. 25.3.1.2, Ulpian). Similarly, to interpret a law that allowed a Roman to take home (*domum ducere*) duty-free from Sicily slaves for his own use, the jurist Alfenus Varus had to explain more precisely that *domus* is "where each person had his abode and accounts, and put his own affairs in order" ("ubi quisque sedes et tabulas haberet suarumque rerum constitutionem fecisset," Dig. 50.16.203). Despite a certain vagueness and circularity in this explication, these comments suggest that a man's home, *domus*, might be distinguished from his other houses by a sacred quality (the *lar*) and a practical managerial function (the account books).[20] In other circumstances, however, the jurists defined *domus* more broadly, as any residence. The *lex Cornelia de iniuriis* allowed a man an action for insult against one who forcefully entered his *domus*, construed as any residence, including an urban apartment or a rustic villa (*Dig.* 47.10.5.pr-5, Ulpian).

(2) In its sense of the people comprising the household establishment, *domus* comes close to one of the definitions of *familia* – that is, a man's servile dependants – but normally there is some distinction. Whereas *familia* is frequently used for the group of slaves under a *dominus*, to the exclusion of the free members of the household, *domus* is often rather broader, including the wife, children, and others in the house. Seneca castigates the man who complains of the loss of *libertas* in the *res publica*, but then destroys it in his own *domus* by forbidding his slave, freedman, wife, or client to talk back to him.[21] The *domus* here clearly includes more than the *familia* in the

---

[18] Cicero *Cat.* 4.12, *Verr.* 2.5.80, *Cael.* 60, *Mil.* 64, *Phil.* 2.91; Valerius Maximus 5.7.3; Columella *Rust.* 4.3.1; Seneca *Constant.* 12.2, *Ep.* 41.7 (*familia formosa et domus pulchra*); Quintilian *Decl.* 337, p. 325; Pliny *Ep.* 7.27; Tacitus *Ann.* 13.18, 15.38, 41, 43, 50, 52, *Hist.* 3.33; Suetonius *Aug.* 5, 72.1, *Cal.* 22.4, *Ner.* 16.1, *Dom.* 1.1.
[19] E.g., *Har. Resp.* 16.
[20] Ernout's definition of *domus* as the sphere of *dominium* does not account for the way in which the jurists singled out one *domus* for certain purposes, since a wealthy Roman possessed *dominium* over all his houses and their staffs.
[21] *Ira* 3.35.1. Other examples where *domus* clearly includes the wife are Cicero *Cat.* 1.14, *Phil.* 5.11.

limited sense of slaves and freedmen. It is presumably this broader group
that is meant by the phrase *tota domus*, as when Cicero closes a letter to
Atticus with the line "our whole household sends its greetings" (*domus et
nostra tota salutat*).[22]

The most self-conscious attempt to define the circle of people who
constituted the living unit of the household comes in the juristic discussion
of *penus*, the "stores" of the house. Testators sometimes bequeathed the
penus as a legacy to their spouses or other family members, and it was
essential to agree on what was included in the *penus* (as opposed, say, to
stocks being kept for sale). The Republican jurist Q. Mucius Scaevola
defined *penus* in these words: "*Penus* is what is for eating or for drinking,
which has been secured for the sake of the *paterfamilias* himself or the
materfamilias or the children of the *paterfamilias* or his slaves (*familia*), who
are around him or his children and do not work."[23] This passage, in
specifying who was expected to live "around the *paterfamilias*," provides
insight into what propertied Romans perceived to be the standard living
unit. It included father, mother, children, and household slaves. The jurists
explicitly excluded the agricultural slaves housed in the villa and did not
envisage the possibility of a joint household, either one headed by two
brothers in *consortium* or one of three generations including daughters-in-
law.[24] Of course, in reality Roman households were not so neatly bounded,
owing to death, divorce, and reconstitution, yet the point remains that for
certain purposes, such as interpreting legacies, the Romans used standard,
abstract definitions, which informed their view of what a household ought
to be.

It is worth stressing, since the lexicons give the opposite impression, that
domus, like the English "family" in the sixteenth and seventeenth centuries,
normally refers to all those living in the household and not just the nuclear
family within it. This is the implication of Cicero's statement in the *De officiis*
(1.54) on the pseudo-historical hierarchy of family obligations. First came
the husband–wife bond, then the parent–child, and third the bonds of those

---

[22] *Att.* 4.12. Because *domus* is usually understood to include the whole group living in the
household, Columella does not use it in his discussions of the organization of the slave
staff; he invariably uses *familia*, a more precise word for slaves alone. For the feeling of
the family among slaves in the household, see Flory 1978: 78–95.

[23] Quoted by A. Gellius, *NA* 4.1.17: "nam Quintum Scaevolam ad demonstrandam penum
his verbis usum audio: 'Penus est,' inquit, 'quod esculentum aut posculentum est, quod
ipsius patrisfamilias aut matrisfamilias aut liberum patrisfamilias aut familiae eius, quae
circum eum aut liberos eius est et opus non facit.'"

[24] *Dig.* 33.9.3.6, where Ulpian does allow for the possibility that those around the
paterfamilias might include *amici* and *clientes*. Since the jurists did include grandchildren by
a son among a man's *liberi*, it could be argued that the definition of *penus* automatically
encompassed three generations. But women marrying sons in the household would not
have been included among *liberi* and are not envisaged in the definition.

within the *domus*. This order would make no sense if the Romans usually thought of *domus* as the mother–father–children triad. In Cicero's *commendationes* freedmen are assumed to be part of the recommended *domus*, and Seneca and Pliny write of the *domus* as a miniature *res publica* in which the slaves participate as citizens.[25] Of course, humbler households did not necessarily have slaves, and in these cases the *domus* might coincide with the nuclear family. A couplet from Ovid's *Fasti* (4.543–44) offers an example of this. When the goddess Ceres enters the poor cottage of Celeus and heals his little son, "the whole *domus* is happy, this is the mother and father and daughter: these three were the whole *domus*" ("tota domus laeta est, hoc est materque paterque / nataque: tres illi tota fuere domus").[26] Ovid expects to raise a smile here with the hyperbolic use of *tota domus* for a small nuclear family. The lines would be tediously flat and repetitious if *domus* had regularly brought to his well-to-do readers' minds only mother, father, and children.

Although *domus* normally encompasses the whole household, free and slave, it is occasionally used with reference to the slave staff alone, like *familia* in Mucius Scaevola's definition of *penus*. Seneca reports that when the aging *praefectus annonae* Turannius was asked by the emperor to retire, Turannius had his *familia* mourn him as if he were dead; and the *domus* did not stifle its grief until he was reinstated.[27] The two words seem to be used synonymously here for the servile establishment. Similarly, both *familia* and *domus* appear in connection with the emperor's servile staff.[28]

In sum, neither *domus* nor *familia* had as a usual meaning in literary Latin "family" in the primary sense of the word today. When writers wished to signify that core family unit, they employed the phrase *uxor* (or *coniunx*) *liberique*: so Cicero referred to Sex. Roscius having his *domus* and his *uxor liberique* at Ameria, and Seneca listed among a man's worst misfortunes his having to bury *liberos coniugem*.[29]

(3) The broader kinship group. As with the English word "family" in the

---

[25] Cicero *Fam.* 13.23.1, 13.46; Seneca *Ep.* 47.4; Pliny *Ep.* 8.14.16.

[26] In most passages the composition of the *domus* is not so clearly specified, and it is possible that the nuclear family is sometimes meant, but I have not found any other examples where this is certainly the case, and only a few where it might be the case (e.g., Lucretius 3.894 where it is unclear whether *domus laeta* is equivalent to the explicitly mentioned *uxor* and *liberi* or to a wider group).

[27] *Brev. vit.* 20.3. Tacitus uses *domus* with reference to Agricola's servile staff while he governed Britain (*Agr.* 19).

[28] Seneca *Cons. ad Polybium* 2.4; Tacitus *Hist.* 2.92; Suetonius *Claud.* 40.2. For *familia Caesaris* see Weaver 1972: 299–300.

[29] Cicero, *Rosc. Amer.* 96; Seneca, *Prov.* 3.2. See also Cicero *Phil.* 12.5, *Quinct.* 54; Quintilian *Decl.* 337, p. 325. In *Pro Deiotaro* 15, Cicero argues that Deiotarus would not have been foolish enough to plot against Caesar, since even if he had succeeded he would have been destroyed *cum regno, cum domo, cum coniuge, cum filio*. The position of *domus* in this series suggests that it was an entity of intermediate size between *regnum* and *coniunx et filius*.

early modern period, *domus* could be used for a kinship group (not including servants) but was normally more inclusive than the nuclear family. *Domus* could refer variously to a man's circle of living kin or to his descent group including ancestors and descendants. The extent of the kin encompassed by the *domus*, as by the *familia*, could be more or less great, from the whole *gens* to a much narrower circle of relatives. In these respects, *domus* is very much like *familia*, but there is one notable difference: *domus* does not generally have the formal agnatic connotations that *familia* has.

With regard to living relatives, *domus* could refer to a group as narrow as brothers. In his *Consolatio* addressed to Polybius (3.4), Seneca chastised Fortuna for breaking up *optimorum adulescentium domum* – that is, Polybius and his recently deceased brother. As a freedman, Polybius had a necessarily very limited circle of relatives. Usually *domus* encompassed a larger group, not limited to the *familia*. In several recommendations Pliny stressed the quality and standing of the *domus* of his protégé. In the letter to Minicius Fundanus on behalf of Asinius Bassus, Pliny described Bassus' father, brother-in-law, and nephew "so that you may know how abundant, how numerous a house you would put under obligation by a single favor" ("ut scias quam copiosam, quam numerosam domum uno beneficio sis obligaturus," *Ep.* 4.15.4). Sextus Erucius Clarus was said by Pliny to be a young man of virtue *cum tota domo*, from which Clarus' father and *avunculus* (maternal uncle) Septicius Clarus the future praetorian prefect were singled out for mention (*Ep.* 2.9.3). When Iunius Mauricus asked Pliny to suggest a husband for his orphaned niece, Pliny nominated Minicius Acilianus, in part for the virtues of *tota domus* including his father, his maternal grandmother and uncle (*avia materna, avunculus, Ep.* 1.14.6). It is striking that Pliny places as much stress, or more, in these letters on cognate kin as on agnates, and for this group *domus* rather than *familia* was the appropriate label. Pliny regarded even distant kin as part of his *domus* and deserving of his patronal support, as illustrated by his letter of thanks to Trajan for transferring to his own staff Caelius Clemens, *adfinis* of his previous wife's mother. Pliny was pleased that Trajan extended his beneficence to Pliny to his whole *domus* (*Ep.* 10.51).

These passages from Pliny can be paralleled by uses of *domus* in other authors. Seneca (*Ben.* 5.16.4) wrote of Caesar as being part of the *domus* of Pompey, his son-in-law, and Tacitus regarded himself as a member of Agricola's *domus* by virtue of his marriage to Agricola's daughter (*Agr.* 46). Nephews were included in the *domus*. Whatever their faults, Otho and Vitellius had the common decency to avoid harming each other's *domus*, in which Otho's brother and nephew were counted (Tac. *Hist.* 1.75, 2.48). The kin included were sometimes very distant: as a show of *liberalitas* Tiberius gave to Aemilius Lepidus the unclaimed *hereditas* left by the wealthy Lepida

"from whose house he seems to be" (*cuius e domo videtur*, Tac. *Ann.* 2.48).
The fact that Lepidus could not claim the estate through the normal
procedure indicates that his kinship must have been beyond the sixth
degree. Tacitus' wording suggests that a common cognomen may have
been Lepidus' only evidence of being from the same *domus* (that is, *familia*).

The emperor's relatives of all types constituted the *domus Caesarum*. Pliny
judged it praiseworthy that Nerva, in contrast to most of his predecessors,
did not confine his search for a successor *intra domum* (*Pan.* 7.5). That the
imperial *domus* was a broader group than the *familia* is made clear by Tacitus'
statement that Tiberius entered the *domus Augusti* first as a *privignus*
(stepson), when his mother married Octavian.[30] Only later did he become a
member of the *familia* by adoption. Altogether, a comparison of the
frequency with which *domus* is used for cognates and affines with the very
rare uses of *familia* for non-agnatic kin suggests that *domus* is the more
general term.

Often the context does not indicate whether *domus* means the living kin
group, as in the above passages, or the kin of earlier and later generations,
as with *familia*. For example, Valerius Maximus (5.2.ext.4) reports that
Masinissa, known for his loyalty to the *familia Cornelia*, advised his wife and
children to continue their contact with the *domus Scipionis*. In the scene from
Tacitus' *Histories* (3.66) in which Vitellius' supporters urge him to be worthy
of his father's consulships and censorship, *honores egregiae domus*, Tacitus
could have substituted *familia* without altering the meaning.[31] Occasionally
the two words are found in sequence, as when Seneca writes of a son being
domus ac familiae perpetuitas.[32] Is this a case of hendiadys or is there a
difference of nuance? The context here offers no answer.

Domus certainly could be used for a broader descent group than that for
which *familia* would be appropriate. In Virgil's version of the founding
legend of Rome the native king Latinus lacked a son, and consequently "his
daughter alone preserved the house and so great a foundation" (*sola domum
et tantas servabat filia sedes*).[33] A *domus* could be extended through a
daughter's children, but a *familia* could not without adoption. Seneca also
considered the mother's ancestors to be part of the *domus*: comparing the
deaths of Marcia's father and grandfather with that of her son, Seneca
summoned up the spirit of her father to console her with the thought that
her son's was the least painful death *in nostra domo*.[34]

---

[30] *Ann.* 6.51. See also *Ann.* 6.8 and Suetonius *Aug.* 25.1.

[31] So also in *Ann.* 2.48, 3.24.

[32] *Ben.* 3.33.4. See also *Ad Heren.* 4.51; Livy 22.53.11; Curtius 10.7.15; Petronius *Sat.* 64.7.

[33] *Aen.* 7.52. Anchises refers to his *domus* in *Aen.* 2.702: here *familia* would also be
      appropriate since he is referring to agnatic lineage.

[34] *Cons. ad Marciam* 26.3. Pliny writes of Helvidius' last living child, a daughter, as being the
      hope for continuation of his *domus* (*Ep.* 4.21.3).

Given Augustus' practice of securing marriage ties with leading aristocratic families, the *domus Caesarum* became extensive. At the core of the imperial dynasty were the two *familiae*, referred to as the *domus Iuliorum Claudiorumque* or the *Claudia et Iulia domus*, but the circle of cognatic kin extended much further.[35] Among the ancestors in *nostra domus* Claudius would have included, in Seneca's view (*Cons. ad Polyb.* 15.3), his maternal grandfather M. Antony. The *domus Caesarum* was in fact such a large group that there were bound to be factional houses or *domus* within it. So, for example, Germanicus, who was part of the imperial family, was also represented as having his own *domus* made up of Agrippina, his children, and their descendants, toward whom Tiberius was represented as implacably hostile. Awareness of the *domus Gemanici* continued to shape popular opinion and to provoke family infighting after his death. Titius Sabinus suffered for his loyalty to the *domus Germanici* from other factions in the *domus Caesarum*, and in the popular view the birth of Drusus' twins was a further misfortune for the *domus Germanici* (though in the broader sense they were all part of the same imperial house).[36] Because Tiberius felt compelled in the end to select his successor from the *domus Caesarum*, he had to turn, after the misfortunes of his once *florens domus*, to Germanicus' house and to select Gaius.[37] The use of *domus* for the imperial dynasty continued with the *domus Flavia* which included Vespasian's brother and sons (Tac. *Hist.* 2.101, 3.75). According to Tacitus, one of the reasons Mucianus conceded primacy to Vespasian was that the latter had two sons in his *domus* – some assurance that the dynasty would survive more than one reign (*Hist.* 2.77).

(4) The patrimony. The survival of a *domus* depended not only on having children, but also on having the financial resources to preserve their social standing. For this reason *domus* in the sense of lineage is closely related to *domus* meaning patrimony. *Domus* in the latter sense does not occur frequently in classical texts, but it is not an archaic or legal usage, as *familia* is with regard to *res*. One of the son's responsibilities as heir of a patrimony, according to Seneca, is to hand on the *domus* "in an undiminished state" (*in integro statu*) when he dies.[38] In his *Apologia* (76) Apuleius accuses his arch-enemy Rufinus of being a wastrel with a *domus* "drained and full of children" (*exhausta et plena liberis*). Clearly, the only sense in which a house with children could have been *exhausta* was with regard to its financial resources, and that is the sense in which L. Volusius strengthened his *domus* with great riches (Tac. *Ann.* 3.30).

In sum, all of the above meanings of *domus* are related and shade into one

---

[35] Tacitus *Hist.* 1.16, *Ann.* 6.8.
[36] Tacitus *Ann.* 4.68, 4.40, 2.84. Germanicus' son Drusus includes his whole family in Tiberius' *domus* in *Ann.* 6.24.   [37] Tacitus *Ann.* 4.1, 6.46; Suetonius *Cal.* 13.
[38] *Cons. ad Marciam* 26.2; a similar comment using *domus* appears in Tacitus *Ann.* 15.1.

another. When a Roman spoke of the pleasures of his *domus*, it is often impossible to discover whether he meant his physical house or the family and servants in it over whom he exercised *potestas*. Or again, when pride is expressed in a *domus*, it could be pride in a physical *domus* or the household establishment or the wider circle of kin who derived from a single household.[39] Further, the distinction between *domus* as the living extended family and *domus* as the descent group is often not worth specifying. When the deaths of Gaius and Lucius left Augustus with a *domus deserta* (not literally true on any definition of *domus*), the reader is meant to understand that Gaius and Lucius were lost from the *domus* as the living circle of kin, but also, and more important, that they were lost as potential successors in Augustus' *domus* in the sense of dynasty.[40]

The range of meaning made *domus* a more widely applicable measure of social respectability than *familia* in the Principate. Cicero always used *familia* when speaking of a man's prestige through his family background (though he was not oblivious to the mother's pedigree), and he rarely employed *domus* to mean the extended family.[41] The very nature of Republican politics ensured a concentration on *familia*: in the popular assemblies the renown of a man's *nomen*, transmitted through the *familia*, was an important asset in securing a successful political career.[42] The change in thinking about family background in the Principate is evident in Pliny's letters: in contrast to Cicero, Pliny never refers to the *familia* of his friends or clients in recommendations, but always to the *domus* including cognate kin. Pliny's contemporary, Tacitus, associated *familia* in the sense of lineage mainly with Republican noble families and the imperial house.[43] Such noble families were

[39] Tiberius rejected a proposal for selection of magistrates five years in advance, arguing that it would be impossible to foresee a candidate's *mens*, *domus*, and *fortuna* so far in the future (Tacitus *Ann.* 2.36). *Domus* is used as a measure of status, but which sense of *domus*, if a particular one was intended, is difficult to discern.

[40] Seneca *Cons. ad Marciam* 15.2. Similarly, in Tacitus *Ann.* 4.3 *plena Caesarum domus* refers not so much to the size of the kin group as to the number of potential male successors, as the enumeration of the members of the *domus* makes clear (*iuvenis filius* and *nepotes adulti* of Tiberius).

[41] I find only a few certain examples in Cicero's letters and speeches. In *Ad familiares* 10.3.2 Cicero refers to his bond of *necessitudo* with the *domus* of Plancus which began before Plancus' birth. The other three examples appear in letters to C. Marcellus (*cos.* 50 BC) in comments on the services rendered to Cicero by *domus tua tota* (*Fam.* 15.8, 15.10.2, 15.11.1). In these instances, Cicero wishes to include P. Cornelius Lentulus Marcellinus who had left the *familia Marcellorum* through adoption – consequently *familia* would not have been an accurate description of the extended family (see Shackleton Bailey [1977] on 15.10.1). In general, Cicero does not use *domus* where *familia* would be appropriate, as imperial authors do.

[42] Wiseman 1971: 100–107. I do not mean to suggest that office-holding was hereditary in the Republic, only that a distinguished *nomen* was perceived to be an asset in competition in the popular assemblies and the law courts; see Hopkins 1983: ch 2.

[43] By my count, of the forty-one passages in which Tacitus uses *familia* to refer to lineage, eleven involve the imperial family and twenty-two involve families which established

increasingly rare as the turnover in senatorial families continued at a very rapid pace.[44] Consequently most senators of the empire could not boast a long, illustrious agnatic lineage, nor was there the same need for a great *nomen* since its recognition in the assemblies was no longer of political consequence. The value of the old, great *nomina* was in any case diluted when new citizens acquired the same names. Membership in an ancient Republican *familia* continued to carry prestige in a society still concerned with birth: the funeral of Iunia in AD 22 must have been an impressive sight with *imagines viginti clarissimarum familiarum* (Tac. *Ann.* 3.76). But for the vast majority of recently promoted senatorial families, it was enough to boast a respectable circle of kin whether related by blood through males or females, or by marriage. This change in thinking away from an emphasis on agnatic line is nicely reflected in the development in nomenclature, from the agnatically transmitted *nomen* and *cognomen* of the Republic to the monstrously long names of the second century AD taken from maternal as well as paternal ancestors.[45]

"Domus" as symbol of status and family

The "Mactar harvester" has long interested imperial historians as an instance of remarkable upward social mobility. His success in rising from the poverty of a fieldhand to the wealth of a local aristocrat was no doubt exceptional.[46] But the terms in which his tombstone (*ILS* 7457) describes his life story provide a fascinating insight into the symbols of status stressed by an ordinary provincial far from the capital city. He was born of a "poor *lar*" and an "insignificant father" (*parvus parens*), who had neither a *census* nor a *domus*. Years of hard work in the fields under the hot African sun made this successful laborer master of his own *domus*, a *domus* (he stresses) that lacked nothing (*nullis opibus indiget ipsa domus*); the local curia honored him with

their nobility in the Republic. Among the remaining eight *familiae*, one is said to be consular, three praetorian, one senatorial, and three equestrian. Already in the Republic the rights of cognates had begun to appear in praetorian law. On the diminishing power of the agnatic principle, see Thomas 1980: 362.   [44] Hopkins 1983: ch. 3.

[45] The practice of adopting names from the mother's family appears clearly in the stemma of the Dolabellae in *PIR²* C 1348 (chosen *exempli gratia*): Cn. Dolabella and Petronia produced a son named Ser. Dolabella Petronianus; L. Nonius Asprenas and Quinctilia had a son named Sex. Nonius Quinctilianus; another L. Nonius Asprenas and Calpurnia named their son (Nonius) Asprenas Calpurnius Serranus; related to the family was the emperor Galba, who added to his name the name of his stepmother Livia Ocellina, becoming L. Livius Ocella Ser. Sulpicius Galba. Unfortunately, there seem to have been no rules with regard to adding cognate relatives' names, and nothing more concrete can be deduced from a name like Ti. Iulius Candidus Marius Celsus (*cos. ord.* II AD 105) than that "parentela coniunctus videtur et cum Mariis Celsis" (*PIR²* I 241). For a cautious assessment of the difficulties of deductions from nomenclature, see Salomies 1992.

[46] Rostovtzeff 1957: 331.

membership and office. The terms used in this epitaph to describe success differ somewhat from our modern success tales in the idiom of "rags to riches": here the idiom of mobility is the rise to the status of a man with an opulent *domus* from the impoverished condition of a man without a *domus*. The physical house in itself marked the harvester's wealth and also provided a domain in which he could exercise social power as a *dominus*. Clearly, the *domus*, apart from kinship, was central to the Roman construction of social status.

Of course, still today the size and elegance of a house are thought to symbolize status, but the nature of Roman public life dictated that the *domus* be of markedly greater importance, as implied by some malicious remarks about Roman leaders. Among other things for which Antony is ridiculed in the *Second Philippic*, Cicero includes the fact that Antony had no *domus* of his own even before Caesar's confiscations, when nearly everyone had his own house.[47] A century later it was thought to cast a grave light on Vitellius' character that he had to lease out his *domus* when he went to Germany as a legate.[48]

Religious, political, and social factors contributed to the value of the *domus* as a symbol for the Romans. Since a man's *domus* was where he kept his *lar* (*Dig.* 25.3.1.2), the Roman house had a sacred aura, embodied in the *lares* or *dii penates*, that houses in more recent societies have not had.[49] Cicero refused to believe that the goddess Libertas would want Clodius to build a *porticus* on the site of Cicero's house during Cicero's exile. Would Libertas want to eject Cicero's own *dii penates*? "What is more sacred, what is more protected by all religion than the house of each and every citizen?"[50] Cicero was not above rhetorical exaggeration to support his argument, but the interchangeable use of *domus* and *dii penates* in other authors presumes a general belief in the sanctity of the house.[51] So too does the association of *domus* with temples and altars in other passages. The worst of the excesses of Vitellius' army in AD 69 included polluting houses and altars with blood (*domus arasque cruore foedare*).[52] This was particularly repugnant

[47] *Phil.* 2.48. See Cicero *Pis.* 61 for a similar, but less direct, insult against L. Calpurnius Piso.
[48] Suetonius *Vit.* 7. In contrast, Petronius has the freedman C. Pompeius Diogenes put up a sign stating that he has moved to his own *domus* as an advertisement of his rise in the world (*Sat.* 38).
[49] Prudentius *C. Symm.* 2.445 ridicules the pagans for investing each *domus* with its own *genius*. For the epigraphic evidence, see the dedications to *Genius domi* given in E. de Ruggiero, *DizEpigr.* 2.2.248, together with the useful discussion of how the "famiglia" and "casa" senses of *domus* are united in inscriptions.
[50] *Dom.* 108: "Quid est sanctius, quid omni religione munitius quam domus unius cuiusque civium?"
[51] Valerius Maximus 5.6, 9.1.6, 9.15.5, Seneca *Clem.* 1.15.3, Tac. *Hist.* 3.70, *Ann.* 13.4. On household cult, see Orr 1978.
[52] Tacitus *Hist.* 3.84. The association of *arae* and *foci* in passages such as Cicero *Phil.* 2.75 and Sallust *Cat.* 52.3 also reflects the Roman feeling of the sanctity of the house.

to Romans who felt that a man's *domus* was his last refuge, a *perfugium sanctum*.[53] The sacred quality of the *domus* made it an especially emotive symbol for generals to employ in appeals to their soldiers: whereas more recently armies have been called on to fight for "God and country," Romans were called on to fight for *patria domusque*.[54] The Roman generals were probably not referring to the physical houses alone, but rather to the whole complex of meanings of *domus*. The very range of meanings allowed for manipulation, so that Tiberius Gracchus is reported to have turned the standard appeal to *patria domusque* against the senatorial leaders by pointing out to the poor voters that in fact they had no house for their wives and children (Plutarch *T. Gracch.* 9).

As a symbol the physical *domus* could give expression to the family's sentiments. After the Pisonian conspiracy was discovered, at the very time when leading Romans were burying their relatives and friends, they were also decorating their *domus* with laurel as an expression of gratitude and joy for Nero's safety.[55] Commentators have noted Tacitus' sarcasm about the hypocrisy,[56] but the irony may be more subtle than they suggest: the survivors were decorating their physical *domus* at the same time that their kinship *domus* were being destroyed in the bloodbath.

For all Romans the *domus* was closely associated with wives, children, and other relatives; for aristocrats it was also associated in a concrete way with lineage, for which it could stand as a symbol. Pliny the Elder describes the various aspects of the house related to lineage: *imagines* were displayed in the atrium with strings running between them to indicate genealogy; records of family achievements were kept in archive rooms; and the trophies of battle victories were fastened to the outside of the *domus* and around the *limina*. Altogether, the physical *domus* was an impressive symbol of the glory and continuity of the great Republican lineages. Pliny notes that this continued to be so even after the great *familiae* died out because the spoils of victory were not to be taken down by the new occupants: "the enduring houses were triumphing even after the owners were changed" (*triumphabant etiam dominis mutatis aeternae domus*).[57] For the great families some of the symbolic significance of the house was lost if the *imagines* were taken down.

---

[53] Cicero *Cat.* 4.2, *Vatin.* 22, *De domo sua* 109. The refuge was even protected in law: a man could not be dragged out of his *domus* into court (*Dig.* 2.4.18, 50.17.103, Gaius).

[54] Tacitus *Hist.* 1.29. In defeating the Carthaginians, Scipio was said to be taking revenge for *patria* and *domus* (Silius Italicus 16.593). Virgil has Aeneas exclaim upon landing in Italy *hic domus, haec patria est* (*Aen.* 7.122).

[55] Tacitus *Ann.* 15.71. Earlier, one of the charges against Piso, the adversary of Germanicus, was that his *domus* was festively decorated after Germanicus' death (*Ann.* 3.9).

[56] For example, Koestermann 1963: 4.321.

[57] *HN* 35.7. Suetonius notes that many of these *domus priscorum ducum* were destroyed in the great fire of Nero's reign (*Nero* 38.2). The association of the house with the glory of the triumph is found in Propertius 1.16.

That this was thought to be a considerable diminution of honor is suggested
by the fact that one of the penalties established by the severe *lex Calpurnia
de ambitu* of 67 BC was the loss of the right to display family *imagines*. In his
defense of P. Sulla, Cicero tried to draw the sympathy of the jury by
stressing Sulla's already wretched state after having lost his *imagines*
through a previous conviction.[58] Given this emphasis on the *domus* as a
symbol of high birth and family renown, it is not surprising that the old
families resented upstarts moving into great houses. Cicero expresses
exasperation at the snobbery of those who said that he was not worthy of
occupying a villa that once belonged to Catulus or of building a house on
the Palatine.[59]

With the influx of new families into the senatorial aristocracy in the
Principate, few houses could display an impressive string of their own
imagines. At this point the symbolic importance of the *domus* shifted
somewhat, and it became more a visual sign of the current wealth and power
of the owner.[60] Because of the connection between a fine *domus* and social
standing, Seneca repeatedly included the *domus* with *pecunia* in his list of
transient material things which did not bring goodness or happiness. When
he preaches "put me *in opulentissima domo* ... and I will not admire myself"
or that "a *domus formosa* makes you arrogant," he presumably chooses the
domus because his readers did think that a house was a manifestation of
worth.[61] The epitaph of the "Mactar harvester" shows that this valuation
extended beyond Rome and Italy to the provinces, where Apuleius listed a
well-appointed house among the standard markers of status.[62]

It was vital for a Roman aristocrat to have a fine house because, unlike his
classical Athenian counterpart, he had to carry out most of his dealings with
his public there. In particular, the morning *salutatio* was an open
demonstration of a man's position in the social hierarchy.[63] If friends or

[58] *Sull.* 88. On the *lex Calpurnia de ambitu* and the *ius imaginum* see Mommsen 1887: 1.442–43, 492, n. 3.
[59] *Att.* 4.5.2 with Shackleton Bailey's commentary 2.186. See Allen 1944: 3. Earlier Clodius had taunted Cicero with the comment *domum emisti* (*Att.* 1.16.10).
[60] I want to stress that this was only a shift of relative emphasis which must have occurred with the great flow of new aristocratic families from Italy and the provinces into Rome (Hopkins 1983: ch. 3). That continuity of the family in the physical house was still valued is evidenced by the few *fideicommissa* in the *Digest* which prohibit the heir from alienating the house (*Dig.* 3.69.3, Papinian; *Dig.* 32.38.4, Scaevola).
[61] *Ep.* 41.7, 87.6, 110.17, *Vita beata* 25.1, 26.2.
[62] *Flor.* 22: wealth, a large retinue of slaves, and a *domus amplo ornata vestibulo* (a house adorned with a large vestibule).
[63] Seneca *Ep.* 68.10, 76.12 and 15, 84.11–12, *Cons. ad Marciam* 10.1. Vitruvius 6.5.1–2 distinguishes between the men of high rank who fill public office and the ordinary man who has no need of "magnifica vestibula nec tabulina neque atria, quod in aliis officia praestant ambiundo neque ab aliis ambiuntur." Friedlaender 1908: 1.207–9, describes the *salutatio*. For an excellent, detailed discussion of house and status using archaeological evidence, see Wallace-Hadrill 1988 and 1991.

clients needed a man's help, they approached him at his *domus*. Consequently, the *domus frequentata* (crowded house) repeatedly appears in texts as an indication of power in an active public life. Among the signs of prominence picked out by Seneca is the *domus frequentata*, and Aper, Tacitus' ambitious orator in the *Dialogus*, claims as one of the rewards of forensic oratory a *domus* filled with high-ranking persons.[64] Examples show that this was taken for granted in the Republic and Principate. Cicero took the quantity and quality of his callers as a barometer of his current prestige: as evidence of his popularity he wrote to Atticus in 59 BC that "the house is filled" (*domus celebratur*).[65] As a sign of the corruption of public affairs in Sicily during Verres' governorship Cicero pointed to the fact that the *domus* of the jurisconsults were empty, while that of Verres' mistress was full of crowds hoping to secure favorable legal decisions. Honorable men had to debase themselves by going to "a prostitute's house" (*meretricis domus, Verr.* 2.1.120, 137). Patronage remained central in social and political life under the emperors, and so too did the symbol of the *domus frequentata*. Sejanus' power grew in the 20s AD to the point that he became concerned about arousing Tiberius' suspicions. According to Tacitus, since the praetorian prefect was unwilling to diminish his power by prohibiting "the crowds in constant attendance at this house" (*adsiduos in domum coetus*), he decided to encourage Tiberius to retire from Rome so that he could not see the manifestations of Sejanus' power.[66] The nexus of the *domus frequentata*, *potentia*, and public prestige could not be brought out more clearly.

Cicero's comment in the passage quoted above from the Verrine orations points up the fact that who went to whose *domus* was a matter of honor, an indicator of relative social status. Augustus was praised by Seneca for his common touch when he participated in another man's family *consilium* "at the *penates*" of the other rather than insisting on it being held at his own *domus*.[67] One sign of the inversion of the social order during the heyday of the imperial freedmen was that Callistus' former master stood in line before Callistus' doors to pay his respects. Even more repugnant to Seneca's readers was the subsequent turning away of the former master by Callistus on the ground that he was unworthy *domo sua* (*Ep.* 47.9). This points to another use

---

[64] Seneca *Ep.* 21.6, Tacitus *Dial.* 6 (compare Maternus' wish in *Dial.* 11 to avoid *frequentia salutantium* as part of his retirement from public life).

[65] *Att.* 2.22.3, cf. 1.18.1, *Fam.* 9.20.3, 11.28.1, *Comm. pet.* 35, 47.

[66] *Ann.* 4.41. When Vespasian's accession to the throne seemed imminent, senators, *equites*, and soldiers filled the *domus Flavii Sabini* (Tacitus, *Hist.* 3.69). Nero moved Agrippina out of his *domus ne coetu salutantium frequentaretur* (*Ann.* 13.18). One sign of Seneca's retirement was that he stopped the *coetus salutantium* at home (*Ann.* 14.56). See also Seneca *Ep.* 84.12 and Suetonius *Claud.* 25.1.

[67] *Clem.* 1.15.3. Cicero remarked on Appius Claudius Pulcher's courtesy in coming to Cicero's *domus*, an action that was not taken for granted among social equals outside the circle of immediate friends (*Fam.* 3.13.1).

of the *domus* as a symbol in social interactions: in breaking off a friendship a Roman prohibited the former friend from his house (*interdicere domo sua*).[68]

One last extreme indication of how closely a man was associated with his house may be considered. It was not enough in the Republic to punish with execution an aristocrat suspected of aiming at tyranny: his *domus* was razed to the ground as well.[69] Cicero (*Dom.* 101) and Valerius Maximus (6.3.1) review the famous examples of this: Sp. Maelius, Sp. Cassius, M. Vaccus, M. Manlius, M. Flaccus, and L. Saturninus. Clodius tried to exact the same penalty from Cicero, but his actions were reversed by the senate.[70] The demolition of the *domus* constituted a symbolic destruction of the offender and his family root and branch. Not only was he eliminated but also all reminders of his house, in the senses of household and lineage. In Valerius Maximus' words, "the senate and Roman people, not satisfied to inflict on [Sp. Cassius] capital punishment, after his destruction threw over his *domus*, so that he would also be punished by the trashing of his *penates*."[71] These examples are traditional Republican ones, and it is likely that in the Empire there was some loosening of the link between lineage and *domus*, with its sacred embodiment the *penates*. But the link did not disappear, to judge from a comment by Seneca that one of the terrible consequences of the mob's anger was "whole houses burnt with all the lineage."[72] Here there is an explicit connection between the physical destruction of a *domus* and the destruction of a man and his family, root and branch. Philosophers, such as Seneca, might teach that the *domus* was just another of man's transient worldly possessions. Cicero acknowledged these lessons in the conclusion of his oration *De domo sua* (146), but went on to say that the seizure and destruction of his house was not just a material loss, but a "dishonor" (*dedecus*) and a source of "grief" (*dolor*).

Domus in the sense of human household, as well as physical house, was a focus of honor for Romans: the honor of the *paterfamilias* depended on his ability to protect his household, and in turn the virtue of the household contributed to his prestige.[73] Upon discovering the conspiracy of Cinna, Seneca claims that Augustus took Cinna aside for a long talk. As one means of embarrassing him, Augustus is said to have pointed out to Cinna that he

---

[68] Seneca *Ira* 3.23.5 and 8, Tacitus *Ann.* 3.12, 6.29, Suetonius *Aug.* 66.2.
[69] For the Greek parallel, see Connor 1985.   [70] Allen 1944: 8–9.
[71] 6.3.1: "senatus populusque Romanus, non contentus capitali eum [Sp. Cassium] supplicio adficere, interempto domum superiecit, ut penatium quoque strage puniretur."
[72] *Ira* 3.2.4: "totae cum stirpe omni crematae domus."
[73] Pitt-Rivers 1977: ch. 2 comments on the dual nature of the honor of the Mediterranean family: the male virtue of being able to dominate in competition with the outside society and the female virtue of purity (sexual purity in particular) at home. As is evident from the examples adduced here, these two aspects were not strictly divided along male–female lines in Rome (though Rubellius Plautus' *domus casta* is associated with a withdrawal from public competition). On sexual chastity and honor in imperial Rome, see Cohen 1991.

was hardly capable of seizing and holding imperial power: "you are not able to protect your own *domus*; recently you were defeated in a private law suit by the influence of a freedman."[74] Seneca's Augustus chose not Cinna's inability to protect himself but his inability to protect his *domus* as a way of belittling him.

The virtue of one's *domus* was something to be praised: Livia preserved the *sanctitas* of her household and Rubellius Plautus had a *domus casta* (chaste house), while Verres' and M. Antony's households were marked by *dedecus* (disgrace).[75] Violations of this virtue were treated particularly harshly and thought to be a matter of pollution. The Augustan adultery law permitted a father to kill his daughter and her *adulter* only if he caught them in his own *domus* or that of the daughter's husband, and the husband could kill an *adulter* of low status if discovered in the husband's house.[76] In Valerius Maximus' version of the legend of the rape of Verginia (5.10.2), Verginius her father went to the extreme of spilling his own daughter's blood so that his *domus* would not be contaminated by *probrum* (shame). In historical times Iullus Antonius "violated the house of Augustus" (*domum Augusti violasset*) through his affair with Julia; Seneca was taunted by Suillius with being an adulterer of the *domus Germanici*; and Fabius Valens, Vitellius' general, abused his power by polluting the houses of his hosts (*stupris polluere hospitum domus*).[77] The language of pollution and violation in these passages once again underlines the sacred nature of the *domus* and the honorable duty to protect it. In law both violent entry into a man's physical house and insult by sexual advances or physical blows to those under his protection gave rise to an action for *iniuria* (insult, *Dig.* 47.10).

Less serious offenses than adultery and rape could diminish the honor of the household. In the choice of a new Vestal Virgin in AD 19 Fonteius Agrippa's daughter was passed over through no fault of her own: "for Agrippa had diminished his house by divorce" (*nam Agrippa discidio domum imminuerat*, Tac. *Ann.* 2.86). Of course, divorce was common at this time, and it was frowned on only in special situations where religious purity was required.[78] But the point remains that Tacitus focussed on the *domus* in choosing his language regarding family purity and honor.

---

[74] Seneca *Clem.* 1.9.10: "domum tueri tuam non potes, nuper libertini hominis gratia in privato iudicio superatus es." I have no confidence that this anecdote accurately represents events, but it does express the common values of Seneca's readers, which is enough for my purposes.

[75] Tacitus *Ann.* 5.1, 14.22, Cicero *Verr.* 2.4.83, *Phil.* 3.35. Crassus' *domus* was also described as *castissima* by Cicero (*Cael.* 9). In a discussion in which associations of the *domus* with continuity and virtue come together, Pliny lamented Fannia's death on the ground that it would shake her *domus* because she was the last of her line in virtue (*Ep.* 7.19.8).

[76] *Pauli Sententiae* 2.26.1 and 7, *Dig.* 48.5.23.2, 24.2, 25.pr, *Coll.* 4.2.3–7, 3.2.

[77] Tac. *Ann.* 3.18, 13.42, *Hist.* 3.41.   [78] Humbert 1972: 31, 77.

Familia and domus95Given the various aspects of honor and status involved in the *domus*, it is
not surprising that it became increasingly emphasized as *familia* became less
suitable. A few senators might still look back to their agnatic ancestors in
their claim to *dignitas*, but most of the new senatorial families had to find
other standards of social status. Wealth was indispensable and was
publicized by a fine house capable of accommodating the morning crowds
seeking the "influence of the enriched house" (*quaestuosae domus gratia*, Sen.
Constant. 8.2). A respectable and well-connected circle of kin was another
measure of a man's position. As Livia clearly demonstrated, these kin did not
have to be agnatic relations to be valuable patronal links;[79] consequently, it
became more important in a description of family background to include
relatives traced through females and through marriages. The new political
reality was a web of friendship and patron–client ties emanating from the
emperor. To this new reality the agnatic principle, enshrined in Roman
family law, was irrelevant, as it had been to the real household units in Rome
for some time. As alternative criteria of social status became more solidly
entrenched, *familia* as lineage could begin to appear somewhat empty. Pliny
was pleased at the show of talent by the young Calpurnius Piso – after all,
it would be sad if "our nobles were to have nothing of beauty in their *domus*
except their ancestral deathmasks."[80]

Conclusion: representing household and family after death

For the living, the *domus* was the organizing unit to satisfy basic needs and
to reproduce the next generation. Romans of means assumed that it would
be more inclusive than a couple and their children. As the jurists' definition
of *penus* shows, those "living around the *paterfamilias*" would normally
include household slaves and other dependants. What conclusion should be
drawn from the fact that the Romans did not define the boundary of *domus*
or *familia* around the nuclear family to the exclusion of other household
residents? Does the failure to isolate the nuclear family with a single word
suggest that the sense of familial obligation and affection was diffused in a
way to weaken the bonds between father, mother, and children in the larger
unit? The inference is an attractive one, and has been drawn for the Roman
world and later Europe.[81] For all its plausibility, the argument is difficult to

[79] Saller 1982: 65.
[80] *Ep.* 5.17.6: "nobiles nostri nihil in domibus suis pulchrum nisi imagines habeant." New men
of the Republic might have made the same point, but not in the same patronizing tone,
since *nobilitas* still dominated.
[81] Stone 1977 is perhaps the most notable exponent of this view for the early modern era.
Bradley 1991 has argued along these lines for the Roman family, as did I (Saller 1987b)
in thinking about the impact of slavery on the Roman family.

evaluate. How would the diffusion of affection and obligation be measured, and what would be used as a standard of comparison to judge "weakness"? Is it right to assume a sum-zero game where bonds with household slaves necessarily weakened children's bonds with their parents?

Whatever the diffusion, clearly the bonds between husband, wife, and their children were dominant in the Romans' conception of familial obligations and affection, despite the fact that they had no single word to identify that group. That conceptualization was not always easy to put into practice in everyday life, where, as Bradley has stressed, death and divorce gave rise to a shifting and reconstitution of family living arrangements.[82] To say that the nuclear family was the starting principle in the organization of a Roman household is not to suggest that the nuclear family was static over a whole generation. Indeed, because in reality the membership of Roman households was changing, it is useful to examine how the representation of family bonds of affection and duty were crystallized following death, in burial arrangements and commemoration. Given the unevenness or lack of evidence of other types for the shape of Roman households and families, it is important to consider the evidence of Roman burials and epitaphs, which bulk so large among the materials extant from classical antiquity.[83]

To interpret the burials and many thousands of epitaphs, we must begin by asking what meaning the Romans assigned to them. What were they intended to represent? Morris has recently stressed the need "to embed inscriptions in the rituals for which they were created."[84] He argues for a holistic approach to the interpretation of burials and funerary monuments, taking "ritual" in a wide sense to include the making of a will and burial arrangements before death, as well as funeral rites and annual feasting at the tomb after death. As he notes, however, only in rare individual cases is this approach possible: most inscriptions have been detached from the graves, and in virtually no case do we know the full history of arrangements resulting in commemoration. Yet, imperfect though the evidence is, we have more explicit testimony for the meanings attached to burial and commemoration than for most other forms of symbolic behavior, and we have direct and indirect evidence for how the Romans believed the act of

---

[82] 1991: chs. 6–7.
[83] The following draws on Saller and Shaw 1984a, with some modifications to answer the criticisms of that paper.
[84] Morris 1992: 157. It should be emphasized that "rituals" are not meant in the narrow sense of funerary rites, since some monuments and inscriptions were erected well before or well after burial and could be put up by individuals who were not central actors in the ritual (for an extreme case, see Pliny *Ep.* 6.10, regarding the remains and memorial of Verginius Rufus, whose instructions had not been carried out ten years after his death and cremation). Furthermore, Romans hoped that their epitaphs would perpetuate their memories long after the rituals associated with burial had ceased.

commemoration flowed from previous social relationships with the deceased.[85] Although limited in distribution, the burials and funerary inscriptions derive from a wider geographical and social cross-section of the population than any other type of source material from the western empire.

For some burials the architecture of the monument and the contents of the graves give obvious clues about representational intentions. The house-tombs of the first, second, and third centuries, best preserved in the Isola Sacra and Vatican cemeteries, are relevant here. As Toynbee and Ward Perkins remarked,

the Vatican house-tombs, and their counterparts elsewhere, so simple without, so richly decked and colourful within, were surely regarded as places in which the dead, in some sense or at some times, resided. Hidden away behind stout doors and seen only by members of the owners' families on anniversaries and feast-days, when sacrifices, ceremonial meals, and ritual washings took place, all this luxuriant internal ornament and art must have been designed as much to delight the dead as to gratify and to instruct the survivors. The souls of the former, visiting, perhaps intermittently, the tombs where their relics reposed, could be made to feel at home there by renderings in paint, stone, or stucco of the useful and familiar objects – the toilet-articles, the tools, the writing-materials, which once had served them.[86]

Whatever the specific beliefs about the afterlife, it is apparent that these tombs were meant as analogues to the houses of the living. Other representations are not so straightforward to interpret. Nevertheless, Purcell argues on the basis of the archaeological remains that "the social background to the growth of the later Roman urban cemeteries [was] linked closely to the associative structures of town life." In particular, the *columbarium* reflects "the growth of the huge *familiae* of freedmen, slaves and free dependants which characterized the Roman aristocracy between 50 BC and AD 150 ... The housing which parallels it is the *domus*, with its endless attics and

[85] Beard (Reynolds, Beard and Roueché 1986: 142) rightly notes that "the gap between recording practice and 'social reality' must remain a problem for all work of this kind," arguing that "the absence of any mention of 'mother' on a tombstone cannot prove that the mother was not important in the scale of familiarity and affection – still less that she did not exist." This is right but misleading. First, Saller and Shaw (1984a) did not argue a one-to-one correspondence between the commemorative bond and any single aspect of "social reality." Secondly, the absence of a mother in any one commemoration could be explained in many ways; that is why it is important to analyze the *overall patterns* and not to press fine details further than warranted. The absence of a mother in any one commemoration or the variable proportions of mothers and fathers from one area to another may not be explicable, but a total absence of mothers would be a noteworthy cultural phenomenon. In fact, mothers are not absent, but kin beyond the nuclear family are quite rare in the epitaphs, whether by comparison with the nuclear family or with unrelated *familiares*, to a degree that must be indicative of the extensiveness of the sense of family duty. [86] 1956: 113–14.

tabernae and ramifications for the long and short-term stay of the dependants."[87] At a general level, then, for some types of burial the organizing principle was similar to that of the living, that is, the *domus*.

If the architectural form provides a starting point of interpretation, written texts permit more specification. The jurists discuss burial and commemoration as a matter of obligation to the deceased.[88] The obligation might derive from inheritance or from familial ties. The jurists point to a strong popular association between heirship and burial – so strong that the arrangement of burial was widely interpreted as tantamount to acceptance of the inheritance of the deceased. Although Ulpian (*Dig.* 11.7.14.8) firmly points out that the inference is legally incorrect, his comment underlines the common notion of reciprocal duty between the deceased and the heir: if a potential heir proceeds to arrange burial without intending to commit himself to the inheritance, he should say that he is doing so out of *pietas*. That bond of duty was often expressed in writing in the epitaph. In many, though not all, of the Latin-speaking, urbanized areas of the western empire, the commemoration was phrased in standard terms such as "X made this monument for Y, well-deserving" or "most dear" or "most devoted." So standard were the terms that the formula could be abbreviated to X *f(ecit)* Y *b(ene)m(erenti)* or *k(arissimo)* or *pientissimo*. As brief and formulaic as the epitaph might be, its basic wording points to commemoration as a consequence of prior, reciprocal bonds of duty and affection between the living. The bonds that Romans chose to represent were overwhelmingly (though not exclusively) between husband and wife or parents and children: more than two-thirds of the relationships expressed in the civilian populations under study fall into these categories.[89]

Since these bonds were in life multi-stranded, involving duty, affection and property, it would be misguided to try to isolate any single strand and argue that it correlates with the pattern of commemoration: normally lines of inheritance and bonds of family duty and affection would have coincided in a way to make it futile to attempt to disentangle them. It has been suggested that the act of commemoration represents, above all, the fulfillment of the heir's duty and that the geographical spread of the standard Roman commemoration is a consequence of the spread of Roman citizenship

[87] 1987: 39–40.   [88] Saller and Shaw 1984a: 125–27, give more detail.
[89] To summarize the numbers presented in the tables in Saller and Shaw 1984a: 147–51, the proportion of expressed relationships falling into the husband–wife and parent–child categories are: Republican Rome & Latium: 68 percent; Rome: Senators & Equites: 73 percent; Rome: Lower Orders: 70 percent; Italy: Latium: 70 percent; Italy: Regio XI: 72 percent; Gallia Narbonensis: 75 percent; Spain: 75 percent; Germania Inferior: 69 percent; Germania Superior: 78 percent; Noricum: 87 percent; Africa: Lambaesis: 83 percent; Africa: Auzia: 84 percent; Africa: Caesarea: 80 percent; Rome: Ostia, Portus: 77 percent; the only group with less than two-thirds in these categories was Britain: 60 percent.

and testation. This is corroborated, it is suggested, by the very noticeable underrepresentation of children among the commemorated.[90] If this were true, the corpus of funerary inscriptions would preserve an invaluable record of patterns of property transmission. Unfortunately, the interpretation cannot be so direct. Although in many large categories of epitaphs the commemorator is likely to be the heir of the deceased,[91] it is highly unlikely that the commemorator is the heir in others. First, although children under ten years of age tend to be underrepresented, children in their teens and early twenties commemorated by their parents are in fact overrepresented: most of these parents must have been motivated by affection and duty, since the Roman legal system did not give children in their father's *potestas* the capacity to own or bequeath property.[92] Secondly, numerous commemorations took the form of "X made this for him/herself (*sibi*) and his/her spouse and his/her child."[93] These obviously cannot be interpreted in terms of the duty of an heir. Finally, although some epitaphs identify the commemorator as "heres," far more common are those memorializing family sentiments such as *pietas* and *caritas*.[94] On some monuments the iconography reinforces the family aspect of the representation through a portrait of the couple and child; this iconography cannot be explained on the assumption that heirship was the primary motive for commemoration.[95]

Most of those who died in the Roman world did not have their names preserved on a funerary monument. Many were not sufficiently Romanized to adopt this Roman cultural form; others were too poor to afford proper

[90] Meyer 1990: 78. While recognizing that heirship and family bonds often coincided, she concludes that "heirship, not family, is the primary basis of commemoration."

[91] See ch. 7 below.

[92] With the exception of Roman senators, in every civilian population sampled in Saller and Shaw 1984a: 147–50 the number of commemorations from father to child equalled or exceeded (sometimes by a very large margin) the number from child to father. Unless an astonishing proportion of children were emancipated, this pattern cannot possibly be explained in terms of an heir commemorating a testator. Table 2.2 breaks down the commemorations by age of deceased and relationship of the commemorator: in all populations under study except the Theveste region of North Africa males who died between ages fifteen and twenty-four and were commemorated by parents bulk disproportionately large in the samples, even though these age cohorts must have had among the lowest mortality rates. Shaw 1991 discusses the ideological and cultural bases for the observed preferences for commemorating those of certain age groups, but it must be remembered that his study cannot take account of the commemorations (very numerous in some regions) where the commemorator chose not to specify age at death.

[93] This form of commemoration was especially popular in Republican Rome, Italian Regio XI, Noricum, and the Familia Caesaris in Rome; see Saller and Shaw 1984a: 147–51.

[94] Note that the "heredes" group of commemorations rarely exceeds 5 percent of the relationships tabulated in Saller and Shaw 1984a: 147–50; the exception once again is Britain, where heirs constituted 11 percent of the commemorators. This is not to say that other commemorators were not heirs, but they did not choose to represent themselves in that way. Curchin 1982 examines the qualities ascribed to the deceased and their commemorators. [95] Kleiner 1977.

burial and commemoration; still others were incorporated anonymously in the tombs of their masters or patrons.[96] A standard formula recognized this third group, indicating that the tomb was made for X and Y and "their *liberti* and *libertae* and the freedmen's descendants." Eck has pointed to the existence in the house-tombs of the Isola Sacra and Vatican cemeteries of the numerous *ollae* (vases) for ashes of unnamed deceased. He plausibly suggests that these were provided for the household slaves of the owners named in the inscriptions of the tomb, and concludes that the inscriptions do not name all of the dead housed in the tombs. If Eck is right, then here is another parallel between the living household and the house of the dead.[97] Cicero's hierarchy of bonds — husband–wife, parents–children, then the domus as a whole — is neatly replicated in these tombs, where the most honored bonds, those between spouses and their children, receive explicit acknowledgement by name in the context of a larger social group whose anonymity left it less honored.

As in life, so in death various contingencies could alter the neat representation of household and family bonds. In the best-preserved house-tombs in the Vatican odd, extraneous individuals or groups are found in the same monument. Nevertheless, the basic organizing conception is clear enough: the father, mother and children surrounded in the house during life and in burial afterwards by other members of lower status. The assortment of others including slaves, freedmen and other dependants does not obscure the central bonds that dominate in the representation. The master or patron had a general responsibility to his whole household, including the decent disposal of their remains, but in choosing which relationships to memorialize for all time (so it was hoped) the bonds between husband and wife, and parents and children, are pushed to the fore. It may be that the formality of funerary commemoration served to exaggerate the focus on the immediate family. On the other hand, the pattern of commemoration should invite reconsideration of what seems a plausible inference about diffusion of sentiment and obligation in the large *domus*: the inclusion of slaves and dependants may have blurred the boundary between the immediate family

---

[96] This limitation of the evidence was recognized in Saller and Shaw 1984a. Evans 1991: 20 criticizes the urban focus of that study, and then attempts to describe marriage patterns of the rural *Italian* family, indeed of rural families of all classical antiquity, on the basis of evidence such as Dio Chrysostom's Euboean Oration (VII), the extended family of which was certainly not Italian and may have been no more than a figment of Dio's literary imagination (cf. Jones 1978: 61: "It cannot be denied, however, that many of the ingredients of this idyll have a literary flavor: some resemble comedy, others recall conventional descriptions of rustic or primitive virtue.") In my view it is best to admit that our knowledge of family life in antiquity will remain partial owing to lack of evidence.

[97] Eck 1988. Morris 1992: 166 points out that the Vatican house-tombs have not been preserved intact and so it is impossible to be certain about how many of those buried received named commemorations.

and others or, alternatively, it may have encouraged an enhancement of the core unit by a continual contrast between those members with honor – father, mother, and children in the standard conception – and those without honor, consigned to the anonymity of a nameless grave. The next two chapters pursue these alternatives by exploring the notions of obligation and authority through examination of the central family virtue of *pietas* and an analysis of the symbolic behavior associated with coercion.

5

Pietas and *patria potestas*: obligation and power in the Roman household

The relation of authority, obligation, and coercion within the Roman household constitutes the subject of this chapter and the next. Over the centuries the Roman *paterfamilias* has served as a paradigm of patriarchal authority and social order; *patria potestas* has been seen as the embodiment of arbitrary, even tyrannical, power.[1] By "arbitrary," I mean here the sort of power a master exercises over his slave, a power more or less unanswerable to higher principles or formal procedures. On this view, Roman family relationships were almost wholly asymmetrical, with power in the hands of the father, and the obligation of obedience imposed on the rest of the household and underwritten by the core family value of *pietas*. In this chapter I will first analyze how the Romans construed *pietas*: was it a value designed in such a way as to encourage obedience in asymmetrical relationships between the *paterfamilias* and other members of the household? Next, the formal elements of *patria potestas* will be enumerated. Finally, consideration will be given to how those powers were exercised within the field of family obligations, the norms of the wider society, and the social and economic dynamics of the household.

The image of the Roman father endowed with nearly unlimited power over his household goes back to antiquity, especially Greek commentators. Dionysius of Halicarnassus (2.26.4) enumerated the powers that Romulus granted to fathers for life over their children: the power to imprison, to beat, to hold in the country, even to kill their sons. Sextus Empiricus placed the Roman father's powers in a wider, mythico-historical context: "Cronos decided to destroy his own children, and Solon gave the Athenians the law 'concerning things immune' by which he allowed each man to slay his own child; but with us the laws forbid the slaying of children. The Roman lawgivers also ordain that the children are subjects and slaves (*doulous*) of

---

[1] The element of arbitrariness or "caprice" in patriarchy was pointed out by Maine 1861.

their fathers, and that power over the children's property belongs to the fathers and not the children, until the children have obtained their freedom like bought slaves; but this custom is rejected by others as being despotic" (3.211). The comments of Dionysius and Sextus Empiricus exhibit two elements of the image of the despotic *paterfamilias*: it is an image based on legal powers and is associated with the legendary past.

The despotic *paterfamilias* has been used as a touchstone in various modern views of social evolution. For Lewis Morgan, a founder of modern kinship studies, the Roman family epitomized the fourth stage of his developmental scheme of primitive societies as they evolved toward order and hierarchy:

Authority over its members and over its property was the material fact. It was the incorporation of numbers in servile and dependent relations, before that time unknown, rather than polygamy, that stamped the patriarchal family with the attributes of an original institution. In the great movement of Semitic society, which produced this family, paternal power over the group was the object sought; and with it a higher individuality of persons. The same motive precisely originated the Roman family under paternal power (*patria potestas*); with the power in the father of life and death over his children and descendants, as well as over the slaves and servants who formed its nucleus and furnished its name; and with the absolute ownership of all property they created ... the Hebrew and Roman forms were exceptional in human experience ... In the patriarchal family of the Roman type, paternal authority passed beyond the bounds of reason into an excess of domination.[2]

In his influential collection a century later, L. DeMause used a similar image of ancient fathers as the starting point for the development of parent–child relations: referring to Greek authors of the Roman empire, he characterized the ancient world up to the fourth century of our era by the "infanticidal mode": "The history of childhood is a nightmare from which we have only recently begun to awaken. The further back in history one goes, the lower the level of child care, and the more likely children are to be killed, abandoned, beaten, terrorized, and sexually abused."[3]

The evolutionary view expressed by DeMause finds support in the work of some professional historians of classical Rome. In analyzing the Romans' taste for blood sports, M. Grant found one of the causes in "the absolute mastery of the early Roman *paterfamilias* over his children." The familiar

[2] Morgan 1877: 466.
[3] DeMause 1974: 1, 51. DeMause argues that from the "infanticidal mode" Europeans moved on to a millennium in the "abandonment mode" (fourth–thirteenth centuries), then to "the ambivalent mode" (fourteenth–seventeenth centuries), the "intrusive mode" (eighteenth century), the "socialization mode" (nineteenth–twentieth century), to arrive in the late twentieth century at the "helping mode." Wiedemann 1989 effectively critiques this crude perception of antiquity.

evidence is then quoted: "'The Roman lawgiver,' wrote Dionysius of Halicarnassus, 'gave the father complete power over the son, power which lasted a whole lifetime. He was at liberty to imprison him, flog him, to keep him a prisoner working on the farm, and to kill him.' And though the laws were modified, much of the spirit remained."[4]

More recently, P. Veyne in *A History of Private Life* invoked the image of the despotic father/master to paint a striking picture: the Roman family and household of the Republic and early Principate were units bounded not by affection, but by the limits of the father's power. In so characterizing the family, Veyne deliberately minimized the distinction between *filiusfamilias* and slave, over whom the *paterfamilias* exercised similar *potestas*.[5] The language of affection and love appear in his discussion of parent–child relations only briefly in a passage dismissing "the so-called maternal or paternal instinct." Treated virtually like chattels, "children who were moved about like pawns on the chessboard of wealth and power were hardly cherished and coddled." Consequently, for children the father's death "signalled the end of a kind of slavery."[6]

If some historians see the spirit of the despotic father remaining throughout antiquity, others discover a change as the early asymmetry of paternal severity and filial duty gave way to mutual affection and devotion in the late Republic or early empire. *Patria potestas* came to encompass a father's duty to protect those in his power.[7] To the contemporary eye this may appear as progress, but to the great sixteenth-century political theorist of absolute sovereignty, Jean Bodin, it was a fundamental cause of the breakdown of good order in the Roman empire, which had been underwritten by paternal authority:

So the fatherly power being little by little diminished upon the declination of the Roman Empire; so also shortly after vanished away their ancient virtue, and all the glory of their Commonweale: and so in place of piety and civility, ensued a million of vices and villainies. The first stain, and beginning of taking away the power of life and death from parents, proceed from the ambition of the Magistrates, who seeking to increase their jurisdiction, and little and little drawing unto them the deciding of all matters, extinguished all domestical powers: which happened especially after the death of Augustus Caesar; at which time we read the magistrates to have been almost always occupied in punishing of such as had murdered their parents.[8]

---

[4] Grant 1967: 114–15.
[5] Veyne 1987. Watson 1987: 46–47 notes the similarity of *potestas* over the *filiusfamilias* and the slave, but goes on to remark that "it goes without saying that in practice sons and slaves would be treated very differently."   [6] Veyne 1987: 16–17, 18, 29.
[7] Rabello 1979: 246; Néraudau 1984: 168–70.
[8] *The six bookes of a commonweale*, from the 1606 translation by R. Knolles, ed. K. D. McRae (Cambridge, Mass., 1962): 24H.

The exaggeration in Bodin's summary of the decline of the Roman empire now appears slightly comical, but recent historians' image of the despotic Roman father is also a product of caricature rooted in Roman legends about their past and in law. J. Crook in a fundamental article written in 1967 warned against too heavy a reliance on legal principles in the analysis of the Roman family, pointing out that "the Romans in law ... pushed things to the limits of logic, so that, given that *paterfamilias* had certain roles, their implications were rigorously drawn; they also kept law sharply apart from religion and morals, so that the legal character of *patria potestas* stands out in sociologically misleading clarity." He concluded that "the all-powerful *paterfamilias* of Rome, in the standard contrast with Athens, is, then, too crude a figure to correspond to the nuances of reality."[9] We may now turn to the moral system within which the father exercised power in the household.

Pietas

At the core of the Romans' ideal of family relations was the virtue of *pietas*, represented by the image of Virgil's Aeneas carrying Anchises on his shoulder from Troy. The *Oxford Classical Dictionary* defines *pietas* as "the typical Roman attitude of dutiful respect toward gods, fatherland, and parents and other kinsmen."[10] This definition captures several connotations commonly associated with *pietas*. First, the emphasis is on duty rather than affection or compassion.[11] Secondly, it is a virtue displayed primarily toward a higher power, whether it be the gods, the fatherland, or parents.[12] Within the family it is thought to have been an attitude particularly appropriate for children to show to parents, as reflected in the common English translation, "filial piety."[13] As such, it is a virtue that promoted obedience to paternal power. Balsdon expressed the common view of the interrelationship of these quintessentially Roman values: "Roman society was built on the idea of deference (*obsequium*) in the family as in the State. Whatever their age, sons and daughters owed deference to their father, who had the sanction of power over them (*patria potestas*); their wholehearted and sincere submission

[9] Crook 1967b: 114, 122.
[10] A similar stress can be found in the entry in Berger 1953 and Ferguson 1964: 164, though both also recognize the possibility of *pietas* toward other relatives.
[11] Lee 1979: 17–23, stresses that Aeneas is *pius* because he places duty above his feelings of tenderness and compassion.
[12] Néraudau 1984: 121: "C'est une vertu fondamentale de la morale romaine. Elle est d'abord respect envers les dieux et les parents, c'est-à-dire qu'elle est reconnaissance d'une principe hiérarchie qu'il faut admettre et aimer." Manson 1975: 22–24 asserts that in Republican literature *pietas* within the family is *pietas erga parentes*, and never *pietas erga liberos* – in other words, the virtue is asymmetrical.
[13] The great Cambridge anthropologist Meyer Fortes used *pietas* as the focal point for his influential treatment of father–son relations in Roman, African and Chinese societies: 1970: esp. 184.

was an exaltation of *obsequium*; it was *pietas*."[14] In other words, the success of Rome flowed from obedience to authority, especially paternal and state authority, celebrated in the virtue of *pietas*: success, authority, and obedience went hand in hand. Some scholars see an evolution in the conception of *pietas* beyond these particular connotations, parallel to the broader evolution in parent-child relations, as the virtue came to have overtones of affection and compassion, and to be applied to parental attitudes toward their children.

Does the image of the dutiful son submissive to his father's authority fully capture the nuances of *pietas* in Roman culture? On first consideration it might seem so. Cicero repeatedly refers to *pietas* before higher authorities: the gods, the *patria*, parents.[15] Valerius Maximus includes in his collection of moral *exempla* a title "De pietate erga parentes et fratres et patriam" (5.4). Yet a close reading of these *exempla* and other stories told to illustrate *pietas* suggests that its essence lay in devotion, not merely in obedience or submission. In some situations, to be sure, devotion entailed submission, but in most of the *exempla* about *pietas* obedience is not at stake.

Many of our basic ideas about *pietas* come from Virgil's national epic featuring *pius* Aeneas. It would not be practical to enter the discussion about the *Aeneid*, with its vast bibliography. Suffice it to say that for Aeneas *pietas* is a virtue of duty, yet *pietas* in the epic is not solely a matter of obedience to higher powers: a father could display *pietas* to a son, as could a son to his father, and the virtue encompassed compassion as well as duty.[16]

The enduring cultural prestige of the *Aeneid* should not be allowed to overshadow other evidence for the meanings of *pietas*. Aeneas did not figure in the founding legend of the Republican Temple to Pietas, nor does he appear in the *exempla pietatis* catalogued by Valerius Maximus and the elder Pliny. Both authors retell the story of the foundation of the Temple to Pietas, built by the Acilii Glabriones and dedicated in 181 BC.[17] According to Valerius Maximus,

the praetor at his tribunal condemned a woman of freeborn blood on a capital charge and handed her over to a triumvir to be killed in prison. The man charged with guarding her there, moved by pity (*misericordia*), did not strangle her

[14] Balsdon 1979: 18.
[15] *Inv.* 2.65–66, *Planc.* 90, *Off.* 2.11, 46, *Rep.* 6.16. On Cicero's changing ideas about *pietas*, Wagenvoort 1980: 1–20.
[16] Lee 1979: 45, on *pietas* from father to son; Manson 1975: 26 stresses that Aeneas is not explicitly said to be *pius* toward Ascanius, but concedes that Mezentius displays *pietas* toward his son (10.824). See also Johnson 1986 for *patria amor* as an element of Aeneas' character. Lee 1979: 19 points out that the duty of *pietas* sometimes stands in opposition to compassion, but Johnson 1965 shows the connection between *pietas* and *miserere* in the lament of Euryalus' mother. The textual evidence is enough to show that Virgilian *pietas* was not merely obedience to higher powers.
[17] *R.E.* XX, col. 1223 (Koch); Richardson 1992: 290.

immediately. He granted access to the woman to her daughter, whom he thoroughly searched lest she bring in any food, thinking that the old woman would waste away from lack of food. However, when more days went by, he asked himself how she was sustained for so long. Out of curiosity he watched the daughter and observed her, with her breast uncovered, easing the mother's hunger with the aid of her own milk. The novelty of such an admirable sight, having been reported by him to the triumvir, by the triumvir to the praetor, and by the praetor to the council of iudices, demanded remission of the punishment for the woman.[18]

After the old woman's release a temple to Pietas was built on the site of the prison. For Valerius Maximus the episode shows that "the prize of dear (cara) pietas is not cheapened by the bitterness of fortune or meanness of station." He concludes the story by remarking that one would think this incident a violation of the natural order, "except that the first law of nature is to love (diligere) parents." The elder Pliny (NH 7.121) describes the episode more briefly and specifies that the women were humble (humilis et ignobilis). For him, this exemplum surpasses all others from around the world as an act of pietas.[19]

By the time of Valerius Maximus and Pliny, the temple no longer existed, its site occupied by the Theater of Marcellus. The story had Greek antecedents and is no doubt apocryphal,[20] but that makes the details all the more interesting to the cultural historian, since the elaboration of the tale as an exemplification of pietas was unconstrained by reality. What essential qualities does the story associate with pietas? It is a tale of a daughter's devoted protection of her mother; the object of pietas here is not a father or any other male authority figure, but a poor woman under sentence of death – the antithesis of power in the Roman world. The pious daughter acts out of loving devotion (diligere) to the helpless mother and against the higher authority of the state. The helplessness of the mother, stressed in the narratives, leads the reader to associate compassion with the daughter's devotion. Finally, both authors take this to be a memorable example of a

---

[18] 5.4.7: "Sanguinis ingenui mulierem praetor apud tribunal suum capitali crimine damnatam triumviro in carcere necandam tradidit. quo receptam is, qui custodiae praeerat, misericordia motus non protinus strangulavit: aditum quoque ad eam filiae, sed diligenter excussae, ne quid cibi inferret, dedit existimans futurum ut inedia consumeretur. cum autem plures iam dies intercederent, secum ipse quaerens quidnam esset quo tam diu sustentaretur, curiosius observata filia animadvertit illam exerto ubere famem matris lactis sui subsidio lenientem. quae tam admirabilis spectaculi novitas ab ipso ad triumvirum, a triumviro ad praetorem, a praetore ad consilium iudicum perlata remissionem poenae mulieri impetravit."

[19] Much later Festus (209) told the legend, but substituted for the mother Glabrio's father – presumably a late attempt to reconcile with the legend the fact that the temple was built by the Glabriones.

[20] Richardson 1992: 290. The Greek origin does nothing to diminish its value as testimony for Roman culture, since the Romans chose this story to illustrate pietas, which they regarded as a natural devotion.

virtue that they assume to be natural and universal. Clearly, to identify *pietas*
as the filial virtue that complements and underwrites *patria potestas* is to fail
to understand this founding legend, which has nothing to do with fathers
and sons. *Pietas* was not simply a virtue of social order applicable only to
aristocratic males. The image of a poor, nameless young woman nursing her
mother, in addition (and contrast) to that of Aeneas carrying his father, lends
a rather different and interesting meaning to this cardinal Roman value.

Pliny's other four *exempla pietatis* have equally little to do with paternal
power and obedient sons. (1) Tiberius Sempronius Gracchus voluntarily
accepted death in place of his wife Cornelia: his *pietas* lay in sparing his wife
and taking thought for the best interests of the republic (*uxori parcere et re
publica consulere*). (2) M. Aemilius Lepidus manifested his *pietas* by dying on
account of his love (*caritas*) for his divorced wife.[21] (3) P. Rutilius' devotion
to his brother was such that he died of a mild illness upon hearing of his
brother's electoral defeat. (4) The freedman P. Catienus Philotimus loved
(*dilexit*) his patron to the point that, although his patron instituted him heir
to his entire estate, he threw himself on his patron's funeral pyre and died.
These four *exempla* illustrate *pietas* pushed to its limits, each ending with the
death of the pious protagonist. None concerns *obsequium*. Nor is it easy to
construe the deaths of Lepidus, Rutilius or Philotimus as exemplifying duty
(had Philotimus dutifully followed his patron's wishes, he would have
chosen to live on to accept the inheritance); rather, the stories are about
selfless, loving attachment, as indicated by the language of *caritas* and
diligere. Finally, that devotion is appropriate to bonds between husband and
wife, brothers, and freedman and patron; these *exempla* do not feature *pietas
erga parentes, patriam,* or *deos*.

Parents are the center of attention in Valerius Maximus' catalogue. His
first *exemplum* is the legend of Coriolanus, who ceased hostilities against
Rome when confronted by his mother, wife, and children. This is not a
narrative of obedience to a higher power, since Coriolanus is explicitly said
to have rebuffed official authority in the form of the state's legates and
priests before yielding to his mother's pleas (*preces*). In the second *exemplum*,
Scipio Africanus, spurred by *pietas* and in spite of his youth, went on to
defeat Hannibal after his father's death. Africanus was acting out of devotion
to his dead father's memory, not obedience to orders. The third *exemplum* is
especially complex and interesting. A tribune of the plebs, Pomponius,
charged L. Manlius Torquatus. Torquatus' son, usually kept by his father out
on the farm doing hard labor, came to the city, entered the tribune's house,
and threatened him with a sword until he promised to withdraw the charge.
Valerius Maximus remarks that while *pietas* toward gentle parents is

[21] The identity of this M. Aemilius Lepidus is a subject of debate; Syme 1986: 126–27 places
him in the Augustan age.

commendable, young Torquatus' *pietas* toward his rough (*horridus*) father is all the more laudable, "since he had not been induced to esteem him beyond natural love by any lure of indulgence."[22] *Pietas* in this story is not obedience to the rough, old-fashioned father; rather, it is the loving devotion exhibited by a son *in spite of* the severity of his father. It is remarkable, in Valerius' view, precisely because it is not the more usual response to parental kindness. Here again, the act of *pietas* – a threat against the life of a tribune – is shown in conflict with official power. In the fourth *exemplum*, another *pius filius*, M. Cotta, upon taking up the *toga virilis*, revenged his father's conviction by accusing his father's prosecutor, Cn. Carbo. Like Torquatus, Cotta was notable for devoted protection of his father's reputation. The sole *exemplum* about filial obedience in Valerius' catalogue is the fifth, in which the populist tribune C. Flaminius (232 BC) came down from the rostra in submission to his father's orders. Here we find the *auctoritas patria*, which is notably absent from the other stories. Valerius Maximus explains that his sixth and seventh *exempla* show that *pietas* is not only a male virtue. In addition to the founding legend of the Temple to Pietas, he tells the familiar story of Claudia, who used her prestige as a Vestal Virgin to prevent a tribune from stopping her father's triumph. Far from being submissive to authority, Claudia was extraordinarily spirited in her devotion to her father, according to Valerius (5.4.6).

These eleven different *exempla pietatis* have warranted individual consideration because the Romans traditionally perpetuated their moral values through retelling such *exempla* (rather than through systematic moral philosophy or sacred texts).[23] In all seven of Valerius Maximus' stories a parent is the object of *pietas*; four concern the father–son relationship, of which only one emphasizes the value of obedience; the rest celebrate filial devotion, associated with love and esteem both during the parent's life and after death (through protection of reputation). Pliny's *exempla* go beyond the parent–child relationship to the conjugal and fraternal bonds, and beyond duty to love and esteem. A glance beyond Valerius' title, *De pietate*, reveals that his conception of *pietas*, too, encompassed more than "filial piety": another title "de parentium amore et indulgentia in liberos" (5.7, "concerning parental love and indulgence toward children") offers examples of "pius et placidus adfectus parentium erga liberos" ("dutiful and gentle affection of parents toward children"), pointing to the reciprocal quality of *pietas* and its association with family love.

In Roman society the experts at the invocation of the conventional values

---

[22] 5.4.3: "quia ad eum diligendum praeter naturalem amorem nullo indulgentiae blandimento invitatus fuerat."

[23] See, e.g., Plutarch, *Cato maior* 4.2 on the importance of paradeigmata; Horace, *Sat.* 1.4.105–6, on the instruction he received from his old-fashioned father through *exempla*.

illustrated by Valerius Maximus were the rhetoricians, for whom *exempla* were the tools of persuasion. The rhetoricians' manipulation of virtues in debates over imaginary conflicts provides insights into the meanings and associations of moral values. The fact that these rhetorical exercises are fictitious and highly contrived does not diminish their value as evidence for the meanings of virtues and the logic of the Roman moral system. In several of the elder Seneca's *Controversiae* the interlocutors invoke *pietas* in ways that reveal that its most basic sense cannot have been filial obedience or submission, because it is used to justify disobedience to a *paterfamilias*. In one debate, a son is disinherited by his father for helping his uncle in a time of need; the young man is later adopted by his uncle, who orders him not to offer support to his natural father; nevertheless he does help his natural father and suffers disinheritance as punishment for disobedience of the command of his *paterfamilias* (the uncle). The son justifies his support for his natural father by appeal to *natura* and *pietas* (1.1.16; also 7.1 for a similar case). In another *controversia* (1.4.5), a son is disinherited for disobedience of his father's order to kill his adulterous mother; the son claims that disobedience toward his *paterfamilias* was an act of *pietas* toward his mother. In these rhetorical exercises, as in the *exempla*, *pietas* is represented as a natural devotion to family that may come into conflict with, and override, the demands of the legal constructs of authority.

Non-literary texts corroborate the argument that the fundamental essence of *pietas* lay in a reciprocal devotion to family members that was broader than the notion of filial obedience.[24] One might expect to find in the legal texts, with their interest in obligation and authority, a strong association of *pietas* with filial obedience. In his *Classical Roman Law* Schulz indeed limits his comments on *pietas* to the three respects in which it bound children: children could not bring their parents into court without the praetor's permission and could not bring infaming actions against them; nor could a child effect execution on the person of a parent.[25] Schulz's stress here is not surprising in view of the *Digest* title "De obsequiis parentibus et patronis praestandis" (37.15) in which it is laid down that *pietatis ratio* calls for *obsequium* toward parents. More concretely, this *ratio* meant that children were not to abuse their parents, but it did not impose unilateral, positive obligations of obedience.[26]

The few positive legal obligations derived from *pietas* were symmetrical. In the Roman view *officium pietatis* obliged parents to bequeath at least part of their estate to their children, and this was given legal sanction by the end of the Republic in the *querela inofficiosi testamenti*.[27] Those children who accumulated property had a similar duty: "For although the estate of

[24] Renier 1942: 75.   [25] Schulz 1951: 160.
[26] Rabel 1930: 296–98; Voci 1980: 78.   [27] Renier 1942: 39–76.

children is not owed to parents on account of parents' desire and natural concern for children: yet if the order of death is upset, it is owed *pie* no less to parents than to children."[28] Before death *pietas* obliged parents and children to provide maintenance for one another in case of need, a reciprocal duty sanctioned by law at least as early as the reign of Antoninus Pius.[29]

Beyond legally sanctioned duties, the jurists recognized that considerations of *pietas* could modify the usual legal rules where family members were involved. For example, if relatives provided *alimenta* for a fatherless child (*pupillus*) out of a sense of *pietas*, they could not recover the costs from the *pupillus'* estate under the rules for unauthorized administration, as an outsider could.[30] Or if a woman paid a dowry under the false belief that she was obliged to do so, she could not recover, as could others who paid under false belief: "for after the false belief is set aside, there remains the motive of *pietas* from which release cannot be sought."[31] Considerations of *pietas* also affected the rules about fraud. In general, debtors and freedmen could not give away their property to defraud creditors or patrons, but the fulfillment of an obligation imposed on a father by *pietas* was not interpreted as fraud. For this reason, an indebted father could turn over the whole *hereditas* left to him by his wife with a *fideicommissum* to restore it to their son; the immediate emancipation of his son, restoration of the full *hereditas*, and his refusal to keep the Falcidian quarter for himself was accepted as a reasonable show of *pietas*, and so not interpreted as fraud on his creditors.[32] Similarly, "if a freedman provided a dowry for his daughter, by this act he does not seem to defraud his patron, since a father's *pietas* ought not be criticized."[33] Finally, the limitations on women bringing legal cases were eased in situations where they were motivated by *pietas*: though in general women could not bring charges against unworthy *tutores* (guardians), mothers, grandmothers, and *nutrices* (nurses) were allowed to do so if "led by *pietas* toward some close relation" (*pietate necessitudinis ductae*).[34]

A survey of all uses of *pietas* in the *Digest* leads to several conclusions about how the jurists conceived of this virtue. First, the great majority of references concern relations within the nuclear family, reinforcing the argument of the previous chapter about the differential nature of obligation within the household and the wider kin network. Secondly, the reciprocal quality is clear from the fact that there are as many references to parental *pietas* as filial *pietas*: parents were obliged to look after the best interests of their children, just as children were obliged to respect and protect their

---

[28] *Dig.* 5.2.15 pr, Papinian.   [29] Voci 1980: 87–88.
[30] *Dig.* 3.5.26.1, Modestinus, for an *avunculus*; 3.5.33.pr, Paulus, for mother and grandmother, with Paulus stressing the importance of the intent of the grandmother.
[31] *Dig.* 12.6.32.2, Julian.   [32] *Dig.* 42.8.19, Papinian.   [33] *Dig.* 38.5.1.10, Ulpian.
[34] *Dig.* 26.10.1.7, Ulpian; cf. 49.5.1.1, Ulpian, for the mother's right to appeal a decision bringing ruin on her son — "a concession to *pietas*."

parents.[35] Spouses should feel *pietas* toward one another.[36] Thirdly, the jurists subscribe to the view of Valerius Maximus, Pliny, and the elder Seneca that *pietas* is natural (as opposed to a consequence of relations created by civil law). Not only did emancipation not sever the bonds of *pietas* (the point of the first *controversia* discussed above), but slave families, though not recognized as such in law, were regarded as bound by *pietas*. Consequently, *pietas* was due from a freed son to his freed mother, and, in connection with the Aediles' Edict regulating sales, "usually slaves who are not sick are returned [to the seller] with sick slaves, if they cannot be separated without great inconvenience or offending against *pietatis rationem*."[37]

As indicated above, some scholars have taken an evolutionary view of *pietas*, arguing that the reciprocal or affective qualities were developments of the late Republic, or the Augustan age, or the later Principate, or the age of established Christianity. Lee argued that prior to the Augustan age *pietas* was understood as "strict adherence to the principle of duty" without any affective dimension.[38] Manson discovered the precise point at which *pietas* broadened from a filial virtue to include parental affection in the Augustan age with the poet Ovid.[39] Roberti asserted that references in the *Digest* to *paterna pietas* must be post-classical interpolations, because they do not fit comfortably in the classical era with the image of the severe, all-powerful father.[40]

These developmental views start from a conception of the early Roman *paterfamilias* as a severe, authoritarian figure.[41] It is important to ask what evidence exists to support this conception. Among the *exempla* discussed above are some Republican episodes that emphasize love (*caritas*) and affection (*diligentia*).[42] Of course, one might dismiss these examples on the

---

[35] By my count, there are actually more references to *pietas paterna* and *materna* (16) than to filial *pietas* (12); conjugal *pietas* appears much less frequently (2). I do not mean to argue that the jurists believed in equality of duties among family members: for instance, Daube 1953 shows that in the classical period a father could undertake actions against a son's *peculium*, but the son did not enjoy the same capacity against his father.

[36] *Dig.* 12.6.32.2 for wife to husband; 32.41.pr for husband to wife. In the *Digest* references to conjugal *pietas* are noticeably rarer than to *pietas* between parents and children.

[37] *Dig.* 37.15.1.1, Ulpian; 21.1.35, Ulpian, the awkward grammar of which may admittedly indicate compression or interpolation; see also 36.1.80.2, Scaevola, for a father's *pietas* toward his *filius naturalis* who is a slave.   [38] Lee 1979: 22.

[39] Manson 1975: 26.   [40] Roberti 1935; rightly rejected by Rabello 1979: 237–38.

[41] Eyben 1991: 121–25 presents the evidence for paternal severity of early Rome, but recognizes that already in Roman comedy the severity was softening – in other words, in the earliest contemporary evidence the early evolutionary phase had already passed. The stories of early severity come from much later Latin authors whose accounts are highly dubious because they derive more from a schematic, idealized vision of their own past than from any reliable evidence.

[42] The founding legend illustrates *cara pietas*, according to Valerius Maximus 5.4.7; Torquatus' action on behalf of his father illustrates *diligentia* "praeter naturalem amorem" (5.4.3).

grounds that the affective qualities are early imperial glosses on older versions concentrating solely on duty. It is better, then, to examine Republican literature for expressions of the dimensions of *pietas*. In Roman comedy, the earliest substantial body of extant Latin literature from the first half of the second century BC, *pietas* most often characterizes children's proper attitude toward parents, but it is not so limited. In the *Poenulus* (1137) Plautus refers to a father's *pietas* in rescuing his daughters, and in the *Stichus* (7a) two young women oppose their father's wish for them to remarry, out of *pietas* for their husbands. The latter passage makes it particularly clear that even in our earliest evidence *pietas* cannot be construed solely as filial submission to *patria potestas*. The reciprocal aspect is plainly expressed in the early first-century rhetorical treatise *Ad Herennium*: "There is a natural law, observed *cognationis aut pietatis causa*, by which parents are esteemed by children and children by parents."[43] In the rhetorical treatise of his youth Cicero defined *pietas* as "benivolum officium" (*Inv.* 2.161). The adjective is noteworthy: *pietas* is more than just duty, "officium"; it is "well-wishing duty" – that is, it includes an affective element.[44] Overall, one would expect differences of emphasis in the connotations of *pietas* between Roman authors, and between works of the same authors.[45] There may have been a general shift of emphasis toward the affective dimension and paternal *pietas* toward children over the centuries, but it would be difficult to show because of the scarcity of the evidence for the period before Cicero. Enough has survived, however, to prove that the affective and reciprocal qualities were not late or post-Republican inventions.[46]

---

[43] 2.19; the ascription of this reciprocity to Stoic influence by Renier 1942: 54–65 does not seem to me to be provable or necessary. Néraudau 1984: 121 recognizes the *pietas* directed toward children but ascribes it to a belief in the child as sacred.

[44] Lee 1979: 17–23 shows that *pietas* might come into conflict with compassion and affection, as when Aeneas abandons Dido, but such conflict does not prove that Aeneas' *pietas* does not have an affective dimension – after all, one could be torn between two different obligations based on love or compassion.

[45] For instance, Cicero does not associate *pietas* with a parent's relationship to his/her children. In describing his brother's devotion to him during his exile, Cicero says that Quintus showed the *pietas* of a son toward him and the *beneficium* and *amor* of a *parens* (*Post red. ad Quir.* 5, 8). Here *pietas* is a filial quality, but not the complement of *patria potestas*. The paternal quality of love fits with the more benign paternal image sketched above.

[46] In an influential essay "*Pietas* in ancestor worship" (1970), Meyer Fortes interpreted *pietas* in terms of "the legal constraint and moral compulsion" binding "a son in loyalty to his father" and found a parallel in Chinese society in the virtue of "hsiao." More recently, however, Freedman 1966: 152 has insisted that to do so is to mistranslate "hsiao," which is the virtue of "obedience": "A man's loyalty to the interests and wishes of his father is supposed to outweigh all other loyalties and attachments. The state supports the father in commanding obedience; a wayward son can in the extreme be hauled into the magistrate's court." The contrast between "hsiao" and "pietas" is instructive. However

To insist that *pietas* was reciprocal is not to say that it was symmetrical in every repect. There was symmetry in the most general sense of devotion of all family members to the interests of the others, and also symmetry in some specific aspects noted above (for example, the duty to protect). Other aspects exhibit asymmetry, based on biological givens and cultural constructs. *Alimenta* was an obligation especially appropriate toward the helpless – that is, a duty of parents toward their young children, and of adult offspring toward their elderly parents. Testamentary duty was normally one of parent to child. Respect and obedience were regarded as the duty of offspring toward parents, who bestowed on their children the incomparable *beneficium* of life.[47] Though we would consider the virtue of respectful obedience as a matter of cultural construction, the Romans themselves saw it as universal, not their own peculiar characteristic like *patria potestas*. The Hadrianic jurist Sex. Pomponius included filial obedience among the elements of the *ius gentium*: "[it is common among men:] so, for instance, religious awe toward the gods, so we obey parents and fatherland."[48] Note Pomponius' use of the plural, *parentes*: it must be emphasized (against Balsdon's and others' association of filial obedience with *fathers*) that the Romans did not discriminate by gender as to the object of *obsequium* – that is, mothers were owed it as much as fathers, whose *potestas* was irrelevant in this regard.

Potestas

Whereas filial respect and obedience was in the jurist's view a universal value among human societies, *patria potestas* was regarded as characteristically Roman. In the often quoted words of Gaius, "there are hardly any other men who have over their children a power such as we have."[49] Indeed, *patria potestas* is so striking and extensive that it has too often dominated historical interpretations of Roman family relations, turning attention away from the negotiation of everyday contacts and the mutuality of obligation in the virtue of *pietas*. There is no doubt that *patria potestas* was a central principle organizing the Roman law of persons and property, but its legal centrality does not warrant reading the nearly absolute legal powers

authoritarian Roman fathers may have been in practice, at least "the core Roman virtue" of family life cannot be interpreted as one of submissive obedience, since it was expected of parents, children, and siblings alike. Freedman adds that obedience is the social ideal, but for social and economic reasons it does not translate into thorough going social control.

47 Implied in Valerius Maximus' version of the founding legend of the temple in his reference to the mother as *genetrix* who nourished her daughter (5.4.7). For *pietas* as the children's response to parental *beneficia*, Seneca *Ben.* 3.36.1.

48 "[Ius gentium hominibus inter se commune est:] veluti erga deos religio: ut parentibus et patriae pareamus" (*Dig.* 1.1.2; O. Lenel, *Palingensia* II, col. 44, discussed by Rabello 1979: 165).   49 *Inst.* 1.55.

of a father over his children as a sociological description of family relationships. This section will present a brief enumeration and description of the principal legal powers of Roman fathers, then ask how those powers were exercised, and, finally, consider how paternal powers played out in the personal dynamics of the household.

The most striking aspect of paternal power was the power of life and death (*vitae necisque potestas*) that a father possessed over his descendants *in potestate*. It is easy to assume that this is what Gaius had in mind in his reference to *talem potestatem*, yet Gaius does not mention the *vitae necisque potestas* in his treatment of paternal power.[50] By the time of Constantine the killing of a child in one's *potestas* was brought under the crime of *parricidium*, where it had not been listed in the *lex Pompeia de parricidiis* of the 50s BC.[51] A review of the Roman examples of fathers putting their children to death, however, does not yield a clear or precise idea of the evolution of the scope or limitations of the power during the centuries before Constantine.

Rabello, Voci, and Harris have recently surveyed the historical examples of the killing of children on paternal orders. Several points from their studies deserve emphasis. Harris underlines "the real rarity of historical instances in which [*vitae necisque potestas*] was relied on with regard to adult sons." The most famous instances come from the legendary era of early Rome, well before the beginnings of Roman historiography, so their details are not reliable and change from version to version.[52] Several of the best-known severe fathers, L. Iunius Brutus, A. Postumius Tubertus and T. Manlius Torquatus, held a high magistracy and invoked magisterial power to order the son's execution for violation of duty to the state. Valerius Maximus and Livy explicitly say that his consular role imposed the dreadful duty on Brutus the father.[53] Though Sp. Cassius is not said to have been holding a magistracy, he also is represented as acting in the interests of the state. In one of the very few examples from the historical era, the senator A. Fulvius, in the interests of state order, put to death his son who was seeking to join the rebel army under Catiline.[54] All of these stories illustrate the value of placing loyalty to the *patria* ahead of loyalty to the *familia* – a value as relevant to sons as to fathers.[55] The jurist Marcellus wrote: "our ancestors

---

[50] Rabello 1979: 181.   [51] Rabello 1979: 146–48.

[52] For references to the ancient sources, Harris 1986, who gives the conflicting evidence about whether Sp. Cassius put his demagogic son to death by virtue of *vitae necisque potestas* or the quaestors put the son on trial for *perduellio*.

[53] Livy 2.5.5: "poenae capiendae ministerium patri de liberis consulatus imposuit"; Valerius Maximus 5.8.1: "exuit patrem, ut consulem ageret."   [54] Sallust *Cat.* 39.5.

[55] Harris 1986: 86. Polybius 6.54 interpreted these examples in the following terms: "There have also been instances of men in office putting their own sons to death, in defiance of every custom and law, because they rated the interests of their country higher than those of natural ties even with their nearest and dearest." In other words, such behavior was not normative, but a display of loyalty to the state against custom and law.

thought there was no need to mourn a man who set out to destroy his country and to kill his parents and children. They all decided that if such a man was killed by his son or father, it was no crime, and the killer should receive a reward."[56]

The other examples from the classical era are no more certain in detail and are more ambiguous in their implications. Q. Fabius Maximus in the late second century BC and an unnamed father during Hadrian's reign had their sons killed for sexual offenses (in the latter case, adultery with the father's wife who was the son's stepmother). Both fathers received official punishment for their actions. Although the specific grounds or charges are not specified, the implication is that the exercise of *vitae necisque potestas* was not unrestricted.[57] Yet it is impossible to define the conditions or justifications for its use. Specificity may be sought in the *lex Iulia de adulteriis*, which laid down the particular circumstances in which a father was permitted to kill his adulterous daughter. The conditions were very strict: the father had to catch the adulterous couple in the act in his own *domus*, or that of his son-in-law, and to kill both adulterer and adultress "as if by a single stroke"; otherwise, a father, like a husband, must proceed against an adulterous daughter through the law courts.[58] *Patria potestas* is one of the relevant conditions, but the right to kill (*ius occidendi*) seems not to be based on *vitae necisque potestas* in the *lex Iulia*.[59] The conditions – e.g., the immediate slaying, only in the act and only in the father's or husband's house – do not make sense if Roman fathers possessed a general power of life and death. The reason given for the father's *ius occidendi* is *iustus dolor*, justifiable pain, which served as the legal basis for the defense of homicide of honor for millennia to come.[60] The distinction between the father's right to kill and the husband's general lack of such a right in classical law does not derive from the husband's lack of *potestas* over his wife, but from the belief, according to Papinian, that a father would be more likely to restrain his anger out of *pietas* for his child.[61]

The one specific case in which an emperor may have defended the paternal *vitae necisque potestas* was that of the equestrian Tricho. According to Seneca, Tricho had his son whipped to death. The crowd in Rome attacked and threatened him, until he was rescued by Augustus. The details

---

[56]   *Dig.* 11.7.35.   [57]   Rabello 1979: 118–21; Voci 1980: 50–57.
[58]   *Dig.* 48.5.23–24; Treggiari 1991a: 282.
[59]   Thomas 1984: 501; Cantarella 1991: 232. Papinian, *Coll.* 4.8.1 (FIRA II.555) does connect the *ius occidendi* here to the *lex regia* granting the *pater* the *vitae necisque potestas* and claims that the novelty lay in ordaining that both be killed, but that does not explain the nature of the restrictions on the father's power to execute his daughter. On the problems of this passage, Rabello 1979: 214.
[60]   Cantarella 1991 offers a fascinating account of the scope of this defense over the centuries.
[61]   *Dig.* 48.5.23.4.

of the account are so vague that it is not certain that Tricho's right to invoke
vitae necisque potestas was in fact at issue.[62] Three centuries later the emperor
Constantine asserted that if a master applied a whip to a slave and killed him,
it was not to be considered criminal homicide on the ground that a man with
homicidal intent would use a more lethal weapon such as a club.[63] By
Constantine's logic, Tricho's use of the whip leaves it unclear whether he
was perceived to have intentionally executed his son on the basis of *vitae
necisque potestas*, and Seneca's account does nothing to clarify the issue.

In sum, there is no clear evidence for the successful invocation in the
classical era of a father's *vitae necisque potestas* against a grown offspring
except in defense of the *patria*. The father's right to expose a newborn was
taken for granted and may have been one aspect of the *vitae necisque potestas*,
but this also is uncertain.[64] Altogether, the evidence for this singular power
is singularly unsatisfactory: no conditions laid down for its use; some
fathers (mostly ancient magistrates) vindicated, others punished for killing
their sons but without specification of the grounds. In a brilliant essay, Y.
Thomas has shown a way out of these difficulties by suggesting that the
vitae necisque potestas, mostly clearly attested in the adoption formula rather
than in practice, was not "a daily reality," "not a fact of social history," but
"an abstract definition of power," "a pure concept."[65] For an adopting
father the *vitae necisque potestas* was a legal formula expressing the most
extreme, limiting case, but one that could be successfully used only in concert
with the state and only in extremely rare circumstances. "In reality, the
cruelty of fathers, when it is attested, is condemned. To kill a son is almost
always sacrilege, except when a father embodies the State or when the State
is badly represented by a son."[66] There is no reason to believe that Roman
children lived their daily lives conscious of this terrible paternal power.[67]

In Roman comedies and *controversiae*, which often feature conflicts
between fathers and sons, the most serious punishment threatened against

[62] Harris 1986: 86.   [63] *C. Th.* 9.12.1.   [64] Harris 1986: 94.
[65] Thomas 1984: 512, 545, 500.   [66] Thomas 1984: 545.
[67] In the past Chinese fathers were endowed with the power of life and death over their
children, but it also was abstract and distant from daily life, according to Hsu 1967: 56,
62–63: "The father has authority of life and death over the son, and the son has to revere
and support his parents. Mourning and worship after the death of the parents are integral
parts of the son's responsibility ... The father has great authority over the son, but the
authority is subject to the fact that socially a father and a son are part of each other. The
older man cannot abuse his power without injury to himself. The son is obliged to please
and support his father, but the latter is also the provider for the son at all times ... The
generally accepted pattern of behavior between father and son, far from being a negative
one of authority and submission, or of exploitation and support, is much better described
by a more positive literary saying, 'The father is kindly toward his son, and the son filial
toward his father.' As soon as the sons have married and have had children, the West
Towner father consults them and defers to their opinion almost as frequently as they do
to his."

a son is repudiation and expulsion from the house.[68] The precise legal standing of *abdicatio* and its relation to the Greek practice of *apokéryxis* are matters of dispute. Scholars of Roman law have been inclined to view *abdicatio* as a Greek import without legal force in classical Rome.[69] Against them, B. Levick has argued that it was a legal institution, effectively punitive emancipation approved by a domestic *consilium* and leading to disinheritance. In Levick's view, Agrippa Postumus was the most famous victim of *abdicatio* at the hands of his adoptive grandfather Augustus. What Augustus did in this case in virtue of what powers is not clear; furthermore, as Levick acknowledges, references to *abdicatio*, absent in classical legal texts, come mostly in the rhetorical writers, from whom legal precision is hardly to be expected. Thomas reasserts the view that "*abdicatio* severed not a legal bond, but a moral one" and should not be confused with the formal legal institutions of emancipation or *exheredatio* (disinheritance).[70] In fact, Quintilian distinguishes *abdicatio* from *exheredatio*, associating the former with the rhetorical schools and the latter with real legal cases.[71] For the purposes of this chapter, the legal standing of *abdicatio* is not as important as the fact that Roman fathers were able to disown and expel their sons from their *domus*. Evidence of actual cases of invocation of this power is scarce. Valerius Maximus offers two historical instances from the late second century in his section "De severitate patrum in liberos." Both sons committed suicide after being disowned by their fathers for failures in public duty, the adopted D. Iunius Silanus following repudiation by his natural father T. Manlius Torquatus for maladministration of the province of Macedonia, and M. Aemilius Scaurus for having deserted the battle against the Cimbri with his cavalry unit.[72] The *exemplum* of Silanus supports Thomas' claim that moral authority, rather than a formal legal power, was involved, since Torquatus declared his natural son "unworthy of my *domus*" and ordered him "to leave my sight" after his formal *potestas* had been severed by adoption.[73]

Exheredatio was one aspect of disowning a son, and was a part of the *paterfamilias'* proprietary power in the *familia*. The *paterfamilias* alone possessed formal ownership (*dominium*) over the property of his *familia*, while those in his *potestas* had no independent proprietary capacity. Anything acquired by a *filiusfamilias*, no matter what his age, became the property of his *paterfamilias*, who then had wide discretion in distributing the property through a written will. It was this life-long monopoly of ownership rights that Sextus Empiricus (3.211) singled out in his remarks

[68] E.g., Terence *Phormio* 425.
[69] Kaser 1971: 61–62; Buckland 1963: 132, n. 6; Voci 1980: 76.
[70] Thomas 1990: 463, 460; Levick 1972.   [71] *Inst.* 7.4.11.
[72] Valerius Maximus 5.8.3–4.   [73] Rabello 1979: 124–25.

about paternal despotism in Rome. In his humorous caricature, Daube drew out the implications of this monopoly for the "rigid control" exercised by the patriarch over his male descendants:

Suppose the head of a family was ninety, his two sons seventy-five and seventy, their sons between sixty and fifty-five, the sons of these in their forties and thirties, and the great-great-grandsons in their twenties, none of them except the ninety year-old Head owned a penny. If the seventy-five-year-old senator or the forty-year-old General or the twenty-year-old student wanted to buy a bar of chocolate, he had to ask the senex for the money.[74]

The law provided an institution, the *peculium*, that could be used to mitigate the proprietary incapacity of the *filiusfamilias*. This was a fund granted by a *paterfamilias* to one in his *potestas* to be used in business or public affairs, or to meet moral obligations, but not for gifts unless permitted by the *pater*.[75] The child's *peculium*, like the slave's, was revocable at the discretion of the *paterfamilias*. The exception to this rule was the *peculium castrense*, a special fund for military income granted to legionaries by Augustus. A *filiusfamilias*, otherwise without testamentary capacity, had the right to bequeath the contents of his *peculium castrense*, unconstrained by the usual rules of testamentary form.

In contrast to sons' general testamentary incapacity, fathers had wide, though not unlimited, flexibility in the transmission of the patrimony upon their death. Testation will be examined in greater detail in chapter 7; suffice it to say here that fathers had the power to disinherit children with good cause, or to give them as little as a quarter of their full share without having to justify the arrangement. Reference to the power of testation occurs far more often in our texts for the classical era than the elusive *vitae necisque potestas* or *abdicatio*, and has been seen as the most potent power in the paternal arsenal.

The law also gave the *paterfamilias* considerable influence over the marriage of his children. In the classical period *iustum matrimonium* required the consent of the spouses and the *paterfamilias* of each.[76] No particular form of consent was specified: participation in the property arrangements and ceremonies, or even informed acquiescence, could be construed as consent.[77] In addition to the right of approval, the *paterfamilias* of either spouse possessed until the mid-second century after Christ the right to break off the marriage.[78]

These legal powers would seem to endow the *paterfamilias* with an overwhelming dominance in the family. Some legal historians point to an evolution in which *patria potestas* was gradually limited by the emperors and

[74] Daube 1969: 85, 79.   [75] Thomas 1981.
[76] *Dig.* 23.2.2, Paulus; Volterra 1948, Matringe 1971.   [77] Treggiari 1991a: 170–76.
[78] Treggiari 1991a: 459–61.

assumed a protective (rather than coercive) quality. Emperors of the second century punished abusive fathers; by the end of the fourth century emperors regarded the father's killing of his child of any age as homicide. In the realm of property rights, children were given recourse to a *querela inofficiosi testamenti* to contest disinheritance without just cause; the first emperor gave sons in legionary service limited property rights. With regard to marriage, the Augustan legislation forbade fathers from preventing the marriage of their daughters, and Antoninus Pius and the Severans prohibited fathers from breaking up harmonious marriages of their children. Rabello sees an important development and ascribes it to *étatisme*, an increasing willingness on the part of the imperial apparatus to intervene in what had been a tight and more autonomous family unit.[79]

But the development should not be overstated, for two reasons. First, the nature of the evidence for these trends, as for others, is likely to exaggerate the change. The *Digest* disproportionately preserves the rulings of the emperors from Hadrian through the Severans, whereas the *notae* of Republican censors are poorly documented. Yet the censors are known to have had the responsibility to watch over the citizenry's mores, including family behavior, and Republican magistrates occasionally took action against abuse of paternal power.[80] As early as the Augustan age, Dionysius of Halicarnassus (*Rom. Ant.* 20.13.3) contrasted Greek fathers, who wielded autonomous power within their houses, with Roman fathers, who were traditionally monitored by the censors. It is necessary to distinguish between *étatisme* as an explanation for the survival of imperial rescripts and as a cause of increasing intervention in family life. The concentration of rescripts from the second and early third centuries is partially an epiphenomenon of the survival of more rescripts, as well as of the increasing intervention by emperors. *Patria potestas* was never in the historical period completely arbitrary and unrestrained. Secondly, the emperors sought to restrict only the extremes of paternal power at the margins of family life. If the behavior of most families stayed well within those margins, then most families would have been unaffected by the imperial rulings. As Matringe in his study of paternal power and children's marriage concluded, "the prudent and exceptional character of imperial and magisterial intervention left practically intact the traditional *patria potestas*."[81]

If the emperors of the Principate left intact the principal powers of Roman fathers, that is not to say that fathers exploited those powers to their fullest. Demographic constraints and social and moral pressures operated to mitigate the effects of the stark legal rules. To begin, the tables of microsimulation results (pp. 48–65 above) offer a guide to answer the simple

[79] Rabello 1979: 246. [80] Rabello 1979: ch. 5; Matringe 1971: 193.
[81] Matringe 1971: 208.

question: what proportion of Romans at a given age had a living father and were likely to have been *in potestate*? The answer will vary according to assumptions about mortality and ages at marriage, but on any reasonable set of assumptions Daube's picture of four generations of offspring at the whim of the *senex* is highly misleading. Given the most optimistic assumption about mortality (Coale–Demeny Level 6 West, $e_0 = 32.5$) and the lower "senatorial" ages at marriage, more than one-quarter of children would have lost their father by age fifteen, when girls were entering marriage; nearly one-half would not have had a living father by age twenty-five, when "senatorial men" were married and thought to be fully competent to manage an estate; by age forty, when senators were competing for the highest magistracies, only one-fifth had a living father. On the more pessimistic (and, in my judgment, more likely) assumption about mortality (Coale–Demeny Level 3 West, $e_0 = 25$), the proportion of fatherless at each age is higher: one-third without fathers at age fifteen, about half at age twenty, six of ten at age twenty-five, and nine out of ten without fathers at age forty. Among the non-elite, given the higher marriage ages and the likely higher mortality (Coale–Demeny Level 3 West), half were fatherless at age twenty, when women typically married; two-thirds had no living father at age twenty-five; and more than three-quarters were fatherless at age thirty, roughly the median age at first marriage for men. To generalize about this range of probabilities, most Romans upon reaching full adulthood, the *aetas perfecta* of twenty-five, did not have to live under the continuing shadow of *patria potestas*. Most "senatorial" girls probably did have a father available to arrange their first marriage, but among the non-elite the requirement of paternal consent to marriage was irrelevant to half of the women. Marrying at a later age, most men would not have had to reckon with paternal consent. It would be wrong, then, to infer from *patria potestas* that in Rome the young generation of adults was in general rigidly controlled by their elderly fathers, still less by their grandfathers. In noting these implications of high mortality, Veyne suggests that the contrast between the independence of the majority of adults *sui iuris* and the lack of rights of the minority still *in potestate* served to heighten the intergenerational tensions and resentment of the minority.[82] In order to evaluate this suggestion, it will be necessary to consider how paternal powers were put into practice.

We have noted that the precise legal rules regarding the father's extreme coercive powers are difficult to delineate because there are so few historical examples, and those are not reported with legal precision. Roman social norms did not encourage the use of such powers. Valerius Maximus, it is true, presents a series of *exempla* to praise paternal *severitas* – all cases in

[82] Veyne 1978.

which sons harmed the public good. With regard to private wrongs, however, Valerius sees virtue in paternal *moderatio*. In two of the four *exempla*, the father forgives his son suspected of adultery with his stepmother, the father's wife.[83] These *exempla* celebrate the triumph of the bond of *amor* between father and son over sexual jealousies and misbehavior within the family. The two other *exempla* in this section show Q. Hortensius and Q. Fulvius leaving their patrimonies to their sons despite filial *impietas*. In so doing, Hortensius was moved by paternal affection "not to upset the order of nature," which called for parents to leave their property to their children. These *exempla* are as extreme and exceptional as those concerning paternal severity, but they show that Roman ideology regarding paternal power and filial respect did not uniformly call for, or underwrite, unforgiving harshness from the father. Rather, the lesson of Valerius' contrast between *severitas* and *moderatio* is that fathers should be unyielding in the interests of the state, even to the point of stepping out of their paternal role, but should display loving forgiveness toward personal injuries, even those as serious as an adulterous affair between son and stepmother.[84]

Paternal moderation toward serious filial misbehavior was not only regarded as a virtue but was also in the father's own interests, which were heavily invested in his children. To repudiate a son, drive him from the house, and disinherit him was considered hurtful to the father as well as the son. The father Menedemus in Terence's *Heautontimorumenos*, unhappy at his son's marriage, did drive him away from home through verbal abuse, and later regretted the behavior that ruined his house (99–157). Though fictional, the story illustrated to the Roman audience the destructive consequences of a father's invocation of his extreme powers – destructive to his *domus* and thus to himself.[85]

The extreme powers of life and death and repudiation, attested in collections of *exempla, controversiae* and drama, were far enough removed from ordinary experience that they do not appear in the letters of Cicero, Pliny and Fronto, our best sources for daily social practices among the elite. By contrast, the testamentary power of parents does appear in the epistolary collections and was a more immediate concern to children. Although quantification is impossible, it is unlikely that many legitimate children were completely cut out of their patrimony.[86] The Romans had a strong sense that duty required transmission of the patrimony to *sui heredes*, usually children. Valerius praised Hortensius for overlooking his son's *impietas* to institute him heir out of affection. More generally, Plutarch suggested that

---

[83] 5.9.1 and 4. In *Dig.* 48.9.5 it was for adultery with a stepmother that a father killed his son and was punished by Hadrian.
[84] On the seriousness of the *iniuria* to the wronged husband, Cohen 1991.
[85] Eyben 1991: 134.   [86] Champlin 1991: ch. 6.

men chose to have children out of love rather than a desire for heirs to bury them, arguing that attentive heirs could be found outside the family, whereas children took their inheritance for granted to such a degree that they did not feel compelled to show respect (*timosin*).[87] Plutarch's claim is tendentious and perhaps overstated, yet it reveals an assumption of strong motives, regarded as natural, that inhibited the paternal exercise of *exheredatio*.[88] Whether natural or not, the inclination to name one's children as heirs was reinforced by social pressure. As Pliny's letter (*Ep.* 8.18) passing judgment on Domitius Tullus shows, the wills of wealthy Romans became public knowledge and a matter of public censure or praise. Domitius Tullus increased his repute posthumously by leaving his vast estate to his family – a display of *pietas*.

If *exheredatio* was regarded as unnatural and appropriate only in extreme circumstances, it is also true that Roman testators had great flexibility within the boundaries of the socially acceptable to show more or less favor to their children in the division of the estate. Which farm should go to which heir, how much should be given away in legacies – these were decisions that would affect the fortunes of sons and daughters. Because a father's testamentary arrangements were often not as simple and automatic as Plutarch implies, children had reason to cultivate their father's favor. How they went about this is suggested by a comment of Ulpian concerning the criteria for adoption. In general, it was appropriate for a man without legitimate children to adopt: if a man with many legitimate children (*plures liberos*) should adopt another, the addition of another prospective heir would diminish the expectation (*spes*) of property that "each of the children has secured for himself by *obsequium*."[89] Here the child's share of the patrimony is not regarded as automatic, but won as a reward for filial respect.[90] Testamentary power gave fathers a potential leverage to require *obsequium* from their children that they used in varying degrees. Arbitrary use of that power brought peer disapproval and ruin to the house.

The significance of the father's monopoly of proprietary rights in the *familia* during his lifetime, like his testamentary right, depended on his wealth.[91] It would seem obvious that *dominium* over property must have given wealthy fathers more power to withhold maintenance or money, and yet it is clear that wealthy fathers did not exploit these powers to their limits. Some children were given a degree of de facto financial independence through the *peculium*; how great a degree depends on how the historian envisages its use. Daube minimizes the independence by stressing the legal rule that the *peculium* was revocable at the father's discretion.[92] Hopkins

---

[87] *Mor.* 497B.   [88] Crook 1967b: 120; Dixon 1986: 93–120.   [89] *Dig.* 1.7.17.3.
[90] This aspect is stressed by Hopkins 1983: 245.   [91] Daube 1969: 81.
[92] Daube 1969: 76, 83.

minimizes the liberating potential of the *peculium* by translating it as "pocket money."[93] On the other hand, Kaser's impression from the legal evidence is that sons were customarily granted a *peculium* and left alone to administer it.[94]

Our evidence is not sufficient to reveal the typical financial situation of a son *in potestate*, but several arguments favor Kaser's view. First, as Kaser points out, the withdrawal of the *peculium* and the attendant problems that would have created are not prominent in the legal sources.[95] Secondly, whatever the etymology of *peculium*, it was plainly more than "pocket money" for many Roman sons. Not only did it provide the basis for *filiifamiliarum* to make contracts and fulfill family obligations, but it also constituted the security for their proper performance of public services.[96] For instance, one of the tasks of local magistrates was to approve *tutores* for the many *pupilli* whose fathers had died. The magistrate was supposed to see that the *tutor* gave proper security for the return of the *pupillus'* estate; if the magistrate failed to do so, he himself was held liable. The jurists asked whether the magistrate's *paterfamilias* was also liable. "Julian says that an action on the *peculium* is available, whether or not he wanted his son to be decurion. Even if he filled the office with his father's permission, his father should not be liable beyond the value of the *peculium*."[97] The sums involved in *tutela* (guardianship) could be quite large. If adult sons serving as magistrates typically had no *peculium* or merely "pocket money," the legal recourse offered to *pupilli* would have been of little value. Given the concern in the law to protect *pupilli*, it seems preferable to follow Kaser in thinking that the jurists were offering a meaningful recourse on the assumption that adult *filiifamilias* of propertied families often had a substantial *peculium*.

Peculium recurs in the juristic writings, but does not figure in the literary sources, where sons are represented as spending family funds with little attention given to the legal niceties. Sons in Cicero's and Pliny's letters do not appear as helpless suppliants requesting funds for each expenditure, as one might expect from the legal rules. The explanation lies in part in the social pressures put on fathers to provide for their sons in a style appropriate to their status. This is especially clear in Cicero's letters to Atticus concerning the arrangements for young Marcus during his studies in

---

[93] 1983: 244. [94] 1938: 85–86; Crook 1967b: 119 takes an agnostic position.
[95] 1938: 86.
[96] Thomas 1982: 573. Thomas (p. 540) claims against Kaser and others that whereas slaves used *peculium* for financial pursuits, *filiifamilias* are referred to in the *Digest* as using *peculium* almost entirely for family and municipal obligations. But there seem to be references to *filii* using their *peculium* for financial transactions: e.g., *Dig.* 15.1.5, 15.1.38.pr, 16.3.1.42, 16.3.19, 16.3.21 (deposit); 14.1.1.22; 15.1.27.pr (commerce); 3.5.45.pr, 17.1.12.2ff. (mandate); 6.1.41.1, 18.5.1, 20.6.8.5, 21.1.23.4, 41.2.14.pr (sale); 2.11.5.2, 22.1.32.2–3. (contract); 2.13.4.2 (banking); 3.5.5.8 (*actio gestorum negotiorum*).
[97] *Dig.* 27.8.1.17.

Athens. Cicero wished to provide an allowance that would be "as much as Publilius and Lentulus gave their sons." This standard turned out to be more than a knight's minimum income. When young Marcus went through his allowance with unexpected ease, Cicero was at pains to get more to him, because "it is base (*turpe*) for us that in his first year he be in want, whatever kind of son he is." It was a matter of honor for Cicero to supply his son "as honorably and as abundantly as possible."[98]

Fathers sometimes reacted against supporting their sons' extravagance, as Pliny reports. "A certain man was chastising his son because he was spending rather too extravagantly on horses and dogs. After the youth went away, I said to him: 'Well, what about you, have you never done something that could be criticized by your father? Dare I say you have? Do you not do something now and then which, if suddenly he were the father and you the son, he would criticize with equal severity? Are not all men led astray by some error? Does he not indulge himself in this while someone else indulges in that?'"[99] Several aspects of this letter are especially interesting. The son was able to spend first and take the consequences later. Then the consequences of spending too much on dogs and horses were nothing more severe than verbal chastisement from his father (recalling the harangues of fathers in Roman comedies three centuries earlier).[100] Finally, the father's reprimand (which we might regard as not unreasonable by contemporary standards) won him a moralizing lecture from Pliny to the effect that he should not expect a different standard of behavior from his son than he himself meets (again, recalling comic dialogue of the early second century BC).[101] That the conventional Pliny was ready to interfere, and later to recite the story to another friend by way of advice, indicates a level of direct peer pressure restraining the exercise of parental authority that might discomfort modern parents.

Cicero and Pliny articulate the experience and values of the leisured elite, whose income derived from property ownership and not labor. The fortunes of children in this class were especially closely tied to parental decisions about the distribution of that property. Although there is very little evidence, it may be that in families with modest assets (say, a small family farm) the balance of economic power between ageing parents and adult sons was more nearly equal. The son's labor may have been needed to work the land, but the father enjoyed the leverage derived from the testamentary power to bequeath the family farm, or most of it, to someone other than the son. How these competing sources of power – labor and property – worked out in practice is impossible to know. Some fathers partially forfeited their power by transferring their property before their death. This

---

[98] *Att.* 12.7, 12.32, 13.47, 14.7.   [99] *Ep.* 9.12.   [100] Saller 1993.
[101] E.g., Plautus *Epidicus* 382–91.

practice seems to have been much less common in Rome than in later
Europe, but a few examples can be found in the *Digest*.[102] It is also possible
that local custom in peasant communities granted fathers less discretion in
testation than allowed by law, and correspondingly less social power.

To judge from comparative evidence, the dynamics in poor, propertyless
families, who existed by virtue of their labor alone, probably differed from
that of the elite and the smallholders.[103] In the absence of a welfare system,
poor, ageing Romans must have depended on their children for support –
hence the moral maxim that "it is evil not to provide maintenance for
parents."[104] The need of a father to be cared for by his son was accepted by
Javolenus as a legitimate reason to allow an adoptive father to stipulate a
penalty if he were pressed to emancipate his adopted son.[105] The alimentary
obligation was reciprocal between parents and children and can be traced
back in the legal evidence as far as the reign of Pius. The *Digest* title "De
agnoscendis et alendis liberis vel parentibus vel patronis vel libertis" (25.3)
contains a ruling by Pius in a case involving a humble artisan: "But if the son
can support himself, the judges ought to decide that they should not decree
maintenance for him. For the divine Pius issued a rescript to this effect: 'The
appropriate judges approached by you will order that you be supported by
your father in accordance with his resources, only if, since you say that you
are a craftsman, you are in such a state of health that you are not able to
support yourself by your own labor.'"[106] This rescript is of particular
interest for the assumptions it makes about a working family. The situation
envisaged by Pius is one in which a healthy adult son would normally
"support himself by his *operae*," implying an independence that is rather
different from the picture based on the father's technical proprietary rights
to all of his son's income. If it is accepted that adult sons of poor families
achieved a certain independence by virtue of their income-earning capacity,
that no family property offered them an incentive to maintain family ties,
and that the legal machinery was hardly adequate systematically to enforce
the alimentary obligation, then it follows that ageing, propertyless parents

---

[102] 31.87.4, Paulus; 32.37.3, Scaevola; 34.4.23, Papinian; 41.10.4.1, Pomponius.
[103] According to Arthur P. Wolf and Chieh-shan Huang 1980: 66, ageing fathers in poor
   Chinese families find it difficult to maintain their authority over adult sons, because they
   have no property to use as leverage. Consequently, as a father grows weak in old age
   and comes to depend on his sons' labor for support, he finds the traditional distribution
   of power reversed to the point that he "might have to beg his adult sons for cigarette
   money"; for a similar argument, Hsu 1967: 9; Freedman 1966: 47.
[104] Cicero *Att.* 9.9; the same principle is found much later in Augustine's work; see Shaw
   1987b. Bradley 1991: ch. 5 discusses the need among the poor to exploit their children's
   labor.
[105] *Dig.* 45.1.107; how often sons were adopted for this reason is impossible to know, but
   in Chinese society adoption was a standard, though not especially desirable, way for
   childless men and women to find someone to care for them in old age.
[106] *Dig.* 25.3.5, Ulpian.

were highly vulnerable and dependent on their children's goodwill and their success in inculcating the virtue of *pietas*. Such parents are unlikely to have been in a position to insist on parental authority.

The legal rule requiring paternal consent for a child's marriage appears deceptively straightforward. In reality, as Treggiari has shown, the arrangement of marriage was a complex matter, because it involved the interests of more than just the spouses and their fathers.[107] In accepting consent expressed tacitly, by silence, the law left open the direction of the initiative in making the arrangements. Interconnected assumptions about age and gender influenced the dynamics of the decision-making. At first marriage, women, particularly in the elite, were usually quite young. It is difficult to envisage a Roman girl of a senatorial family at the age of ten or twelve taking a leading part in arranging a betrothal to a husband ten years her senior. And, in fact, Pliny's letters take it for granted that the decision in such circumstances belongs to the father. He congratulates Julius Servianus on his choice of Fuscus Salinator as a son-in-law endowed with the virtues of *simplicitas, comitas*, and *gravitas*. "It remains for him as quickly as possible to make you a grandfather of grandchildren similar to yourself" (*Ep.* 6.26). In another letter praising Musonius Rufus' selection of Artemidorus as his son-in-law, Pliny barely mentions his daughter, treating his decision as evidence of Musonius' excellence (*Ep.* 3.11.5, 7). Centuries earlier Roman comedies had portrayed decisions about a young woman's marriage as part of her father's *ius* in principle, but in reality manipulated by the daughter's appeals to the father's sense of affection and duty to his children's welfare.[108] A woman remarrying later in life (and many did so after divorce or a husband's death) was likely to exert greater influence on the decision, even in the unlikely circumstance that her father was alive. Cicero during his governorship of Cilicia in 51–50 BC left the arrangement of Tullia's third marriage largely to Terentia and Tullia back in Rome. Even though the choice of Dolabella caused Cicero some political embarrassment, he went along with the decision.[109] This example illustrates particularly well the fact that paternal powers in law constituted a potential that a father might or might not use in reality.

As males marrying later, sons were probably more active participants in choosing their first spouse. Cicero's nephew Quintus took it upon himself to look over the field of eligible women while still *in potestate* (*Att.* 15.29.2). A son's independence could lead to tension, since fathers may have been especially concerned that their sons marry women from honorable families to produce descendants worthy of their name. A stock question among

---

[107] Treggiari 1991b; Dixon 1985c.
[108] Saller 1993, citing Plautus, *Stich.* 68–72 and Terence, *Hec.* 243–45.
[109] Treggiari 1984.

moralists was whether sons should obey their fathers in taking a wife.[110] The jurist Celsus addressed the issue of the validity of a marriage which a *filiusfamilias* entered unwillingly (*invitus*) under paternal compulsion (*patre cogente*).[111] Celsus considered the marriage valid, since the *filiusfamilias* went ahead with it. Unfortunately, there is no hint in this passage of the form of compulsion, but in Roman comedies fathers tried to push their sons away from *amicae* and into honorable marriages by hectoring and threatening loss of patrimony. Of course, the plots end happily with the sons having their own way.[112] The end of Terence's *Heautontimorumenos* is revealing about how the choice might be made. The father Chremes is pressing his son Clitipho to give up his lower-class *amica* and to take a legitimate wife. Clitipho gives in to the pressure, but insists, against his mother's proposal, on his own choice from among the possibilities; his parents agree to his decision (1059–66). This plot suggests how conflicts might be resolved and mutual consent reached, as the father achieves his general aim of an honorable marriage for his son, who is allowed to make the particular choice. Fathers had good reason not to force unwanted marriages on their sons and daughters: not only did a father have an *officium* to protect his children's interests, but marriages in pre-Christian Rome were not lifetime commitments. A son or daughter forced into marriage was not trapped for life (as in later Europe), since *iustum matrimonium* ceased when conjugal affection (*affectio maritalis*) no longer existed.[113] A father desiring a successful marriage for his child would presumably seek an arrangement appealing to all sides.

The analysis up to this point has concentrated on the dyadic relationship of father and child and has shown that the *potestas–obsequium* polarity is inadequate as a sociological description of the dyad. The participation of Clitipho's mother in the decision about his marriage suggests that it is also misleading to focus solely on the father–child relationship, because fathers and children interacted within a larger context of family and household. The presence of slaves affected the expectations and experiences of fathers and children, just as it affected everything else in Roman society. The differentiation of children and slaves is the subject of the next chapter. With regard to the father–mother–children triad, the common characterization of the Roman family as patriarchal is misleading. From a legal point of view, the father–child bond was indeed patriarchal, but the husband–wife relationship (to which the term is usually applied in other societies) was certainly not in the classical era. By the end of the Republic, marriage *sine manu* appears to have been the norm, leaving fatherless wives with independent property rights. As a result, it is right to say that the *paterfamilias* had a monopoly

---

[110] Treggiari 1991b: 93.   [111] *Dig.* 23.2.22.   [112] Saller 1993.
[113] Volterra 1948.

over property in the *familia*, but wrong to say that he had a monopoly in the household. Just as the Roman father enjoyed leverage derived from his discretion in disposing of property, so did his wife, and the dynamics of influence would depend very much on the assertiveness and relative wealth of husband and wife.[114] That the women's property often gave Roman husbands an incentive to be attentive to their wives' wishes is attested by Papinian in connection with the legal rules against the exercise of undue influence on people drawing up their wills: "I replied that there was no crime in the case where a husband had intervened, not by force or trick, so that his wife would not add a codicil to her will when her sentiments changed against him, but, as usually happens, he soothed the offended sensibilities of his angry wife by husband's talk."[115]

The need to keep a wife with property in good humor must have tempered some husbands' arbitrary exercise of power over their children. After all, the wife's goodwill and money might be needed to dower a daughter or to support a son in his studies abroad. The significance of the mother's influence is highlighted by the negative case, the bad influence of the stepmother who diverted the goodwill of the father from her stepchildren to her own children.[116]

If a husband had reason to pay heed to a propertied wife's wishes, so also their children might find it as important to cultivate the favor of their mother as of their father. Following the acrimonious separation of his parents, young Quintus Cicero played a double game to keep his father and his mother happy; through his mother's goodwill he hoped for access to his uncle's money. Similarly, Cicero admitted after his divorce from the rich Terentia that it would be a good idea for Atticus to take young Marcus along to see his mother because "he has some interest in appearing to have wished to please her."[117] A century and a half later, Voconius Romanus was dependent on the generosity of his mother to meet the census requirement for a senatorial career.[118] The jurist Scaevola discusses a different situation: "A son who was accustomed to deal with his mother's property and used his mother's money with her consent to buy slaves and other property drew up bills of sale in his own name. He died in his father's *potestas*." The jurist gave the opinion that the woman could recover the property by an action on the *peculium* or to the extent of the father's enrichment.[119] Since Roman

---

[114] For a general statement on women's social power and testamentary rights, see Crook 1986a: 58. Dixon 1988 provides a systematic treatment of the authority of the mother.

[115] *Dig.* 29.6.3.

[116] *Dig.* 23.3.82, Proculus; 24.1.34, Ulpian, for dowry; Marcus Cicero's allowance came from dotal property, see above n. 98 for references; *Dig.* 5.2.4, Gaius, for the evil influence of the *noverca* (stepmother).

[117] *Att.* 13.38, 39, 41, 42 for Quintus; 12.28.1 for Marcus.   [118] Pliny *Ep.* 10.4.

[119] *Dig.* 24.1.58.2.

fathers clearly did not have a monopoly of financial resources in the family (as opposed to the *familia*), it would be unrealistic to impute to them a monopoly of leverage derived from property.

At the extreme, a mother (or other relative) could use her property posthumously to apply pressure to break a father's *potestas*. Both the literary and the legal sources provide examples of mothers bequeathing property to their children only on the condition that their fathers emancipate them.[120] Pliny describes with relish how his bête noir, Regulus, emancipated his son so that the boy could inherit his mother's estate and how Regulus then engaged in a disgusting show of obsequious indulgence toward his son so that the boy would name him heir.[121] No doubt most sons were not emancipated and few were cultivated by their fathers, but Pliny's story nevertheless illustrates the potential that a mother's wealth had for undermining paternal authority in the family, even if it was usually brought to bear in less extreme ways.

Conclusion

A survey of the non-legal evidence reveals that day-to-day behavior did not correspond to the abstract characterization of the Roman family as a paternal despotism. Is it true, as Morgan thought, that paternal power in Rome was so great that family life suffered under "an excess of domination"? Should we think of the Roman family as wholly asymmetrical, with fathers endowed with *potestas* on the one side, demanding total submission from their children constrained by *pietas* to obey on the other? Were the demands for filial obedience so severe that sons were driven to patricide? Were tension and violence between father and child a special characteristic of Roman culture?

In their nature, family relationships are bound to be asymmetrical, since the different members have different physical and mental capacities and needs through the life course. Undoubtedly, Roman family relationships were more asymmetrical and hierarchical than those characteristic of contemporary European societies. But were they more hierarchical than in other pre-industrial societies? How much of the hierarchical quality was a special cultural trait of the Romans and how much was a common characteristic of agricultural societies structured by private ownership of land? Definitive answers to such broad questions may not be possible, but several points from the preceding material are worth considering.

---

[120] *Dig.* 5.3.58, Scaevola; 29.7.6.pr, Marcianus; 35.1.70, Papinian; the father could refuse to emancipate and forfeit the bequest, Voci 1980: 46.
[121] *Ep.* 4.2, on which see Tellegen 1982: 63–67, who gives references to other examples.

(1) The Romans regarded filial obedience as natural, part of the *ius gentium*. Certainly, Romans were not unique in their inculcation of filial obedience. Whether they were less tolerant of disobedience than other pre-industrial societies is difficult to say. Against the legends of execution of sons for disobedience to the state, we have the stories of tolerance toward sons guilty of adultery with their stepmothers and the more ordinary accounts of fathers verbally chastizing wayward sons for spending too much on dogs, horses, and other luxuries.

(2) *Pietas*, the Roman family virtue, was not merely filial obedience, but more broadly affectionate devotion among all family members. Most of the *exempla* repeated to illustrate this virtue had nothing to do with filial obedience, and many had nothing to do with fathers. To be sure, *pietas* could be invoked by parents to claim submission from children, but it was also invoked to justify disobedience in the name of a higher family duty.

(3) If Roman law gave to fathers powers that were unusual on account of their lifetime duration, other aspects of law and social custom softened the impact of those powers. Sons and daughters in propertied families relied for resources on their mothers, who had a remarkable potential for financial independence, and on other relatives, as well as their fathers. Moreover, it was common in elite families for young adult sons to live outside the house and beyond the daily reach of their father's authority.[122]

(4) Whereas most sons lost their fathers before reaching adulthood, for other sons a living father hanging on to the family estate could be a source of tension. Far from being uniquely Roman, such tension has been widespread in European agrarian societies, arising from the fundamental problem of supporting more than one adult generation from a single, fixed patrimony.[123] In some societies it was customary for elderly fathers to retire and hand over the farm, but this practice (unusual in Rome, as far as the evidence goes) did not solve all the family problems, as a reading of some of the retirement agreements from modern European families shows. It was thought necessary by some fathers to specify, occasionally in minute detail, the basic foodstuffs and comforts that the son was obligated to supply down to the last pound of pork and pot of milk. The reason was that sons were thought capable of refusing even basic subsistence to retired parents. Further perspective on the Roman situation can be gained from later European tracts of advice on family life, which gave attention to the problem of hostilities between fathers and sons and how to avoid them. Clearly this has been a common problem in the history of the European family, with or without *patria potestas*. To quote D. Gaunt, "the problems of the unfriendliness

---

[122] Saller and Shaw 1984a: 137.
[123] The contrast here is with modern economies in which the primary form of individual capital is education, which is expandable rather than fixed.

between the generations seemed universal, from Lithuania to Finland and southern Germany."[124]

Was the father–son relationship in Rome peculiarly oppressive and hence peculiarly tense and violent, as one might think from Bodin's reference to magistrates "almost always occupied in punishing of such as had murdered their parents"?[125] The exaggeration is apparent. Of course, there were some instances of patricide, such as that of Macedo, which prompted the *Senatusconsultum Macedonianum* barring creditors from legal action to recover loans made to *filiifamiliarum* in anticipation of the death of their fathers.[126] On the other hand, Cicero could claim in his defense of Sex. Roscius of Ameria that "such an awful deed … has occurred so rarely, that if even the name of the crime was heard, it was counted as resembling a portent or prodigy."[127] Cicero's statement is tendentious, but must have appealed to the sense of social truth held by some of his listeners in court. That patricide occasionally happened there is no reason to doubt, but it has also happened in other societies, including contemporary America. Indeed Jean Bodin recalled two French instances, recent in his day, and for him the cause was obvious: French fathers, lacking the power of life and death over their children, had lost all authority and respect. Thus, to quote Bodin, "the health and life of parents [are] subject to a thousand dangers, except their children either by the fear of God, or the goodness of their own nature, be kept within the bounds of their duty."[128] Bodin's statement reminds us that general claims about the relation between authority and violence were and are ideologically charged. In truth, we have neither clear criteria by which to measure tensions within families, nor systematic evidence necessary to determine whether the Romans were more prone to extreme violence within the family than other peoples. The Roman attitude toward the less extreme violence of corporal punishment is the subject of the next chapter.

---

[124] Gaunt 1983: 261; a similar point has been made by others, e.g., Laslett 1977: 78; Held
        1982: 227–54; Comaroff and Roberts 1981: 189.
[125] A view recently echoed by Veyne 1978: 36, who suggests that Roman sons murdered
        their fathers with "surprising frequency."   [126] Daube 1947.
[127] *Rosc. Amer.* 38.   [128] *Commonweale* 24 I.

6

Whips and words: discipline and punishment in the Roman household

In his powerful interpretation of slavery in the American South, Eugene Genovese discusses the conception of the plantation as a "family, white and black." Like the *domus* in Rome, the planter's family encompassed his wife and children and his slaves, "and therein lay dangerous implications."[1] In suffering merciless beatings, the slaves "did not always fare much worse than the master's wife and children. From ancient to modern times we hear this theme. According to Roman legend, Manlius Torquatus beheaded his son, who had just returned victorious from combat, for breaking ranks."[2] Genovese quotes planters on the virtues of corporal punishment of children and slaves alike, concluding: "The slaveholders' vision of themselves as authoritarian fathers who presided over an extended and subservient family, white and black, grew up naturally in the process of founding plantations."[3] In the cultural matrix of the slave society, then, the categories of the master's slaves and of his children were assimilated, both subject to patriarchal authority enforced by violent coercion. As Genovese's reference to Manlius Torquatus shows, the stereotype of the Roman *paterfamilias* invites projection of such an assimilation back to Roman society, apparently confirmed by the similarities in the legal position of the slave and the *filiusfamilias*.[4]

Despite the law, the Romans did not assimilate children and slaves in their reflections on the nature of authority. Cicero, following Greek philosophers, wrote that "different kinds of domination and subjection (*et imperandi et serviendi*) must be distinguished." A father governs his children who follow out of readiness to obey (*propter oboediendi facilitatem*), but a master must "coerce and break (*coercet et frangit*) his slave" (*Rep.* 3.37). The primary

---

[1] 1972: 73.   [2] 1972: 73.   [3] 1972: 74.
[4] Watson 1987: 46–47. After noting the legal similarities, Watson adds: "It goes without saying that in practice sons and slaves would be treated very differently." In a paper on slaves in the household (1987b) I was tempted to argue for assimilation.

instrument deployed to "break" slaves in antiquity and later was the whip:
"Whipping was not only a method of punishment. It was a conscious device
to impress upon slaves that they were slaves."[5] This chapter will examine
how the whip was used in Roman society, particularly in the household, to
make distinctions of social status. The first section seeks to elucidate the
general meaning of whipping as a highly charged form of symbolic
behavior. The second presents a summary of the evidence for how the
application of the whip served to make status distinctions in public life
between the dominant honorable and the subservient honorless. The third
section will explore how associations with the whip in the wider cultural
matrix influenced Roman thinking about the discipline of children and slaves
within the household. We will find that classical Roman authors, far from
advocating the virtue of corporal punishment for children and slaves alike,
condemned the use of the whip on children precisely because it was
important to differentiate children from slaves.

The meaning of corporal punishment

In reading about the instruments of corporal punishment that were part of
a Roman's ordinary experience – spiked whips, clubs, racks, hot irons – a
modern is likely to react initially with revulsion.[6] Romans regularly *and
legitimately* inflicted on their fellow men corporal punishments that maimed
and even killed. It is important to move beyond fascinated horror at the
cruelty of Roman civilization in order to consider the fact that more was at
stake than raw physical pain: to the Romans the anguish was in significant
measure a result of a cultural construct, an insult to *dignitas*. Seneca describes
the slave whose sense of pride leads him to consider it better "to be beaten
with whips than with fists and thinks death and whips to be more bearable
than insulting words."[7]

The notions of honor and insult underlie much of the legal writing about
corporal punishment. Official exemption from beating is explicitly associated with honor by the jurists: "all who are exempted from beating with
rods ought to have the same *honoris reverentiam* as decurions have" (*Dig.*
48.19.28.5, Callistratus). The rules regarding the legal action for insult (*actio
iniuriarum*) illustrate how illegal beatings had to be considered in terms of
both the physical harm done and the infringement of honor. The *lex Cornelia*

---

[5] Rawick 1972: 59, quoted by Patterson 1982: 3.
[6] Wiseman 1985: 5–10 stresses the foreignness of the cruelty and gives additional
references to the torturer's instruments.
[7] *Constant.* 5.1: qui flagellis quam colaphis caedi malit et qui mortem ac verbera tolerabiliora
credat quam contumeliosa verba.

de iniuriis gave an action in three cases: *verberatio, pulsatio,* and entry into another's *domus* by force (*Dig.* 47.10.5.pr, Ulpian). According to the jurist Ofilius, the difference between *verberatio* and *pulsatio* was that the former was "with pain" (*cum dolore*) and the latter "without pain" (*sine dolore, Dig.* 47.10.5.1). *Pulsatio,* though causing no physical pain, nevertheless required compensation for the insult. Furthermore, in addition to the victim of a beating, those responsible for protecting him or her could bring an *actio iniuriarum* because of the diminution of honor suffered by those whose power was thus mocked. A *paterfamilias* could bring an action for the beating of his child or slave by a third party, and also for insults inflicted on certain others not in his *potestas,* such as his wife and daughter-in-law (*Dig.* 47.10.1.3, Ulpian). Since the law clearly demonstrates that beatings inflicted both physical pain and dishonor, the philosophers must have been arguing in vain against conventional values when they claimed that as unpleasant as beatings and mutilations were, they did not constitute true insults (*iniuriae*).[8]

The degradation and humiliation felt by a Roman who was struck by another may be illustrated with a few examples. Horace sneered at an upstart whose base status in the past was evoked by the characterization that he had been "beaten by triumviral whips."[9] Tacitus believed that Sejanus in his scheme to take the imperial throne chose to destroy Drusus first among members of the imperial family on account of Sejanus' undiminished anger over an earlier episode in which Drusus had lost his temper and struck Sejanus on the face (*os verberaverat*). Because of the insult to his honor – recall Seneca's freedman who preferred almost any punishment to being struck in the face – Sejanus set about revenging himself by cuckolding Drusus in the process of bringing his house to ruin.[10]

Why did the Romans regard beatings with such gravity? The answer lies partly in general considerations of social psychology and partly in the particular social milieu of the Roman empire. The sociologist Erving Goffman, in writing about deference, stressed "rituals of avoidance," by which he meant "those forms of deference which lead the actor to keep at a distance from the recipient and not violate what Simmel has called the 'ideal sphere' that lies around the recipient."[11] It was Simmel's view that "although differing in size in various directions and differing according to the person with whom one entertains relations, this sphere cannot be penetrated, unless the personality value of the individual is thereby destroyed. A sphere of this sort is placed around man by his honor. Language poignantly designates an insult to one's honor as 'coming too close'; the radius of this sphere marks, as it were, the distance whose

---

[8] Seneca *Constant.* 16.1–2, where Epicurus' view is also cited. See also Seneca *Ep.* 85.27.
[9] *Epod.* 4.11: "sectus flagellis triumviralibus." *Flagella* were thought particularly appropriate for slaves (see below, p. 138). [10] *Ann.* 4.3. [11] Goffman 1967: 62.

trespassing by another person insults one's honor."[12] Goffman's analysis of various kinds of everyday behavior suggests that the relative status of two parties in an interaction is asserted by the differential liberties they take in invading each other's private sphere, the party of higher status deserving the deference of greater distance. Goffman traces this phenomenon to a fundamental feeling "that the self is in part a ceremonial thing, a sacred object which must be treated with proper ritual care and in turn must be presented in a proper light to others."[13]

Considered in terms of violation of person, the Romans' attitude toward corporal punishment becomes intelligible: it was the grossest form of invasion and hence a deep humiliation. Furthermore, aspects of the ritual of infliction were designed to exacerbate the degree of invasion and degradation. Aulus Gellius offers three comparable accounts of beatings, from speeches by the elder Cato, Gaius Gracchus, and Cicero, in order to contrast the rhetorical power of three of the greatest Republican orators. All three condemn the arrogance of Roman magistrates in the strongest possible terms, employing certain common motifs. In each account, a Roman official ordered local notables to be led into a public place, to be stripped, and then to be beaten. It is difficult to imagine a greater violation of the personal sphere than to be exposed naked in front of peers and dependants and then to be reduced by the *virgae* (rods) to cry out in pain. Indeed, Cato emphasizes not so much the physical pain as the humiliation: "many men looked on. Who can bear this humiliation, this power, this slavery?"[14] It was Cato's view that the *verbera* (whips) exposed honorable men to "dishonor and the greatest humiliation, as their own people and many men look on."[15] The very fact that Gellius chose passages about whipping to illustrate highly emotive oratory is suggestive about the importance attached to it as a form of symbolic behavior.

The common elements in Gellius' stories – the stripping of the victims and the public nature of the punishment – can be found in other examples. In his anger at the insolence of two actors, Stephanio and Hylas, Augustus had them flogged before onlookers (Suetonius *Aug.* 45.4). After St. Paul had been stripped in Philippi and given a public beating, from which his citizenship should by law have protected him, he would not accept the permission of local officials to leave prison quietly, but demanded as a matter

---

[12] Simmel 1950: 321. In America today the common colloquial expression comparable to "coming too close" would be "in your face."

[13] Goffman 1967: 91. The elder Cato referred to beating of wife or children as a violation of the "sacred"; see below, p. 145.

[14] A. Gellius *NA* 10.3.17: "videre multi mortales. Quis hanc contumeliam, quis hoc imperium, quis hanc servitutem ferre potest?"

[15] A. Gellius *NA* 10.3.17: "dedecus atque maximam contumeliam, inspectantibus popularibus suis atque multis mortalibus."

of honor that they come to him personally to grant release (*Acts* 16:22–38).[16] The public nature of Roman punishment (in contrast, say, to our own) has been ascribed to the intention to deter other potential criminals who might be looking on and to the need to provide entertainment for urban crowds so fond of blood sports.[17] These motives are no doubt part of the explanation, but it should not be overlooked that another important aim was to punish the victim by public humiliation.

In the case of wrongful beatings, the connection between the public visibility of the *iniuria* and the degree of harm to a man's honor is made clear by the jurists. The rules concerning the *actio iniuriarum* included a distinction between an ordinary *iniuria* and one that was *atrox* or aggravated. An insult could be *atrox* by virtue of the place where it occurred: striking another person, even lightly, was considered *atrox* if publicly committed "in the theater or the forum" (*Dig.* 47.10.9.1, Ulpian; see also 47.10.7.8). The *actio iniuriarum* offered the victim at least a possibility of recompense. The humiliation must have been all the more acute in situations where a response was precluded by the position and authority of the one inflicting the beating. Of course, the archetypal case of the helpless victim in the ancient world was the slave.

The special potency for Romans of the symbolic act of beating hinged on its association with slavery. One of the primary distinctions between the condition of a free man and a slave in the Roman mind was the vulnerability of the latter to corporal punishment, in particular lashings at another man's private whim. Roman comedies portray the slave's mind as constantly preoccupied with corporal punishment through repeated references to past beatings and to the anticipation of future beatings. Much of the humor derives from the threat of infliction of pain on slaves; as Plautus has one of his characters say, a stock comic motif is the master lying in wait for his slave, ready to attack with goad or whip.[18] Slaves are addressed in the plays by variations on the word *verber*, with *verbero* or "whipping post" being common, and a slave might be regarded as "eminently beatable" (*verberabilissime*).[19] Indeed, the distinguishing marks of slaves in these plays are the scars on their backs from past whippings; conversely, the slave's metaphor for staying out of trouble was "to protect his back" from the

---

[16] Similarly, during the Second Punic War the Pontifex Maximus flogged to death a Vestal Virgin's lover in the comitia (Livy 22.57.3).

[17] MacMullen 1986: 159; Wiseman 1985: 6.

[18] *Pseud.* 1239–40; Segal 1968: 137–69. Parker 1989 discusses the nature of the humor and concludes that it lies in part in the displacement of punishment from son to slave; like other scholars, he views the son's position in legal terms (p. 243).

[19] E.g., Plautus, *Amph.* 180, 284, 565, *Asin.* 416, 669, *Cas.* 380, *Curc.* 196, *Mostell.* 1132, *Merc.* 189, *Pseud.* 1045; for *verberabilissime*, *Aul.* 633.

whip.[20] A free man, on the other hand, when threatened with a beating, could protest that he was not to be abused like a slave.[21]

Since *verbera* were fit for slaves, to suffer *verbera* symbolically put a free man in the servile category and so degraded him. Tacitus more than once employed the rhetoric of servitude and beatings in the words that he placed in the mouths of rebelling provincial subjects. For example, Calgacus' speech points to the violation of women, and the *verbera* and other insults (*contumeliae*) suffered by the Britons at the hands of Roman officials, as evidence that "Britain daily purchases its own slavery."[22] Though the basic distinction between slave and free with regard to corporal punishment declined in the second and third centuries, the classical jurists still referred to it in their arguments. Ulpian wrote that in some noxal actions, especially for capital cases and *iniuriae*, it was important that a slave be produced in the same legal condition that he committed the wrong and not be manumitted, because after manumission the culprit as a free man would be subject to one set of punishments, such as a fine, whereas a slave would give satisfaction *verberibus* (*Dig.* 2.9.5). More grimly, Callistratus wrote that those condemned to work in the mines must lose their freedom and become "penal slaves" (*servi poenae*), because "they are coerced by servile beatings" (*Dig.* 49.14.12). Callistratus' logic rested on the premise that "servile whippings" were not fit for free men.[23] *Servilia verbera* were particularly distinguished by the use of the *flagellum*, the whip. Beatings administered to free men by magistrates were typically done by *fustes* or cudgels, to judge by the juristic sources.[24] A beating with *flagella* was reckoned a harsh form of beating.[25]

In sum, whipping can be interpreted from several angles as a form of symbolic behavior in Roman culture. From the standpoint of the law, certain categories of men were legally subject to certain types of *verbera* from those with authority over them. To those who suffered other, illegal beatings legal recourse was offered. But the legal interpretation does not exhaust the social significance of beatings, as the jurists themselves recognized. The act of being whipped affected a Roman's status by detracting from his honor through public humiliation and association with the lowest human form in the Roman world, the slave. The seriousness of the matter was expressed by the jurist Macer in his statement that "a single blow of the cudgels is more serious than a monetary penalty."[26] Callistratus regarded petty traders as

---

[20] Plautus *Amph.* 446, *Men.* 970.   [21] Plautus *Asin.* 485, *Men.* 974, *Mostell.* 869.
[22] *Agr.* 31.2: Britannia servitutem suam cotidie emit.   [23] Millar 1984.
[24] *Dig.* 47.9.4.1, Paulus quoting Caracalla; 47.10.45, Hermogenianus; 48.2.6, Ulpian. In *Dig.*
48.19.7 Callistratus associates admonition with *fustes*, *castigatio* with *flagella*, and *verberatio*
with *vincula*.
[25] Horace *Sat.* 1.3.121. For a discussion of the varieties of corporal punishment, Garnsey
1970: 136–47.
[26] *Dig.* 48.19.10.2: "solus fustium ictus gravior est quam pecuniaris damnatio."

"lowly persons" (*viles personae*), being beaten by aediles policing the marketplace. Although not absolutely disqualifying them from admission to the curia, Callistratus thought that it would be "dishonorable" (*inhonestum*) to recruit for the curia such men who are "subject to the blows of whips" (*personas flagellorum ictibus subiectas, Dig.* 50.2.12). The centrality of the symbolism of the whip to Roman thinking about status is apparent in the jurist's choice of subjection to the magistrate's whip as the feature to characterize the baseness of a certain category of men.

"*Verbera*" in the public sphere

In a general discussion of modes of discipline in family history, Casey rightly points out that "it is inadequate to talk simply of indulgence or severity ... these attitudes have to be related to some kind of social context."[27] In Roman public life the whip was such a powerful marker distinguishing status that its connotations were bound to affect its meaning within the household. It is relevant, then, to inquire briefly in which social and political relationships authority was exercised with the aid of beatings. Two particular public roles made a free inhabitant of the empire vulnerable to beatings: service as a soldier and subjection as a provincial.

Corporal punishment to enforce discipline was part of the soldier's way of life. Among the punishments listed for soldiers by Modestinus is a beating with *fustes* (clubs), an appropriate punishment, for example, for a soldier falling out of line (*Dig.* 49.16.3.16). Of course, the traditional fate for a whole unit guilty of a more serious breach of discipline was decimation, the beating to death with *fustes* of every tenth man in the unit. The centrality of *verbera* to the experience of military life is brought out clearly in Tacitus' account of the rebellions of the troops at the beginning of Tiberius' reign.[28] Tacitus has both the Pannonian and Rhine legionaries angrily display their marks from whippings (*verberum notas*) as part of their complaint (*Ann.* 1.18, 35). In an attempt to restore discipline, the Pannonian commander Junius Blaesus ordered a few of the rebellious soldiers punished by *verbera* and imprisoned in the hope that the others would be terrified (*Ann.* 1.21). The most patent sign that the officers had lost control of the German legions was the reversal of roles dramatized by the beatings the soldiers gave to the centurions, "the oldest object of the soldiers' hatred" (*Ann.* 1.32).[29] That an author as

---

[27] Casey 1989: 153.
[28] Brunt 1988: 522 presents the evidence to suggest that a Porcian law may have exempted soldiers from the magistrates' *virgae*, but not from corporal punishment with *fustes*.
[29] In Pannonia the soldiers made a special effort to find and kill the centurion Lucilius, known as "cedo alteram" for his habit of breaking a switch over his soldier's back and then calling for another (*Ann.* 1.23).

sensitive to Roman institutions as Tacitus should use *verbera* as a recurrent motif in his story of the breakdown of military discipline and authority is evidence of its symbolic power in Roman thought.

The free, civilian population of the empire was divided into citizens and subjects, a distinction marked, respectively, by exemption from and subjection to magisterial beatings. The issue of the magistrate's authority to inflict beatings had long been a very sensitive one for the Romans. As a symbol of authority, on the one side, the magistrates with *imperium* had their *virgae*. On the other, a perennial issue for humble citizens was protection from the *virgae*. It was not just a matter of exemption from painful punishment for the plebs, but could be expressed rhetorically as an antithesis between *libertas* and subjection. The plebs symbolically established their *libertas* with the *lex Valeria* and in the second century the *leges Porciae*, which gave citizens the right of protection from the magistrate's arbitrary use of the rods.[30] The achievement of the Porcian laws was celebrated by the sponsor's descendants on the reverses of two late second-century coins, the first depicting the figure of Libertas crowned and the second showing a Roman citizen being protected by the cry of PROVOCO ("I appeal") from a magistrate's lictor wielding rods.[31] Later Cicero in his speech on behalf of Rabirius (12) could claim that the infliction of *flagella* and death on a citizen amounted to the loss of *libertas*. Later still, Tacitus pointed as a sign of the Germans' *libertas* to the fact that their kings and generals did not have the right to inflict *verbera* (*Germ.* 7). Historians of the Republic are so familiar with *provocatio* that it is easy to take for granted the connection between the freedom of citizens and the exemption from corporal punishment. But it was not at all inevitable that the connection should have been formulated in this way. In other ancient societies other issues – taxation or freedom to speak – rather than protection from corporal punishment have been central to the rhetoric about freedom.[32]

Without the citizen's protection of *provocatio*, provincials were subject to coercion (*coercitio*) at the hands of Roman officials. M. Marcellus chose precisely the flogging of a leading citizen of Transpadane Gaul as a dramatic symbol of his contemptuous rejection of Caesar's extension of political rights in the region. The action was regarded as extreme even by Marcellus' political allies.[33] The *Acts* narrative portrays Paul in the mid-first century

---

[30] Lintott 1972: 249; Brunt 1988: 331, 522–23.   [31] Crawford 1974: 293, 313–14.
[32] Brunt 1988: ch. 6 presents a detailed study of the Roman conceptualization of *libertas*. In his discussion of the Social War (128–29) Brunt argues that despite the play given in the ancient narrative to subjection to corporal punishment the *ius provocationis* should not be overrated as an Italian motive. This may be right, but it is still noteworthy that beatings were believed to be a highly emotive symbol of subjection. (In Diodorus Sic. 37.12.3, the actor Saunio is made to describe himself as "no Roman" but subject to the "rods" like other Italians.)   [33] Cicero *Att.* 5.11.2; Plutarch *Caes.* 29.2; Appian *BCiv.* 2.26.

after Christ being prepared as an ordinary provincial for a flogging until he protested his citizenship. By a process that cannot be clearly documented, this *civis/peregrinus* distinction ceased to be the dividing line between those exempt from and those subject to corporal punishment. The late second and early third century jurists, though they still referred to the citizen's right to *provocatio*, more often distinguished between the *honestiores*, who were exempt from beatings because of their honorable station, and the humble (*humiliores* or *tenuiores*), who are "accustomed to be beaten with rods."[34] As Finley notes, "it was an important symbol of the changing social structure and accompanying social psychology which set in by the second century AD that so-called humiliores were transferred by law to the 'slave category' in this particular respect."[35] The assimilation of categories went so far in the matter of legal punishment that Macer could reverse the direction of the association and write that "in the case of slaves it is to be observed that they are punished like humiliores."[36]

Because of its symbolic potency, Roman authors and orators could assume that an illicit beating would provoke the outrage of their audiences. Cicero repeatedly drew attention to Verres' abuse of flogging. A generation later Livy wrote that the first plebeian secession was prompted by the sight of an old man's back "deformed by the fresh marks of whippings" (*foedum recentibus vestigiis verberum*, 2.23.7). The historicity of the incident is open to doubt; what is important for my argument is that Livy expected his Augustan readers to find it plausible that one of the major events in Republican history started from *verbera*. Another generation later Tiberius horrified senators, according to Tacitus, by publicizing the fact that his grandson Drusus at the end of his life suffered "under the centurion's whip, in the midst of slaves' blows" (*sub verbere centurionis, inter servorum ictus, Ann.* 6.24). In his treatment of the civil wars Tacitus again uses role reversal to evoke the horror of the scene: after the Flavian army broke into Cremona, the soldiers greedily collected booty; some were not satisfied with what they could see and tried to discover the location of buried fortunes "by the whipping and torture of masters" (*verberibus tormentisque dominorum, Hist.* 3.33). The Romans accepted the whipping and torture of slaves as an ordinary part of life, but to have *verbera* and *tormenta* turned against the masters must have aroused the sort of nightmares that Seneca had referred to just a few years before this episode as the worst of a Roman's fears (*Ep.* 14.6).

[34] *Dig.* 48.19.28.1–5, Callistratus: "fustibus caedi solent." For *provocatio*, *Dig.* 48.6.7, Ulpian, but the right of *provocatio* is not in evidence in the Callistratus passage, nor in 50.13.5.2, also by Callistratus. On the difficulty of tracing the development, Garnsey 1970: ch. 5.

[35] Finley 1980: 95.

[36] *Dig.* 48.19.10.pr.: "In servorum persona ita observatur, ut exemplo humiliorum puniantur."

This brief description of *verbera* in the public sphere could be extended, but it is enough to show that whipping was a marker in Roman culture distinguishing social categories of domination and subjection.

The whip and discipline in the household

It would be easy to assume that in Roman society, where beating was a pervasive form of discipline, fathers regularly relied on the whip to discipline their children and their slaves alike. A close examination of the evidence, however, yields a different picture, rooted in the wider cultural associations of the whip.

That the *paterfamilias* had the legal right to apply the whip is beyond question, but what was the Roman attitude toward the use of the whip as a mode of discipline of children? There was no single attitude, but a discussion representing a range of views. Seneca in his work *On Anger* laid out the problem for parents (2.21). Their goal in child-rearing was to steer a middle course in order to avoid encouraging the child's temper and anger on the one hand, and to avoid blunting the child's native spirit (*indoles*), on the other. Treading the fine line between control and repression could be difficult: "the spirit increases by permissiveness and diminishes through slavery (*servitute*)." The child's spirit is led to the good by praise, which in excess may also produce insolence and bad temper. In governing the child, a parent should use a combination of the rein and the spur. "Nothing humiliating or servile should be endured by the child; never should it be necessary for him to beg." In games with peers he should not be defeated nor become angry; he should be praised for winning but should display restraint in victory. He should see his parents' wealth rather than be allowed to use it, and should not be spoiled by limitless gifts, but rewarded for proper behavior. In this passage there is no hint of corporal punishment from parents: the essential mode of socialization is the granting or withholding of praise. Elsewhere Seneca implies that physical punishment of children may be justified on the grounds that they do not understand reason (*Constant.* 12.3).[37]

Seneca's discussion of child-rearing should be interpreted in the context of an overtly hierarchical society. For elite parents the challenge was to imbue a child with a proper sense of his own *dignitas* — he was supposed to

---

[37] Evans 1991: 169 cites this passage as evidence that Roman fathers abused their children like their slaves. Seneca says that a wise man will apply *poena* (punishment) to children, just as he will beat a misbehaving animal. The word for beating (*verber*) is not actually applied to children and must be assumed. By general historical standards, Seneca's suggestion does not amount to child abuse.

win – and with the self-restraint to avoid taking advantage of that superiority to vent his anger. Slaves form the background to the discussion: on the one hand, the child must not be repressed by discipline to the point of servility or forced to beg in an undignified way; on the other hand, he must internalize a sense of self-control because as the head of a slave household he would come to enjoy arbitrary power over others. As for modes of punishment, whereas corporal punishment was appropriate for those incapable of reason, including young children, older children should be guided by the grant or withdrawal of praise or rewards. The goal of proper appreciation of *dignitas* and use of power sets the discipline of children apart from the coercion of honorless slaves.

The imperial tract on child-rearing ascribed to Plutarch, *De liberis educandis*, pushes the consequences of the distinction between honorable children and honorless slaves further. Philosophy teaches men proper conduct: "that one ought to reverence the gods, to honor one's parents, to respect one's elders, to be obedient to the laws, to yield to those in authority, to love one's friends, to be chaste with women, *to be affectionate with children, and not to be overbearing with slaves*" (10). Children and slaves are to be treated differently, as the advice against corporal punishment of children makes clear.

> Children ought to be led to honorable practices by means of encouragement and reasoning, and most certainly not by blows nor by ill treatment; *for it is surely agreed that these are fitting rather for slaves than for the freeborn*; for so they grow numb and shudder at their tasks, partly from the pain of blows, partly also on account of the hybris. Praise and reproof are more helpful for the freeborn than any sort of ill-usage, since the praise incites them toward what is honorable, and reproof keeps them from what is disgraceful. (12)

The means of socialization here, as in Seneca's *On Anger*, is a judicious mix of praise and criticism. Corporal punishment is eschewed precisely because it inculcates a servile mentality by treating children in a servile way.[38]

Words, not the whip, are the appropriate mode of treatment for the honorable freeborn in the household, just as in the public sphere. As Horace put it, "so [my father] was accustomed to shape me as a boy by words."[39] The traditional form of the words in Roman culture was the *exemplum* and the *sententia*. Horace's "best of fathers" (*pater optimus*) taught his son to avoid squandering his patrimony and to steer clear of prostitutes and adultery by holding up examples of vice (*exempla vitiorum*, 105–6). He

---

[38] This passage shows that the issues of *obsequium* and corporal punishment must be distinguished: it was possible to advocate authoritarian relationships based on respect for elders and yet condemn physical punishment.

[39] *Sat.* 1.4.120–21: "sic me formabat puerum dictis." Seneca *Ep.* 33.6 associates the *sententia* with the teaching of children.

sought to instill the habit of asking whether a course of action was "dishonorable" (*inhonestum*) or "disadvantageous" (*inutile*, 122–25). Whether these lines are autobiographical or derive from literary tradition matters little:[40] they show the ideal Roman father working through reasoned appeal to common interests, backed up by a stock of cautionary stories.

The distinction between words and the whip as modes of discipline for children and slaves was not some imperial relaxation of antique severity, but goes back as early as extant Latin literature. Many Roman comedies portray conflict between fathers and youthful sons (*adulescentes*), as fathers attempt to rein in their sons' passions and to guide them toward honorable and financially responsible behavior. In other words, these are stories about the socialization and discipline of youths. It is noteworthy, then, that fathers are never represented in comedies as beating or threatening to beat their sons.[41] In this respect, the contrast with the discipline of mischievous slaves is explicitly drawn. In Terence's *Heautontimorumenos*, the slave Syrus remarks to his master's son Clitipho on the consequences of being caught by the angry *pater*: "for you there will be words (*verba*); for this man [i.e., me] there will be a beating (*verbera*)" (356). Syrus expresses the distinction in modes of treatment as clearly and directly as possible. In different words the slave Geta in Terence's *Phormio* expresses the same idea to the disobedient son Phaedria: "you will hear complaints (*litis*); I will be hung up and beaten" (220–21). Similarly, in Plautus' *Mostellaria* the old man Simo imagines the consequences when the father Theopropides discovers that his son has sold the family's house for money to buy the freedom of his *amica*: the son is expected to receive a verbal dressing down (*increpare*), while the slave will get the whip (*flagrum*) or even worse (*crux*, 743–50). At the end of the play, father and son are reconciled, the father deciding that the son's shame (*pudet*) over the affair is punishment enough; but Theopropides threatens the slave with death by *verbera* (1154–65).[42]

The son's shame points to the general logic and values underlying the distinction in modes of punishment. The father hopes to instill in his son a sense of shame (*pudor*), so that the son will act honorably, whereas he must coerce his honorless slave. As Micio comments in Terence's *Adelphoe*, what distinguishes a father (*pater*) from a master (*dominus*) is that sons are taught to do the right thing "of their own volition" (*sua sponte*) whereas slaves do

[40] On the question, see Leach 1971.
[41] *Pace* Evans 1991: 185, no passage from the comedies cited shows a father beating his child.
[42] This contrast can also be observed in Plautus' *Bacchides*, where the slave expects rods (*virgae*) on his back, while the father protects his son from the *iniuria* of blows from the *magister*.

so out of fear (*metus*). Micio's foil, the severe father Demea, starts out believing that fear in a son is a good thing, but by the end of the play he is brought around to a moderate position: fathers should not be uniformly indulgent, but should "restrain, correct, and fall in with" (*reprehendere et corrigere et obsecundare*) their sons (989). That is, he advocates discipline but not corporal punishment or fear.

Derived from Greek New Comedy, these plays might be thought to represent new, more humane Greek values in contrast to traditional Roman severity. Or, it has been suggested, the humor lay in the displacement of the expected physical punishment from sons to slaves.[43] Against these interpretations stands the advice of the elder Cato, hardly a proponent of new Greek values, suggesting that the plays are expressing a standard cultural distinction between son and slave. Cato projected himself as a figure of traditional severity: flogging his domestic slaves for mistakes in the preparation and serving of dinner, Cato had a reputation for treating his slaves like beasts of burden and so earned Plutarch's disapproval (*Cato maior* 5.1, 21.3). Cato's discipline but not his violence extended to his wife and sons. Priding himself on being a good father and husband, Cato "was accustomed to say that a man who struck his wife or child laid hands on what was most valuable and sacred" (20.2). In this connection Cato remarked that the only commendable thing about Socrates was that he treated "kindly and gently" a difficult wife and stupid sons. This remark implies that Cato saw continuity in Greek and Roman values in the matter of paternal gentleness and restraint in the punishment of family members – a continuity that extended on to Plutarch, who approved of Cato's self-representation as father and husband, but not as master. Rather than an evolution from paternal severity to indulgence, the evidence suggests a continuing debate about how to manage the right balance, a debate based on the opposition between honorable children, for whom the shame of words was a recommended mode of discipline, and shameless slaves motivated by physical coercion. Some Roman authors preached restraint in the punishment of slaves, but none to my knowledge argued that slaves possessed a sense of honor that made corporal punishment wholly inappropriate.

That Cato, Seneca, and the author of the *De liberis educandis* accepted the same essential opposition between *dignitas* and *servitus*, and consequently between words and the whip, can be illustrated through a contrast with some later Christian statements on corporal punishment. Augustine taught that the head of the household had the duty to apply the whip to misbehaving members of the house "for their benefit ... For just as it is not

[43] Parker 1989.

an act of kindness to help a man, when the effect is to make him lose a greater good, so it is not a blameless act to spare a man, when by so doing you let him fall into a greater sin."[44] Augustine therefore preached that the father "who denies discipline is cruel ... When a father beats his son, he loves him."[45] No extant classical writer, as far as I am aware, advocated the value of the whip in such forceful terms.[46] Perhaps Seneca came closest in suggesting that it is the duty of a good parent to criticize and sometimes even to admonish with the whip a wayward son (*Clem.* 1.14.1), but he then added that only a bad father would whip constantly, even for trivial reasons (*Clem.* 1.16.3).[47]

The change in thinking about corporal punishment of children corresponds to an ideological shift in the fundamental polarity between honorable freeborn citizen and shameless slave. In Augustine's view, the condition of the son and the slave may be differentiated in regard to worldly goods, but in regard to the worship of God there is no distinction: since everyone sins, everyone is in servitude (*Civ. Dei* 19.15–16). Sin provides the imperative for corporal punishment, now a manifestation of paternal love, as never before. No one is exempt from the whip, on the logic presented in the *De liberis educandis* that beating is beneath the dignity of the free citizen. The argument in favor of the whip to save sinning children from damnation had a long history in later Christian Europe.[48] Yet against prescriptions in favor of corporal chastisement, Christian writers also saw the need for moderation; and in some Christian societies, as in classical antiquity, parents prized their children as continuations of themselves and so were loath to punish them.[49]

If classical writers offer a sense of how the corporal punishment of children fits into the broader cultural logic, they can give only a vague impression of the actual incidence of whipping.[50] By no means all Romans subscribed to the view that corporal punishment was altogether inappropriate for children. A grandfather in one of the elder Seneca's *Controversiae* points out that no one would question the propriety of him

[44] *Civ. Dei* 19.16: "pro eius ... utilitate ... Sicut enim non est beneficentiae adiuvando efficere ut bonum quod maius est amittatur, ita non est innocentiae parcendo sinere ut in malum gravius incidatur." On Augustine's thought about household order, see Shaw 1987b: 11. [45] *Sermones* 13.8.9 PL 39.111, cited by Eyben (1991): 134.
[46] Shaw 1987b. It is interesting that Wiedemann 1989: 28 has to look as late as a Benedictine rule on discipline for "the normal practice of a Roman household."
[47] The interpretation of this passage is problematic, because the passage is tendentious: Seneca must justify the use of physical coercion by the emperor who as *pater patriae* was certainly not going to give up the disciplinary use of force.
[48] Stone 1977: 167–69; Ozment 1983: 146–48. [49] Casey 1989: 153.
[50] Before ancient historians become too apologetic about the lack of statistical evidence, we should remember that contemporary statistics for child abuse are highly problematic, since increases may represent more incidents of abuse, or greater sensitivity in reporting, or both.

striking his grandson if the boy were naughty or behaving wildly in boyish pranks (*inter pueriles iocos*, 9.5.7). According to Cicero, if boys misbehave, they can expect to be corrected by their mothers and teachers "not only with words but also *verberibus*" (*Tusc.* 3.64). Several points may be suggested from this and other evidence for corporal punishment.

First, Roman authors do not discuss the issue in legal terms as the special prerogative or duty of the *paterfamilias*. The elder Seneca and Cicero indicate that mothers, grandfathers and teachers might strike a child to control his behavior.[51] The father was not the sole figure of discipline in a child's life.

Secondly, the physical punishment of children and slaves was differentiated in terms of age and severity. Just as the Roman male slave had to endure the epithet of *puer* or "boy" as long as he lived in slavery, so he was subject to the whip. Freeborn, citizen children were thought to outgrow physical punishment, even if they remained *in potestate*. The advocate of limited whipping, Seneca, thought that it was appropriate for children before they reached the age of reason.[52] In youth (*adulescentia*) children were thought to have acquired reason and a sense of honor that militated against corporal punishment. Among the bits of wisdom of the mid first-century BC satirist Publilius Syrus is the statement that "by reason, not by force, should youth be mastered."[53] Quintilian asked his readers to imagine the insult that a youth would feel from a whipping received after childhood (*Inst.* 1.3.14). Quintilian's later remarks about P. Servilius Isauricus (consul in 48 BC) imply that the whipping of a *filiusfamilias* after childhood was in fact rare in elite society: M. Caelius and Cicero ridiculed Isauricus by alluding to his having been beaten once by his father, presumably after childhood (*Inst.* 6.3.25, 48). Quintilian regarded Cicero's jest as so humiliating as to be almost indecent (*scurrile*). While the beating was within the father's power, it must have been highly unusual, if Isauricus could be singled out by Cicero and Caelius for derision by mere allusion.

The ranges of punishment applied to children and slaves were overlapping but different. Both might be beaten with rods, but *pietas* was regarded as a moral constraint on paternal punishment of children. Too severe punishment of a son was construed as *saevitia* (savagery) and labelled *impius*.[54] On the other hand, the slave was vulnerable not only to the whip but also to a series of more drastic punishments. Because torture of slaves is usually treated in the context of legal procedures, it should be stressed that torturers (*tortores*) were also available for private hire to masters – a striking indication of the

---

[51] Dixon 1988: ch. 7.
[52] Néraudau 1984: 22–25 discusses the age classifications in Roman culture.
[53] 627: "Ratione non vi vincenda adulescentia est."
[54] In Livy's tale of the conquest of Gabii (1.53.8), the son of Tarquinius Superbus appeals for refuge from his father's *saevitia* and from his *crudelibus atque impiis suppliciis*.

severity of the punishments inflicted on slaves. Administering a brutal beating could be an exhausting job better left to professionals.[55] So Trimalchio is depicted as having two *tortores* on staff ready to punish the inept cook. For Juvenal, a humorous way of evoking a mistress' special cruelty is to allude to her keeping a *tortor* on annual retainer (6.480). Just like other artisans, the *tortor* had his place of business, where the variety of the tools of his trade could be counted on to chill his prospective victim to the bone.[56] The business of the *tortor* – one of the least attractive among many unattractive features of Roman civilization – cannot be discounted as a figment of literary imagination: the jurists discuss the torturer's liability for exceeding the orders of the master (additional evidence that they were available for private hire), and an inscription from Puteoli lists prices for a torturer's services.[57]

Thirdly, Petronius' and Juvenal's *tortores* are part of a literary topos of violence toward slaves. From 200 BC Roman audiences and readers were treated to scenes featuring the whipping of slaves and were expected to laugh. Reference to the stringing up and beating of old female slaves was meant to be funny, to judge from the banter in Plautus' *Truculentus* (775–82) and *Aulularia* (48). A slave need not commit any fault, however slight, to receive *verbera* from an irritable master taking out his or her frustrations on "whipping boys," in the literal sense. In Plautus' *Poenulus* the young man Agorastocles repeatedly beats his slave, with the excuse that he is frustrated in pursuing his love and so not in control of himself (146, 410, 819). Juvenal portrays a slighted wife as a much more vicious character who has her slaves savagely whipped as she transfers the target of her anger from her husband to her helpless servants (6.481). In literature and, more generally, in life, the whip was inextricably linked to the life of the slave. Hence manumission was conceived of as freedom from the cross and *verbera*.[58]

By contrast, parental whipping of children was not a Roman literary topos, as whipping by the teacher (*magister*) was. Martial jokes about the complaints of neighbors living next to a school room: the sounds of students being beaten awakens them annoyingly early in the morning. Juvenal represents even the greatest ancient warrior, Achilles, as afraid of the *virga magistri* (7.210). I know of nothing comparable for fathers and children. St. Augustine's vivid description of episodes from his childhood suggests that the student-beating topos was not far removed from real

---

[55] For the motif of wearing out the torturer, Cicero *Clu.* 177; Seneca *Ep.* 66.18, 21, 29.

[56] Juvenal 6.O29 refers to the "pergula tortoris" summoning the *ancillae*; for the fear evoked see Seneca's comment (above, p. 134).

[57] *Dig.* 47.10.15.42, Ulpian citing Labeo; *AE* 1971, 88 and 89, with HS 4 listed as the fee for a whipping. Additional evidence can be found in Cicero's account in the *Pro Cluentio* (177) of Sasia having her slaves put to the torture before town notables.

[58] Cicero *Rab. perd.* 16.

experience: he lived in dread of the whip of his *magister*, the regular punishment for poor performance (*Confessions* 1.14), but nowhere hints that his own parents beat him. His resentment toward them arose from their indifference to the pain inflicted by the *magister*.[59]

Augustine's account raises the issue of the relevance of literary topos to social practice. Should any significance be attached to the contrast between the beating topos for students and slaves, and the absence of such a topos for children? Clearly, a topos cannot be taken as direct evidence for daily practice. Some classical topoi are contrived, artificial literary products, far removed from social realities. This is surely not the case with the beating of slaves, whose presence and motivation were problems of daily life in propertied households. I would suggest that, like modern stereotypes, the beating topos may be considered a representation and reinforcement of a standard association in Roman culture. As such, it was a part of Roman reality insofar as it contributed to the Roman world view, regardless of its actual, statistical accuracy (which neither the Romans nor we can possibly know). As a part of the world view, the topos informed behavior in a way which may be illustrated through Tacitus' account of C. Petronius' final hours. Having been ordered by Nero to commit suicide, Petronius was determined to maintain a normal life until his death. In his typically frivolous way, Petronius continued his daily routine after slitting his wrists. Instead of weighty discussions about the immortality of the soul, he invited friends to offer light verse. To his good slaves he gave rewards; his bad slaves received *verbera*. After a meal he retired for sleep and died (*Ann.* 16.19). Petronius ended the day with a calling to account of his slaves and the punishment of the bad slaves with the whip – the sort of routine alluded to by Seneca (*Ep.* 122.15). Is this element of Tacitus' account based on topos or reality? It is impossible to know, or even to separate the two in this instance.

Whether statistically frequent or not in reality, the beating of slaves recurs as a topos in moralizing discourse. In his famous Epistle about the treatment of slaves Seneca deplores the fact that even an involuntary sound such as a cough from a slave will draw a beating for disturbing the master's dinner (*Ep.* 47.3). Elsewhere Seneca criticizes the short temper of a master who has slaves whipped for talking during dinner or for giving the master an insolent look (*Ira* 3.24–25). Perhaps most interesting for our purposes is Juvenal's Fourteenth Satire. Its theme is the bad example that parents so often set for

---

[59] The association of classical education with the whip had a long tradition in later Europe, leading John Locke to ask: "Why ... does the learning of Latin and Greek need the rod, when French and Italian need it not? Children learn to dance and fence without whipping; nay arithmetic, drawing, etc., they apply themselves well enough to without beating." Quoted by Stone 1977: 166. Sir Hugh Lloyd-Jones pointed out to me that in his generation boys were whipped at school for misplacing the accent in names in Roman comedy.

children. Parents are criticized for preaching chastity to their children but setting an example by adultery. As one of the bad examples, Juvenal portrays a master of a household, with *virga* in hand, motivating his slaves to clean house in preparation for a guest (14.63). The father is satirized for preaching tolerance and gentleness, and then openly taking sadistic pleasure, in his son's presence, from the groans of slaves under the whip (14.15–24). In modern debates over corporal punishment a comparable argument against spanking children is made by those who claim that it sets an example of violence for the child. But Juvenal's worry is different in a revealing way: the son is brutalized, not by his own suffering, but by watching his father inflict pain on slaves.[60] Thus, the topos of slave-beating contributed to the Roman perception of moral realities and formed a starting point for moral maxims and generalizations. Tacitus apparently accepted the general truth of the frequent beating of slaves: among his oppositions between German virtues and Roman decadence is the German restraint in flogging their slaves only rarely and not in matters of routine discipline (*Germ.* 25).

The whipping *magister* topos had enough substance that Quintilian thought the practice worth criticizing. In a lengthy discussion of the habit of student-beating in the schools, Quintilian argues against its pedagogical value: "I disapprove of flogging, although it is the received practice and meets with the acquiescence of Chrysippus, because in the first place it is a disgraceful form of punishment and fit only for slaves, and is in any case an insult, as you will realize if you imagine its infliction at a later age. Secondly, if a boy is so insensible to instruction that reproof is useless, he will, like the worst type of slave, merely become hardened to blows. Finally there will be absolutely no need of such punishment if the magister is a thorough disciplinarian" (*Inst.* 1.3.13). In his practical advice Quintilian here echoes the fundamental polarity found in the *De liberis educandis* between physical punishments suitable for slaves and verbal reproof appropriate for free children.

In the matter of beating, topos coincided with, and reinforced, perceptions of daily realities. Student-beating was a literary topos and also conventional practice; by contrast, the beating of sons and daughters was not a topos, was infrequently mentioned in literature, and was not regarded as a standard practice or a general moral problem. Indeed, Quintilian, who would not countenance the use of the whip on children, perceived the moral problem for parents to lie in overindulgence of their children (*Inst.* 1.2.6–8) – a view shared by Tacitus (*Dial.* 29).[61]

---

[60] In contrast to the abundant evidence for masters' sadism toward slaves, I know of no comparable evidence for parents' sadistic treatment of children.

[61] Again, lest this be interpreted as an imperial development, it should be noted that in Plautus' *Bacchides* the indulgent father is portrayed as protecting his son from the whip of

Conclusion

The opposition between *pater* and *dominus* was a pervasive and powerful one in Roman culture. While the actual behavior of fathers and masters varied, with some fortunate slaves enjoying kindly treatment, that should not be allowed to obscure the basic distinction in types of household authority drawn by Cicero. The master's authority had to be coercive (to "break" the slave), because the master–slave relationship was inherently exploitative. The servile spirit was one motivated by grudging fear, goaded by the lash; the servile back was marked with scars from past whippings. This was not the mentality that Roman writers wished to instill in their children. The extant literature presents a spectrum of advice on child-rearing, some authors proscribing physical punishment altogether and others recommending words and occasional corporal punishment for younger children. The aim was to imbue the child with a sense of both his honorable position and the shame that would contribute to self-restraint. It was argued by some that physical coercion was not necessary for children, because reason could show the commonality of interests of parent and child. The child stood to inherit his parents' position and wealth; therefore, their relationship was, in the end, not necessarily exploitative but could be based on reciprocal duty and affection, or *pietas*.

That this distinction was widely accepted is suggested by the way in which the emperors manipulated it. In claiming the role of *pater patriae*, they were representing themselves as non-exploitative figures of benign authority looking after the best interests of their subjects. The subjects were bound to obey, just as children naturally (in the Roman view) obeyed their parents. The "good emperors" explicitly or implicitly eschewed the role of *dominus*.[62] This ideology served the emperors well insofar as it denied exploitation, even though in reality their subjects could not hope to succeed to the throne, as a son could expect to succeed to his father's position and estate. Despite the flaws in the metaphor, the *pater–dominus* opposition ran deep in Roman thinking, so that even after Diocletian advertised himself as *dominus*, the image of father continued to provide the positive pole of evaluation. Aurelius Victor described how Diocletian portrayed himself as

the pedagogue, who criticizes such indulgence as a modern decline, which is also part of the topos (437–47). On paternal indulgence, see Eyben 1991: 125–36.

[62] The contrast between *pater* and *dominus* is explicitly drawn in regard to the emperor by, e.g., Pliny *Pan.* 2.3, and Dio Chrysostom 1.22. If the paternal image had been as oppressively negative as some historians have suggested, the emperor's choice of metaphor would make no sense. That the polarity was a commonplace by the beginning of the Principate is suggested by its use in Livy's early narrative to contrast the *lenior* (gentler) consul behaving as a *parens* with the tyrannical consul behaving as a *dominus* (2.60.3).

more than a citizen by his extravagant clothing. "He first after Caligula and Domitian required that he be publicly addressed as *dominus*, and be revered and spoken of as *deus* ... Yet these things in Diocletian were overshadowed by other good qualities; and for this very reason, although he demanded to be called *dominus*, he acted as a *parens*" (*De Caesaribus* 39).

The *pater–dominus* opposition was a significant element of the dominant ideology, rooted in experience and influencing practice. Important as it was, the opposition was also limited in gender and status. The words *liberi* and *filii* in discussions of child-rearing are frustratingly ambiguous: they may refer to daughters as well as sons (as the jurists remind us), yet I know of no clear evidence about corporal punishment of freeborn daughters. The *iniuriae* to women mentioned in the *Digest* are mainly sexual in nature. Slave women were certainly subject to the whip and to sexual abuse as slaves without honor to protect them.

The terms of the discussion about discipline would seem to apply mainly to the elite – the men most preoccupied with honor. In the public sphere only the privileged among the free population (whether citizens or *honestiores*) were exempted from the whip. Whether honor played a formative part in thinking about corporal punishment in the houses of craftsmen and peasants is impossible to know, and facile assumptions should be avoided. Seneca's comment about the freedman insistently struggling for his honor is a reminder that people in danger of being denied may strive particularly hard to assert their honor: the influence of the slave context on cultural categories and moral values was not limited to slave households. Scattered evidence shows that poor freeborn children did suffer corporal punishment as apprentices, but then their wealthier counterparts also suffered under the whip of the *magister*. Augustine wrote that "children are compelled, by dint of painful punishments, either to learn a craft or to acquire a literary education" (*Civ. Dei* 21.14). Wealthier fathers were presumably better placed to protect their children, but Augustine's father chose not to do so.

Ultimately, we cannot know in detail how the free–slave polarity influenced daily behavior in families across the social pyramid. I would suggest, however, that the law granting the *paterfamilias* powers of nearly limitless coercion over his children is an inadequate guide to Roman family relations. In writing about socialization of children, Roman authors do not generally present discipline as a matter of physical coercion regulated by law; rather, they consider much the same range of methods and punishments as can be found in later eras. The stress in Roman texts from the second century BC through the second century after Christ is on reasoned words – *exempla* and *sententiae* – and the aversion to use of the servile whip on children was perhaps more pronounced than in later, Christian literature. Close examination of the evidence for corporal punishment suggests, once again, that there is no strong evidence for holding up Roman fathers as a paradigm of brutal severity. In all likelihood the Romans, in drawing the line between punishment and abuse, accepted more severe physical punishment than we would today, but no more severe than later Europeans.

PART III

The devolution of property in the Roman family

To translate *paterfamilias* as "head of the household" is to capture only a part of its semantic range. For modern students of Roman society the term evokes that most powerful image of the Roman family, the authoritarian father exercising autocratic control over the members and property of his house. The classical Romans, however, more often used the term to mean simply "property owner." The opposition between the *bonus* and *malus paterfamilias* involved a judgment about estate management: whereas the *malus paterfamilias* handled his property carelessly,[1] the *bonus paterfamilius* diligently managed his patrimony and came to represent a legal standard of sound administration in juristic thought.[2] Although classical prose authors frequently use *paterfamilias* without any thought of a family, for fathers the responsibilities for family and property were closely linked. In a society in which property was essential to the well being and status of the family, good husbandry was among the most important duties to the generations to come. Seneca expressed the ideal succinctly (*Ep.* 64.7): "Let us act as the *bonus paterfamilias*. Let us increase what we received. Let that inheritance pass enlarged from me to my descendants."

Seneca's words make the matter of transmission of property to the next generation sound simple, but it was not. For those Romans who made use of the written wills and dotal pacts available in law, nothing was automatic. Decisions had to be made in the face of unpredictable mortality and in the context of a legal system that permitted divorce and gave the right to own property to wives but not to adult children *in potestate*. The chapters of Part III aim to delineate three basic aspects of the transmission of property within the family: strategies of succession, guardianship of underage heirs, and dotal exchange. Inheritance and dowry were the two primary vehicles for

---

[1] Seneca *Ben.* 4.27.5; 4.39.2.
[2] Valerius Maximus 8.13.1; Pliny *Ep.* 7.25. On *diligentia* and the *bonus paterfamilias* in law, see Buckland 1963: 556.

transfer of the patrimony to the next generation; guardianship was an institution intended to protect the patrimony until the heir came of age.

Sources.[3] The Roman social historian studying transmission of property between generations has a peculiar set of sources from which to work: an assessment of what follows must be colored by an awareness of the limitations of those sources. No archives of testamentary or dotal documents have survived from the empire. A few Roman documents related to inheritance, guardianship, and dowry have been preserved on papyri found in the eastern empire, mainly Egypt. It would be rash to claim that these documents are representative of practices across the empire (or even in Egypt), yet they illustrate ways in which citizens outside the elite orders and far from Rome deployed Roman legal instruments. From Italy and the western provinces fragments of testaments have been preserved in inscriptions, but nearly all are concerned with testators' instructions concerning funeral arrangements. An exception is the famous will formerly attributed to Dasumius: only fragments of the long inscription have survived, and recent discoveries have undermined confidence in restorations that would reveal the testator's identity and full intentions.[4]

The historian is left with legal sources, rich in material about inheritance, guardianship and dowry, and scattered comments in literature. Among the legal sources, the juristic writings fall into several categories. First and best known perhaps are the two textbooks, the *Institutes* of Gaius (mid second century after Christ) and of Justinian (nearly four centuries later). The *Institutes* offer a set of rules, and as such they offer more insight into Roman law as a system than into the ways in which it was brought into play. Nevertheless, Gaius' *Institutes* provide an important landmark for judging how far legal developments had progressed by his day. A better source for understanding the uses of legal instruments is the *Digest*, a compilation of excerpts from the treatises of the classical jurists, especially those of the second and early third centuries. The excerpts go well beyond the textbook rules, giving opinions about real cases and imagined scenarios. Sometimes the real cases can be distinguished by the specificity of names and circumstances, but often the distinction between real and imaginary cannot be clearly made – a problem for the historian more interested in social practices than in the jurists' dialectical reasoning. The historian can take some comfort in the comment of Celsus that "the law ought to be related to those things which happen often and easily rather than those which occur very rarely" (*Dig.* 1.3.5). Even imaginary cases can be valuable to the historian interested in the possibilities made available by the law and in the situations that the jurists thought worth discussing.[5]

---

[3] For a more detailed description of the sources of law, see Buckland 1963: ch. 1.
[4] Eck 1978; Champlin 1986.   [5] Boyer 1965: 336.

The jurists were interested in common occurrences among the propertied classes. What proportion of the population that encompassed cannot be known. D. Daube's assertion that nine-tenths of the population were more or less propertyless seems extreme, and many of the cases in the *Digest* and the few surviving documents concern modest sums rather than senatorial fortunes.[6]

One other caution about the *Digest*: the procedure of excerpting means that the passages are out of context. How far Justinian's compilers distorted their excerpts or interpolated new phrases to suit their own Byzantine interests is a subject of debate among historians of Roman law. In the earlier part of the twentieth century, infelicitous usage or a mistake of logic constituted adequate grounds for marking a passage as interpolated. Now students of Roman law are prepared to salvage these passages in the belief that disjointed texts could be the result of abbreviation rather than change of the classical texts. Yet D. Johnston has warned against too easy an acceptance of the texts as genuinely classical, since some clearly were altered to take account of later changes in law. Imperial rulings preserved in the Theodosian and Justinian Codes of the fifth and sixth centuries, respectively, may help the historian to identify significant legal developments in the later empire which might have been retrojected into the classical materials. Unfortunately, there are no decisive grounds for accepting or rejecting the authenticity of many passages in the *Digest* attributed to classical jurists, and the arguments for and against become circular.

Another means of assessing the juristic writings is to look to non-legal sources. Roman literature, especially the letters of Cicero, Pliny and Fronto, contains numerous passing references to, and the occasional discussion of, wills, legacies, dowries, and guardianship. These authors were from, and wrote for, the narrow circles of the imperial elite, and yet after allowing for their special point of view they provide valuable evidence to compare law and practice. Orators like Cicero, Pliny, and Fronto spoke in court about matters of family property and had reason to be informed about the law. Although there is not enough literary discussion to make systematic comparison possible, a recent legal analysis of the younger Pliny's comments about succession finds no glaring contradictions with what is known of the law circa AD 100.[7]

Law and social practice. Since the sources for the Roman empire are so heavily juristic, not archival documents or court records, it is crucial to reach

---

[6] Daube 1965, against which see Crook 1973.
[7] Tellegen 1982. Tellegen's optimistic conclusion about Pliny's legal knowledge should be tempered by recognition that Pliny's discussions of cases are never complete or precise enough, and our knowledge of the law of succession circa AD 100 is not exact enough, to permit detailed comparison.

some preliminary theoretical understanding of the relation between the jurists' rules and principles, and social practice. The following remarks will no doubt be obvious to lawyers, but it may be worthwhile to draw to the social historian's attention some of the views and assumptions of those who have written about Roman law and society. In this regard there is much to be gained from H. L. A. Hart's *The Concept of Law* which presents a critique of the understanding of law as "elements of commands and habits."[8] Since "commands" and "habits" seem to underlie much of the social historian's unexpressed concept of law, Hart's argument deserves our attention.

Law is often conceived as a system of restraints on behavior, which some philosophers have tried to reduce to a set of coercive orders.[9] The statement, in a recent, valuable treatment of the position of women in Roman law, that law "is about what people may or may not do, not what they actually do" is likely to be understood in this way.[10] The point seems to be that law is a body of rules which people may or may not obey. As will be seen, this concept accounts for parts of the Roman law of succession, dowry and guardianship, but not most of it.

If law embodies a society's "habits," then Roman law can be interpreted as a guide to Roman mores. A. Momigliano advocated this view in 1966 when he congratulated a gathering of Roman lawyers and historians on overcoming the disciplinary boundaries separating them. It was only fitting, since "a large part of what is called the sociology of the ancient world is in fact custom or law, seen in a synchronic rather than a diachronic arrangement."[11] It is true that jurists sometimes sought to interpret legal instruments in terms of the linguistic usage and social practices typical of the parties involved, and in doing so offer valuable insights into the expectations shared by the elite.[12] Yet Momigliano's assertion cannot be accepted at such a high level of generality, since it is possible to find in the evidence for Roman succession numerous instances of disparities between law and practice, or even between legal prescriptions and social norms.

In the face of the disparities, the notion of law as "habits" can be saved by seeing law as gradually responding to prevailing attitudes and practice: the law "therefore gives a general guide to social standards."[13] The disparities provided the impetus, after a lag time sometimes measured in centuries, to change the law to conform to new mores. This approach is attractive because in numerous areas of Roman law it is possible to find general legal rules anticipated by individual behavior and social values. The legal instruments and rules regarding the transmission of family property can be seen as evolving over the centuries of the empire in this way. But

8 Hart 1961: 18.   9 Hart 1961: 27ff.   10 Gardner 1986: 3.
11 Momigliano 1966: 242.   12 Boyer 1965: 401.   13 Dixon 1988: 41.

again this is only part of the story: some laws were issued by Republican assemblies or emperors in attempts to turn the tide of mores viewed as deleterious.[14]

Moreover, the most notable feature of the Roman law of succession and dowry is that it did not prescribe or allow for only one pattern of behavior, but presented an array of instruments and rules to allow citizens to pursue an almost infinite variety of goals. For this reason, D. Daube, M. Corbier and others have interpreted Roman testamentary law as liberating Romans to disperse their estates outside the family if they wished. But as Corbier also stressed, the testamentary freedom enjoyed by classical Romans was considerably restrained by social pressures and goals.[15]

It would be possible to press this point further and to argue that in the face of social pressures and custom the law had little impact on the way people behaved and so is irrelevant to the concerns of the social historian. The legal historian Jolowicz expressed just this view on wills and guardianship in Greek-speaking Egypt: the Greeks were perfectly happy to accept fluid informality and ignore legal forms. But in his view the correspondence between law and behavior in the Roman world was much closer, because "the Romans, being lawyers, could not rest satisfied with such a position."[16] An assertion based on such a stereotype may not seem very convincing, but extreme skepticism about the influence of law on social practice is unwarranted in the case of the Romans. Some areas of the western empire and some strata of the population undoubtedly remained unaffected by Roman law. There were also spheres of daily life where formal powers in law, such as the father's right to execute his child, had little practical bearing on behavior. Then as now, however, there were certain crises or transitions in life in which law and legal documents were expected to come into play, the most important of those being the transfer of property at marriage and divorce, and after death. The separation of husband's and wife's property, and the ease of divorce with the prospect of restoration of the dowry, made it prudent to document the exchange of assets upon marriage. Propertied Romans clearly believed that dotal agreements and wills would determine or at least influence outcomes during these transitions – hence their creativity in developing legal instruments to guide their property into the desired hands upon specified future conditions.

Although some attention will be given to "law as restraint" and "law as freedom" and "law as reflection of mores" in Part III, the emphasis will be on the laws of succession and dowry as instrumental. Hart noted that "such laws do not impose duties or obligations. Instead, they provide individuals with facilities for realizing their wishes, by conferring certain legal powers

---

[14] Ancient doubts about the efficacy of such laws may be found in Tacitus *Ann.* 3.52–55.
[15] Daube 1965; Corbier 1985: 520.   [16] Jolowicz 1947: 88.

upon them to create, by certain specified procedures and subject to certain conditions, structures of rights and duties within the coercive framework of the law."[17] The reference to "realizing wishes" may appear similar to Corbier's interpretation of testamentary law as potential freedom from social norms, but there is more to it. The *Digest* illustrates the ingenious use of legal instruments not only in pursuit of freedom from social norms but perhaps more often *in strategies to cope with various contingencies on the way to meeting social norms*. In this sense, the law is indeed about "what people actually do" precisely because it is among the institutions that enable them to pursue their interests. It is that enabling capacity that explains why Babatha, a Jewish woman in the newly annexed province of Arabia, was so quick to adopt Roman forms and institutions in an effort to influence the guardians of her son by her first husband.[18] Consequently, the ways in which propertied Roman citizens did and did not manipulate their flexible legal instruments have much to tell us about their principal concerns and aims in the transmission of property from one generation to the next.

[17] Hart 1961: 27.
[18] Goodman 1991: 171. For more on the Babatha case, see ch. 8 below.

7

Strategies of succession in Roman families

After young Calpurnia's miscarriage, Pliny wrote as a concerned husband to her grandfather, Calpurnius Fabatus, to soothe his disappointment at being deprived of *posteri* (descendants) late in life: "You do not desire great-grandchildren more passionately than I desire children, to whom I expect to leave, from my side of the family and from yours, an easy path to honors with names widely known and ancestral masks of respectable age" (*Ep.* 8.10.3). Fronto two generations later expressed a similar hope for posterity from the marriage of his daughter. The concern for posterity and the reference to *imagines* (death masks) may summon up notions of lines of descent through the generations. The difficulties of successfully planning male lines of descent have been elucidated: in order to have male descendants with property to maintain their status, families had to try to strike a delicate balance between bearing too many children and bearing too few.[1] A Roman father producing many was more likely to have male heirs to succeed him, but also to have to divide his property in a partible system among so many heirs that each would be left with too little to maintain the family's status; a father producing two or three children lessened the risk of fragmentation of his estate, but also was unlikely to have a son to succeed him. The unpredictability of high mortality often spoiled the most careful strategy to leave one and only one male heir to perpetuate the family name with its splendid patrimony intact. Pliny and Calpurnia died before having heirs (though old Fabatus died too soon to know that); Fronto, though his first four children died, was more fortunate with his fifth, a daughter who bore a grandson who brought distinction to the orator's cognomen with a consulship.

The Roman law of succession provided testators with a remarkable array of options in distributing their property, unstructured by conventions of

---

[1] Goody 1976; Hopkins 1983; Corbier 1990.

primogeniture or ultimogeniture. Though not wholly unconstrained, testators could use intricate written legal instruments in pursuit of widely varied ends. Historians have supposed that Romans employed these flexible instruments in strategies to achieve the glory of male descendants through the generations, in the way English noblemen used perpetual entail.[2] At first glance, it would seem that Roman aristocrats were especially well supplied with the means to success in this endeavor: not only did they have the legal power to dispose of three-quarters of their patrimonies in whatever way seemed best, but they also possessed the means to construct and dissolve kinship ties through adoption and emancipation and through divorce and remarriage, with a freedom quite remarkable by later European standards.[3] Given the possibilities for overcoming the natural obstacles to a male line of descent, the Roman elite should have been more successful than their counterparts in later eras. But, in fact, senatorial families of the early empire were conspicuous for their failure to perpetuate their families in the highest ordo – much less successful than even some later aristocracies known for their rapidly declining numbers. More than two-thirds of old Roman consular families were replaced by new ones in each generation, an astonishing rate of disappearance in comparison with, say, the nobility of Elizabethan England or the Danish aristocracy of the seventeenth century.[4]

A wholly satisfactory explanation for the senators' failure to produce sons to fill their places, an essential reason for the influx of provincial families into the senate, is elusive. In view of the prerequisite of property for rank, an analysis of Roman strategies for the transmission of patrimonies may shed light on this problem. No direct illumination is at hand, because we do not have a series of senatorial wills, nor even a single complete one, to show how they disposed of their estates. Literary accounts of cases of succession are scattered and very partial. Adopting an indirect approach, this chapter will examine in a broader manner how Roman legal instruments of succession were developed and put to use, and how they were not used. Starting from D. Johnston's important study, *The Roman Law of Trust* (1988), the following examination of the terms of wills suggests that the Roman strategies of succession were generally planned with a view to a much shorter temporal horizon than often imagined by historians. Roman testators did take an interest in guiding their property beyond the hands of the primary heir or legatee, but, to judge from the *fideicommissa* (trusts) in the

---

[2] Thomas 1958; Corbier 1990: 228 also discusses strategies to continue the *nomen*.
[3] Corbier 1991a.
[4] Compare Hopkins 1983: ch. 3 with Stone 1965: 168; the latter shows that forty-one of sixty-five English noble families failed to produce male descendants in each of three generations from 1559 to 1641. Hansen 1972: 106 gives a 73 percent decline in the numbers of the Danish aristocracy over six generations.

juristic writings, their strategies were far more concerned with the destination of the property within the circle of living kin and freedmen than with grand designs for *posteritas*. It is easier for historians today to think of strategies abstractly in terms of generations of descendants than it was for the realistic Roman who first had to plan for the more immediate contingencies of high mortality and shifting family bonds among his immediate beneficiaries. There is no evidence that the Romans ever tried to develop a system of perpetual entail to maintain an indefinite line of male successors on an undivided estate – perhaps because they were too realistic about the difficulties presented by high mortality to such a system.[5]

The Roman law of succession

By the classical period the Roman law of succession comprised several layers of rules from different periods, organized on different principles and reflecting different conceptions of kinship. Roman testation has been comprehensively studied both as a legal system and as a cultural phenomenon, and there is no need to go into detail here.[6] What follows is a schematic account of the development of the relevant laws and legal instruments to serve as a basis for a discussion of how the law was manipulated toward various ends.

Intestacy, agnates, and the nomen. It is reasonably assumed that the oldest stratum is reflected in the law of intestacy found in the XII Tables (451–450 BC). If a Roman *paterfamilias* died without a valid will, the order of succession was (1) *sui heredes* or "his own heirs" (those who became independent of paternal authority on his death, usually his children and possibly grandchildren by sons, but also a wife married *cum manu*), (2) *proximus agnatus* or "closest agnate" (nearest relative linked by males, most commonly brothers, sisters, or paternal uncles), (3) *gentiles* or clansmen of the same nomen.[7] This was a system based on agnatic ties, giving no recognition to kinship links through women.

The XII Tables already allowed for the possibility of a written will by a testator who wished to supersede the rules of intestacy. How common the written will was in the fifth century BC is impossible to know, but several centuries later propertied Romans expected to write wills, and intestacy was avoided.[8] Nevertheless, the intestate rules giving first claim to all *sui heredes*

---

[5] Bonfield 1979.
[6] For the standard legal accounts, see Voci 1963–67; Amelotti 1966; Kaser 1971: 560–637; Watson 1971a. Crook 1967a: ch. 4 and Thomas 1976: part VI provide more manageable introductions to the subject. See Champlin 1991 for a social and cultural study.
[7] Watson 1975: ch. 5.
[8] Crook 1973, against Daube 1965. Moreau 1986: 180 points out that in Larinum the local elite made wills and that failure to do so required an explanation.

continued to reflect certain elements of Roman mores and expectations at a general level. All sons and daughters were thought to deserve a substantial share of their father's estate, even if not the equal shares that came to those whose fathers died intestate. That underlying sentiment can be found in the apologetic clauses included in some wills: for instance, the father of *Dig.* 31.34.6 asked his daughter "not to be angry because I shall have left a more substantial inheritance to your brother, who, as you know, will be sustaining great burdens and will be discharging the legacies which I have made above." The need for explicit comment on a lesser share for a daughter, whether in a real will or in an imaginary example, suggests that a larger share for sons or eldest sons was not taken for granted (as also in *Dig.* 32.27.1).

Even if most propertied Romans left wills to distribute their estates unequally, the rules of intestacy did not become an irrelevant archaism. *Testamenta* had to be written in fixed formulae and could easily fail on technicalities, leaving the deceased intestate. Therefore, it seems unlikely that the Romans would have tolerated a system of intestacy widely at variance with their general standards for equitable division of patrimonies. Furthermore, from the end of the Republic close relatives came to be able to bring a *querela inofficiosi testamenti* ("complaint of an undutiful will") against a will which flouted standards of equity and responsibility without good cause.[9] If a testator did not name all children in his will or explicitly disinherit them for bad behavior, sons or daughters could bring a complaint to break the will partially so that the rules of intestacy would come into operation. The testator could preempt the complaint by leaving to *sui heredes* at least one-quarter of what would have been due to them on intestacy. The rules were more complex than just stated (e.g., sons had to be disinherited by name, daughters could be disinherited in a general clause), but the point is that the *querela* can only be understood against the background of a belief in the continuing legitimacy of the rules of intestacy rooted in a moral sense that a Roman father ought to see to all his children in the settlement of his property.[10] Here the law constitutes a restraint in accordance with Roman mores; moreover, the need for a remedy such as the *querela* suggests that some testators were deviating from the mores. According to Ulpian, "it must be known that complaints of undutiful wills are frequent: to all parents as well as children it is permitted to dispute an undutiful will" (*Dig.* 5.2.1).

After *sui heredes*, the *proximus agnatus* stood next in line to inherit, followed by *gentiles*. The property interests of agnates were further recognized in the early law of *tutela* or guardianship, to be explored in the next chapter. Women, and children before puberty, no longer in paternal

[9] Watson 1971a: 62.   [10] Renier 1942.

power, came under the guardianship of the nearest agnate, unless otherwise arranged, on the principle that the *tutor* should be the one who stood to inherit the property from those who by definition could not have *sui heredes*. At a general level, emphasis on agnatic relationships in property transmission and guardianship corresponded with Roman elite thinking about dignity and honor which were transmitted through the *familia* marked by the *nomen*.[11] While *sui heredes* remained at the center of moral and legal ideas about succession, by the end of the Republican era in the mid-first century BC both the rules of succession and conceptions of family honor had broadened beyond agnatic kin.

The praetorian edict, cognates and the domus. When contemporary sources first become available for Roman social history in the second century BC, kinship reckoning and property transmission were not strictly along agnatic lines.[12] Despite legislative efforts to limit them, women were inheriting large estates from their natal families and leaving them to their children (see below). These cognatic lines of transmission were eventually recognized in the Edict of the praetor, the senior Roman magistrate who interpreted and developed the law by issuing an edict outlining how he intended to apply the law. In the late Republic praetors were denying unjust claims based on the letter of the *ius civile* in favor of equitable settlements. In the later first century BC the contemporary sense of equity in succession led praetors to include in the Edict a new title, "Unde cognati."[13] As a result, cognates were formally recognized in the residual rules of succession. The new order was children, *legitimi* (closest agnates as recognized in earlier law), *cognati*, and spouses. Among close kinship ties agnatic links were still given preference, but the recognition of kinship bonds to and through mothers, as well as the bond of husband and wife, must have eliminated *gentiles* from succession in most cases.[14]

The legal change was part of the broader trend, discussed in chapter 4, toward taking account of non-agnatic kin in considerations of honor and posterity. Callistratus expressed the readiness of imperial aristocrats to incorporate women in their notions of posterity: "we conceive and produce sons and daughters so that from the continuing stock of both we may leave a memory of ourselves for all time" (*Dig.* 50.16.220.3). The Roman law of succession evolved in response to social mores regarding rights of cognates,

[11] See above, ch. 4.
[12] Boyer 1950 rightly insists that by the time of Polybius the law of primitive Rome, whatever that might have been, had given way to something much closer to the classical system; the change must have taken place by the beginning of the third century BC. Much of the argument of Evans 1991 about the causes of the change from the primitive "rigidly patriarchal" system (p. x) are vitiated by his failure to recognize how far the developments had already progressed by the time of Rome's transmarine wars.
[13] Watson 1971a: 181.   [14] Watson 1971a.

but the change was very slow. The claim of the mother on the child's estate and the claim of the child on the mother's estate in intestacy received full recognition in the *ius civile* only in two laws, the *Senatusconsulta Tertullianum* and *Orfitianum*, of the second century after Christ – three centuries after the literary evidence shows mothers passing on estates to their children through written wills and two centuries after the Praetorian Edict gave a claim to cognates including mothers and their children.[15]

Legal instruments of succession. Written legal instruments, already available under the XII Tables of 451/450 BC, were developed to a high degree of sophistication and flexibility over the next millennium. The law of *testamenta* combined "freedom and formality." As Johnston has recently described it, "civil law provided that formal requirements must be met. No will was valid if it was not duly made and witnessed, if it did not begin with the institution of an heir in prescribed form; no legacy was valid if it did not follow the institution and itself satisfy the time-honored wordings."[16] As long as the formalities were met, the written testament in principle allowed the testator, male or female, very considerable freedom.

Two laws of the middle Republic, the *lex Furia testamentaria* and the *lex Voconia*, attempted to restrict the freedom of testation, neither with enduring success.[17] The *lex Furia* limited legacies to 1,000 asses to protect the heirs against dissipation of the *hereditas*, but the rule did not apply to legatees within six degrees of kinship. Moreover, as Gaius later pointed out (*Inst.* 2.225), the law failed to achieve its purpose because no limit was placed on the number of legacies. By the second century BC women as well as men were using the written will to leave estates to other kin. A close reading of the second century historian Polybius led S. Dixon to conclude that in his day "it was usual for women of the propertied classes to make wills. The general expectation that a mother should regard her children as her proper beneficiaries is likewise established, whatever her legal relation to them by the rules of *agnatio*."[18] The prominence of women in the transmission of patrimonies became such a concern that in 169 BC the *lex Voconia* was passed to bar women from being instituted in wills as heirs to estates of the top property class (100,000 asses or more). They could still take the estate on intestacy; they could also take legacies specified in the will, but not more than the principal heir. The *lex Voconia* represents law as restraint, but one, as it turned out, that was ineffective because it ran counter to the strong feeling that fathers ought to provide for their children, daughters as well as sons. As we shall see, the Romans displayed their creativity in adapting legal instruments, particularly the *fideicommissum*, to circumvent this law –

---

[15] Crook 1986a; Dixon 1988: 54.   [16] 1988: 3.   [17] Watson 1971a: ch. 12.
[18] Dixon 1985a: 170, developing the position of Boyer 1950.

"breaking the law to do the right thing," as Dixon has neatly put it.[19] The ultimate failure of these laws meant that testators could dispose of three-quarters of their estates as they pleased, even after the development of the *querela inofficiosi testamenti* at the end of the Republic. If social pressures and family strategies added extra-legal constraints, it was still true that the Romans were notable for the dispersion of wealth beyond the family.[20]

Despite the freedom allowed in testamentary law, the formal requirements apparently chafed. Through the centuries of the imperial era the jurists developed a different legal instrument, the *fideicommissum* or trust. The *fideicommissum* is attested in the Ciceronian age as an extra-legal means of circumventing the Voconian law. If propertied fathers were barred from naming a woman as heir, they could institute a male third party as heir and instruct the heir by a *fideicommissum* to hand on the estate to the woman (often a daughter) as a gift. Initially the instructions had no legal standing, and the testator could rely only on the heir's *fides* or faith. A famous ethical discussion from Cicero's *De finibus* (2.55, 58) points to the weakness of the Republican trust. Quintus Fadius Gallus instituted Publius Sextilius Rufus as heir with the agreement, it was believed, that he hand over the estate to Gallus' daughter who was ineligible to be named heir because of the Voconian law. Rufus disavowed the agreement and claimed responsibility to uphold the laws, including the Voconian. Cicero and other contemporaries saw this as self-interested hyperlegalism, but the daughter had nothing beyond Rufus' good faith to stand on. A generation later Augustus saw such behavior as a flagrant breach of morality and recognized the *ius codicillorum* giving legal force to *fideicommissa*.[21] Trusts could be set up either in codicils attached to formal *testamenta* or in other documents to stand in place of *testamenta*. Over the centuries of the imperial era the latter sort of *fideicommissum* was developed as a legal instrument, subverting the older testamentary system. Eventually, in the age of Justinian, the alternative forms of succession were brought together in a single form more resembling the *fideicommissum* than the legacy.[22]

If the *fideicommissum* was initially used to transmit property to those who had no capacity to receive in civil law, its attractions went much further. It was a legal instrument in which form was relatively unimportant: whereas a flawed testament would fail and give way to intestacy, the trust had the advantage of respecting the intent of the testator as long as it could be discerned. This feature was valued for reasons expressed in the beginning of a will quoted as an example by the second century jurist Scaevola: "'I, Lucius Titius, have written this, my will, with no legal adviser, following the reason

---

[19] Dixon 1985b.   [20] Corbier 1985.
[21] Justinian *Inst.* 2.25. pr; on the date, Champlin 1986.   [22] Johnston 1988.

of my own mind rather than excessive and wretched pedantry; and if I should happen to have done anything without due legality or skill, the intention of a sane man ought to be held valid at law.'"[23] As a *testamentum*, this document did not meet the requirements of form and therefore was invalid, but because of the opening it was construed by the jurist as a trust and respected. The advantage of putting intent above form was patent, while the corresponding disadvantageous potential for ambiguity was easily overlooked by non-lawyers. Consequently, after Vespasian and Hadrian closed the loopholes so that those incapable of taking under civil law also became incapable of taking under trusts, the popularity of trusts continued to grow. Precisely because *fideicommissa* embodied intent without the structure of formalities and were developed in the early imperial period, it is especially interesting to examine how they were manipulated in the pursuit of certain ends; because they were so flexible, it is meaningful to ask in addition how they were not used.

Goals and strategies

If minimal legal restraints and flexible written legal instruments gave Roman testators a remarkable degree of freedom to express their last wishes, to what ends was that freedom used? Corbier has discussed the social pressures that encouraged Romans to behave properly in their wills toward family and friends.[24] Moreau's case study of the local elite of Larinum, based on Cicero's *Pro Cluentio*, has led him to similar conclusions.[25] More recently, Champlin has stressed that the public quality of wills, together with Roman concern for reputation, caused testators to favor their families, especially their children, in the distribution of their estates.[26] Similarly, Boyer in a valuable survey of the juristic evidence for legacies demonstrated that most clauses benefitted the immediate family or freedmen.[27]

If testation was mostly a matter of distributing property to children who in any case would have received it on the rules of intestacy, in what sense did "strategies" come into play? What use had Romans for elaborate *fideicommissa*? A ready answer has been found in more recent historical experience. As J. A. C. Thomas put it, "it is evident that the Roman of imperial times was no less eager for posthumous power and recognition than his English successor."[28] With the enforceability of *fideicommissa* in the early empire, it became "possible to charge a *heres* with a direction to transmit the property in turn to his successors."[29] The purpose of testamentary clauses banning alienation of property outside the family "was

---

[23] *Dig.* 31.88.17, translated and discussed by Johnston 1988: 139.
[24] Corbier 1985, 1990.   [25] Moreau 1986, esp. 182.   [26] Champlin 1991.
[27] Boyer 1965.   [28] 1958: 571.   [29] 1958: 572.

certainly to transmit the property down through the family line like English entail, by preventing the holder from time to time from alienating outside the relevant group."[30] In a detailed study, Johnston has decisively shown that this interpretation of perpetuities and fideicommissary substitutions is a result of anachronistic preconceptions and misrepresents the intentions of Roman testators.[31] His arguments are worth summarizing as a starting point for analysis of the strategies implicit in *fideicommissa*.

Johnston carefully distinguishes three different types of clause that have been interpreted in terms of perpetuities. First, there were the clauses prohibiting alienation of certain property. The jurist Scaevola decided that the word "alienare" in such clauses referred only to alienation by the beneficiary *inter vivos* (for example, by sale or pledge), thus in no way restricting the beneficiary from bequeathing the property to whomever he or she wished.[32] Scaevola's interpretation meant that this type of clause could not establish a perpetuity.

The second type required that the property continue to be held by those of a certain *nomen* through a phrase like "ne de nomine exeat" ("let it not leave from the name"). This may appear to be an effort at perpetual entail along agnatic lines, but Johnston shows that "almost without exception *nomen* clauses are found, where perpetuities are concerned, only with reference to freedmen."[33] The partial exception among the texts is instructive. Scaevola presents a case in which "a testator instituted his daughter as heir and provided as follows: 'I forbid the building (*aedificium*) to leave from my name, but I wish it to go *to the home-bred slaves*, whom I have named by this will'" (*Dig.* 32.38.2). Patently, the intent of these clauses was far from that of perpetual entail, having nothing to do with familial lines of descent but with the perpetuation of a man's name in the widest sense.

Of the third type of clause establishing a proper perpetuity, Johnston discovered only five examples in the texts of jurists before Caracalla. These

---

[30] 1958: 585, giving as the only example *Dig.* 31.88.15, which is written in Greek and concerns houses, not an estate. On the significance of the Greek of this passage, see Johnston 1988: 77–78. Thomas 1958: 571, n. 2, defines the English perpetuity as "an entail with the addition of a proviso conditional, tied to his estate, not to put away the land from the next heirs."   [31] 1985.

[32] Apart from Scaevola's interpretation of "alienare," it is clear that these clauses were not intended for a social goal comparable to that of English perpetual entail. In only one of the cases examined by Johnston is the heir a son (*Dig.* 32.28.3); in another case the heir is daughter (*Dig.* 32.38.4; 32.93. pr); in two cases, freedmen (*Dig.* 31.88.14; 32.38.5). In the other case a mother left property to her children with a prohibition on alienation and instructions to preserve it for *successio sua*. How deep the preconception runs is shown by the fact that Johnston mentions "descendants" in connection with *successio*, though it need not refer to family members at all (*Dig.* 32.38.7).

[33] 1985: 237. One of the principal faults of Thomas' study, from the social historian's point of view, is that it gives no attention to the statuses and relationships of the parties involved in the *fideicommissa*.

took the form of a *fideicommissum* instructing the heir to keep the property "in familia." Johnston concluded that such clauses provided only "severely limited protection," insofar as the duration was restricted and "no pressure was put on the beneficiaries except by their own members."[34] In other, social, respects these texts are also quite different from the perpetual entail envisaged by Thomas. Among the five, one perpetuity was established for freedmen and their children (*Dig.* 33.1.18. pr, Scaevola). Two of the texts, including the only one with ambitions of limitless duration, concern houses rather than estates (*Dig.* 31.88.15, Scaevola [in Greek]; 31.69.3, Papinian). The other two are about farms to go to sons and grandsons, but even one of these is not as focussed as a perpetual entail in a male line: the father instituted his son as heir with a prohibition on alienation of the *praedia* and a *fideicommissum* to leave the property to "*liberis et ceteris cognatis*" ("children and *other cognatic relatives*," *Dig.* 32.38. pr, Scaevola). In allowing the property to go to cognates, this testator was not insisting on keeping the property within any descent group, agnatic or otherwise.[35] Marcellus in *Dig.* 35.2.54 offers the sole example of a perpetuity involving the transmission of a *fundus* "in familia" from father to son to grandchildren (not necessarily male).

For the period before Caracalla, Johnston concludes that the most restrictive clauses were those affecting *liberti* of the same *nomen*. "The manner in which prohibitions on alienation imposed on family members are interpreted suggests a reluctance to restrict their powers of disposal greatly."[36] Tracing the historical development into the Severan period, Johnston shows that freedmen became more prominent and "in nomen-related settlements ... predominant in Papinian."[37] In their frequent inclusion of *liberti* and their lack of discrimination by gender, these texts are striking to the social historian not for their similarities, but for their contrasts, to English perpetual entail. Behind the Roman practices lay entirely different attitudes toward posterity, much less dominated by a preoccupation with male "blood" lines so evident in later European aristocracies.

Johnston's studies provide a more precise idea of how prohibitions and perpetuities were and were not used in family settlements. Yet the *fideicommissa* of interest to Johnston for his legal purposes represent only a fraction of those to be found in the *Digest*. Most of the *fideicommissa* involving family members have nothing to do with perpetuities, but are instructions to the beneficiary to pass on the bequest to another person, either immediately or at some future time. It is the latter, with instructions

---

[34] 1985: 248.
[35] Again, Johnston 1985: 244 reveals the strength of the preconception that he is exploding when he refers to this perpetuity only with respect to "the testator's grandchildren."
[36] 1985: 271.   [37] 1985: 220.

for the future, that is of particular interest here to illuminate the strategies pursued by Romans.

A survey of the *fideicommissa* discussed by the jurists in the *Digest* suggests that Roman strategies of transmission of property were usually planned with reference to the generations currently living in the household rather than to generations of the indefinite future. The specific clauses reveal testators trying to cope with numerous scenarios and personal circumstances. Several features of Roman society contributed to the notable variety of *fideicommissa*. First, the general obligation of Roman testators to take care of their children was not translated into precise, fixed formulae for transmission of the patrimony; consequently, testators could carry out their duty in innumerable ways within the legal framework. In particular, mothers making wills might wish to find ways to deal with the legal fact that any children *in potestate* would not be able to inherit property in their own right. Secondly, testators repeatedly attempted to deal with the many contingencies of high mortality, divorce and remarriage within their immediate families through conditions, substitutions and *fideicommissa*. Thirdly, with the weakening of the agnatic conception of kinship, the Romans were left with many socially acceptable options in the absence of a sharply defined "system" of kinship to designate which relatives deserved what. Fourthly, as the many perpetuities in favor of freedmen show, the testator's sense of duty to his household extended beyond his kin.[38]

Taken together, these features yielded a profusion of strategies for the transmission of property. A simple social classification of the *fideicommissa* discussed in the *Digest* books on legacies and *fideicommissa* (30, 31, 32) suggests the many possibilities. Among the fifty-eight clauses designed to guide the property through the hands of the heir or legatee into the hands of some other member of the family or household at some later date, there are at least seventeen different permutations in the ordering of the relatives and/or freedmen to benefit.[39] Within the nuclear family alone there are four permutations: property to be transmitted from father to mother to offspring, from mother to father to offspring, from father to offspring to mother, and from parent to offspring to offspring's sibling. If all ascending and descending relatives are included, an additional six permutations are represented. Inclusion of collateral kin adds another four, and three other possibilities occur within the circle of kin and freedmen.

Among the possible lines of transmission, the historian concerned with inheritance most readily imagines the simple, paradigmatic case of an ageing father writing a will to divide his property among his children. Even in the

---

[38] Moreau 1986: 186–87.
[39] I have not included the numerous other texts where the beneficiary was instructed to restore property immediately.

paradigmatic case, transmission was not necessarily automatic, because testators used legal instruments to adjust the shares of their children and the timing of the transfer. There is no reason to repeat here Boyer's details of the ways legacies were often deployed to give particular assets to certain children.[40] Although ownership of the patrimony was normally transferred after the testator's death, Roman law provided more than one way for a father wishing to pass on his estate during his lifetime to do so *inter vivos*. For instance, before his death "a father divided his possessions between his children, confirming the division in his will and providing that each of them should have sole responsibility for the debts he had incurred or would incur in the future" (*Dig.* 10.2.39.5, Scaevola). In this case the children seem not to have been emancipated, leaving the father the right to reclaim his estate. In another example a father transferred virtually his entire estate to his emancipated son, but with a stipulation that he could reclaim it in case of his son's death or bad faith (*Dig.* 32.37.3, Scaevola). The rarity of arrangements like these in the *Digest* suggest that transfer of the patrimony before the father's death was not the norm.[41]

If a testator was fortunate enough to live to see his children reach adulthood and produce children, then he could draw up his will, comfortably foreseeing the direction in which his estate would descend to his posterity. In such circumstances, testators are sometimes found using *fideicommissa* to ensure transmission of their estate to their grandchildren. Ulpian discusses the wording of a testator who wrote, "'I ask you, my son, that you cherish with all your diligence the estates that will come to you, and so look after them that they may pass to your children'" (*Dig.* 32.11.9); though not properly worded, the jurist decides to treat it as a *fideicommissum* in favor of the *nepotes*. This seemingly normal line of descent of the patrimony is represented in four of the fifty-eight *fideicommissa*, one of which was noted above as specifying *cognati* as well as *nepotes*.[42] In three others a father left property to a daughter with instructions to bequeath it to her children, in one instance to the child bearing his grandfather's name.[43] Direct, lineal transmission was a goal of some testators, but one represented in only a handful of the jurists' discussions of *fideicommissa*.

The microsimulation shows that most Roman fathers did not have the good fortune to live to see their grandchildren and to make concrete plans to transmit their patrimonies in a simple, descending fashion. To judge by the jurists' writings, testators who made wills before their children reached

---

[40] 1965: 356–59.

[41] See also *Dig.* 10.2.20.3, 41.10.4.1. *Dig.* 31.87.4 shows that a father needed to take care in such arrangements; here an emancipated son was given most of the patrimony before his father's death, then tried to invoke the rule about the Falcidian quarter to avoid carrying out a *fideicommissum* in favor of his sister; the emperor ruled in the sister's favor.

[42] *Dig.* 30.114.15–18, 31.77.4, 32.38.pr; also 35.2.54.   [43] *Dig.* 31.76.5; 31.77.10, 25.

adulthood gave attention to more immediate decisions about whom to trust and how to arrange the first steps in the devolution of their property. It was probable that one parent would die before a child reached adulthood, but unlikely that both would die.[44] Many of the testamentary arrangements in the *Digest* seek to address situations created by the death of a father or mother. If a wife predeceased her husband in whom she had faith, the matter was fairly straightforward: she could bequeath the property to her children or her husband. Either way, the husband would assume ownership of the property, no matter what the age of the children, in the expectation that he would pass it on to them upon his death (that is, when they became independent and capable of owning property in their own right). If the wife wished to add some legal force to that faith, she could charge her husband with a *fideicommissum* to restore the property to her children, a practice well attested by the jurists.[45] Variations on this practice were possible: a husband might be allowed usufruct of the wife's property in the meantime (*Dig.* 31.34.7), or a son could be given an allowance as long as he was in his father's power (*Dig.* 33.1.25). Not all fathers deserved such trust and some were known to defraud the *fideicommissum* on behalf of their children; Hadrian and later emperors increasingly intervened to protect property intended for children (*Dig.* 36.1.52; 36.1.17.10). During the late empire the *dominium* of the father over maternal property bequeathed to the children continued, but his discretion was drastically reduced in order to protect the children's interests.[46]

When a *paterfamilias* with underage children predeceased his wife, it was conventional to institute the children as heirs and to name guardians to manage and protect the patrimony (see chapter 8). However, legal contrivances were available to a husband with complete faith in his wife to circumvent the traditional prohibition on women fulfilling the duty of *tutela*. He could disinherit his children and institute his wife as heir with a charge to restore the property to the children. Historians tend to think of disherison as a penalty for unfilial behavior (as it often was), yet Ulpian pointed out that "many men disinherit their children not as a mark of disgrace nor to prejudice them, but so as to provide for their interests, as, for example, where they are *impuberes*, and they give them the inheritance by *fideicommissum*" (*Dig.* 28.2.18). The transmission of property in this way – from father to mother to children – appears repeatedly in the *Digest*. For

---

[44] The simulation suggests that in the "ordinary" population with level 3 West mortality about 10 percent of children lost both parents before puberty and another 20 percent lost both parents before age twenty-five. In the "senatorial" population with level 6 West mortality, about 5 percent of children lost both parents before puberty, and an additional 12 percent before age twenty-five.

[45] *Dig.* 35.2.95.pr; see also 31.77.7, 32.41.12 [a foster child], 36.1.80.10, 36.3.7.

[46] Dixon 1988: 58–59.

example, "Fabius Antoninus left an *impubes* son Antoninus and a daughter
Honorata; disinheriting them, he instituted their mother Junia Valeriana as
heir and left three hundred and certain things to be paid by her to the
daughter; he wished the rest of the inheritance to be restored to the son
Antoninus when he reached his twentieth year of age."[47] The trust between
spouses implicit in this arrangement was highly valued: "the Emperor
Marcus [Aurelius] ruled in a rescript that the words in which a testator had
provided 'that he did not doubt that his wife would deliver to the children
whatever she had taken' [from his estate] should be taken as a *fideicommissum*.
This rescript is highly salutary to ensure that the honor of a well-conducted
marriage, and confidence that children are held in common, does not deceive
a husband who thought too highly of the mother" (*Dig.* 31.67.10).

Aside from a *fideicommissum*, the husband could reach much the same goal
by instituting his children as heirs but giving his wife, together with the
children, *usufructus* (profit) and *usus* (use) of the property.[48] This strategy, in
evidence from the late Republic, was a convenient means of entrusting
management of the inheritance to the mother and taking care of her needs,
while ensuring that the children's ownership was protected.[49] Alternatively,
the testator sometimes saw to the interests of his wife and child by asking
them to hold his property in common. Scaevola discussed the case where
"Lucius Titius about to die intestate, since he had a wife and by her an
emancipated daughter, put these words into a codicil: 'This codicil applies
to my wife and daughter. First I ask that you carry on living as you did while
I was alive, and I ask that you hold in common whatever I have left and what
you yourselves have.' The daughter received *possessio bonorum* from her
intestate father. It was asked whether some part of the inheritance of Lucius
Titius is due from the daughter to the mother by way of *fideicommissum* and
how much. I answered that according to the circumstances described a half
share is owed, as long as the wife is ready to place her assets in common"
(*Dig.* 31.89.3; see also 36.1.80. pr). This is a good illustration of the jurist
respecting the vaguely expressed intentions of the deceased and giving
precision to them.

The fact that the mother was often felt to be the most natural protector
of her children's interests is reflected in the attempts of husbands to leave
management of their children's estates in their wives' hands even though
women could not legally serve as their children's *tutor*. Some husbands
instructed the *tutor* to pay heed to their wife's wishes, and that occasionally
put *tutores* in an awkward dilemma, caught between the will of their ward's

---

[47] *Dig.* 36.1.76.1, Paul; Fabius' intentions were upset when his wife and his son died before
the son reached the specified age. Other cases include 35.1.77.3, 31.88.2, 36.1.80.14,
36.2.26.2, 31.77.12.   [48] Humbert 1972: 233–39.
[49] Cicero *Caecin.* 11–12; cf. *Dig.* 7.2.8; for later times, *Dig.* 33.2.37, Scaevola.

mother and their own best judgment about the child's interests.[50] But the law was not irrelevant and ignoring legal rules carried risks.[51] There were other compromises to compensate for the mother's inability formally to act as *tutor*. Her husband's will might grant her the choice of residence for their children or the choice of a husband for their daughter, though neither was legally binding.[52]

Some Roman fathers were inclined to trust their widows only as long as they did not bring a second husband into the house.[53] The threat to the mother's devotion posed by remarriage was not taken lightly. On account of the Augustan legislation intended to encourage marriage and child-bearing, conditions on bequests prohibiting marriage or remarriage were void. But it was acceptable to bequeath property to one's wife on condition that she not remarry as long as the children were *impuberes* (*Dig.* 35.1.62.2). Gradually the law came to accept mothers as *tutores*. Around AD 100 the jurist Neratius allowed for the possibility that mothers could petition the emperor for special dispensation to act as *tutor* for their children. In the later empire this possibility was generalized, but only if the mother took an oath that she would not remarry – an oath that was more acceptable with the new Christian attitude toward remarriage.[54] Here as in other matters of succession, what was a matter of individual arrangement through legal instruments in earlier periods became a general rule under the Christian emperors.

Hostility and distrust between husband and wife increased the need for careful manipulation of legal instruments. The mother who predeceased her children's father faced the problem that the children were likely to be in the *potestas* of the father, who would therefore acquire ownership of anything left to them. The law offered solutions to this obstacle. The mother could leave the property to the children on the condition that they be emancipated from the father's power (*Dig.* 5.3.58). The father could not be compelled to emancipate his children, but his refusal would cost his family the bequest (*Dig.* 30.114.8; 35.1.92). The father in such circumstances would naturally be eager to acquire the property, as in Pliny's account of Regulus and his son (*Ep.* 4.2); if he did meet the condition, the law tried to honor the mother's intention by preventing the father from retaking control of his child's affairs (*Dig.* 26.5.21.1). We hear of other relatives, especially grandmothers, who also included the emancipation condition in their wills to ensure that their property reached the children for whom it was intended.[55] The emancipation

---

[50] *Dig.* 4.4.47.pr, 26.7.5.8, 38.17.2.23, chapter 8 takes up the relationship between mother and tutors in greater detail.   [51] *Dig.* 46.3.88, Scaevola; cf. 3.5.30.6.
[52] *Dig.* 33.1.7; 23.2.62. pr.   [53] Humbert 1972: 208–13.
[54] Humbert 1972: ch. 3; Dixon 1988: 65; Evans 1991: 187–95.
[55] *Dig.* 28.7.18.1, 35.1.77.pr, 35.1.93, 27.10.16.2.

condition was the extreme case of the way in which the separation of husband's and wife's property in Roman families could operate to undermine the monopoly of *potestas* granted to the *paterfamilias* in law (see chapter 5).

As a less drastic strategy, the mother could resort to the institution of a third party as heir with a *fideicommissum* to restore the property to her children when they became *sui iuris*. The woman's relatives were regarded as natural choices for this role.[56] Yet trust was a very personal matter that sometimes flew in the face of stereotypes, as where "a woman who had left two sons in the power of their father and married another man instituted her second husband as heir and asked him to restore her inheritance to her children or to the survivor of them after the death of their father." To everyone's surprise, the distrusted father emancipated the sons before his death; the emperor Marcus Aurelius ruled that the estate could then be restored in accord with the woman's implicit intention (*Dig.* 36.1.23. pr).[57] Though the general tendency of the law was to protect children's property from stepparents, legal instruments offered the flexibility to override general rules. When late imperial law came to recognize and protect children's property while it was technically in the father's *dominium*, these legal devices may have become less necessary.

Testators wishing to leave property to children sometimes felt that the ages established by law as the end of *tutela* (fourteen for boys and twelve for girls) were unsatisfactory. A testator uneasy at the thought of a teenage son making decisions about his patrimony could use the *fideicommissum* to raise the age at which the estate would be turned over to the child.[58] A husband could leave his property to his wife to be restored to their son at age twenty-five, perhaps with the profits being handed over to him in the meantime (*Dig.* 36.2.26.2). Testators might also choose sixteen or eighteen or twenty as the appropriate times for restoration.[59] For girls marriage was sometimes set as the point at which to pay the bequest. The jurists then asked whether it should be paid if the girl moved to the house of her husband before the minimum age for marriage; Labeo and Ulpian ruled that it was not due until the girl reached twelve years of age.[60]

The *fideicommissum*, infinitely flexible, could be used in the opposite way, the child being instituted heir under instructions to hand over the estate to another's management, as in Scaevola's example: "A man instituted as heirs his son to three-quarters and his wife to one-quarter, and imposed on his son a *fideicommissum* that he should hand over his inheritance to his stepmother. Of her, however, he asked that she should take thought for the youthful weakness of his son and pay him ten *aurei* a month until he reached his

[56] *Dig.* 22.1.3.3, Papinian; 36.3.18.pr, Scaevola.   [57] Gardner 1987.
[58] Humbert 1972: 214–23.   [59] *Dig.* 36.1.48, 33.2.37, 34.3.28.8, 36.1.76.1.
[60] *Dig.* 36.2.30, 35.1.10.pr.

twenty-fifth year, but when he reached that age she should hand over to him half the inheritance" (*Dig.* 33.1.21.2). The manipulation of legal instruments to meet personal circumstances at odds with the usual stereotypes is again in evidence here with trust placed in the stepmother.

Roman legal instruments permitted testators the discretion to judge at what age their ultimate heirs would be responsible; some decided that they could not predict, or could not trust their normal heir at all. Again, *fideicommissa* offered solutions to such difficulties. A testator could leave property to a third party with instructions to restore it when the beneficiary began to demonstrate a sense of responsibility (*Dig.* 34.4.30. pr). A woman who distrusted her sons but did not want to take the extreme action of disinheriting them instituted the sons as heirs and instructed them to hand over management of the estate to a third party until the property could be divided among her grandchildren when they reached age twenty-five (*Dig.* 36.1.80.1).

Finally, the *fideicommissum* enabled Romans to bequeath property to other relatives or dependants without shirking the ultimate duty to their children's interest. Paulus refers to a case in which "a testator asked that whatever had gone from his estate to his father should be restored by his father to his daughter so that she would have as much more than what she would have had from the father's estate" (*Dig.* 32.8.2). Scaevola discusses a will in which "a testator left to his sister as a legacy slaves whom he named with a *fideicommissum* to restore the same property to his children when she died" (*Dig.* 32.41.10). The same jurist also envisages legacies to freedmen given on condition or in the expectation that the property would eventually be restored to the testator's children (*Dig.* 31.89.6; 32.39. pr).

The varied examples in the preceding pages show Romans using *testamenta* and *fideicommissa* not to avoid their basic obligations to their children or to pursue grand strategies, but to deal with individual circumstances in diverse ways to fulfill their duty to their offspring.

After arranging for their children's welfare, thoughtful Roman testators had to reckon with the prospect that those offspring might not live long enough to produce heirs. If matters were left to the residual rules of intestacy, the estate could move off in unforeseen directions that might not satisfy the testator's wishes or sense of obligation. Therefore, in wills it was common to name a substitute to the main heir; if the heir died as a *pupillus* (below the age of puberty and not in *patria potestas*), the substitute heir would have a claim.[61] This sort of instrument, known as a pupillary will, lapsed when the *pupillus* reached puberty (*Dig.* 28.6.14, Pomponius). The will of the soldier Antonius Silvanus, who instituted his *impubes* (below the

---

[61] Thomas 1976: 491–93.

age of puberty) son heir and appointed his brother as substitute, must have been a common type.[62] If the heir was an older child capable of making a will, the testator could use a *fideicommissum* to instruct the son or daughter to pass the property on to a third party upon death. That person might be the beneficiary's sibling or parent.[63] Members of the immediate family are most often found as the secondary beneficiaries, but more distant kin, such as the testator's brother's children, are occasionally also specified.[64]

A testator who felt daunted by all the permutations created by the vagaries of mortality among his kin could decide that it was easier to place the estate in the hands of someone close, with general instructions to pass it on to whatever descendants had survived in accordance with good judgment. Papinian offers an illustration (*Dig.* 36.1.59.2): "'I request of you, my dearest wife, that when you die you restore my inheritance to my children or to one of them or to my grandchildren or to such of them as you wish or to my kinsmen, should you wish to choose any from among my whole kindred (*cognatio*).'" A testator without firm ideas about which relatives should receive his estate could still be definite about who should not receive it: "A testator appointed his mother and wife as heirs and provided as follows: 'I ask you, my dearest wife, that you should not leave anything after your death to your brothers. You have sons of your sisters to whom you may leave property. You know that one of your brothers killed our son while robbing him; and another, too, has done me an injury'" (*Dig.* 31.88.16, Scaevola). Though the wife's intestacy in this example gave her brothers a claim to her property, this clause was interpreted as a *fideicommissum* in favor of the nephews. Clauses like these and the one referring to *cognati* (discussed above at n. 30) reflect a Roman view of kinship that has evolved a long way from the sort of sharply defined agnatic system attributed to early Rome that would determine a testator's choices.

Finally, to develop Johnston's conclusion about the prominence of freedmen in *nomen*-settlements, it is perhaps worth observing more broadly that among all the *fideicommissa* in Books 31, 32, and 33 of the *Digest* freedmen are mentioned as beneficiaries more often than kin beyond the immediate family.

Conclusion

Out of the welter of testamentary and fideicommissary clauses considered by the jurists, several characteristics of significance to the social historian emerge. Written instruments were used, for the most part, by Roman men

---

[62] *FIRA* III, 47.

[63] *Dig.* 30.123.pr, 32.27.1, 31.77.pr; cf. 31.89.5 where a father asks his daughter to have her brothers stipulate for the return of her dowry.

[64] *Dig.* 34.9.16.pr; see also 31.70.2 in which a father institutes his son and brother as part heirs and asks the brother to include the son as heir along with the brother's own children.

and women to gain not *freedom from* familial obligations so much as *freedom to* design an individual strategy to meet both their own personal circumstances and the general conditions of unpredictable mortality and shifting family bonds. Most of the *fideicommissa* were concerned with members of the immediate family; relatively few went beyond the family and household; fewer still had pretensions to dictating the fate of family property for generations to come.

The value of these conclusions to the social historian rests on the premise that the jurists' writings provide a guide to the concerns and strategies of propertied testators. Of course, that premise is open to challenge. A defense of this use of the jurists' writings may be offered along several lines. First, even if the frequency of certain clauses in the *Digest* is no sure guide to the frequency of testamentary practices of Roman citizens, those clauses indicate the range of the possible. A survey of them will at least reveal the inadequacies of schematic interpretations of strategies in terms of *a system* of Roman inheritance. Secondly, although it would be rash to argue for a direct correspondence between the frequency of legal practices in the *Digest* and in the wider society, it would be odd if the two were completely divorced from one another. It would be hard, for example, to think of a plausible explanation for the focus on freedmen in juristic discussions of *nomen* clauses if in fact those clauses had normally been employed in relation to agnatic descendants. In this connection, the demographic background can be very helpful in understanding that testators did not usually have a tidy, full circle of kin whom they could assume would reproduce in an orderly and predictable way in future. As the micro-simulation suggests, to the extent that the classical jurists dealt with a wide variety of clauses for the transmission of property within the family and household, they were in closer touch with the varied realities of family life than those twentieth-century social and legal historians who have assumed simple, direct lines of devolution. In view of the jurists' practice of responding to cases, it is not surprising that their interests reflect to some degree the demographic patterns which they themselves did not necessarily understand. Finally, there is some corroboration for the arguments of this chapter in the general correspondence between the juristic evidence and the epigraphic evidence of funerary commemorations. In general, though by no means always, the heirs had the responsibility for the burial and commemoration of the deceased. Given this attested link, it is significant that in both the jurists' testamentary clauses and the thousands of epitaphs the bonds between members of the immediate family predominate.[65] Next in frequency (a distant second) in the jurists and in the corpus of Italian

---

[65] Boyer 1965: 341. See chapter 4 on the social meaning of funerary commemoration.

inscriptions comes the relationship between ex-master and freedman. Much less common in both are the appearances of more distant kin.[66] Moreover, the epigraphic evidence confirms the wide use of *nomen*-clauses in trusts to benefit *liberti* in the manner discussed by jurists.

As Crook concluded, "by and large, the Roman will looks a very 'family' thing: the sentiment is that something should be done for everyone."[67] Roman trusts also were "a very 'family' thing" in the sense of the living kin and household unit, not a "*familia*" thing in the sense of the agnatic descent group. Any association with perpetual entail of later eras obscures the essential characteristics of most *fideicommissa*: their relatively short temporal horizon and their diffuseness in terms of the gender and generation of the beneficiaries. Historians of early modern Europe who have attached great weight to the reintroduction of Roman law as a fundamental root of the differences in family patterns between southern Europe, with primogeniture inheritance, and northern Europe, with traditional partible inheritance, appear not to appreciate the complex richness of that law.[68] Perhaps the most important characteristic of the classical law of succession was its flexibility, which could be used to validate any number of patterns of devolution of property (though not primogeniture in a strict sense). Roman law could have been used in the empire and in later eras to validate many customary patterns of division of the patrimony, and cannot in itself explain any particular pattern.

[66] Saller and Shaw 1984a; Meyer 1990. *Patronus–libertus* dedications are more common than those between extended kin among the populations of Italy (except senators and equestrians) and Gallia Narbonensis, but not in other western provinces with smaller slave populations.   [67] 1986a: 79.   [68] E. g., Macfarlane 1980: 10; cf. Saller 1991b.

8

Guardianship of Roman children

The vagaries of high mortality in the Roman world resulted in weak links, to be taken into account by any Roman planning the perpetuation of his family name and the transmission of his patrimony. There was uncertainty whether he would have children and whether any of them would live long enough to inherit his fortune and status. If not, the institution of adoption was available to repair the deficiency, though it was not regularly used.[1] When children did survive their father, the transmission of the estate was not necessarily unproblematic. The prospect of one or more heirs being underage required the testator to reckon with a significant problem: how to protect his child-heir and patrimony from a greedy world.

The solution lay largely in the Roman institutions of guardianship, *tutela impuberum* and *cura minorum*, which have received little attention in social histories of Rome. Guardianship of women, *tutela mulieris*, has attracted more interest than *tutela impuberum*, even though the former came to have little force in the classical era, while the latter gained in strength and legal rigor. Moreover, the forty-year-old man still subject to *patria potestas* looms larger in many classicists' image of the Roman family than the twelve-year-old fatherless child, even though the latter was fivefold more common in Roman society. Some historians who have commented on the subject of fatherless children have treated the phenomenon as a result of special crises, in particular bloody wars.[2] Yet, though wars certainly exacerbated the problems, fatherless children have been a pervasive and perennial issue in all societies before the demographic transition to modern mortality and birth rates. The Roman jurists' and moralists' extensive and careful treatments of the problem have drawn detailed treatises from twentieth-century Roman lawyers and perceptive comments from a few historians with a special

---

[1] Corbier (1991a) describes the flexibility that Romans had in constructing kinship bonds, but does not explain why the institution of adoption was used as rarely as Hopkins 1983: 49 suggests.   [2] Syme 1986: 348; Evans 1991: 3.

interest in the law.[3] But the fact that guardianship is ignored in a recent book on Roman adults and children suggests a continuing lack of understanding of the scope of the phenomenon.[4]

In the broadest sense, the subject of guardianship leads us to explore the interaction between nature and culture in family life, and to assess competing interpretations of the family both as a natural biological unit and as a wholly malleable cultural construct. Nature presents a situation common to all societies before the demographic transition, the child whose father has died.[5] Such children are especially problematic in societies, widespread in Eurasia,[6] which are organized in nuclear families supported by inherited private property in need of protection. The many societies with these general characteristics have developed different institutions and practices to cope with the problem in their various legal and cultural contexts. My aim in this chapter is to delineate the peculiarly Roman configuration of institutions and practices, and then to understand how they relate to the legal, demographic, and cultural contexts. The chapter begins with a description of the legal institutions of *tutela* and *cura*. Having identified the ages defining *tutela* and *cura* in Roman law, we can use the microsimulation of the Roman kinship universe to suggest the pervasiveness of the need for guardians. The widespread need invites a brief survey to identify the significance attached to *tutela* within the traditional Roman hierarchy of moral duties. It will then be possible to discuss the ways in which the Romans used the legal institutions within their demographic and cultural contexts, and finally to suggest the potential impact of the practices related to guardianship on the wider society and economy.

The legal background[7]

The law of guardianship of children underwent a development resembling, and linked to, broader developments in Roman family law. Legal historians suppose that in early Rome the orphan and his or her inheritance automatically came under the power of the closest agnates or clansmen, whose role was preserved in later ages in the form of the *tutor legitimus*. Their interest in the guardianship lay in the fact that they stood to inherit the orphan's property, should he or she die before the age of puberty. On the basis of the late Republican jurist Servius Sulpicius' definition of *tutela* as

---

[3] Solazzi has written a series of papers (1955, 1957, 1958, 1960) and books (1913, 1917) on legal aspects of guardianship. See Crook 1967a: 113–16 and Dixon 1988: 63–65 for comments on the social context of legal practices.   [4] Wiedemann 1989.

[5] The jurist Gaius (*Inst.* 1.189) claimed that all states place underage children under guardianship as a matter of "natural reason."   [6] Goody 1990.

[7] For general discussions, Crook 1967a: 113–16; Kaser 1971: 76–81, 299–311; Solazzi 1973.

"vis ac potestas in capite libero ad tuendum eum" (*Dig.* 26.1.1. pr, Paulus), it used to be argued that the orphan was not legally independent (*sui iuris*), but under the formal *potestas* of a *tutor* whose legal powers were comparable to *patria potestas*.[8] But Servius may well not have been using *potestas* in a special technical sense; certainly by the time he wrote underage children without a *paterfamilias* (*pupilli*) were *sui iuris* and not in the *potestas* of guardians.[9]

Whatever the earliest law of guardianship, in the XII Tables (5.3) testators were already able to leave a *testamentum* specifying the choice of a *tutor* (labelled *testamentarius*) as well as the division of the patrimony. The third principal type of *tutor*, appointed by magistrates, was added during the middle Republic by the *lex Atilia* (? 210 BC). Since the Roman jurists elaborated the law of guardianship in terms of these basic types, they require some detailed attention.[10]

The testamentary *tutor* was the primary type, in the sense that a Roman father was felt to have a strong responsibility to leave a will dividing his property and naming guardians. A Roman who failed to settle the matter of guardianship was labelled *intestatus* on this count, just as the Roman who failed to leave valid instructions regarding his property. In a proper *testamentum* the guardian was named through the formula "Lucium Titium liberis meis tutorem do" or "Lucius Titius ... tutor esto" (Gaius, *Inst.* 1.149; 2.289). Owing to the strong presumption in favor of the father's intent, if his will was somehow flawed, the magistrate was supposed to confirm the father's choice, barring unforeseen changes in circumstances (*Dig.* 26.3.8).[11] The fact that a testamentary *tutor* was the father's special, trusted choice affected the rules of this type of guardianship. For example, the testamentary *tutor* was not required to put up security (*cautio*) to guarantee proper performance of the duty.

If a father left no will or specified no guardian, the duty fell to the orphan's male agnates of the nearest degree, the *tutores legitimi* (older brothers, then paternal uncles). The general rule, stated as early as 100 BC by Q. Mucius Scaevola (*Dig.* 50.17.73.pr), was that the inheritance followed the guardianship, except that women could inherit but not serve as guardians.[12] Thus, the *pupillus* and the inheritance were protected by the male heirs next in line. But kinship was not regarded as an adequate safeguard by jurists in the imperial era, and *tutores legitimi* could be required to give security.

In the absence of a *tutor testamentarius* or *legitimus*, the magistrate could be approached to appoint one. In Republican Rome the appropriate authority was the urban praetor, together with a majority of the plebeian tribunes; in

[8] Guarino 1948; Kaser 1971: 76. [9] Watson 1967: ch. 9.
[10] Solazzi 1960: 81. The *tutor praetorius*, appointed by the urban praetor for particular legal cases or in special circumstances, is not relevant here. [11] Solazzi 1957: 297.
[12] Watson 1967: 117.

the provinces it was the governor, following the late Republican *lex Iulia et Titia*. The emperor Claudius replaced the praetor with the consuls in this job, and later Marcus Aurelius added a special *praetor tutelaris* (Hist. Aug., *Marc.* 10.11). There is disagreement among historians of Roman law over whether local magistrates or councils also had the power to appoint guardians for citizens of modest wealth.[13] Although the evidence does not clearly settle the legal principle, an early second-century document of the remarkable Babatha archive from Arabia Petrea reveals the boule of Petra taking upon itself the responsibility for such an appointment.[14] A magistrate might make an appointment with or without an inquiry (*inquisitio*) into the character and finances of the prospective *tutor*. In the absence of an inquiry, it was incumbent on the magistrate to demand security, and there was incentive to do so, inasmuch as the magistrates could be held liable for the shortcomings of a *tutor* who turned out to be insolvent at the time of the appointment.[15]

The guardian's responsibilities for the ward's estate during the *tutela* and his financial liability at the end made the *officium* a significant burden. It was standard practice for the guardian to begin by drawing up an inventory of the estate. He then had the responsibility to manage the property with a view to providing the *pupillus* with maintenance until puberty and to turning over the estate, preferably enriched, at that time (*Dig.* 27.2.3.1, Ulpian). Management would have routinely included the sale of the produce from the estate, the collection and payment of debts, and the investment of any profits to yield further income. The precise nature of the legal duties depended on the age of the *pupillus*. While the ward was an infant and too young to participate in legal transactions, the *tutor* had full responsibility for the administration of business (*negotiorum gestio*). But in this capacity the *tutor* could technically bind only himself in contracts with third parties; moreover, he could alienate property from the estate only by *traditio* (handing over), not by *mancipatio* (the form required for sale of land, slaves and major livestock). Various legal devices were developed to circumvent the limitations, for instance the use of the *pupillus'* slave to acquire on the infant's behalf. When the *pupillus* was old enough to speak for himself (fixed at age seven in later Roman law), the role of the guardian changed to one of validation of the *pupillus'* acts through his authority (*auctoritatis interpositio*). Transactions of this sort were simpler insofar as they were directly between the third party and the *pupillus*, not the guardian.[16] Without the *auctoritas* of a *tutor*, any transaction by a *pupillus* could be nullified through *restitutio in integrum*, if it turned out to be to his

[13] Solazzi 1956, Arangio-Ruiz 1956, Grelle 1960.
[14] P. Yadin 12–13 in Yadin 1989; see also Biscardi 1972.
[15] *Dig.* 27.8.8.12–13, Ulpian. Lecomte 1928: 237, 250.
[16] For a clear and succinct statement, Zulueta 1953: II, 49; also Solazzi 1955: 89–129.

disadvantage. The formal rules governing the management of *tutela*, minimal during the Republic,[17] became increasingly elaborate and restrictive in the classical and post-classical eras. In a major step Septimius Severus in AD 195 flatly prohibited *tutores* from selling their wards' rural or suburban estates, or using them as security (*Dig.* 27.9.1.2, Ulpian).

At the end of *tutela* upon the child reaching puberty (fixed at age twelve for girls and eventually at fourteen for boys[18]), the guardian turned over management of the property and gave a final accounting. Improper administration made the *tutor* liable to legal action by the ward. Along with increasing regulation came higher standards of liability, to the point that, in the judgment of W. W. Buckland, "the interests of the *pupillus* were in the foreground and were safeguarded to an almost unreasonable extent."[19] During the *tutela* a testamentary *tutor* could be charged as *suspectus* for fraudulent management (*crimen suspecti tutoris*); if *dolus* (fraud) on his part was proven, he was removed and suffered infamy.[20] Upon the end of the *tutela* the *actio rationibus distrahendis* ("action for the pulling apart of accounts") was available against the *tutor* for embezzlement; already available in the XII Tables (8.20b), this may have been for a time the only action against a *legitimus*, with conviction carrying *infamia* and a double award.[21] After coming of age, the young heir could also bring the broader *actio tutelae* on the ground that the tutor had not carried out his duties in accordance with good faith, *bona fides*. A successful action brought compensation for the ward and *infamia* for the *tutor*. The *actio tutelae* was available by the time of Q. Mucius Scaevola against *tutores* appointed by testators or magistrates, and by the classical period was probably extended to *legitimi* as well.[22] The standard of liability in this action is a subject of disagreement among Roman lawyers. It increased from *dolus* to *culpa* (fault without fraudulent intent), and eventually, under Justinian, to failure to exercise the utmost *diligentia*, but the chronology is uncertain. It used to be thought that *culpa* was a post-classical extension, but MacCormack has argued for its existence as early as the late first century after Christ on the basis of a reference to it by the jurist Aristo (*Dig.* 26.7.61, quoted by Pomponius), and Watson has suggested that it may be implied in a comment

[17] Watson 1967: 131.
[18] The classical jurists debated whether fixed age or physical inspection was the appropriate means of establishing puberty for boys; see Dalla 1978: 191–99.
[19] Buckland 1963: 154.
[20] This charge initiated a criminal proceeding in the XII Tables (8.20a), but later in classical law resulted in removal rather than public punishment. It is uncertain when it was extended to other types of *tutores*. Classical law also allowed for the removal of a merely incompetent *tutor* without infamy. Kaser 1971: 80; Solazzi 1913: 259–85; 1957: 101–46; Watson 1967: 139.   [21] Solazzi 1957: 201–10, 287–97; Watson 1967: 139.
[22] Kaser 1971: 309; Watson 1967: 140; *contra* Solazzi 1957: 292, who believes in general that the legal actions were extended only in later law.

of Q. Mucius Scaevola before the end of the Republic (*Dig.* 33.1.7).[23] If Watson and MacCormack are right, their cases show that in the early empire actionable fault on the part of the *tutor* included even the payment of a maintenance allowance for the *pupillus* in a way not specifically authorized in the will, loss of produce stored in the *tutor's* house through a fire, and negligence in failing to charge a fellow *tutor* as suspect.

As the last example of *culpa* indicates, the appointment of two or more *tutores* (*contutores*) for a *pupillus* raised whole new sets of legal questions, enough to require a monograph to analyze.[24] The *tutela* could be administered by the *contutores* together or by one managing *tutor* (*tutor gerens*), or the *tutela* could be divided by region among the *contutores* – each arrangement with its own legal consequences. *Tutores legitimi* had no choice: because the institution was originally designed to protect their collective interest, they had to act as a group, all giving their *auctoritas* to every transaction and all liable as a group *in solidum* for shortcomings.[25] The situation of testamentary *contutores* was different: because the testator demonstrated his trust by choosing them, each had the power individually to validate a transaction by his *auctoritas*. It was recognized that joint management by *contutores* was not the most efficient way to run a consolidated estate (*Dig.* 26.7.3.1). Therefore, a father might specify his intention in his will that one *tutor* should undertake active management, in which case his *auctoritas* was needed and he was liable in the first instance. In the case of a very extensive and dispersed patrimony, the testator could divide the *tutela* into spheres and assign one *tutor* to each, in which case that *tutor's auctoritas* was valid only in the sphere for which he was primarily liable. If the father did not assign responsibilities, then the matter could be settled among the *contutores* by one putting himself forward as manager and giving security to the others for proper performance.[26]

Although in all these arrangements the managing *tutor* bore primary liability for his own actions, the others still had a subsidiary liability on the ground that they had responsibility to supervise the managing *tutor* and to bring his mismanagement or his personal financial insolvency to the magistrate's attention. As Ulpian wrote in Book 35 on the Edict,

---

[23] MacCormack 1970; Watson 1967: 143. The inconclusiveness of the debate stems from the circularity of the interpolation arguments, with references to *culpa* in the classical jurists being excluded as intrusions of the compilers. Arangio-Ruiz 1927 argues that the only classical standard is *dolus*, but sees *dolus* as including a *tutor's* failure to draw up an inventory or to dispose of produce.

[24] Lecomte 1928; also Solazzi 1957: 37–62. Voci 1970 is less influenced by the interpolationist current and more convincing.

[25] Lecomte 1928: 76; Voci 1970: 82.

[26] Against those arguing that in classical law there was only liability *in solidum*, Voci (1970) shows that *beneficium divisionis* goes back to the classical era.

The other *tutores* do not administer, but are those commonly called honorary. Let no one think that no risk falls back on them: for it is agreed that they ought to be sued, after the resources of the one who managed have been exhausted. For they have been appointed as observers of his behavior and custodians, and sometimes it will be asked of them why, if they saw him behaving badly, they did not charge him as suspect. It is also incumbent upon them assiduously to demand an accounting from him and to show solicitous care over what sort of life he is living. And if there is money that can be invested, they are to see to it that it is invested in the purchase of estates. For those who think that honorary *tutores* are in no way held liable are fooling themselves.[27]

This joint liability amounted to a joint guarantee by all *contutores* to safeguard the *pupillus'* property, because, as Papinian points out, "if certain of them are not able to pay, without doubt the rest will bear the burden" (*Dig.* 26.7.38.1). Even in a case where municipal magistrates in appointing two *tutores* failed to demand security as they should, and one *tutor* died in poverty, the other *tutor* was liable for the whole sum owing to the *pupillus'* estate, because "it was the *tutor's* fault that security was not taken from his fellow *tutor* or that he was not proved untrustworthy" (*Dig.* 27.8.2). Ultimately, if the *pupillus'* claims exhausted the resources of all the *tutores* in such a case, the magistrates failing to take the proper security were held liable.[28]

The greater regulation and liability made avoidance of *tutela* more desirable. During the Republic withdrawal from the duty (*abdicatio*) was available to testamentary *tutores*. *Legitimi* could not abdicate the duty, but did not have to take an active part in management. The appointment by a magistrate was regarded as a public *munus* or duty, not to be refused without good cause. Claudius made testamentary guardianship similarly compulsory unless the appointee had a valid excuse.[29] By the mid second century *abdicatio* was no longer allowed, and a body of law on valid excuses was elaborated, growing to the point that Modestinus in the late classical period devoted six books to the subject, also treated in a title of the *Digest* (27.1) and a substantial proportion of the Vatican Fragments (123–247). Acceptable excuses ranged from private circumstances, such as poor health, numerous children, old age, and living an impractical distance from the estate, to other public obligations, such as three other *tutelae* at the time,

---

[27] *Dig.* 26.7.3.2. Kaser 1959: 166 accepts the authenticity of this passage, but Lecomte 1928: 94 judges it heavily contaminated by the legal duty of charging a *contutor* as suspect, a duty believed by him and earlier Romanists to have been post-classical. Voci 1970 defends the classical origin of this and other passages, interpreting them in terms of mutual guarantee.

[28] On the complex issues of magistrates' liability, Voci 1970: 137–54.

[29] Kaser 1971: 301.

public office, and military service.[30] By the end of the classical era, a *tutor* chosen by a magistrate could nominate another, more suitable candidate before the magistrate to take his place (*Frag. Vat.* 157, Ulpian). The one member of the household who had no valid excuse was the testator's freedman, whose obligation to the family required service.

The end of *tutela* at puberty came well before the child was regarded as having reached the *aetas perfecta* of twenty-five and hence fully competent to manage his property. As Ulpian wrote with reference to youths younger than twenty-five, "all agree that anyone of this age is not strong and is weak in good sense" (*Dig.* 4.4.1.pr). Not long after the Second Punic War, the *lex Laetoria* was passed to provide protection for *minores* (that is, youths between puberty and age twenty-five) by imposing penalties on anyone perpetrating a fraudulent deal on them.[31] In addition, the praetor would grant a reversal through *restitutio in integrum* of any inadvisable, disadvantageous transaction made by a youth. To protect himself against such consequences, the party dealing with the youth could ask him to have present an experienced adult, a *curator*, as an advisor whose *consensus* certified the transaction as fair. In the late empire, the institution of *cura minorum* was regularized in a way effectively to extend guardianship from puberty to age twenty-five. Its legal rules were assimilated to the rigorous rules of *tutela impuberum* (including the Severan prohibition on alienation of land), so that the two institutions tended to be conflated by Justinian's compilers. The steps in the 700-year evolution of *cura minorum* seem to have been: (1) the *lex Laetoria* encouraging the voluntary and ad hoc use of *curatores* to safeguard the interests of youths in individual transactions; (2) *curatores* serving on a continuous but still voluntary basis for minors until they reached age twenty-five; (3) continuing *cura* regularized, as the *curator* took over administration of the minor's estate; (4) permanent *cura* made compulsory on much the same terms as *tutela*. Given the unfortunate loss of the relevant passage in Gaius' *Institutes*, the precise chronology of this evolution through the classical era is unclear.[32] It would seem that from the time of the *lex Laetoria* anyone in a significant transaction with a minor would have had considerable incentive to ask for the presence of a *curator*. In a surviving paragraph (*Inst.* 1.199), Gaius does refer to a *curator* being required by the praetor to give security that the ward's property would be safe, suggesting that in the mid-second century after Christ *curatores* were managing the estates of *minores* on a continuing basis. The biography of Marcus Aurelius (Hist. Aug. *Marc.* 10.12) credits him with regularizing permanent *cura minorum* as an institution. The *curator*'s management of the

---

[30] Kaser 1971: 304; Solazzi 1957: 93–99, 239–48, 421–63.
[31] Evans 1991: 190 argues that the law was prompted by the unusually large number of orphans left by the Hannibalic War.   [32] Zulueta 1953: II, 53–54.

estate made him liable to the *actio negotiorum gestorum* for improper decisions. When *cura* became compulsory in the late empire, the body of law on excuses was carried over from *tutela*.

This is a sketch of the Roman law of guardianship (passing over the finer legal details). It must now be asked how it was used within the Roman demographic, social and economic context.

The demographic background

As a result of the agnatic roots and assumptions of Roman law concerning gender, the institutions of guardianship were defined in terms of the *fatherless* child. As a guide to the pervasiveness of guardianship, it is useful to examine the kinship tables generated by the microsimulation in order to discover the proportions of *pupilli* (fatherless children under puberty) and *minores* (between puberty and twenty-five). The questions of proportion can be posed from several viewpoints, each necessary to answer different social and economic questions. The three viewpoints might be described as the orphan's, the father's, and the aggregate.

From the child's point of view we would like to know what proportion were likely to have lost their fathers before puberty, and between puberty and age twenty-five. The tables suggest that just over one-third of Roman children lost their fathers before puberty, and another third then lost their fathers before age twenty-five.[33] In other words, it was usual, rather than exceptional, for children to be left with their patrimonies before they were regarded as mature enough to manage them. The proportions are so high because of the high mortality and the pattern of late male marriage. As a result, the average age at paternity was between thirty-five and forty, at which point the Roman father with a newborn had about the same chance of dying within the next ten years as a sixty-year-old in a contemporary western European society today (about 20 percent).

A father drawing up his will would have looked at the situation rather differently: if he had any underage children, or if there was a possibility that his wife might be pregnant at his death, he would have to make arrangements for guardianship. Conscious of their mortality, most married men with substantial property were likely at one time or another in their lives to draw up a will appointing guardians.

---

[33] Of the "ordinary" population, Level 3 West, 34 percent were fatherless by age fourteen; 63 percent were fatherless by age twenty-five. Of the "senatorial" population, Level 3 West, 32 percent were fatherless by age fourteen; 57 percent were fatherless by age twenty-five. Of the "senatorial" population, Level 6 West, 26 percent were fatherless by age fourteen; 50 percent were fatherless by age twenty-five.

In order to assess the overall economic and social implications, the aggregate question is worth posing: what proportion of all citizens *sui iuris*, hence potential property owners, were under the age of puberty or under the age of twenty-five? This can be calculated by taking each age cohort in the population pyramid and multiplying the size of the cohort by the percentage in that cohort without fathers. As each cohort grew older, naturally it decreased in numbers, but the fraction without fathers increased. As a result, the absolute numbers of *sui iuris* males in their twenties, in their thirties, and in their forties must have been more or less the same, each comprising about a fifth of the whole *sui iuris* population. The median age of all *sui iuris* men was between thirty and thirty-five years, and there were more legally independent males under fifteen than over fifty years of age. Thus it would be wrong to imagine that old men in Rome owned the empire's wealth with the consequent political leverage. Roughly one-sixth of all independent property owners in the Roman world were children under the age of puberty and another one-fifth were between ages fourteen and twenty-five. In other words, a very substantial minority of the property owners in the Roman world, more than a third, were too young to be fully competent to manage their estates. The economic implications of that conclusion are considerable and worth exploring.

Tutela in Roman morality and literature

This demographic background explains why the jurists treated *tutela* at such length: orphans must have been a pervasive concern in Rome, as in other societies before the demographic transition. Nor was the concern limited to lawyers: *tutela* appeared prominently in Roman moral thought and consequently figured in Roman rhetoric and literature as a relatively common topos. Romans were much concerned about questions of duty, *officium*, and strove for an explicit ordering of priorities. Aulus Gellius (*NA* 5.13) reports a discussion *de gradu atque ordine officiorum* ("concerning the hierarchy and order of duties") in which there was some disagreement about the order of *officia* among those experts in *morum disciplinarumque veterum doctrina* ("special knowledge of ancient customs and right practices"). Yet these moral authorities had no disagreement with regard to the top of the list: setting aside duty to parents, the first duty on the list was *tutela* of *pupilli*. After *tutela* came, in one order or another, hospitality, *clientela*, kinship and so on. To settle their differences, Gellius' unnamed interlocutors appealed to authoritative figures from the past. The ostentatiously moral elder Cato of the early second century BC was quoted on the importance of duty to clients, ahead of which came only *pupilli*: "'our ancestors (*maiores*) held it more sacred (*sanctius*) to defend *pupilli* than not to deceive a client.

One testifies against kin (*cognatos*) on behalf of a client; no one gives testimony against a client. They hold the name of father first, then patron next'" (Gellius *NA* 5.13.4). The recurring language of sanctity, found in this passage, is noteworthy. A different opinion was quoted from Masurius Sabinus, who two centuries later in his *Ius Civile* claimed that the ancestors placed *hospitium* ahead of *clientela*, which came ahead of duty to *cognati* (kin by blood) and *adfines* (kin by marriage); but before all these came the responsibility of *tutela*. In addition, Sabinus explicitly distinguished *tutela* of women from that of *pupilli*, and assigned *pupilli* priority (Gellius *NA* 5.13.5). Cicero reported that the great Republican jurist Q. Mucius Scaevola attached special importance to good faith in guardianship (*Off.* 3.70), and Cicero himself, in his *De natura deorum* (3.74), picked out *tutela* as among the most sacred trusts. That the Romans placed *tutela* among personal *officia* is perhaps not surprising, but that they should rate it above all but bonds within the immediate family deserves emphasis.

Cicero in his speeches against Verres (*Verr.* 2.1.153) explains why *tutela* should have been an *officium* held so sacred: "We all have small children. It is uncertain how long a life each of us will have. While still living we must take counsel and forethought so that our children's deprivation and young years may be protected by as firm a protection as possible." For Roman fathers, then, higher mortality made death more imminent, and the need to protect the vulnerability of their children more immediate, than in our experience. It was critical for them to be able to trust in the proper performance of *tutela*. As Quintilian indicates (*Inst.* 4.1.13), *pupilli* were regarded, along with women and the old, as among the weak in society needing protection.

The sanctity of the trust opened the way for orators and satirists to manipulate the theme of violation. Good men were described as virtuous *tutores* who felt love (*amor*, Quintilian *Inst.* 11.1.59) and parental affection toward their wards, as the excellent Verginius Rufus had shown toward Pliny (*Ep.* 2.1.8). Conversely, a stock accusation against an evil enemy was that he preyed on helpless *pupilli*. Cicero used the ploy repeatedly. Verres as *tutor* robbed the estate of his *pupillus* Malleolus (*Verr.* 2.1.90–94); so also one Staienus (*Cluent.* 68). Even more nefarious, archenemy Clodius was said to be engaged in murdering orphans (*pupillos necavit*, *Har. Resp.* 42). The *spoliator pupilli* ("despoiler of his ward") is a recurring figure in satire. Persius cynically imagines a man praying aloud for a good reputation and *fides* while secretly wishing for the death of his *pupillus*, whom he will succeed as *proximus heres* (2.12). The figure of the *spoliator pupilli* illustrates Juvenal's satiric vision of a corrupt society without *fides* (10.223, 15.135). What could be a more damning commentary on the greed of Roman society than the image of such a despoiler enjoying the attention of "herds of companions" eager for a share of the plunder (1.46–47)? Poets may be mad, according to Horace, but not as mad as the man who goes in for fraud on *socio puerove pupillo* ("partner or orphaned boy," *Epist.* 2.1.123).

Law and practice

It is within the context of the sacred duty of the *tutor* and the vulnerability of the ward that we should consider the specific configuration of Roman legal arrangements and social practices that put the *pupillus* at the center of a web of legal, social and administrative relationships, and economic interests. The legal rules reviewed above offer a general insight into the relationships and responsibilities but are by no means a simple reflection of how families actually behaved. As suggested in previous chapters, legal rules cannot be imposed on men and women as a kind of straightjacket thoroughly fixing behavior. It is necessary, then, to examine the literary, legal and documentary evidence to understand how these institutions were used and enforced in the Roman empire.

With regard to the social location of guardianship institutions, it goes without saying that the propertied elite had the greatest interest in, and were most influenced by, the intricacies of the law and recourse to the courts. Yet clearly many modest Romans – soldiers, smallholders, artisans – also had assets that they wished to transmit to their children under the protection of a guardian. A tombstone from Rome witnesses a centurion commemorated by his son with the help of his *tutor* (*CIL* 6.3331). From Egypt comes the papyrus *testamentum* of a soldier who appointed a fellow soldier as *tutor* to his young son (*FIRA* III.47, 23–27). Another *pupillus* living in Rome seems to have been of a modestly prosperous family, to judge by the sum of 225 denarii spent by his *tutor* on the burial of his mother (*CIL* 6.25144). More broadly, the jurists took up the problem of the obligations of *tutela* for members of artisanal *collegia*: different *collegia* and *corpora* received various privileges of exemption, with many (including the *collegium fabrorum*) being required to serve as *tutores* only for children of their own members (*Dig.* 27.1.17.3, Callistratus; 27.1.41.2, Hermogenianus).

The propertied child whose father had died presented a range of needs and responsibilities: nurturing, management of his inheritance, and appointment of the nurturers and managers. Those duties have been distributed in different ways in different societies. Perhaps the most obvious way of dealing with the orphan is to leave the whole responsibility to the mother.[34] This may well have been the most common practice among the humble classes in Rome. Classical Roman law, however, separated the duties of

---

[34] Carron 1989: ch. 4 provides evidence for the tendency in regions of medieval France to assign guardianship to the mother.

nurturing and property management. Although in classical law mothers were generally not eligible to manage their children's patrimony (*Dig.* 26.2.26. pr), it was assumed that they would continue to have custody (*custodia*) and to live with their children after the father's death. If a mother was not available or suitable, the praetor was supposed to appoint another caretaker, kinsmen by blood or marriage and freedmen being obvious choices. The jurists argued over whether an unwilling relative could be compelled to undertake the responsibility: Ulpian believed that it was sometimes necessary for the magistrate to insist (*Dig.* 27.2.1.2). Testators sometimes asked trusted freedmen (perhaps the ones who had had a part in child-care) to stay on with the children in return for a legacy or annuity.[35]

As indicated above, it was encumbent on propertied Romans to write a will with instructions on how their estate was to be distributed, and the Roman who failed to leave a valid will was *intestatus* (*Dig.* 26.4.6, Paulus) – not just a legal label but a serious social criticism of imprudence.[36] Therefore, the fact that it was also applied to the father-testator who failed to make provision for a guardian deserves more emphasis than it is usually given. The judgment makes pragmatic sense, since without a dependable and effective guardian, a rich estate of a child heir was an invitation to plunder. So a Roman father's discretion in naming a *tutor* might be just as important as his well-known discretion in dividing his property. The significance becomes apparent if the alternatives are considered. Had guardianship always devolved automatically to the nearest male relative, as in some societies, the father would have had less opportunity to choose the man most likely to protect his child's interest. In late medieval and early modern England noble wards were treated as plums in the hands of the king to distribute, producing a considerable income for the crown.[37]

Where a father failed to designate a *tutor testamentarius*, or the *tutor* died and no close agnate was available, it was up to the mother, the family's freedmen, or other relatives to approach the magistrate to request the appointment of a *tutor*. It was expected that mothers would do so out of natural concern for their children (*Dig.* 26.6.1, Modestinus), but it was also a legal requirement for them and freedmen. Septimius Severus ruled that mothers who neglected this responsibility forfeited their right to inherit their children's estates (*Dig.* 26.6.2.1).

The jurists tried to maintain the division between the mother's custodial function and the *tutor*'s proprietary function. Even if fathers left instructions in their wills that women be allowed to decide how much income to devote to the daily maintenance of the child, Scaevola believed the provision to be

---

[35] *Dig.* 40.5.41.16; on the role of slaves and freedmen in child-rearing, see Bradley 1991: chs. 2–3.   [36] Crook 1973; Champlin 1991: ch. 1.
[37] Buckland and McNair 1952: 47–48.

invalid, since such a decision ought to lie with *bonus vir* (*Dig.* 26.7.47.1). The reason for the separation of duties was in part that widowed mothers often remarried, and there was a danger that a mother in her second marriage might try to divert her children's patrimony to her new family. In the late empire, when the formal law was changed to permit mothers to be *tutores*, the condition was that they not remarry until their children came of age.

Despite the jurists' best efforts, the separation between *custodia* and *tutela* could not always be neatly maintained. The *tutor* did not have authority in personal decisions such as the choice of a spouse, but certain responsibilities were bound to involve him in the upbringing of the child. So, the *tutor* had to provide an allowance out of the patrimony; too large a sum risked spoiling the *pupillus*, according to Seneca (*Ira* 2.21.6–8). The guardian was seen to have an influence on the *mores pupilli* in appointing and paying a teacher (*Dig.* 26.7.12.3, Paulus). Nor were *tutores* always autonomous in managing the estate. A father-testator might want the mother to be involved with the child's property, instructing the *tutores* to manage *consilio matris* (with the advice of the mother, *Dig.* 26.7.5.8). Mothers are credited with supervising their children's property by authors of the late Republic and early empire.[38] The impossibility of a neat separation comes through in the literary sources which sometimes credit mothers with *tutela* in a loose sense (for example, Seneca *Cons. ad Marc.* 24.1). Livy could imagine a contest between mother and *tutores* over the selection of a husband for a young girl (4.9.5–6). This sort of confusion of responsibilities was perceived to have its dangers. In Livy's account (39.9.2–3), the Bacchanalian conspiracy was revealed in 186 BC through the orphan Publius Aebutius under the *tutela* of a mother and stepfather, who needed to cover up their peculation by corrupting the youth.[39]

Although not sharply delineated, there was a general division of the nurturing and proprietary responsibilities for the fatherless child, and it had significant consequences. The mother and the *tutor* were brought into contact and potential conflict by the *tutor*'s duty to provide the *pupillus* with income from the estate to support him and his slave retinue and to pay for clothes, shelter, and education. The *tutor*'s interest in preserving the estate, and thus protecting himself from a lawsuit, was sometimes at odds with the mother's wish for funds to maintain the household in style. The potential for conflict was all the greater insofar as the mother, as the closest relative, was regarded as an obvious watchdog over the *tutor*'s administration and one likely to initiate charges against the *tutor* for corruption. The mother was first in the list of females permitted to bring a charge against a suspect *tutor* on account of their *pietas* toward the *pupillus* (*Dig.* 26.10.1.7, Ulpian). The

---

[38] Cicero *Verr.* 2.1.105–6; Seneca *Cons. ad Helv.* 14.3, with Dixon 1988: ch. 3.
[39] Pailler 1990: 77.

Babatha archive shows a mother bringing charges against her son's *tutores* for an inadequate allowance and peculation.[40] But mothers were not held accountable for failure to bring such charges, "since it is for the masculine mind to judge and determine facts of this kind and a mother can be ignorant even of criminal acts" (*Dig.* 26.6.4.4, Tryphoninus).

It appears that the division of responsibilities for the child-heir, and the resulting potential for adversarial relationships, was to a certain extent intentional – a means of protecting the child from the arbitrary actions of any one adult. This would help to explain one of the most interesting features of Roman guardianship, the propensity to appoint multiple *tutores*, *contutores*. Juristic discussions, legal documents, and casual references to guardianship in Latin literature suggest that multiple *tutores* must have been the norm.[41] Cicero was one of several *contutores* appointed for T. Pinnius' son, as was Verres for young Malleolus (*Fam.* 13.61, *Verr.* 2.1.92). Elsewhere in Cicero's speeches orphans are also represented as having multiple *tutores* (*Sest.* 111; *Verr.* 2.1.104–6, 130–51; 2.3.16). For his unborn child, Julius Caesar appointed in his will *tutores*, many of whom (*plerique*) turned up among his assassins – a sorry story of unrequited trust (Suetonius *Iul.* 83.2). In his consolation to Marcia on the death of her son (24.1), Seneca refers to the son's *tutores* during childhood. Multiple *tutores* also turn up in Roman funerary commemorations and in chance finds of papyrus documents from the eastern provinces of the empire.[42] If *contutores* were a typical arrangement, then it is not surprising to find authors like Livy (4.9.5–6) and Apuleius (*Met.* 1.6) writing stories with passing references to multiple *tutores*. The jurists also repeatedly imagined cases involving *contutores*: sometimes the fact of more than one *tutor* had a bearing on the case, but sometimes it was apparently gratuitous (for example, *Dig.* 26.7.57.1, 58.3; 33.1.7 quoting Q. Mucius).

Since the practice of appointing multiple *tutores* complicated questions of authorization and liability, and was generally not followed in the modern civil law tradition in France, Germany, Switzerland, and Spain, it should be asked why it was so popular in Rome.[43] At least four reasons may be suggested. First, a single *tutor* might not be able to complete the duty. The jurist Scaevola pointed to the testator's concern that a *tutor* might die or be excused as a motive for appointing more than one.[44] It is impossible to know

---

[40] P. Yadin 13–15 in Yadin 1989; Biscardi 1972 points out that the form seems to be that of an *actio tutelae*, which in classical law could not properly be brought until the end of the *tutela*.   [41] Lecomte 1928: 16.

[42] *CIL* 6.24773, 29602; *FIRA* 3. 29, 30, 31 (in the latter two documents one of the *tutores* has withdrawn or is requesting to be excused); P. Yadin 12 in Yadin 1989.

[43] Lecomte 1928: 1–5.

[44] *Dig.* 26.2.34. Scaevola is here concerned specifically with a clause concerning *tutores* added in a codicil, but the same motive would presumably operate in the *testamentum* itself.

how often an appointee was excused by the magistrate, but model life tables suggest a not negligible risk that a *tutor* would die before his *pupillus* reached puberty.[45] Secondly, since it was an honor to be named *tutor*, just as it was to be named to a legacy, multiple *tutores* may have tended to become numerous for much the same reason as honorific legatees (see below). Thirdly, Roman fathers may have judged it wise to appoint *tutores* with a range of aptitudes and resources, from the trusted freedman with experience running the estate to a friend of highest status and greatest influence as a patron. For instance, in choosing Cicero as one of the *tutores* for his son, T. Pinnius recruited a powerful senator who could ask his friend the governor of Bithynia and Pontus to be sure that the city of Nicaea paid off his *pupillus* first among its creditors (*Fam.* 13.61). Pinnius may also have known Cicero well enough to realize that he was not the best choice to undertake direct management, being unable to administer his own estate without assistance. Finally, a motive perhaps not articulated by testators but implicit in juristic discussions: multiple *tutores* provided legal and practical safeguards in their joint liability and responsibility to watch over each other.

Who were chosen as guardians? Paulus wrote in general terms that "parents are accustomed to choose as *tutores* for their children those who are their closest and most faithful friends, *amicissimi et fidelissimi*, and then to reward them for undertaking the burden of *tutela* by the honor of a legacy" (*Dig.* 27.1.36.pr). The choice of the trusted friend as guardian can be found in Latin literature. In his narrative of the legendary regal period Livy supposed that Ancus Marcius' institution of Tarquinius Priscus as *tutor* to his sons followed from their intimate friendship (1.34.12). When Tarquin later usurped the sons' rule, they denounced the *tutoris fraus* (1.40.2). The theme of *fides* is echoed in an imperial funerary commemoration to a *tutor* "on account of the most faithful return of the estate by him" (*CIL* 6.2210). In addition to probity of character, it was important that the guardian be solvent to cover his liability. The father's designation of *tutores* was usually respected by the magistrates without any inquiry, but if it could be shown that since the father had written his will the appointee had suffered impoverishment or had been tainted by improbity or had quarrelled with the father, then the magistrate could appoint someone else to take his place (*Dig.* 26.3.8).

Certain relations appear repeatedly in the literary and juristic texts as common candidates for *tutela*. Close male relatives were the most obvious choices: a brother over the age of twenty-five or a paternal uncle.[46] The

---

[45] Perhaps one out of seven forty-year-old *tutores* would have died before completing five years of service, and one out of four before completing ten years.

[46] Brother: Apuleius *Apol.* 68; *Dig.* 26.7.39.17, 27.1.28.1, 27.3.9.1. *Patruus*: Cicero *Verr.* 2.1.135; *Dig.* 26.7.39.8, 43.1, 47.6.

Table 8.1. *Proportion of pupilli with at least one living kin at time of father's death*

Kin	"Ordinary" Level 3	"Senatorial" Level 3	"Senatorial" Level 6
Brother over age 25	.01	.03	.02
Paternal uncle over age 25	.41	.44	.47
Maternal uncle over age 25	.41	.42	.36*
No adult brother or uncle	.34	.32	.34

This table is based on the simulations described in chapter 3.
* Note
Though more *pupilli* had a living maternal uncle than a living paternal uncle (because women married at younger ages and hence mothers had more siblings still alive), fewer *pupilli* had maternal uncles over age 25 and legally able to accept the duty of *tutela* (because senatorial women married so young, hence their brothers were more likely to be under age 25).

paternal uncle was the expected choice to such a degree that, according to Scaevola, a *tutor* appointed by will had legitimate grounds for being excused if a *patruus* was available (*Dig.* 27.1.37. pr). Table 8.1 , however, shows that on demographic grounds many *pupilli* would not have had close male agnates over age twenty-five: perhaps only 1 or 2 percent had a brother over twenty-five and just over 40 percent a *patruus* at the time of their father's death. About one-third would not have had an adult brother, or paternal or maternal uncle, still alive. Freedmen are mentioned as *tutores* several times by the jurists, in one case as the *tutor* of a senator's child (*Dig.* 27.1.43, Hermogenianus). They were an especially practical choice insofar as they could not refuse and were experienced in carrying on the family's business interests (*Dig.* 26.7.58. pr, Scaevola; 27.3.1.6, Ulpian; also 26.2.32.2 for freed *tutores*).

In the longest passage about guardianship outside the legal sources, Cicero tells of Verres' attempt to plunder the estate of the *pupillus* of the publican Publius Iunius, and in so doing provides a small insight into one man's choice of a variety of *tutores*.[47] Among the close male relatives Iunius appointed the boy's stepfather (*vitricus*) and his paternal uncle; he also selected Publius Titius, identified as a *homo frugalissimus*, and Marcus Marcellus, a great senator. While the others handled the business, Marcellus was called on to bring his considerable *auctoritas* to bear to protect the boy's property from Verres' depredations. Cicero represents Verres' indifference

[47] On this family, see Nicolet 1974: 916.

to that authority as shocking, indicating why a father would want his child-heir to have a guardian in high places (*Verr.* 2.1.130–53).

In trying to gauge the extent to which these *tutores* were influenced to act in accordance with the legal rules, we need to know how often cases for maladministration were brought to court, or at least how common they were perceived to be. If guardians were never held to the legal standards, there is no reason to suppose that the body of law described above had much influence on the way *tutores* acted. On the other hand, if *tutores* perceived a significant risk of an *actio tutelae*, then it is reasonable to suppose that they managed their wards' estates in a way to avoid legal liability. Of course, there are no figures for rates of prosecution, but Ulpian does say that the clause on suspect *tutores* is very necessary, "for every day *tutores* are charged as suspect" (*Dig.* 26.10.1.pr). There are various indications to corroborate Ulpian's assessment. As early as the late Republic, before the era of rigorous regulation, Cicero claimed that a young girl's guardians would hesitate to pay money from the girl's *hereditas* to bribe the corrupt governor Verres because they would be held accountable later (*Verr.* 2.1.104–6). An Egyptian papyrus from the Augustan era shows a former *tutor* taking a receipt from his *pupillus* to prove that he had returned to the boy "everything that his father had in his estate."[48] As evidence of the desire to take precautions against an *actio tutelae*, this document is perhaps more revealing of expectations and fears than the papyri in Babatha's archive documenting an actual lawsuit of her son against his *tutores*. The frequency of lawsuits must have contributed to the perception of *tutela* as a burden in Rome, unlike other societies where guardianship was counted a bonanza because the guardian could milk or at least manipulate the ward's estate. In Rome, the *tutor* was commonly rewarded for his troubles with a legacy, which was taken away if the *tutor* tried to excuse himself. Nevertheless, an elaborate body of law on legitimate excuses from *tutela* was developed in the early empire. Surely underlying these phenomena was the fact that *tutores* were by and large held to high standards of conduct by the threat of legal action.

Even honest intentions were no sure protection against legal action, because the guardian had to make delicate decisions. In principle, it was the praetor's job to set the level of maintenance to be provided for the *pupillus* and his retinue out of the profits of his estate (*Dig.* 27.2.3. pr, Ulpian), but the Babatha documents show that *tutores* sometimes used their own judgment and could be challenged in court as a result. Just who was a member of the *pupillus'* retinue and deserved support was not altogether obvious. Should a *pupillus'* income be used to support his mother or sister? Ulpian's answer was

[48] *FIRA* 3.31, with translation and comment by Crook 1967a: 116.

yes, but only in certain circumstances: "If the *tutor* provides support for the mother of the *pupillus*, Labeo thinks that he can charge the estate. But it is truer to say that he ought not charge the estate unless he has given support to a needy mother out of plentiful resources of the *pupillus*." If Ulpian did not quite agree with Labeo over the provision of maintenance to a mother, they took the same view that a wedding gift for a mother was an unjustifiable expense (*Dig.* 27.3.1.4–5, Ulpian). If payments to immediate family members should be limited to necessary expenses, then what met that criterion? Was the cost of a teacher for a sister justified? Julian thought that it was, and the *tutor* would not be liable to a legal action, even if he had provided the funds without a magistrate's decree (*Dig.* 27.2.4). These and other passages in the *Digest* concerning appropriate expenditures from the *pupillus'* estate offer very interesting insights into what the Romans considered to be unnecessary or frivolous expenses and what was deemed necessary in accordance with the *pupillus'* station in life and social obligations: education of a young sister did meet the standard, support for a mother only if she was needy. The pressure to sort out such standards must have come from the risk of litigation: if he felt threatened by a lawsuit, a *tutor* would be eager to know just what constituted a chargeable expenditure.

Needless to say, not all *tutores* were conscientious, and the sources reveal some of the possibilities for dishonesty. A stock explanation for the diminished size of one's patrimony was a corrupt guardian – an explanation offered by Apuleius for his own circumstances in his *Apologia* (21). The jurists Marcian and Ulpian can envisage bribes being exchanged to acquire a *tutela* (*Dig.* 26.1.9; 26.10.3.15). The means of cashing in on a rich *tutela* were somewhat limited by the fact that the Roman guardian, unlike those later in England, did not have power over the person of the ward, and so could not legally arrange a marriage of a wealthy ward to a member of his own family. Ulpian envisages the possibilities that a corrupt *tutor* might make use of his *pupillus'* funds without paying interest or might purchase on behalf of his *pupillus* unsuitable lands "on account of meanness or influence" (*per sordes aut gratiam, Dig.* 26.7.7.2). Babatha charged the guardians of her son with lending his money at an unduly low rate of interest, to the profit of the borrower.[49]

Although dishonest *tutores* certainly existed, the jurists devote much less effort to them than to the liability of *tutores* who were not intentionally corrupt. Overall, one is left with a much stronger impression of *tutela* as a burden than as a source of profit. That is the only context in which it is

---

[49] P. Yadin 13 in Yadin 1989. A *contutor* was allowed to take loans from the *pupillus'* estate with the *auctoritas* of the fellow *tutores* as long as it was at the statutory rate of interest, which was not necessarily the highest rate available (*Dig.* 26.7.54, Tryphoninus).

possible to make sense of this passage from Modestinus (*Dig.* 27.1.6.17): "A deadly enmity conceived by the person appointed [*tutor*] toward the father of the person orphaned provides an excuse from *tutela*, except a *tutor* appointed by a provision in a will, unless the deadly hatred arose between them after the will was made or, although the hatred preceded the will, it was considered [by the father] a good move to appoint [his enemy] to the *tutela* so that he would be loaded with its burdens and administrative cares." In a world with ineffective legal protections for wards, Modestinus' scenario would be unthinkable.

Tutela in its social and economic context

The social ramifications of *tutela* must be understood in relation to a culture that placed great emphasis on the maintenance of honor and the competition for social status. For a Roman proper performance of guardianship was not just a matter of honesty but more broadly a matter of honor. Cicero in his oration *Pro Q. Roscio* 16 wrote that the three *iudicia privata* (private legal judgments) that most affected a man's *existimatio* or public reputation were breaking *fides*, defrauding a *pupillus*, and cheating a *socius*. In all three cases a man's honor was tainted by violation of a personal bond. The word *existimatio* recurs often in the jurists' discussions of *tutela*. In general, a *tutor* who was relieved of his duty suffered *infamia* – that is, disgrace and diminution of his citizenship rights – but under certain circumstances a *tutor* could be replaced "with his reputation intact," *integra existimatione* (for instance, if the position was taken away "on account of slowness or rusticity or inertia or simple-mindedness or ineptitude" [*Dig.* 26.10.3.18]). Ulpian urges magistrates to be explicit about the causes for removal in order to be clear about the consequences *de existimatione* (*Dig.* 26.10.4.1). Precisely because of the deleterious consequences for *existimatio*, Modestinus recommended that *tutores* bound to their *pupilli* as kinsmen (*necessarii* and *adfines*) or as patrons of the freed father should not be removed *cum notata fide et existimatione* (with tainted faith and reputation), but should be joined by a *curator* appointed to take over management (*Dig.* 26.10.9). Given Roman sensitivity to reputation, it is reasonable to suppose that the threat of losing it for despoiling a *pupillus* was a significant sanction.

Guardianship had the potential of contributing to a man's honor as well as diminishing it. No doubt in many societies men perceive others to be honest and honorable in varying degrees. In Roman culture there were vehicles for clear and public expression of those perceptions. The last will and testament, read out in public, was one of these.[50] In naming *tutores* for his children in his will, a Roman indicated whom he thought to be honorable

[50] Champlin 1991.

and trustworthy among those around him. Conversely, the omission of someone expected to be *tutor* implied distrust and was a dishonor. To blacken the reputation of the elder Oppianicus, Cicero in his *Pro Cluentio* pointed, as an indication of his ruthlessness, to the fact that his brother-in-law Cn. Magius conspicuously refused to entrust him with the *tutela* of his unborn child (33). Indeed, Oppianicus was so corrupt that "no one out of his very many kinsmen by blood and marriage (*cognati et adfines*) ever wrote down his name as *tutor* for their children" (41). Cicero later used the same rhetorical ploy in defense of Sestius against L. Gellius Poplicola, whom his sister's son did not appoint among the many *tutores* in his will (111). The efficacy of this rhetoric depended on the public quality of wills, the frequent need for guardians, social expectations about the appropriateness of certain kinsmen, and the testator's free choice to name multiple guardians as an honor.

The honor to be derived from being named as *tutor* depended in part on the status of the testator and *pupillus*. It seems likely that as a practical consideration a testator would have been inclined to name at least one *tutor* of greater power and wealth as the best protection for his children's estates – rather like the tendency to choose godparents of higher status in some recent Mediterranean societies. In response to that tendency to look upwards in the social hierarchy for guardians, the jurists developed rules about social rank and guardianship. The general principle was that one could be compelled to serve as *tutor* only for children of fathers of equal or greater status. So Marcus Aurelius issued a ruling (*Dig.* 26.5.27.1; 27.1.1.4) that only freedmen should be appointed as guardians to freedmen's children, but freedmen could also be compelled to undertake the duty for the freeborn as well. In general, honorable military service exempted veterans from *tutela* of civilians, but not *tutela* of fellow soldiers' children beyond the first year after discharge. The legal obligation was carefully differentiated by rank: ex-legionaries could be required to serve for children of other legionaries and *vigiles*; a *primipilarius* was obligated to serve only for children of other *primipilarii*; as a *beneficium* Septimius Severus and Caracalla gave former tribunes of the Praetorian Guard complete exemption from *tutela*, a privilege that not even senators enjoyed (*Dig.* 27.1.8, Modestinus; 27.1.9, Ulpian). Marcus Aurelius decided that senators could be compelled to serve as *tutores* for children of other senators, but not those of lower status (*Dig.* 27.1.15.2–3, Modestinus). The principle of obligatory *tutela* for children of men of equal or higher rank was not always straightforward to apply, and questions arose: for instance, what should be done in the case of a non-senator who undertook the *tutela* of a child below the senatorial order and then was promoted into the senate? Modestinus' answer was that he was released from the duty (*Dig.* 27.1.15.3). Did the principle of rank excuse a senator of higher office from serving as *tutor* for a child of a senator of lower office? Just like the distinction between legionary and *vigiles*, this one was not regarded as sufficient for an exemption (*Dig.* 27.1.15.2, Modestinus).

These passages show why we should not think of the Roman social hierarchy as some reified structure; rather, the hierarchy was a matter of cultural norms and distinctions worked out and reaffirmed in interpersonal relationships. *Tutela* was one of the institutions that regularly brought Romans into such relationships in a way that forced them to elaborate and fix rules about which distinctions counted for what.

Similarly, *tutela* required Romans to formulate standards for sound financial decision-making, so that they could assess a *tutor's* liability if his decisions were challenged by his ward or ward's mother or other relative. Implicit in the juristic writings is the Roman perception of sound estate management by the *bonus paterfamilias*. Where feasible, the goal was to produce profits at a level to support the *pupillus* and to have some left over to increase the capital of the estate (*Dig.* 27.2.3.1, Ulpian). Consequently, it was incumbent on the guardians to keep the *pupillus'* wealth invested to produce a profit. The standard investments mentioned repeatedly in the *Digest* are two: loans at interest and, above all, land.[51] *Tutores* were liable if they deposited money without interest and neglected to use the accumulated sum to buy a farm (*Dig.* 26.7.7.3; 26.7.49). Septimius Severus further tightened the regulations on *tutores'* administration in AD 195 with the prohibition of the sale of any of the *pupillus'* rural or suburban properties. Severus insisted on his rule even when the piece of land was barren, on the grounds that such land would not bring a price any higher than justified by its potential for income (*Dig.* 27.9.1.pr). Legal passages like this offer insights into the Roman economic mentality and should be a part of the discussion of the' ancient economy. They appear to me to reflect a somewhat sophisticated yet highly conservative attitude to investment – there is no thought of investing money in urban businesses or trade.[52]

The implications of this conservatism for the economy as a whole are not negligible. In the debates over Roman economic attitudes, there is often an unexpressed assumption that the decision-maker was an adult male, who either acted rationally or was constrained by social and economic values. Among adult males distinctions are sometimes made between economic attitudes of different classes, particularly aristocratic as opposed to freed.

---

[51] *Dig.* 26.7.5.pr, 26.7.7.7, 26.7.8, 26.7.54, 26.10.3.16, 27.4.3.6.
[52] The only apparent exception concerns two slaves who continued in the same business after being granted their freedom on the master's death. The legal question was whether they owed the *pupillus* the actual profits from the business or a standard rate of return on the value of the business. Scaevola favored the former (*Dig.* 26.7.58.pr). Since the case did not involve the *tutores* in making new investments, it is not really an exception to the rule of investment in land.

Yet a case could be made that much of the capital, possibly even most, was not owned by adult males or managed by adult males with a free hand. Aside from the property owned by women, the fact that perhaps one-sixth of the *sui iuris* males were *impuberes* suggests an economy in which a significant fraction of capital was managed by *tutores* within a legal and social framework that encouraged the safest investments, rather than the most profitable, as protection against later litigation. The property owned by the additional one-fifth of *sui iuris* males who were *minores* was probably also conservatively managed for the most part. By the end of the classical period much of that property was administered by *curatores* under much the same constraints as *tutores*. Even before the regularization of permanent *cura*, the *lex Laetoria* and the praetorian *restitutio in integrum* were intended to make adults cautious about engaging in risky transactions with youthful owners. In sum, perhaps as much as one-third of property-owning males were not of an age freely to manage their property. It is impossible to be precise about the economic consequences, but any discussion of economic mentalities in ancient Rome should start from the fact that much of the capital – not only property in *tutela* and *cura* but also, for example, dotal land in Italy – was subject to laws encouraging safe management or restricting alienation.[53]

In sum, the institutions related to guardianship pervaded the networks of social relations among propertied Romans. Any prudent, propertied Roman with children, or with even the prospect of children, needed to make arrangements for guardians in his will, to judge, in a fashion that would be made public, who among his relatives and friends was most trustworthy. High mortality lent these decisions greater importance and immediacy than felt by testators today. That minority of mature Roman propertied men fortunate to live long enough to see their children through to adulthood must have been called upon time and again to serve as *tutor* of others' children: three currently running *tutelae* was the standard for exemption. We would prefer to have quantitative empirical data to document these conclusions and to add precision. In the absence of such evidence, the value of the microsimulation becomes apparent in that it draws attention to an issue previously neglected. Once examined, the qualitative evidence shows that, whatever the exact extent of *tutela*, the bond between *tutor* and *pupillus* was regarded in Roman culture as more intense and more sacred, and in law was more highly regulated, than other pervasive forms of social relations such as *amicitia* or *hospitium*. That regulation, in turn, suggests some important ways in which *tutela* contributed to the structuring of social relations and economic decisions.

---

[53] Osborne (1988) discusses the rental of orphans' property in ancient Athens.

9

Dowries and daughters in Rome

Dowry was an institution of legal, economic and social dimensions that Roman fathers and mothers used to transmit property and status to their daughters. Although legitimate marriage in Roman law did not require validation by a dowry, the provision of one was a paternal duty (*officium paternum*) enforced by social expectation and law among the propertied classes. Like a creditor who automatically expected repayment of a debt, a husband expected payment of a dowry, "since he would not take a wife without one (*indotatam uxorem*)" (*Dig.* 42.8.25.1, Venuleius). Since lack of a dowry could effectively prevent a woman of the propertied classes from entering marriage, Augustus legislated against fathers who tried to stop a daughter's marriage by refusing to finance a dowry.[1] My aim in this chapter is not to repeat the recent systematic treatments of the legal rules and other evidence for dowries.[2] Rather, I wish to examine dotal exchange within the Roman legal and demographic context as one element related to others in the devolution of familial property. Although no systematic evidence for dowries is available, and the scattered testimony points in various directions, it may be possible to generalize beyond the assertion that "almost everything about Roman dowry is ambivalent."[3]

As one element in the devolution of property before the death of the parents, dowries in historical societies have varied in function and size – so much so that it could be argued that "dowry" as a catch-all category is

---

[1] *Dig.* 23.2.19, Marcianus. I follow the interpretation of Treggiari (1991a: 65), who traces the rule back to Augustus and finds the Severan innovation in the extension of the enforcement of the rule to provincial governors. *Contra*, Gardner 1986: 97.

[2] Gardner 1986: ch. 6 and especially Treggiari 1991a: ch. 10; these books, together with Gardner's response (1985) to my earlier article on the subject (1984), have helped me develop a better appreciation for the details and flexibility of the law. As will become clear, the central point of my earlier paper still seems right to me and worth elaborating here.   [3] Treggiari 1991a: 323.

misleading.[4] Since *dos* is a specific category in Roman law, even though dowries could differ widely in size and purpose, it does not seem sensible to drop it from the analysis. But it is essential carefully to distinguish the possible uses. Drawing on comparative evidence from other European societies, one may imagine a spectrum of uses and sizes. At one end would be small dowries that are little more than modest wedding gifts (say, a wife's small trousseau) and serve no maintenance or patrimonial function in the distribution of capital to the next generation. At the opposite end would be large dowries that give a daughter and her descendants a substantial share of her father's patrimony. Large dowries, implying in Goody's words a system of "diverging devolution," have regularly posed serious financial problems in societies where there is a strong urge to keep the patrimony consolidated in order to maintain the status of families. Between these two ends of the spectrum would be significant but modest dowries, intended to maintain the wife in her husband's household but not to satisfy her claim to the estate of her natal family. To understand Roman dowry it is useful to discover where it should be placed on this spectrum, and what were the various uses for and claims on it by the parties to the marriage.

A few comparisons

A casual survey of European agrarian societies of the past suggests that dowries have most often served to satisfy the daughter's claim on her father's estate. In ancient Greece dotal law varied from polis to polis. Where evidence has survived, dowries legally settled the daughter's claim, thus leaving the patrimony to be divided among the sons on the father's death. Athenian law stipulated that a daughter should have no share of the inheritance in a family with legitimate sons, and so the dowry provided a daughter with her portion of the family's wealth (sometimes as much as a quarter or more of the whole estate).[5] In the fifth-century law code of Gortyn on the island of Crete the dowry was explicitly treated as an alternative to the daughter's receipt of an inheritance, neatly illustrating Goody's general argument.[6] There, daughters had a right to one-half the share of their brothers, which they might receive either on their marriage as a dowry or on their father's death as an inheritance. Although in the laws of both Athens and Gortyn dowry had a patrimonial function, fathers in Gortyn apparently had less discretion in deciding the size of the daughter's share.

Later, in some societies of medieval and early modern Europe, dowries

---

[4] Brettell 1991: 340–53. For dowry as part of a larger system, see Goody and Tambiah 1973: 17–47; also Goody 1976. [5] Schaps 1979: ch. 6. and app. 1.
[6] Goody 1976: 6–7. Goody recognizes that the two means of transmission of property to daughters carry with them some noteworthy differences. Gortyn code iv.

constituted the daughter's share of the family estate, or at least the bulk of it. Customs regarding dotal settlements varied from place to place and time to time, but in general dowries were substantial, in many places several times the family's annual income. On the basis of far more extensive data than are available for the ancient world, Herlihy and Klapisch-Zuber have described the situation in fifteenth-century Florence, with its pattern of late male/early female marriage comparable to that in Rome. "Delayed marriage for men inevitably affected the treatment and the fate of urban girls. In the wealthy classes, high mortality and inevitable shrinkage in the age pyramid at its upper levels reduced the number of men near age thirty who might take as brides girls between the ages of fifteen and twenty. The families of these young girls thus entered a desperate competition for grooms; this competition drove up the value of dowries to ruinous levels ... In the early fourteenth century, Dante deplores the excessive amounts that Florentine dowries had already attained ... Near 1427 and, as in Venice, already for some time past, it seems that the sums paid for dowries had begun to rise ... The difficulties in dowering a daughter preoccupied family heads and even the communal government." The data from the catasto suggest that dowries represented, on average, 14 percent of the bride's family's estate and augmented the groom's wealth by 23 percent.[7]

The sizeable settlements found in Florence and later Europe had important consequences for family strategies.[8] First, large dowries required some families to allow only one daughter to marry, since it was not feasible to provide settlements for more (England appears to have been an exception in this respect, in part because dowries were relatively small). Secondly, dowries were seen as a major cause of debt, driving aristocratic families to borrow cash in order to avoid selling land. Thirdly, as a result there were widespread complaints about extravagant dowries leading to the ruin of great families (the Venetians, for instance, passed laws to limit their size). Nevertheless, aristocratic competition to achieve the most prestigious marriages possible for daughters continued to inflate dotal settlements from Venice to England. Fourthly, large dowries tended to result in endogamy within aristocracies, since wealthy aristocrats were the ones who could provide large dowries to secure prestigious marriages with other aristocrats. But a _nouveau riche_ could also use his money to buy a good match for his daughter, thus affording an opportunity to a poor noble family to re-establish its fortunes by offering a son in such a marriage. Some noble families were able to trade on their status in this way and to make a profit from dowry exchange over several generations, but most families in the

---

[7] Herlihy and Klapisch-Zuber 1985: 223–24, 227.
[8] For the European evidence I have depended on Cooper 1976: 249, 269, 283, 286, 301; Forster 1960: ch. 6; Davis 1975: 106; Stone 1965: 175; Litchfield 1969: 203.

long run probably paid out for their daughters' marriages roughly what they received from their sons'. I offer these broad generalizations as a heuristic device to call attention to important features of Roman dotal exchange.

Scanty though the evidence is, it is possible to suggest how Romans used the legal rules and dotal practices in their strategies for marriage and the transmission of wealth. A schematic description of function is to be avoided, however, since the law and practices changed over the centuries, and the classical law of *dos*, just like that of inheritance, offered fathers, mothers, daughters, and husbands alternatives to reach individual ends.

Legal rules and purposes of dowry

In early Rome, as far as it is possible to know from the inadequate and unreliable sources, marriage and dotal exchange were fairly straightforward, and in certain central respects resemble dotal customs in later, Christian Europe, when marriage was again conceived of as an arrangement for life. In early Rome marriage *cum manu* was the normal form.[9] Upon her marriage the woman passed from her father's *potestas* into her husband's and took her place *loco filiae* (in the position of a daughter). Along with her the dowry passed into the *dominium* of her husband or his *paterfamilias*, where it was added to the family's single pool of property. A woman married *cum manu* gave up her right to intestate succession in her father's family and became one of her husband's *sui heredes*, to inherit an equal share along with her children. Marriage was an arrangement for life, and divorce was heavily penalized. A wife divorced for moral faults lost her dowry, and a husband who divorced without just cause lost his entire estate. In this system of property devolution the dowry effectively served to satisfy the daughter's claim to the paternal estate, as it did in Athens and Gortyn.

Through the second century BC major developments, impossible to trace in our scanty sources, changed marriage customs. By the Ciceronian age, *matrimonium sine manu* (sometimes called "free marriage") was the dominant form. In such marriages the wife remained in her father's *potestas* and, when he died or emancipated her, she became *sui iuris* with an independent right to own property, which in law was entirely separate from her husband's. Under the new arrangement dowries continued to be customary and to come under the *dominium* of the husband or his *paterfamilias*. It is conventional to suppose that the bride's father turned over property or money to the groom, in three annual installments in the case of money or other fungibles, and this must have been a common pattern. Dowry given in this way from the estate of the bride's *paterfamilias* was called *dos profecticia*. Very often, however, the standard pattern must have been

---

[9] Watson 1971b: 17; 1967: 29–31; Treggiari 1991a: 324–26.

prevented by the father's death or his lack of financial resources, so that other arrangements had to be made. At the time of women's first marriage, one-third to one-half of the brides would not have had a living father as they went through this crucial rite of passage, and of course this would have been true of a much higher proportion of women entering subsequent marriages. Without a father, a woman might provide the dowry herself out of her own property, or look to others for resources. Such dowries fell into the legal category of *adventicia*, and the legal sources tell of brides, mothers, brothers, and friends providing them.

Family history rarely produces private individuals as catalysts of major changes, but Sp. Carvilius Ruga was one in Roman memory. Later authors identified him as the first (230 BC) to divorce his wife without the justification of moral fault and without paying the penalty of forfeiture of his property.[10] With this precedent, Roman marriages could no longer be conceived of as lifetime arrangements. Precautions had to be taken to secure the return of the dowry upon divorce, and a legal action, the *actio rei uxoriae*, was developed to allow the woman and her father to make the claim. Furthermore, during the marriage the husband's discretion as *dominus* came to be partially limited in order to protect the dotal assets: Augustus' law on adultery prohibited the sale of dotal real estate in Italy without the wife's approval.

The rules for its return in various circumstances show that the dowry was no longer primarily a device for transmitting a share of the woman's patrimony to her children. In the absence of a dotal agreement, the law provided that different types of dowry be treated in different ways, depending on who gave the dowry and how the marriage ended. In the case of the husband's death the *dos* could be recovered by the wife together with her *paterfamilias* (if alive) by an *actio rei uxoriae*. The children of the marriage had no legal claim in such a circumstance. If the marriage was brought to an end by divorce at the husband's instigation without moral cause, again the entire dowry was recoverable by the woman. On the other hand, if the divorce was at the instigation of the woman or her *paterfamilias* or on account of her moral lapses, the husband was allowed to retain one-sixth of the *dos* for each child up to three (*retentio propter liberos*) and up to one-sixth for moral offenses (*retentio propter mores*).[11] Thus the rules were such that if the wife lived on after the dissolution of the marriage, she would have at least part of her original *dos*. On the wife's death *dos adventicia* went to the husband unless specific agreement had been made for its return to the donor (in which case it was *dos recepticia*); *dos profecticia* from the woman's

[10] Treggiari (1991a: 442) accepts the tradition as genuine and gives the sources.
[11] Corbett 1930: 182–201. Schulz (1951: 126–28) offers a brief summary of the rules. The rules are set out in *Ulp. Reg.* 6.3–13 (in *FIRA* II.269–70).

paterfamilias went back to him on the wife's death, but that must have been a relatively infrequent occurrence since the daughter's life expectancy was probably nearly three times longer than her father's at the time of her first marriage.[12]

As in succession, the Romans achieved great flexibility by superseding these residual rules with written documents, dotal agreements called *pacta dotalia*. The terms of the pacts varied considerably and might favor either the husband's or the wife's side.[13] The frequent appearance of certain terms in the *Digest* suggest that they were common. By agreement the dowry could be promised for some future time, rather than delivered at the time of the wedding. Another common clause stipulated that the wife's father forfeit his right to recovery of *dos profecticia* where the wife died leaving children.[14] Since the right to claim *dos profecticia* could not be inherited, there was another common term to the effect that the *paterfamilias'* heirs, particularly the wife's brother, be able to claim return of the *dos* or part of it (again often under the condition of no children of the marriage).[15] The jurists placed some limits on the terms of the agreement: a "sterile" dowry in which all of the income was added to the dowry was invalid (*Dig.* 23.4.4); so also was an agreement that forfeited the woman's right to reclaim the dowry in the event of her husband's death (*Dig.* 23.4.2).

One other set of legal rules related to dowry is of interest here to clarify the relation between *dos* and *hereditas*: the procedure called *collatio dotis*. Where a father's will was upset, issues of equity in the division of the patrimony arose. From the second century BC the praetor allowed emancipated sons and daughters to make a claim on the *hereditas* along with the children who had been *in potestate*, but the emancipated children had to bring into the pool for division any property they had been able to accumulate as a result of emancipation. In particular, emancipated daughters had to bring in their dowry through *collatio dotis*. Married daughters who had remained *in potestate*, on the other hand, did not have to count their dowry as part of their share, until Antoninus Pius (*Dig.* 37.7.9) decided that these daughters also had to bring their dowries into account, if they had interfered with the will or wished to take a larger share than specified in the will.[16]

These legal rules carry significant implications about the functions of

---

[12] The microsimulation suggests that about half of the women marrying at age twenty did not have a living father (see table 3.1.b, p. 49). In Coale–Demeny Model Life Table 3 West, a twenty-year-old woman has a life expectancy of an additional 31.3 years in comparison with her sixty-year-old father's life expectancy of an additional 10.4 years.

[13] Crook 1967a: 105.

[14] In the title on *pacta dotalia* 23.4 see 2, 12.pr, 23, 24, 26.pr, 26.2, 30. For further discussion and references in other titles see Humbert 1972: 284–92.

[15] Humbert 1972: 284 n. 6.   [16] Gardner 1985: 451–52.

dotal exchange, as the jurists and emperors saw them. It is appropriate to
think in terms of function because those formulating and developing dotal
law reasoned in such terms. The rules show that the primary function of
dowries was *not* to give the daughter her portion of her father's estate or to
transmit that share to her descendants, as in so many European societies. The
distinction between dowry and daughter's inheritance is clearly evident in
the limits on *collatio dotis*: prior receipt of a dowry by a *filiafamilias* was *not*
counted against her share of the *hereditas* unless she took action to upset the
will. Nor was the dowry regularly transmitted to the woman's children: *dos
profecticia* went back to her father if she died; and if her husband died, the
dowry went back to her without any *retentiones* for the children.[17] All of
these features, however, were subject to alteration by legal instruments. A
father could decide to give his daughter only a dowry as her share of the
estate, and a husband could stipulate in an agreement that he should keep a
dowry from the *paterfamilias* upon the wife's death if the marriage produced
children.

Several aims emerge from these legal rules. P. E. Corbett, in *The Roman
Law of Marriage*, begins his chapter on dowry with the assertion: "In its
essential character and purpose dowry is a contribution from the wife's side
to the expenses of the household." In other words, the profit (*fructus*) and
use (*usus*) of the *dos* were intended to help offset the burdens of marriage
(*onera matrimonii*).[18] There has been considerable debate among Roman
lawyers concerning the significance of *onera*, and detailed studies have
shown that the matter is not so straightforward as Corbett's introduction
might suggest. Koschaker and Wolff argued in the 1930s that the phrase
onera matrimonii should be discounted as a post-classical interpolation in the
Digest.[19] Its genuineness in most texts has been defended by F. Dumont,
who points out that much of the legal reasoning about dowries is based on
the idea that an income was needed to support the wife; and Crook has
recently stressed that the *onera* were the expenses of the wife, not of the
household in general.[20] This basic function, Dumont notes, is implicit in
dotal agreements stipulating that the father not deliver the capital to the
husband until the father's death but in the meantime pay the husband
interest on the capital or support his daughter himself through an allowance
in lieu of the dotal *fructus* going to the husband.[21] A woman might even

---

[17] Treggiari 1991a: 353.
[18] Corbett 1930: 147. While stressing *onera matrimonii* he recognizes (p. 178) that "there
were cases of legal separation of *dos* from the *onera*." Schulz (1951: 124–25) and Kaser
(1971: 332–33) also stress *onera matrimonii*.
[19] Koschaker 1930: 3–27; Wolff 1933: 297–371.
[20] Dumont 1943: 34; Crook 1990: 60–62.
[21] Dumont 1943: 12, 20, citing *Dig.* 23.4.12, 23.3.20, 23.3.69.3, 23.3.76, 24.1.11.10, 24.1.54,
24.3.42.2, 24.3.44.1.

make a pact to the effect that she be given the dotal *fructus* to maintain herself. Such pacts did not violate the rule against sterile dowries precisely because the support of the wife was provided for. Treggiari traces the concept of *onera matrimonii* back as early as the late Republican jurist Servius Sulpicius.[22] The dowry was certainly associated with the wife's lifestyle much earlier, for example in Plautus' comedies in the early second century BC, even though the husband was not required by law to spend the revenues of the dowry on the wife until the later empire.[23]

The dowry was also intended to support the woman after the end of the marriage by divorce or husband's death, and to facilitate her remarriage. M. Humbert in his important book on remarriage in Rome emphasized the state's interest in keeping the woman *dotata* (with a dowry) so that she could remarry as "le fondement du droit à la restitution."[24] The residual rules for restoration made it likely that a woman would receive much or all of her dowry back at the end of the marriage, and the law limited the discretion of women or their fathers to make pacts forfeiting their right to restoration. Overall, however, a comparison with the more extensive regulations of later Roman law to preserve the dowry highlights the relative freedom and flexibility of dotal instruments in the classical era. How was this flexibility put to use?

Customs and practices: functions and strategies

As with succession, the literary and legal evidence shows that social convention and peer expectations produced clearer patterns of behavior than might be expected in view of the limitless options permitted by the law. The law did not directly require a dowry for *iustum matrimonium*, but the husband's expectation of one meant that a father could not refuse one to his daughter as a means of preventing her marriage. Although no classical author has much to say directly about the purposes of Roman dotal exchange, Tacitus' comments about German dowries offer a mirror for reflections on Roman practices. The historian believed that the Germans practiced a system of "indirect dowry" (that is, from husband to wife) as opposed to Roman "direct dowries" from the wife's family to the husband.

---

[22] Treggiari 1991a: 332.
[23] Dumont 1943: 33 minimizes (rightly in my view) the significance of the late date of the formal legal requirement: "Il s'agissait de questions trop intimes pour que le droit classique cherche à intervenir davantage, et puis n'y avait-il pas là le divorce toujours possible, permettant à la femme délaissée de reprendre sa dot pour recouvrer ses moyens d'existence?"
[24] 1972: 275. The State's interest in remarriage certainly explains the restrictions on dotal pacts to the detriment of the wife.

A second aspect of the contrast is that German dowries comprised productive things, such as oxen, horses, spears and shields, while the Romans gave dowries of *deliciae muliebres* (feminine delights). This passage is tendentious and problematic. Tacitus no doubt misunderstood German dowries, which were not provided so much for the wife as for the common household. Moreover, Tacitus is exaggerating in his reference to *deliciae muliebres*: it is certain that some Roman dowries included farms.[25] Nevertheless, behind the exaggeration there may lie a real and significant distinction of purpose: whereas the German indirect dowry was a transfer of capital designed to establish a basis of production to support the new household, the Roman dowry of the classical period was intended more modestly to maintain the wife and *sui* including her children and slaves. A letter from Pliny to Quintilianus (6.32) lends support to this interpretation. Pliny offered to contribute HS 50,000 to the dowry for the daughter of Quintilianus, an otherwise unknown man of modest means.[26] As an explanation of the need for his contribution, Pliny wrote: "Since your daughter is about to marry a distinguished man, Nonius Celer, on whom the requirements of public duties impose a certain need for splendor, she ought to have clothing and a retinue in accordance with her husband's position; of course such things do not increase her *dignitas* but nevertheless adorn it and provide for it." This letter concerns only one dowry, but it does support Tacitus' general contrast: the dowry of Quintilianus' daughter was not intended to contribute substantially to the production or wealth of Celer's household, but to maintain the daughter in a style appropriate to her new position.

Closely related to the questions of purpose and function is the customary size of dowries. As mentioned above, dowries in many early modern European societies commonly amounted to several times the family's annual income, hence a considerable fraction of the family's wealth and rightly interpreted as the daughter receiving her inheritance before the death of her father. It is impossible to work out such averages for Rome, but enough literary passages with figures have survived to give us an idea of the customary range of value. These passages fall into two categories: (1)

---

[25] *Fundi* and *praedia* are frequently mentioned in the *Digest* titles concerning dowry, e.g. from title 23.3: 6.1, 10.1, 32, 47, 50.pr, 52.

[26] Though this letter does not include the word *dos*, from the context it seems to me all but certain that Pliny's contribution was intended for the dowry (Duncan-Jones 1982: 28 includes this among contributions to dowries). The context and language (*confero*) are parallel to Pliny *Ep.* 2.4, which explicitly involved dowry. *Digest* 23.3.10.pr makes it clear that the wife's clothing, mentioned by Pliny, might be included in a *dos aestimata* (though it was to the husband's disadvantage to have it valued in this way). A Latin dotal agreement from Egypt of *c.* AD 100 has been preserved on papyrus and includes clothing and jewelry as a part of the *dos aestimata*, but unfortunately this is not strong evidence for the custom in Rome and Italy (*FIRA* III.17).

statements of values of real dowries, and (2) the moralists' and satirists' stock figures for extravagant dowries. Taken together, they produce a coherent idea of dowry sizes.

Among the real dowries Pliny generously contributed HS 50,000 and HS 100,000 to daughters of a friend and a relative in the class of local worthies. Pliny's donations did not constitute the whole of the dowries, but in view of what he says about the fathers' financial situations Pliny's contributions were surely a large part.[27] Customs about the appropriate size of dowries for families of the municipal elites would be expected to vary from town to town and region to region, so it is surprising that a chance survival of a papyrus from Oxyrhenchus in Egypt attests a closely comparable figure. In AD 276 a decurion Aurelius Hermogenes made a will dividing his estate among his five children. His two daughters each received, in addition to bequests of land, a dowry of four silver talents (HS 96,000).[28] At a somewhat higher social level, that of the very wealthy provincial elite, was Apuleius' wife Pudentilla, a widow *sui iuris* and worth HS 4,000,000. She offered a dowry of HS 300,000, to revert to her sons by her first marriage should the marriage with Apuleius produce no children.[29] The interpretation of this figure is a delicate matter: Pudentilla as an older woman in her second marriage would be expected to need a larger dowry to attract a husband, yet Apuleius described the *dos* as *modica* (modest) – but then his interest lay in minimizing it in order to answer the accusation of marrying Pudentilla for her money. If Apuleius intended to be plausible, presumably HS 300,000 as a *dos* for someone of Pudentilla's wealth was nothing out of the ordinary, though perhaps somewhat on the low side. Apuleius then proceeded to compare this with the sum settled by his arch-enemy Rufinus on his daughter – HS 400,000, an extravagant dowry from Rufinus, who had squandered his HS 3,000,000 estate and had to borrow the money.[30] After the rhetorical exaggeration has been stripped away, two useful points remain. First, Rufinus' provision for his daughter was at roughly the same level as Pudentilla's dowry, suggesting that several hundred thousand may have been a customary dowry for the wealthy provincials of North Africa worth several millions. Secondly, the fact that the HS 400,000 was borrowed could be levelled at Rufinus as a criticism, a sign of his extravagance in spite of his poverty. The implication is that for *patres* pursuing sound financial management borrowing was not usually necessary to provide a dowry.

For the senatorial class a handful of figures scattered over the four centuries of the classical era have survived. In the early second century BC Scipio Africanus, the conqueror of Carthage, promised for each of his daughters fifty talents (about HS 1,250,000) and left his grandson by

[27] *Ep.* 2.4, 6.32.   [28] FIRA III.51.
[29] *Apol.* 71, 77, 92; 91 for the description of the *dos* as *modica*.   [30] *Apol.* 92.

adoption, Scipio Aemilianus, to pay them. Aemilius Paullus, another leading
senator, received 600,000 sesterces with his second wife. Cicero, at a time
when his reputation in a senatorial career was yet to be made, was given HS
400,000 as a dowry in his marriage to Terentia.[31] Tacitus reported that when
it was necessary to fill a vacancy in the college of Vestal Virgins two
generations later in AD 19, the daughters of two prestigious senatorial
families were presented as candidates. As a consolation to the unsuccessful
one, the daughter of Fonteius Agrippa, Tiberius bestowed on her a dowry
of HS 1,000,000 ("et Caesar quamvis posthabitam deciens sestertii dote
solatus est").[32] This figure is particularly useful: unless Tiberius wished to
look ridiculous with a show of imperial beneficence that was in reality
niggardly, this gift must have represented a generous *dos* among the
wealthiest of Roman society. From the end of the Principate we hear of one
other senatorial dowry from Papinian: "Our Emperor Severus ordered the
imperial treasury to pay Athenagora, daughter of Flavius, whose estate had
been confiscated, HS 1,000,000 by way of dowry, because she alleged that
her father had paid interest on her dowry." The issue arose because the
father had promised a dowry and was paying interest on it until delivery,
which was prevented by Severus' confiscation of his estate. Under these
circumstances Severus was prepared to treat the dowry of HS 1,000,000 as
the daughter's.[33]

These scattered numbers for dotal sizes correspond well to the
assumptions of the moralists and satirists of the early empire. Seneca,
Martial, and Juvenal, when referring to extravagant dowries, picked figures
of HS 400,000 and 1,000,000. Among his remarks on how little good the
wealth of the very rich does them, Seneca commented that Scipio's

[31] Polybius 31.27, 18.35.6; Plutarch *Cic.* 8.2. Treggiari 1991a: 344–45 for a collection of
evidence. Shatzman (1975: 414), followed by Gardner (1986: 101), gives a far higher
figure for Terentia's dowry. Shatzman believes that Plutarch's number of 400,000 must
refer only to the cash in Terentia's dowry because the *insulae* were said to produce an
annual income of HS 100,000 and hence must have been worth much more. However, the
context, a list of Cicero's assets, makes it clear that Plutarch intended the reader to
understand that the number represented the value of the whole dowry. Perhaps the two
figures can be reconciled by the fact that the figure for rent comes from a time more than
two decades after the dowry was constituted during a period of inflation of housing costs.
Shatzman also gives HS 1,200,000 as the size of Publilia's dowry, but the passage used to
deduce this (Cicero *Att.* 16.2.1) does not give enough information to calculate the value
of the whole dowry.
[32] *Ann.* 2.86. It has been suggested to me that Tiberius simply contributed to the dowry, but
the Latin says that Tiberius consoled the loser with a *dos*, not a contribution to one.
Furneaux implies in his comment on the passage an understanding similar to mine. This
passage and others quoted below have been used as evidence that HS 1,000,000 was a
customary size for dowries: see e.g. Balsdon 1962: 187 and Mayor's commentary on
Juvenal 10.335.
[33] *Dig.* 22.1.6.1. This father and daughter are otherwise unknown, but probably related to
the senatorial family of Carminius Athenagoras (*PIR*² C 224).

daughters, who enjoyed the great honor of a dowry provided by the state, were in a more enviable situation than someone of a disreputable profession such as a *pantomima* with a dowry of one million.[34] In one of his epigrams about a woman trying to lure him into marriage, the reluctant Martial required as one of his outrageous conditions a *dos* of one million.[35] The same figure was used twice by Juvenal: In *Satire* 6 he said sarcastically that for a dowry of one million a husband will call the most immoral wife chaste, and then in *Satire* 10 the notorious wedding of Messalina and Silius is mentioned along with a dowry put at a million. Finally, in *Satire* 2 Juvenal talked of a rich man who celebrated a mock wedding with a male horn-player, a wedding with all due ritual including a HS 400,000 *dos*.[36] Of course, these are stock figures, representing the senatorial and equestrian census requirements. Nevertheless, it seems to me that these passages would lack point if one million had not been conventionally thought to be an exceedingly large dowry suitable for the wealthiest class – that is, if dowries of five to ten million had been common among senators. The only passage with a dowry of this order of magnitude comes from Petronius' *Satyricon* (74) where in his quarrel with his wife Fortunata the boorish Trimalchio claims that he could have had a wife with a HS 10,000,000 dowry. This outsized number has as little value for the social historian as Petronius' other fantastic exaggerations.[37]

Scattered though these figures are, both geographically and chronologically, they exhibit some consistency. At the peak of Rome's very steep social pyramid, senatorial families exchanged dowries of the order of HS 1,000,000, the sum that stuck in the satirists' imagination as huge. Among the municipal elite dowries appear in the range of tens to a hundred thousand. Equestrians and other wealthy families of the provincial aristocracies bestowed dowries in an imtermediate range of several hundreds of thousands.

A counsel of caution might warn against making too much of this fragmentary evidence, yet there is justification for talking of typical sizes here.[38] The jurists clearly and repeatedly indicated that there existed standard expectations for sizes of dowries by rank and class. Papinian

[34] *Cons. ad Helv.* 12.6. Seneca makes it clear in this passage that he is not referring to the modestly rich but to the very rich.
[35] *Epig.* 11.23; the same figure appears in 2.65 and 12.75.
[36] *Sat.* 6.136; 10.335; 2.117.
[37] Treggiari (1991a: 345) takes this number more seriously than I would, referring to Duncan-Jones' comment about Petronius' "lack of inventiveness with sums of money." However, the lack of inventiveness noted by Duncan-Jones lies in the repetition of certain numbers by Petronius who "did not attempt realism" (1982: 241–42).
[38] Treggiari (1991a: 346) believes that the round numbers are to be distrusted since farms were often included. But all the passages suggest that the Romans thought in terms of round numbers for dowries, and it may well be that the Romans estimated the value of estates in round numbers, which in any case could always be topped off by cash.

discussed the case where "a son-in-law stipulated with his father-in-law for the payment of a *dos* at a fixed date, without specifying its nature or quantity, but leaving this for the father-in-law to decide. This stipulation is valid ... unlike cases involving land which is not specified. A legacy or a stipulation of land is held to be void here, because there is a great difference between constituting a dowry and providing an unspecified piece of property; the amount of a dowry can be fixed on the basis of the father's wealth (*facultates*) and the husband's status (*dignitas*)" (*Dig.* 23.3.69.4). How difficult was it to fix the size by these criteria? Not at all, according to Celsus, citing the Augustan jurist Labeo: "If a father had directed that a dowry should be given to his daughter at her *tutor*'s discretion, Tubero says that this is to be taken just as if it had been bequeathed at the discretion of a *bonus vir*. Labeo asks: How can you tell how much dowry ought to be provided for the daughter of this person or that, by the judgement of the *bonus vir*? He says that it is not difficult to estimate on the basis of the status (*dignitas*), wealth (*facultates*), and number of children of the person making the will" (*Dig.* 32.43). The clarity of the standard could even ease the awkwardness in a situation where a *tutor* wished to marry his son to his own female ward at her father's request. Whatever dowry the *tutor* fixed would become his own property as *paterfamilias* of the groom – a conflict of interest that could be resolved by setting the size in accordance with the wealth and rank of her family, "pro modo facultatium et dignitate natalium" (*Dig.* 23.3.69.5, Papinian).

Given the jurists' confidence in clear standards, it is not reckless to generalize from the coincidence of the random and the stock numbers in our sources. At least two factors probably pressed Romans to make less use of their flexibility than they might have. Guardians needed standards for setting aside dowries out of their wards' estates in order to protect themselves from litigation (see also *Dig.* 23.3.60, Celsus). In addition, the *paterfamilias* must have been more limited in the exercise of his discretion in settling dowries than in dividing his patrimony in his will, because dowries were the outcome of two families negotiating on the basis of shared social expectations. As Pliny indicated, a young wife marrying a husband of a particular rank was known to need certain items and a certain level of maintenance.

To be understood as one element in the transmission of property to the next generation, the dowry figures of several hundred thousand to a million HS for families of senatorial wealth must be put into context. Pudentilla's *dos* is the only one that can be compared with the value of her estate. It represented about 7 percent of her estate, or something of the order of one year's income on the conventional reckoning. More generally and less precisely, it can be said that the conventional very large dotal settlement of one million was of the same order, one year's income, for moderately wealthy senators, such as Pliny.³⁹ Thus, for well-off senators dowries were comparatively smaller than in many early modern European societies, where they could range from three to five times annual income. On the other hand, they were substantial enough to encourage endogamy within status groups: only a very wealthy family could have provided the hundreds of thousands or the million customary for a senatorial marriage. Endogamy within status groups may explain the differences among jurists over whether it was in accordance with the husband's or the woman's father's wealth and rank that the dowry was to be fixed: in most cases, they would not be too different. The comparatively modest size of Roman dowries fits well with the custom of paying the cash in three annual installments on the assumption that over three years the sum could be paid out of current income without borrowing. Hence, the need to borrow to constitute a dowry could be levelled as criticism by Apuleius. Naturally, some families found themselves in financial straits that made payment or return of a dowry difficult.⁴⁰ Cicero's problems with paying Tullia's dowry to Dolabella and repaying Terentia's dowry are well known, but should be kept in perspective. As Crook writes in connection with Tullia, "what is ... worth noting is the ease with which (apart from minor inconveniences over payment and repayment of dowries, which do not seem to have had the restraining influence on divorces that scholars sometimes attribute to them) people made and unmade marriages."⁴¹ As awkward as Cicero's position was, Tullia did divorce Dolabella, and financial need did not compel Cicero to prolong his marriages to Terentia or poor young Publilia.

Within the constraints of social expectations and legal duty, women and their fathers and brothers had considerable room to manoeuvre. The jurists could envisage a father giving his daughter her whole portion of the patrimony as dowry, but there are hints that this was sufficiently unusual to warrant explanation. So a man who wished to disinherit his daughter could feel the need to explain his action in his will: "'But I have disinherited you,

³⁹ Duncan-Jones 1982: 32. Treggiari (1991a: 345) finds it "hardly credible that Pliny ... could have offered as little as one million sesterces if he had had a daughter," but it must be remembered that a dowry could be supplemented by a *peculium* and there were good reasons to limit the size of a dowry, as will be shown below.
⁴⁰ I do not mean to suggest that dowries were trivial or did not require advance planning. Cicero *Parad.* 44, among other passages, reveals a consciousness of the costs.
⁴¹ Crook 1990: 164. It should be pointed out that one example of borrowing for a dowry given by Treggiari (1991a: 348) may be irrelevant to this issue: *Dig.* 23.3.5.8, Ulpian, concerns a *filiusfamilias* who borrows to constitute a dowry for his daughter and so obligates his *paterfamilias*; the borrowing may have been a consequence of the legal position of the *filiusfamilias* rather than of the family's inability to come up with the resources. What is interesting about this passage is that the family duty to provide a dowry meant that the *filiusfamilias* could obligate the *paterfamilias* without prior consent.

my daughter, because I intended you to be satisfied with your dowry.'" Modestinus was of the opinion that this clause effectively disinherited the daughter (*Dig.* 28.5.62). There are a few other cases in the *Digest* based on the provision of a dowry to a disinherited daughter (*Dig.* 31.34.5, Modestinus), but even if that was the father's clear intention it might be overridden through various circumstances. For instance, if a father disinherited his daughter, instructed his son-heir by *fideicommissum* to provide her with a dowry of a certain sum, and then the son negotiated a smaller dowry after the father's death, the daughter was entitled to be given the difference as her own property (*Dig.* 31.77.9, Papinian). More interesting here is the case where "a father included in the dotal pact a clause to the effect that his daughter had received the dowry without any other expectations from her father's estate; it is certain that this clause has not ousted the rights of succession; for provisions of individuals do not derogate from the authority of the law" (*Dig.* 38.16.16, Papinian). Here the legal presumption in favor of the daughter sharing in the *hereditas* in the absence of disherison in the will (as in Modestinus' case above) overrode the father's intention expressed elsewhere.

The many women without living fathers who provided their own dowries could constitute as dowry all their property, minus any debts they had incurred (*Dig.* 23.3.72. pr, Paulus). That such was not the norm is perhaps suggested by the fact that toward the end of the classical period it could be asked whether it was legal for a woman to do so. Paulus (*Frag. Vat.* 115) replied that it was, in reference to a case of a woman marrying a husband of higher rank (*maioris dignitatis*). For a woman under twenty-five years of age to constitute as dowry her whole estate or an excessive portion of it ("ultra vires patrimonii vel totum patrimonii") raised suspicions that she had been taken advantage of by her husband; if she had agreed to a dowry of a size that no older person would have, she could have recourse to *restitutio in integrum* (*Dig.* 4.4.9.1, Ulpian; 4.4.48.1, Paulus). Here again, the jurists assumed the existence of a broadly accepted standard of what an older person would judge conventional.

In the *Digest* it is more common to find situations where the woman has a dowry and additional property, whether in the form of a *peculium* or a legacy or a share of her father's *hereditas* (as in the case of the Egyptian decurion Aurelius Hermogenes). Although the father might wish his daughter to have a dowry and to be an heir (*Dig.* 36.1.23.4, Ulpian), if the estate was heavily in debt, the daughter could decline the inheritance and keep her dotal property, leaving it to her brother to see to it that the dowry was unencumbered (*Dig.* 19.1.52.1, Scaevola). Unless the father was absolutely clear in his will that a bequest to his daughter was to be treated as her dowry, it was assumed that he wished her to have both. So where a father promised a dowry and left a legacy to his daughter after disinheriting her, the daughter would take both dowry and legacy (*Dig.* 37.7.4, Paulus). If a father wished to give his daughter her whole share from his estate before marriage but not constitute all of it as dowry, he could give her the balance as *peculium*, the *dos* plus the *peculium* then explicitly intended to go to her in lieu of a share of the *hereditas* upon his death (*Dig.* 6.1.65.1, Papinian). Or, alternatively, a father could give his daughter a dowry and *peculium*, and institute her co-heir along with her brothers on condition that she bring her dowry and *peculium* into the account of what was to be divided; the daughter then had the choice of entering into the inheritance or refusing and keeping her dowry and *peculium* despite her brothers' protests (*Dig.* 37.7.8, Papinian). Here is another situation of sibling conflict where the woman has more options in the pursuit of her interests than her brothers. To add to the complexity of the possible arrangements, it must be remembered that the father was not the sole arbiter of his daughter's financial well being. A mother could also bestow a dowry and *peculium* on a daughter still *in potestate* (*Dig.* 39.5.31.1).

A comparison of the Roman legal and literary evidence with that of other societies poses some essential questions. Why did the Romans develop such a varied set of alternatives for the distribution of patrimony to daughters through dowry, *peculium*, and testation? What considerations might have governed a father's choices in allotting resources for his daughter to dowry or *peculium* or legacy or *hereditas*? Related to this question, why do the sizes of dowries appear to have remained more or less stable in contrast to the inflation so lamented in later European societies? To answer these questions, dotal exchange must be considered in the broader context of strategies for the devolution of property in the family.

In answer to the first question, several factors may be suggested. First, dotal law participated in the more general development of Roman law toward remarkable flexibility through written instruments and in response to a multitude of circumstances. Secondly, the variety of circumstances to be met by various strategies was multiplied by the availability of marriage *sine manu* with separate property for wives and easy divorce. Roman marriage was far less unitary, far more fragile and unstable, than in later, Christian societies. In any society before the demographic transition, the chances of a marriage ending by death before the end of the couple's child-bearing years were high. Among first marriages between a twenty-year-old woman and a thirty-year-old man in Rome, one in six would have ended by the death of a spouse within five years, one in three within ten years, nearly one in two within fifteen years, and three in five within twenty years. That inevitable instability due to mortality was heightened by divorce. The frequency of divorce has been the subject of recent debates. The literary sources – and not only those by the moralists – give the impression that divorce was quite common among the elite of the last generation of the Republic. Within the best documented classical family outside the imperial household, Cicero was twice divorced, as was his daughter Tullia, and his brother divorced once despite family pressure. It is possible to pile up examples from this era for which our evidence·is fullest.[42] In regard to the Principate Humbert argued that the pattern of frequent divorce continued, but Raepsaet-Charlier has sought to demonstrate that divorce was not so common: for 562 women known from the senatorial class, only 27 divorces are attested, 15 of those in the imperial family.[43] Unfortunately, the sources for most of this list are honorary and funerary inscriptions, which by their nature would not record divorces. Far more revealing is Syme's comment that "the more that is discovered about a senator, the more wives"[44] – a pattern that cannot be explained solely by mortality since most men would have died before their first wife. The methodological problems inherent in funerary inscriptions, our main source of information for the lower orders, mean that any attempt to judge divorce rates among ordinary Romans will be futile.[45] Although the frequency of divorce in Rome will never be known (and was not known to the Romans themselves), it is safe to say that divorce and remarriage were easy, carried little stigma, and were experiences so common that any prudent woman or father would take the possibility into account in making a dotal pact or will.

In the simple, happy case of a life-long marriage producing children, the destination of the dowry might be unproblematic: it would go to the husband or back to the wife, and then to the children. Even if the simple, happy case was not quite as "rare" as proclaimed in the "Laudatio Turiae," it was certainly not the most likely outcome. The contingencies of divorce, death, and childlessness demanded attention and legal devices, as Humbert has shown.[46] What caused a woman or her father to divide her property in a particular way between dowry and *peculium* or bequest? Although there is little direct evidence to answer the question, it can be shown that the choices were seen to have consequences both for family politics during the marriage and for control of the property after. As early as the plays of

[42] Bradley 1991: 156–76.
[43] Humbert 1972: 76–112, with a few corrections by Syme 1987: 319–20; Raepsaet-Charlier 1981–82. Treggiari (1991a: 479–81) is inclined to agree with Raepsaet-Charlier and concludes that the Republican "examples do not add up to very much," citing Octavian as an example of a man "resolutely wedded." I find it odd to use the example of a twice-divorced man to illustrate the stability of marriage.
[44] Syme 1987: 331.
[45] Kajanto 1969 can identify individual marriages of long duration from the epigraphic evidence, but has no method to identify the typical pattern from inscriptions. Bagnall and Frier (1994) find a pattern of frequent divorce among the ordinary people of Egypt.
[46] Humbert 1972.

Plautus, wives with large dowries, *uxores dotatae*, were portrayed as powerful and demanding, thus upsetting the authority that a husband was supposed to exercise.[47] As Demaenetus lamented in the *Asinaria* (87), a large dowry put him under his wife's rule, "sub imperio uxorio": "I accepted money, for a dowry I sold the right to rule" ("argentum accepi, dote imperium vendidi"). Men in search of a wife might think it better to forego a large dowry in order to preserve their domination: as Megadorus mused in his reflections on marriage in the *Aulularia* (533), "the woman without a dowry is in the power of a husband" ("nam quae indotata est, ea in potestate viri"). Plautus exploited the comic effects of the inversion of conjugal roles, and satiric writers continued to exploit it through the classical era. Horace, Seneca, Martial, and Juvenal all use the topos of the poor husband dominated by a wife with a large dowry. The husband continued in law to have *dominium* over the dowry, but the freedom of the wife to divorce and take her dowry away with her was portrayed as a threat that kept husbands subservient. Many men must have found the prospect distasteful. Martial put the matter with his usual point: he did not want to take a rich woman to be his husband.[48] In later European societies without divorce the acquisition of a well-dowered wife must have been more unambiguously attractive to husbands.

The kernel of truth in the topos of the *uxor dotata* is that a Roman woman could gain standing and power in a marriage through a large dowry; the possession of additional property in her own right could give her even more power and independence. The elder Cato recognized and denounced this potential in the early second century BC: "'At first, a wife brought you a large dowry (*magnam dotem*); then she received a lot of money (*magnam pecuniam*), which she did not entrust into her husband's power (*viri potestatem*); this money she gives to her husband as a loan; later, when she has been angered, she orders a slave of her own to pursue him and fiercely to demand it'" (quoted by A. Gellius *NA* 17.6). What gave the wife uncomfortable power, in Cato's scenario, was her independent wealth, the husband's need to borrow, and the woman's possession of a slave (*servus recepticius*) to press her personal financial interests. With funds at her disposal and slaves at her behest, a wife could support her children or command the solicitude of her husband (*Dig.* 39.5.31.1 and 29.6.3, Papinian). Thus a father, in deciding how to apportion assets for his daughter between dowry and inheritance, could give her more discretion and leverage by favoring the

[47] Schuhmann 1977; Konstan 1983: 47–56.
[48] Horace *Carm.* 3. 24; Seneca *Matrim.*, frag. 87; Martial *Epig.* 8.12; Juvenal *Sat.* 6.136. Treggiari (1991a: 329–31) places more weight than I would on the *uxor dotata* as a real historical phenomenon: the only "historical" example offered is from Cicero (*Scaur.* 7), an old Sardinian woman, who may well be more the product of a rhetorical flourish than anything else.

latter. This strategy would also benefit him by postponing payment of the patrimonial share until his death. Although payment of the dowry could also be postponed by agreement until the father's death, interest on the dowry would be due to the husband for maintenance of the wife in the meantime.

Father and daughter wishing to maintain control over the final destination of her share of the patrimony had further incentive to limit the dowry. In the context of likely premature death or divorce and remarriage, resources placed in dowries were subject to *retentiones* by husbands. If a husband remarried and had more children, there was no guarantee in the classical era that the dotal assets would end up in the hands of the first wife's children. Property that she kept as her own, however, she could take with her upon divorce without debits and could direct to her children or others of her choice by testament or *fideicommissum*.[49]

The interest of the woman and her family usually lay in limiting the dowry, but circumstances did not always permit this. Where a family of declining fortune wished to continue to marry in accordance with their rank, borrowing for the dowry might be necessary, leaving nothing more as an inheritance.[50] The other explanation for constituting the woman's entire estate as dowry was, as we have seen, that she was marrying above her station: the requirements to maintain life with a husband of higher status might not allow her to reserve part of her assets as her own (Paulus *Frag. Vat.* 115).

The separation of the patrimonial function of a woman's property from the maintenance function of dowry, and the interest of the woman's family in limiting the latter, go some way toward explaining the remarkable stability of dowry sizes over a period of four centuries, even as the wealth of elite families was rising. We do not hear from imperial Rome either of the complaints about the crippling effects of extravagant dowries on family fortunes or of the sumptuary laws fixing maximum sizes that were common in later Europe.

Dowries, however, were the result of negotiation of two sides, and it remains to understand why men did not press for larger dotal settlements. A part of the answer may lie in demography: as Herlihy and Klapisch point out, in late medieval Florence the significantly lower age at first marriage for women produced more marriageable women than men, and hence pressure on the women's fathers to increase the size of dowries to attract the husbands in short supply. Conversely, the lack of noticeable inflation in

---

[49] Humbert 1972 deals at length with the problems raised by remarriage and the legal rules and instruments for coping with them.

[50] Another strategy in straitened circumstances, attested a few times in the Republic, was marriage to a kinsman or wealthy friend who was willing to forego a dowry out of duty (Livy 42.34.3–4; Varro *Rust.* 3.16.2); on this motive, see Treggiari 1991a: 110–11.

Roman dowries may indicate that the numbers of marriageable men and women had been brought into balance before the marriage age. Another aspect of the answer may be that the prospect of divorce and return of the dowry restrained the eagerness of men to demand large dotal settlements. A large dowry could not be treated as a permanent acquisition to be used as the husband pleased. A woman on the poorer side in a marriage between two families of differing levels of wealth would perhaps have to accept the subservience that the male ideology represented as natural for wives, but a husband in the weaker position risked ridicule and the taint of servility from the inversion of social roles. Consequently, dowry-hunting was less tempting than legacy-hunting, and we hear much less about it in the non-comic sources.[51] The references to dowry-hunting more often than not characterize the wife as old or sick, because it was only on her death that the husband would acquire secure possession and unrestricted use of the dotal property.[52] The husband in Plautine comedy with an *uxor dotata* looks forward to the day of her demise.[53] As Apuleius tells us, however, in real life even a dowry from an older woman might be only a temporary gain, since the dotal agreement could stipulate for its return to her side of the family if the marriage ended without children. If it is true that Cicero married young Publilia for her dowry, he discovered that the temporary expedient was not worth the psychological cost of a wife whose companionship did not suit him.

Conclusion

In his general treatment of the devolution of family property in Eurasian agrarian societies, J. Goody has conceptualized dowry as a form of inheritance before the father's death for daughters marrying out of their

[51] Though Humbert 1972: 99–100 refers in his text to enrichment through acquisition of a large dowry, in fact none of his references concerns *dos*. In *Att.* 13.28.4 Cicero does not say that Nicias Talna was trying to marry Cornificia for her money; even if that was the case, there is no hint that the enrichment would have been in the form of a *dos*, as opposed to inheritance on her death. In any case Talna suffered what must often have been the fate of would-be fortune hunters: his advances were discouraged because he had an estate worth a mere HS 800,000. Quintilian *Inst.* 6.3.73 again says nothing of financial motives for marriage and not a word about dowry. The motives of the quaestor who divorced his wife after being assigned his province (Suetonius *Tib.* 35.2) are not stated, but the reference to the assignment of the province implies that the quaestor kept his wife just long enough to take advantage of Augustus' marriage laws favouring candidates with wives and children (nothing to do with the wife's money or dowry). Carcopino 1956: 103 portrays Roman husbands as moving from wife to wife in search of ever larger dowries – an exaggerated view of "mariages d'argent" for which he produces no adequate evidence.

[52] Martial's *Epig.* 2.65 and 10.15 refer to the husband acquiring a large dowry, but he is said to enjoy the windfall only on the wife's death rather than from the beginning of the marriage. The wife of the Sardinian Aris is stereotypically old in Cicero's *Scaur.* 7.

[53] Schuhmann 1977: 55.

natal family. In classical Rome daughters normally did not leave their natal families upon marriage from the point of view of property rights, and dowries did not have the primary function of satisfying the daughter's claim on her patrimony. The presumption in the classical legal system was that daughters would receive a share of their father's estate beyond the dowry, which served the more modest function of her maintenance in her husband's household. The law, however, allowed fathers a range of choices including the option to give daughters their full share as dowry. But to judge by the scattered evidence for sizes, family interest and social convention generally kept dowries limited to a modest standard, perhaps roughly a year's income for a propertied family – well short both of the share due to a Roman daughter on intestacy and of the relative sizes of dowries in Greece and later European societies. Thus, social expectations, including the perceived function of dowry, often inhibited all parties to dotal agreements from taking full advantage of the wide flexibility allowed by law.

Whether intended or not, the configuration of legal rights and the pattern of devolution of property during the classical era gave propertied wives a potential for power and independence within families that troubled men. The wives were not trapped in marriages where their dowries were irretrievable contributions to a conjugal fund under their husbands' control. A large dowry and the right of divorce meant that they could leave, or threaten to leave, their husband's house in the knowledge that they could recover most of the dowry for their own support. Furthermore, the right to possess a substantial share of their patrimony in their own right aside from the dowry gave them a capacity to act on behalf of kin, friends and community to an extent not commonly found in other European agrarian societies. Many wives (one suspects especially young ones) did not fully exploit their property rights, and they never approached social equality with men. Nevertheless, there is enough evidence to show that rights of property and divorce enabled some to attract deference from husbands and other men, or at least to break off abusive conjugal relationships. When the Roman jurists envisaged an angry wife leaving her husband's house with her property, they were assuming a degree of freedom not to be underrated.

10

Conclusion

From Jean Bodin to Lewis Morgan to contemporary scholars, Rome has provided the paradigm of patriarchy in western thought. The *paterfamilias*, with his unlimited legal powers over members of his *familia*, has been interpreted as the extreme case in which "paternal authority passed beyond the bounds of reason into an excess of domination."[1] Family relationships are often conceptualized as falling somewhere along a spectrum from affectionless power at one end to loving concern at the other, and the movement along the spectrum is then historicized as social development. The Roman father, who in legend would execute his disobedient son without flinching, is taken to represent affectionless power – the starting point from which the affectionate family gradually evolved.

My study has suggested the inadequacy of such a simple evolutionary view of family history. The Roman family was unquestionably patriarchal, in the sense that it was defined with reference to the father, who was endowed with a special authority in the household. But, I have argued, the characterization of an "excess of domination" has been the result of both a misinterpretation of the legends and, above all, an overly legalistic approach to the family. The law endowed the *pater* with a striking *potestas* encompassing extensive coercive and proprietary rights, yet a purely legal understanding of the Roman family is as incomplete and misleading as would be a solely legal understanding of the twentieth-century family. In certain circumstances, to be sure, legal rights and powers were important in determining the nature of family interactions, but in many other contexts the Romans appear to have been as oblivious to formal legal definitions of power in the family as we are today. In his many letters discussing his own family relationships, Cicero does not contemplate them in terms of legal powers and rights. Rather, Cicero's works present family relationships as a

---

[1] Morgan 1877: 466.

225

central element of moral obligation and as a set of practical challenges in daily practice. Indeed, it turns out on close reading that even the famous legends of early Roman magistrates executing disobedient sons are presented by Latin authors as instances of official public duty superseding paternal devotion. The stories celebrate devotion to the state before even one's own family and do not testify to a time in which the paternal role was defined in terms of power rather than affection.

The jural interpretation of the Roman family often starts from the jurist's definition of *familia* as those in the father's *potestas*. It was on the basis of this legal definition, for instance, that Herlihy argued for a development from the pagan family, in which the father stood outside and above his family, to the symmetrical and inclusive Christian family. Such an argument fails, however, because the semantic study in chapter 4 shows that the Romans themselves did not use the word *familia* in ordinary social discourse concerning the family. As a legal construct, *familia* had a precise meaning and consequences, particularly in regard to property; in daily usage *familia* normally referred to the slave staff and not a Roman's wife or children. In most contexts, *familia* in its legal sense was not appropriate in discussions of the family as the core unit of the household, because it did not include the wife-mother, who in classical times generally did not come under her husband's *potestas* and yet was recognized as an essential member of the household unit.

Moreover, the definition of *familia* in terms of the father's *potestas* elided the crucial distinction in Roman society between free children and slaves, all of whom were in the father's legal power. In certain legal circumstances, children and slaves were conflated, but in most respects the distinction between the two subordinated groups was unmistakably marked in daily social life. The early Christian author Tertullian was drawing on a widely accepted polarity in Roman thought when he contrasted the affectionate duty (*pietas*) characteristic of a father and the legal power (*potestas*) associated with the master of a slave (*Apology* 34). The master's *potestas* was enforced by the whip, the symbol marking the humiliation of slavery in contrast to the honor of free birth, as shown in chapter 6. In contrast to recalcitrant slaves, free children who shared in the family's common interests were to be socialized primarily by words, in the view of Roman authors. Some Republican and imperial writers from Cato to Quintilian specifically eschewed the physical punishment of children on the grounds that it would inculcate a grudging servile character, while other authors recommended restrained use when persuasive words failed.

The implication of Tertullian's contrast is that the moral value of *pietas* offers the historian a better insight into Roman family life than the legal rules of *potestas* – at least, the latter without the former is a serious distortion of family relations. *Pietas* has often been translated as "filial piety" and equated with obedience; as such, it is said to have socialized children to obey paternal power. A survey of the paradigmatic stories told to illustrate the virtue in chapter 5 shows this translation to be inadequate and fundamentally misleading on two counts. First, *pietas* was the virtue not of mere obedience, but of affectionate devotion. The founding legend of the Republican temple to Pietas narrated the tale of a daughter helping her poor, condemned mother to survive in prison, in disobedience to the higher authority of the state. In this story *pietas* was not a value that fit neatly into the Roman system of martial values celebrating male obedience and discipline. Most of the other *exempla* of *pietas* in the lists of Valerius Maximus and the elder Pliny also had nothing to do with obedience (though duty could encompass obedience). Secondly, *pietas* was not narrowly "filial," but was a general, reciprocal obligation primarily within the core family unit of father, mother, and children. Fathers were morally bound by *pietas* to care for the interests of their children, as much as children were bound to respect and to obey their parents, mothers as well as fathers. These basic qualities of *pietas* – reciprocal affectionate duty – can be found in the earliest Latin literature of the early second century before Christ; its early expression gives no empirical warrant for evolutionary views that see patriarchy as starting from severe, affectionless power relations.

Commemorations on funerary monuments provide the historian with the most enduring expression of solemn family duty from the ancient world. The pattern of commemoration points to the centrality of family and household, rather than *familia*, in the Roman's hierarchy of obligation. Dedications to spouses, parents, children and siblings are most common among the tens of thousands of surviving Latin inscriptions. After bonds within the nuclear family, bonds with household dependants such as slaves and freedmen are most frequently represented. Commemorations of kinsmen of the extended family are relatively rare. This ordering of obligation – nuclear family, then the broader household, then extended kin – parallels Cicero's pseudo-historical explanation of the extension of social networks in concentric circles from the individual to the wider society (*Off.* 1.54). The order reflects the Romans' emphasis on house or *domus* in their sense of social identity and duty. As suggested in chapter 4, the house symbolized a Roman's political power and social prestige. The Mactar harvester, who against all odds succeeded in climbing from the working class to the local elite, called attention on his tombstone to his acquisition of a *domus* as the mark of his upward mobility. Within his *domus* a Roman daily exercised power over his dependants and slaves, and it provided the symbolically charged stage on which he managed the relationships with the outside world that extended his influence. In emphasizing the household in their sense of social identity, propertied Romans placed themselves primarily within a set of relationships that were marked as socially hierarchical (slave, freedman, client).

At the normative level, the Latin texts show that the Romans did not conceive of the family as an extreme, wholly asymmetrical patriarchy that placed all power in the hands of the father and the sense of duty solely on the children. In addition, demographic realities placed practical limits on the extent of the father's authority. The core family unit of father, mother, and children – envisioned as the standard household unit in jurists' discussions of household stores (*penus*) – was subject to fragmentation and reconstitution through death, divorce, and remarriage. The historian's model of the Roman family, therefore, must incorporate an understanding of the life course. Chapter 2 presents a survey of the very imperfect data for Roman life expectancy, ages at marriage, and fertility. The scattered and problematic evidence for life expectancy in the empire, especially the household census data from Roman Egypt analyzed by Bagnall and Frier, corroborates the best estimate from comparative studies of similar agrarian societies of later ages. Mortality rates must have been very high, yielding an average life expectancy at birth of around twenty-five years. This should be understood as a rough estimate, both because the data are imperfect and because mortality patterns must have varied by time, region, class and gender. The pattern of funerary commemorations in the Latin-speaking west suggests that women of the class, erecting tombstones tended to marry for the first time in their late teens or early twenties, and men about a decade later in life in their late twenties or early thirties. Over the centuries fertility must, on average, have broadly balanced mortality: in a stationary population with such a low life expectancy women living through their child-bearing years must have given birth to five children on average.

These patterns of mortality, marriage and child-bearing are quite alien to the modern post-industrial experience, in which life expectancy is more than twice as long and the average number of children borne by each woman is less than half. To grasp the consequences of these differences for the shape of the family through the life course, a computer simulation (CAMSIM) may be deployed. Chapter 3 explains how the simulation models the events of the Roman life course and analyzes the resulting kinship universe of the model population. The results are presented in the tables of chapter 3. Since the Roman historian does not possess the precise data necessary to be certain about the input parameters, various simulations were done to capture a variety of possible life expectancies and marriage ages within the range of the probable. The series of tables illustrates the outcomes of differing assumptions and suggests that the differences in outcomes are not great enough to undermine the general conclusions drawn in the following chapters from the tables.

The demographic limitations to patriarchy are apparent from the simulations. Only a small fraction of Roman children would have been born during the lifetime of their paternal grandfather; on demographic grounds alone, most Romans could not have experienced a three-generation, patriarchal household. Furthermore, high mortality and late male marriage meant that many Roman women and most Roman men married for the first time after the death of their father, whose right to approve the choice of spouse was therefore of limited application. Despite a few sensational moral tales to the contrary, only a small proportion of Roman adults suffered under the continuing shadow of *patria potestas*, and for them legal institutions and social custom mitigated the effects of the strict rules of *potestas*.

The tables of simulation results indicate that the child who was orphaned before adulthood (that is, fatherless in Roman terms) was a far more common phenomenon than the Roman adult still in a father's legal power. To judge by the simulations, perhaps a third of Roman children lost their fathers before reaching puberty and another third became fatherless before the age of twenty-five ("the perfect age" in classical Roman law, after which a Roman was thought capable of assuming full managerial responsibility for his property). The pervasive presence of orphans offers a better understanding of the prominence of guardianship in the moral and juristic literature from Rome. Indeed, any account of economic decision-making in the empire should take account of the fact that a substantial fraction of the property was owned by children and managed by guardians whose primary aim is likely to have been protecting themselves from legal liability through conservative management, rather than optimizing profits.

Guardianship is one example of how knowledge of demographic contingencies and of the Roman normative order can provide a richer understanding of the extraordinary development of Roman legal instruments used to transmit property within the family. The emphasis in Roman social values on the house (rather than kin networks) made property a primary concern in the maintenance of the family's standing or the acquisition of higher status: the "good *paterfamilias*" in Roman thought was a man who husbanded his patrimony effectively for the next generation, rather than a good parent in the contemporary sense. *Pietas* stressed the Roman's obligation in his testamentary arrangements to look after "his or her own" (*sui*) – that is, children above all, then spouse, parent and other members of the household. From the beginning of the historical era Romans insisted on their legal power and rights to take care of "their own" in their individual ways through written documents, especially wills, trusts and dotal pacts. They resisted or circumvented legislation, such as the *lex Voconia* of 169 BC, that restricted their ability to distribute their property to their family and household as they saw fit. Roman law developed legal instruments of notable, though not quite unlimited, flexibility to permit the disposition of property according to the owner's wishes. The sources surveyed in chapter 7 suggest that Romans mostly deployed this flexibility not to free themselves from social norms but to meet their obligations to family and household in personalized ways. Within the bounds of normative expectations, Romans were able to use the flexibility allowed them because the moral obligations to "their own" were rather diffuse and vaguely formulated, and not as sharply defined by gender or seniority or blood as in later European societies. Roman inheritance was partible, but in such a loose sense that testators (male and female) enjoyed in the choice of heirs and legatees a wide latitude that translated into social power and influence.

The prominence of written legal instruments in the devolution of property in the upper classes is one of the most salient characteristics of Roman society, and of course one of enduring importance in European culture.[2] As a result of written wills and dotal agreements, there was nothing systematic or automatic about the transmission of property within the family – not choice of the beneficiaries, not the division of wealth, not the timing, not the appointment of a guardian. Although the law permitted a Roman to distribute his or her property before death, custom and individual interest tended to minimize transference of the family estate before that moment. One form of earlier transfer, the dowry, tended to be relatively modest in size and went through no discernible inflation through the four centuries of the classical era. Social expectation required fathers to provide their daughters with dowries large enough to supply maintenance in their conjugal household commensurate with the social standing of the husband. The level of expectation in accordance with status was a matter of common knowledge, according to the jurists, and must have limited the father's latitude in negotiation. Fathers commonly postponed transfer of ownership of the remainder of the daughter's share of the patrimony until their death: the greater the portion turned over directly to the daughter as inheritance, the more leverage she derived from the property in her marriage, and the more likely the property would go only to her children upon her death.

The practice of minimizing the devolution of property between generations before death had the effect of concentrating the decisions about intergenerational transfers in the terms of the Roman will.[3] The importance attached to the will in Roman culture can hardly be exaggerated. Its significance lay not only in the utilitarian function of the distribution of

[2] Comaroff and Roberts 1981 point out that the legal assumptions deeply embedded in European culture, going back to Roman law, have led to a misunderstanding of marriage and property devolution in non-European societies.

[3] Comaroff and Roberts 1981: 176–97 provide an instructive contrast of a society in which the transfer between generations starts at the birth of the child and progresses through his youth.

property, which could make or break the next generation, but also in the final, public expression of the testator's sense of duty and in the public gesture honoring kin and friends. By postponing the devolution until after death, testators retained to the end of their lives the social power that came from discretion over property. On the other hand, after death it was too late to oversee the procedures of division and to address in person all the legal and demographic uncertainties that might affect the division. Romans developed the trust (*fideicommissum*) in part to try to manage the processes of distribution of their patrimony after death in accordance with their personal sentiments and in the face of the unpredictable order of death of those around them. It is revealing of their sense of obligation and their strategies to achieve family status that they did not develop the trust to restrict the patrimony to the male line of descendants down through the generations. Those Roman trusts designed to guide property down through the generations usually benefitted freedmen and their offspring, who perpetuated the testator's name but not his blood.

Waiting until death to transmit the patrimony required testators to place considerable reliance on the legal system and trust in survivors to carry out their wishes. This was particularly so, if the beneficiary was among the substantial minority of heirs too young to protect their own interests – hence the moral imperative to carry out the duty of guardianship in good faith (*fides*) and the extensive elaboration of legal safeguards to protect the ward's estate. Here again the hallmark was the discretion granted to the testator to choose the men he most trusted to look after the interests of his child. That choice and the propensity to appoint multiple guardians for each child offered a testator the means to protect his vulnerable children from the automatic appointment of a close relative who had the reputation of being greedy or irresponsible.

It must be emphasized that the written will, with its potential for broad discretion, goes back to the XII Tables (451–50 BC). By the time Latin texts begin to provide contemporary testimony in the second century before Christ, that potential was already being used to pursue individual wishes within a set of norms socializing Romans in devotion to family after duty to the gods and the fatherland. If there was an early era when devolution was automatic and portions of the patrimony fixed (as there may well have been), it lies in the timeless darkness of prehistory, beyond the realm of social history.

My emphasis in this study on the complex interplay of demographic variables, a wide array of legal options, and mutual social obligations requires revision of the stark patriarchy traditionally associated with the Romans. The simple historical story of development from families marked by harsh paternal authoritarianism to families bound by affectionate concern fails to account for too much of the ancient testimony. At the normative level, it ignores the reciprocal quality of *pietas*. At the practical level, it fails to allow for the demographic realities with which Romans struggled.

There may be some comfort for modern Europeans in a neat, progressive history of development from ancient abuse of children by unsentimental, despotic fathers to loving care for children in the contemporary family. That evolutionary line continues to be repeated, even though it obviously derives from a self-serving, Judaeo-Christian point of view.[4] It must be remembered that it was the elder Cato two centuries before Christ who said that only a fool would lay a hand on what was most valuable and sacred to him, his wife and child. It was the Christian Augustine five centuries later who advocated the use of the whip on all household members to inculcate humility and obedience to God. Both based their quite different precepts concerning the discipline of children on the assumption of the father's loving concern for his household, but they started from different premises about the individual's place in a social system of honor and shame. More grimly, infant abandonment was not, despite assertions to the contrary, exclusively a pre-Christian practice of indifferent pagan parents, to be overcome by the progress of time. D. Kertzer's recent study leaves no doubt about the pervasiveness of infant abandonment and the shocking mortality rates among the abandoned in Christian Europe as late as the nineteenth century.[5] The example of Cato suggests that if a progressive view of history is warranted, it is not because parents have only recently learned to love their children, but because of the disappearance of status distinctions within the household that allowed Cato to treat his slaves as beasts of burden under the whip in contrast to his children, who were too precious to be beaten.

[4] Doniger 1993 offers a salutary challenge to the claim that the European family is especially gentle and humane because Judaism and Christianity have struggled against paternal aggression, in contrast to preceding, pagan cultures that indulged in the sacrifice of children.   [5] Kertzer 1993.

Bibliography

Allen, W. Jr. (1944) "Cicero's House and *Libertas*," *TAPA* 75: 1–9.

Amelotti, M. (1966) *Il testamento romano attraverso la prassi documentale*. Vol. 1. Florence.

Anderson, M. (1980) *Approaches to the History of the Western Family, 1500–1914*. London.

Andreau, J. and Bruhns, H., eds. (1990) *Parenté et stratégies familiales dans l'antiquité romaine: actes de la table ronde des 2–4 octobre 1986*. Rome.

Arangio-Ruiz, V. (1927) *Responsabilità contrattuale in diritto romano*. Naples.

   (1956) "Due nuove tavolette di Ercolano relative alla nomina di tutori muliebri," in *Studi in onore di Pietro De Francisci* 1.1–17. Milan.

   (1960) *Istituzioni di diritto romano*. 14th edn. Naples.

Badian, E. (1981) "The bitter history of slave history," *NYRB* October 22: 49.

Bagnall, R. S. and Frier, B. W. (1994) *The Demography of Roman Egypt*. Cambridge.

Balsdon, J. P. V. D. (1962) *Roman Women: Their History and Habits*. London.

   (1979) *Romans and Aliens*. Chapel Hill, N.C.

Beard, M. (1986) "New lines on ancient life," review of Rawson, B. M., ed., *The Family in Ancient Rome*. *TLS* June 20, 1986: 672.

Benveniste, E. (1973) *Indo-European Language and Society*. Tr. E. Palmer. London.

Berger, A. (1953) *Encyclopedic Dictionary of Roman Law*. Philadelphia.

Biscardi, A. (1972) "Nuove testimonianze di un papiro Arabo-guidaico per la storia del processo provinciale romano," in *Studi in onore di G. Scherillo*, 111–51. Milan.

Bonfield, L. (1979) "Marriage settlements and the 'rise of great estates': the demographic aspect," *Economic History Review* 32: 483–93.

Bourdieu, P. (1976) "Marriage strategies as strategies of social reproduction," in Forster, R. and Ranum, O., eds., *Family and Society*. Baltimore.

   (1984) *Distinction: A Social Critique of the Judgement of Taste*. Tr. R. Nice. Cambridge, Mass.

Boyer, G. (1950) "Le droit successoral romain dans les oeuvres de Polybe," *RIDA* 3rd ser. 4: 169–86.

Boyer, L. (1965) "La fonction sociale des legs d'après la jurisprudence classique," *RHDFE* 43: 333–408.
Bradley, K. R. (1984) *Slaves and Masters in the Roman Empire*. Brussels.
(1986) "Wet-nursing at Rome: a study in social relations," in Rawson, B. M., ed., 201–29.
(1991) *Discovering the Roman Family*. Oxford.
(1993) "Writing the history of the Roman family," *CP* 88: 237–50.
Brettell, C. B. (1991) "Property, kinship and gender: a Mediterranean perspective," in Kertzer, D. I. and Saller, R. P., eds., 340–53.
Brunt, P. A. (1971) *Italian Manpower 225 BC – AD 14*. Oxford.
(1988) *The Fall of the Roman Republic and Related Essays*. Oxford.
Buckland, W. W. (1963) *A Textbook of Roman Law*. 3rd edn. Rev. Peter Stein. Cambridge.
Buckland, W. W. and McNair, A. D. (1952) *Roman Law and Common Law*. 2nd edn. Rev. F. H. Lawson. Cambridge.
Burn, A. R. (1953) "*Hic breve vivitur*: a study of the expectation of life in the Roman empire," *P&P* 4: 2–31.
Cantarella, E. (1991) "Homicides of honor: the development of Italian adultery law over two millennia," in Kertzer, D. I. and Saller, R. P., eds., 229–44.
Carcopino, J. (1956) *Daily Life in Ancient Rome*. Tr. E. O. Lorimer. Penguin edn. London.
Carron, R. (1989) *Enfant et parenté dans la France médiévale: Xe – XIIIe siècles*. Geneva.
Carstairs, G. M. (1957) *The Twice-born*. London.
Casey, J. (1989) *The History of the Family*. New York.
Champlin, E. (1986) "Miscellanea testamentaria," *ZPE* 62: 247–55.
(1991) *Final Judgments: Duty and Emotion in Roman Wills, 200 BC – AD 250*. Berkeley and Los Angeles.
Coale, A. J., Demeny, P., and Vaughan, B. (1983) *Regional Model Life Tables and Stable Populations*. 2nd edn. New York.
Coale, A. J. and McNeill, R. R. (1972) "The distribution by age of the frequency of first marriage in a female cohort," *Journal of the American Statistical Association* 67: 743–49.
Cohen, D. (1991) "The Augustan law on adultery: the social and cultural context," in Kertzer, D. I. and Saller, R. P., eds., 109–26.
Cohen, D. and Saller, R. (1994) "Foucault on sexuality in Greco-Roman antiquity," in Goldstein, J., ed., *Foucault and the Writing of History*, 36–59. Oxford.
Comaroff, J. L. and Roberts, S. (1981) *Rules and Processes: The Cultural Logic of Dispute in an African Context*. Chicago.
Connor, W. R. (1985) "The razing of the house in Greek society," *TAPA* 115: 79–102.
Cooper, J. P. (1976) "Patterns of inheritance and settlement by great landowners from the fifteenth to the eighteenth centuries," in Goody, J., Thirsk, J. and Thompson, E. P., eds., *Family and Inheritance: Rural Society in Western Europe, 1200–1800*, 192–327. Cambridge.
Corbett, P. E. (1930) *The Roman Law of Marriage*. Oxford.

Corbier, M. (1985) "Idéologie et pratique de l'héritage (Ier s. av. J.-C. – IIe s. ap. J.-C.)," *Index* 13: 501–28.

(1990) "Les comportements familiaux de l'aristocratie romaine (IIe siècle av. J.-C. – IIIe siècle ap. J.-C.)," in Andreau, J. and Bruhns, H., eds., 225–49.

(1991a) "Divorce and adoption as Roman familial strategies," in Rawson, B. M., ed., 47–78.

(1991b) "La descendance d'Hortensius et de Marcia," *MEFRA* 103: 655–701.

Coulanges, Fustel de (1980) *The Ancient City*. Baltimore.

Crawford, M. H. (1974) *Roman Republican Coinage*. Cambridge.

Crook, J. (1967a) *Law and Life of Rome*. London and Ithaca, N.Y.

(1967b) "*Patria potestas*," *CQ* n.s. 17: 113–22.

(1973) "Intestacy in Roman society," *PCPhS* 19: 38–44.

(1986a) "Women in Roman succession," in Rawson, B. M., ed., 58–82.

(1986b) "Feminine inadequacy and the *Senatusconsultum Velleianum*," in Rawson, B. M., ed., 83–92.

(1990) "'His and Hers': What degree of financial responsibility did husband and wife have for the matrimonial home and their life in common, in a Roman marriage?," in Andreau, J. and Bruhns, H., eds., 153–72.

Curchin, L. A. (1982) "Familial epithets in the epigraphy of Roman Spain," in *Mélanges Etienne Gareau*, 179–82. Ottawa.

Dalla, D. (1978) *L'incapacità sessuale in diritto romano*. Milan.

Daube, D (1947) "Did Macedo murder his father?" *ZSS rom* 65: 261–311.

(1953) "Actions between *paterfamilias* and *filiusfamilias* with *peculium castrense*," in *Studi Albertario*, 433–74. Milan.

(1965) "The preponderance of intestacy at Rome," *Tulane Law Review* 39: 253–62.

(1969) *Roman Law: Linguistic, Social and Philosophical Aspects*. Edinburgh.

Davis, J. C. (1975) *A Venetian Family and its Fortune, 1500–1900*. Philadelphia.

DeMause, L., ed. (1974) *The History of Childhood*. London.

Dixon, S. (1985a) "Polybius on Roman women and property," *AJPh* 106: 147–70.

(1985b) "Breaking the law to do the right thing: the gradual erosion of the Voconian law in ancient Rome," *Adelaide Law Review* 9: 519–34.

(1985c) "The marriage alliance in the Roman elite," *Journal of Family History* 10: 353–78.

(1986) "Family finances: Terentia and Tullia," in Rawson, B. M., ed., 93–120.

(1988) *The Roman Mother*. London.

(1991) "The sentimental ideal of the Roman family," in Rawson, B. M., ed., 99–113.

(1992) *The Roman Family*. Baltimore.

Doniger, W. (1993) "Why God changed his mind about Isaac," review of Bergmann, M. S., *In the Shadow of Moloch: The Sacrifice of Children and its Impact on Western Religions*. *New York Times Book Review*, August 1: 17.

Dumont, F. (1943) "Les revenues de la dot en droit romain," *RHDFE* 21: 1–43.

Dumont, J. C. (1990) "L'*imperium* du *paterfamilias*" in Andreau, J. and Bruhns, H., eds., 475–95.

Duncan-Jones, R. (1982) *The Economy of the Roman Empire.* 2nd edn. Cambridge.
   (1990) *Structure and Scale in the Roman Economy.* Cambridge.
Eck, W. (1978) "Zum neuen Fragment des sogenannten *Testamentum Dasumii*," *ZPE* 30: 277–95.
   (1988) "Aussagefähigkeit epigraphischer Statistik und die Bestattung von Sklaven im kaiserzeitlichen Rom," in *Alte Geschichte und Wissenschaftsgeschichte, Festschrift für Karl Christ,* 130–39. Darmstadt.
Ernout, A. (1932) "*Domus, fores* et leurs substituts," *RPh* 3rd ser. 6: 297–314.
Evans, J. K. (1991) *War, Women and Children in Ancient Rome.* London and New York.
Eyben, E. (1991) "Fathers and sons," in Rawson, B. M., ed., 114–43.
Ferguson, J. (1964) *Moral Values in the Ancient World.* New York.
Finley, M. I. (1980) *Ancient Slavery and Modern Ideology.* London.
Flandrin, J. L. (1979) *Families in Former Times.* Tr. R. Southern. Cambridge.
Flory, M. (1978) "Family in *familia*: kinship and community in slavery," *AJAH* 3: 78–95.
Fogel, R. W. (1991) "The conquest of high mortality and hunger in Europe and America: Timing and mechanisms," in Higonnet, P., Landes, D. S., and Rosovsky, H., eds., *Favorites of Fortune: Technology, Growth, and Economic Development since the Industrial Revolution,* 33–71. Cambridge, Mass.
Forster, R. (1960) *The Nobility of Toulouse in the Eighteenth Century: A Social and Economic Study.* Baltimore.
Fortes, Meyer (1970) "Pietas in ancestor worship," in *Time and Social Structure,* 164–200. London.
Freedman, M. (1966) *Chinese Lineage and Society.* London.
Friedläender, L. (1908) *Roman Life and Manners under the Early Empire.* Tr. L. A. Magnus. London.
Frier, B. (1982) "Roman life expectancy: Ulpian's evidence," *HSCP* 86: 213–51.
   (1983) "Roman life expectancy: the Pannonian evidence," *Phoenix* 37: 328–44.
   (1992) "Statistics and Roman society," *JRA* 5: 286–90.
Furneaux, H., ed. (1965) *The Annals of Tacitus.* Ed. with introduction and notes. 2nd edn. Oxford.
Gardner, J. F. (1985) "The recovery of dowry in Roman law," *CQ* 35: 449–53.
   (1986) *Women in Roman Law and Society.* Bloomington, Ind.
   (1987) "Another family and an inheritance: Claudius Brasidas and his ex-wife's will," *LCM* 12.4: 52–54.
Garnsey, P. D. A. (1968) "Why penalties become harsher: the Roman case, late Republic to fourth century empire," *Natural Law Forum* 13: 141–62.
   (1970) *Social Status and Legal Privilege in the Roman Empire.* Oxford.
   (1988) *Famine and Food Supply in the Graeco-Roman World: Responses to Risk and Crisis.* Cambridge.
   (1991) "Child rearing in ancient Italy," in Kertzer, D. I. and Saller, R. P., eds., 48–65.
Gaunt, D. (1983) "The property and kin relationships of retired farmers in northern and central Europe," in Wall, R., Robin, J., and Laslett, P., eds., 249–79.

Genovese, E. (1972) *Roll, Jordan, Roll*. New York.

Giddens, A. (1979) *Central Problems in Social Theory: Action, Structure, and Contradiction in Social Analysis*. Berkeley and Los Angeles.

Goffman, Erving (1967) *Interaction Ritual: Essays in Face-to-Face Behaviour*. Chicago.

Golden, M. (1988) "Did the ancients care when their children died?" *G&R* 35: 152–63.

Goodman, M. (1991) "Babatha's story," *JRS* 81: 169–75.

Goody, J. (1962) *Death, Property and the Ancestors*. Stanford.

(1976) *Production and Reproduction*. Cambridge.

(1983) *The Development of the Family and Marriage in Europe*. Cambridge.

(1990) *The Oriental, the Ancient and the Primitive*. Cambridge.

Goody, J. and Tambiah, S. J. (1973) *Bridewealth and Dowry*. Cambridge.

Grant, M. (1967) *Gladiators: Pageants of History*. London.

Gray-Fow, M. J. G. (1988) "The wicked stepmother in Roman literature and history," *Latomus* 47: 741–57.

Greenwood, M. (1940) "A statistical mare's nest?" *Journal of the Royal Statistical Society* 103: 246–48.

Grelle, F. (1960) "Datio tutoris e organi cittadini nel basso impero," *Labeo* 6: 216–25.

Guarino, A. (1948) "Notazioni romanistiche," in *Studi in onore di S. Solazzi*: 26–41. Naples.

Hajnal, J. (1953) "Age at marriage and proportions marrying," *Population Studies* 7: 111–36.

(1965) "European marriage patterns in perspective," in Glass, D. V. and Eversley, D. E. C., eds., *Population in History*, 101–43. London.

(1983) "Two kinds of pre-industrial household formation system," in Wall, R., Robin, J., and Laslett, P., eds., 65–104.

Hansen, S. A. (1972) "Changes in the wealth and the demographic characteristics of the Danish aristocracy, 1470–1720," *Third International Conference of Economic History* III (The Hague): 91–162.

Harkness, A. G. (1896) "Age at marriage and at death in the Roman empire," *TAPA* 27: 35–72.

Harris, W. V. (1986) "The Roman father's power of life and death," in *Studies in Roman Law in Memory of A. Arthur Schiller*, 81–95. Leiden.

Hart, H. L. A. (1961) *The Concept of Law*. Oxford.

Held, T. (1982) "Rural retirement arrangements in seventeenth- to nineteenth-century Austria: A cross-community analysis," *Journal of Family History* 7: 227–54.

Henrion, R. (1941) "Des origines du mot *familia*," *AntCl* 10: 37–69.

(1942) "Des origines du mot *familia*," *AntCl* 11: 253–87.

Herlihy, D. (1983) "The making of the medieval family: symmetry, structure, and sentiment," *Journal of Family History* 8: 116–30.

(1985) *Medieval Households*. Cambridge, Mass.

Herlihy, D. and Klapisch-Zuber, C. (1985) *Tuscans and their Families: A Study of the Florentine Catasto of 1427*. New Haven.

Hinard, F., ed. (1987) *La mort, les morts, et l'au-delà dans le monde romain. Actes du colloque de Caen*. Caen.

Hopkins, K. (1965) "The age of Roman girls at marriage," *Population Studies* 18: 309–27.

(1966) "On the probable age structure of the Roman population," *Population Studies* 20: 245–64.

(1983) *Death and Renewal*. Cambridge.

(1987) "Graveyard for historians," in Hinard, F., ed., 113–26.

Howell, N. (1976) "Toward a uniformitarian theory of human paleodemography," in Ward, R. H. and Weiss, K. M., eds., *The Demographic Evolution of Human Populations*, 25–40. London.

Hsu, F. (1967) *Under the Ancestors' Shadow*. Garden City, N.Y. (originally published 1948).

Hughes, D. O. (1975) "Urban growth and family structure in medieval Genoa," *P&P* 66: 3–28.

Humbert, M. (1972) *Le Remariage à Rome: étude d'histoire juridique et sociale*. Milan.

(1990) "L'individu, l'état: quelle stratégie pour le mariage classique," in Andreau, J. and Bruhns, H., eds., 173–98.

Johnson, W. R. (1965) "Aeneas and the ironies of *pietas*," *CJ* 60: 360–64.

(1986) "The figure of Laertes: reflections on the character of Aeneas," in *Vergil at 2000: Commemorative Essays on the Poet and his Influence*, 85–105. New York.

Johnston, D. (1985) "Prohibitions and perpetuities: family settlements in Roman law," *ZSS rom* 102: 220–90.

(1988) *The Roman Law of Trusts*. Oxford.

Jolowicz, H. F. (1947) "The wicked guardian," *JRS* 37: 82–90.

Jones, C. P. (1978) *The Roman World of Dio Chrysostom*. Cambridge, Mass.

Kajanto, I. (1969) "On divorce among the common people of Rome," *REL* 47 bis: 99–113.

Kaser, M. (1938) "Der Inhalt der *patria potestas*," *ZSS rom* 71: 62–87.

(1949) "Die Rechtsgrundlage der *actio rei uxoriae*," *RIDA* 2: 511–50.

(1959) *Das römische Privatrecht*. Vol. 2. Munich.

(1971) *Das römische Privatrecht*. 2nd ed. Vol. 1. Munich.

Klapisch-Zuber, C. (1991) "Kinship and politics in fourteenth-century Florence," in Kertzer, D. I. and Saller, R. P., eds., 208–28.

Kertzer, D. I. (1993) *Sacrificed for Honor: Italian Infant Abandonment and the Politics of Reproductive Control*. Boston.

Kertzer, D. I. and Saller R. P., eds. (1991) *The Family in Italy from Antiquity to the Present*. New Haven.

Kleiner, D. (1977) *Roman Group Portraiture: The Funerary Reliefs of the Late Republic and Early Empire*. New York.

Koesterman, E., ed. (1963) *Cornelius Tacitus, Annalen: Erläutert und mit einer Einleitung*. Heidelberg.

Konstan, D. (1983) *Roman Comedy*. Ithaca, N.Y.

Koschaker, P. (1930) "Unterhalt der Ehefrau und Früchte der Dos," in *Studi P. Bonfante* 4. 3–27.

Laslett, P. (1977) *Family Life and Illicit Love*. Cambridge.
   (1988) "La parenté en chiffres," *Annales, ESC* 43: 5–24.
   (1989) *A Fresh Map of Life: The Emergence of the Third Age*. London.
Leach, E. W. (1971) "Horace's *Pater optimus* and Terence's Demea: Autobiographical fiction and comedy in Sermo I,4," *AJPh* 92: 616–32.
Lecomte, A. (1928) *La pluralité des tuteurs en droit romain*. Paris.
Lee, M. O. (1979) *Fathers and Sons in Virgil's "Aeneid": Tum Genitor Natum*. Albany, N.Y.
Leonhard, R. (1909) "*Familia*," *RE* XII, 1980–84.
Levick, B. M. (1972) "Abdication and Agrippa Postumus," *Historia* 21: 674–97.
Lewis, N. (1970) "On paternal authority in Roman Egypt," *RIDA* 3rd ser. 17: 251–58.
Lintott, A. (1972) "*Provocatio*: from the struggle of the orders to the principate," in H. Temporini, ed. *ANRW* I.2: 226–67.
Litchfield, R. B. (1969) "Demographic characteristics of Florentine patrician families, sixteenth to nineteenth centuries," *Journal of Economic History* 29: 191–205.
Livi-Bacci, M. (1991) *Population and Nutrition: An Essay on European Demographic History*. Tr. T. Croft-Murray. Cambridge.
MacCormack, G. (1970) "The liability of the tutor in classical Roman law," *Irish Jurist* 5: 369–90.
MacFarlane, A. (1980) "Demographic structures and cultural regions in Europe," *Cambridge Anthropology* 6: 1–17.
MacMullen, R. (1966) *Enemies of the Roman Order*. Cambridge, Mass.
   (1974) *Roman Social Relations, 50 BC to AD 284*. New Haven.
   (1986) "Judicial savagery in the Roman empire," *Chiron* 16: 147–66.
Maine, H. S. (1861) *Ancient Law*. London.
Manson, M. (1975) "La *pietas* et le sentiment de l'enfance à Rome d'après les monnaies," *Revue Belge de numismatique et de sigillographie* 121: 21–80.
   (1983) "The Emergence of the small child in Rome (third century BC–first century AD," *History of Education* 12: 149–59.
Marshall, A. J. (1989) "Ladies at law: the role of women in the Roman civil courts," in Deroux, C., ed., *Studies in Latin Literature and Roman History V. Collection Latomus* 206, 35–54. Brussels.
Matringe, G. (1971) "La puissance paternelle et le mariage des fils et filles de famille en droit romain," in *Studi E. Volterra* 5. 191–237. Milan.
McRae, K. D., ed. (1962) *The Six Bookes of a Commonweale*, by Jean Bodin, 1606. Tr. R. Knolles. Cambridge, Mass.
Meyer, E., (1990) "Explaining the epigraphic habit in the Roman empire: the evidence of epitaphs," *JRS* 80: 74–96.
Millar, F. (1984) "Condemnation to hard labour in the Roman empire, from the Julio-Claudians to Constantine," *PBSR* 52: 124–47.
Mitterauer, M. and Sieder, R. (1983) "The reconstruction of the family life course: theoretical problems and empirical results," in Wall, R., Robin, J., and Laslett, P., eds., 309–45.
Momigliano, A. (1966) *Studies in Historiography*. London.

Mommsen, T. (1887) Römisches Staatsrecht, Handbuch der römischen Alterthümer. Vols. 1, 2, 3. Tübingen.

Moreau, P. (1986) "Patrimoines et successions à Larinum au Ier siècle av. J.-C.," RHDFE 64: 169–89.

(1990) "Adfinitas: la parenté par alliance dans la société romaine (Ier siècle av. J.-C.–IIe siècle ap. J.-C.)," in Andreau, J. and Bruhns, H., eds., 3–26.

Morgan, L. H. (1877) Ancient Society. London.

Morris, I. (1992) Death-Ritual and Social Structure in Classical Antiquity. Cambridge.

Néraudau, J.-P. (1984) Etre enfant à Rome. Paris.

Newell, C. (1988) Methods and Models in Demography. London.

Nicolet, Cl. (1974) L'ordre équestre à l'époque républicaine. Vol. 2. Paris.

North, J. A. (1989) "Religion in republican Rome," in Cambridge Ancient History, 2nd edn. 7.2, 573–624. Cambridge.

Orr, D. G. (1978) "Roman domestic religion: the evidence of the household shrines," in Temporini, H., ed., ANRW II.16.2: 1557–91.

Osborne, R. (1988) "Social and economic implications of the leasing of land and property in classical and Hellenistic Greece," Chiron 18: 279–323.

Ozment, S. (1983) When Fathers Ruled: Family Life in Reformation Europe. Cambridge, Mass.

Pailler, J.-M. (1990) "Les Bacchanales: une affaire de famille," in Andreau, J. and Bruhns, H., eds., 77–83.

Parker, H. (1989) "Crucially funny or, Tranio on the couch: The servus callidus and jokes about torture," TAPA 119: 233–46.

Parkin, T. (1992) Demography and Roman Society. Baltimore.

Patterson, O. (1982) Slavery and Social Death. Cambridge, Mass.

Pitt-Rivers, J. (1977) The Fate of Shechem, or the Politics of Sex. Cambridge.

Platner, S. B. (1929) A Topographical Dictionary of Ancient Rome. Completed and revised by Thomas Ashby. London.

Pollock, L. A. (1983) Forgotten Children. Parent–Child Relations from 1500 to 1900. Cambridge.

Pomeroy, S. (1976) "The relationship of the married woman to her blood relatives in Rome," Ancient Society 7: 215–27.

Purcell, N. (1987) "Tomb and suburb," in Hesberg, H. and Zanker, P., eds. Römische Gräberstrassen: Selbstdarstellung-Status-Standard. Bayerische Akademie der Wissenschaften, Philosophisch-historische Klasse 96, 25–41. Munich.

Rabel, E. (1930) "Negotium alienum und animus," in Studi P. Bonfante 5. 296–98. Milan.

Rabello, A. M. (1979) Effetti personali della 'patria potestas.' Milan.

Raepsaet-Charlier, M.-Th. (1981–82) "Ordre sénatorial et divorce sous le haut-empire: un chapitre de l'histoire des mentalités," ACD 17–18: 161–73.

Rawick, G. P., ed. (1972) The American Slave: A Composite Autobiography. Westport, Conn.

Rawson, B. M., ed. (1986) The Family in Ancient Rome: New Perspectives. Ithaca, N.Y.

ed. (1991) Marriage, Divorce and Children in Ancient Rome. Oxford.

Renier, E. (1942) Etude sur l'histoire de la querela inofficiosi en droit romain. Liège.

Reynolds, J., Beard, M., and Roueché, C. (1986) "Roman inscriptions 1981–5," *JRS* 76: 124–46.

Richardson, L. Jr. (1992) *A New Topographical Dictionary of Ancient Rome*. Baltimore.

Roberti, M. (1935) "*Patria potestas e paterna pietas*," in *Studi A. Albertoni*. 1. 259–63. Padua.

Rostovtzeff, M. I. (1957) *Social and Economic History of the Roman Empire*. 2nd edn. Oxford.

Ruggles, S. (1987) *Prolonged Connections: The Rise of the Extended Family in Nineteenth-Century England and America*. Madison.

Ste. Croix, G. E. M. de (1981) *The Class Struggle in the Ancient Greek World*. London.

Saller, R. P. (1982) *Personal Patronage under the Early Empire*. Cambridge.

(1984) "*Familia, domus*, and the Roman conception of the family," *Phoenix* 38: 336–55.

(1986) "*Patria potestas* and the stereotype of the Roman family," *Continuity and Change* 1: 7–22.

(1987a) "Men's age at marriage and its consequences in the Roman family," *CP* 82: 21–34.

(1987b) "Slavery and the Roman family," *Slavery and Abolition* 8: 65–87.

(1988) "*Pietas*, obligation and authority in the Roman family," in *Alte Geschichte und Wissenschaftsgeschichte: Festschrift für Karl Christ*, 393–410. Darmstadt.

(1991a) "Roman heirship strategies in principle and in practice," in Kertzer, D. I. and Saller, R. P., eds., 26–47.

(1991b) "European family history and Roman law," *Continuity and Change* 6: 335–46.

(1993) "The social dynamics of consent to marriage and sexual relations," in Laiou, A., ed., *Consent and Coercion to Sex and Marriage in Ancient and Medieval Societies*, 83–104. Washington, D.C.

Saller, R. P. and Shaw, B. D. (1984a) "Tombstones and Roman family relations in the principate: civilians, soldiers and slaves," *JRS* 74: 124–56.

(1984b) "Close-kin marriage in Roman society," *Man* 19: 432–44.

Salomies, O. (1992) *Adoptive and Polyonymous Nomenclature in the Roman Empire*. Commentationes Humanarum Litterarum 97. Helsinki.

Schaps, D. (1979) *Economic Rights of Women in Ancient Greece*. Edinburgh.

Schuhmann, Elisabeth (1976) "Ehescheidungen in den Komödien des Plautus," *ZSS rom.* 93: 19–32.

(1977) "Der Typ der *uxor dotata* in den Komödien des Plautus," *Philologus* 121: 45–65.

Schulz, F. (1951) *Classical Roman Law*. Oxford.

Scobie, A. (1986) "Slums, sanitation, and mortality in the Roman world," *Klio* 68: 399–433.

Scott, A. F. (1970) *The Southern Lady: From Pedestal to Politics, 1830–1930*. Chicago.

Segal, E. (1968) *Roman Laughter: The Comedy of Plautus*. Cambridge, Mass.

Shackleton Bailey, D. R. (1977) *Epistulae ad Familiares*. Cambridge.

Shatzman, I. (1975) *Senatorial Wealth and Roman Politics*. Brussels.

Shaw, B. D. (1984) "Bandits in the Roman empire," *P&P* 105: 3–52.

(1987a) "The age of Roman girls at marriage: some reconsiderations," *JRS* 77: 30–46.

(1987b) "The family of late antiquity: the experience of Augustine," *P&P* 115: 3–51.

(1991) "The cultural meaning of death: age and gender in the Roman family," in Kertzer, D. I. and Saller, R. P., eds., 66–90.

(forthcoming) "Death in a large city: Christian Rome."

Simmel, G. (1950) *The Sociology of Georg Simmel.* Tr. and ed. K. Wolff. Glencoe, Ill.

Smith, J. E. (1989) "Method and confusion in the study of the household," *Historical Methods* 22: 57–60.

Smith, J. E. and Oeppen, J. (1993) "Estimating numbers of kin in historical England using demographic microsimulation," in Schofield, R. and Reher, D., eds., *Old and New Methods in Historical Demography.* Oxford.

Solazzi, S. (1913) *La minore età.* Rome.

(1917) *Curator impuberis.* Rome.

(1955) *Scritti di diritto romano, I (1899–1913).* Naples.

(1956) "La *datio tutoris* nelle tavolette di Ercolano," *Labeo* 2: 7–17.

(1957) *Scritti di diritto romano, II (1913–1924).* Naples.

(1958) "Magistrati municipali alla ricerca di tutori idonei," *Labeo* 4: 150–53.

(1960) *Scritti di diritto romano, III (1925–1937).* Naples.

(1963) "Divortium bona gratia," *RIL* 71: 511–24.

(1973) "Tutele e curatela (diritto romano)," *Novissimo Digesto Italiano* 19: 912–18. Turin.

Stone, L. (1965) *The Crisis of the Aristocracy, 1558–1641.* Oxford.

(1977) *The Family, Sex and Marriage in England 1500–1800.* London.

Syme, R. (1986) *The Augustan Aristocracy.* Oxford.

(1987) "Marriage ages for Roman senators," *Historia* 36: 318–32.

Tellegen, J. W. (1982) *The Roman Law of Succession in the Letters of Pliny the Younger.* Zutphen, Holland.

Thomas, J. A. C. (1958) "Perpetuities and fideicommissary substitutions," *RIDA* 3rd ser. 5: 571–90.

(1976) *Textbook of Roman Law.* Amsterdam.

Thomas, Y. P. (1980) "Mariages endogamiques à Rome: patrimoine, pouvoir et parenté depuis l'époque archaïque," *RHDFE* 58: 345–82.

(1981) "*Parricidium* I. Le père, la famille et la cité," *MEFRA* 93: 643–715.

(1982) "Droit domestique et droit politique à Rome: remarques sur le pécule et les *honores* des fils de famille," *MEFRA* 94: 527–80.

(1984) "*Vitae necisque potestas*: le père, la cité, la mort," in *Du châtiment dans la cité: supplices corporels et peine de mort dans le monde antique,* 499–548. Rome.

(1990) "Remarques sur la jurisdiction domestique à Rome," in Andreau, J. and Bruhns, H., eds., 449–74.

Toynbee, J. M. C. and Ward-Perkins, J. (1956) *The Shrine of St. Peter and the Vatican Excavations.* London.

Treggiari, S. (1982) "Consent to Roman marriage: some aspects of law and reality," *EMC/CV* n.s. 1: 34–44.

(1984) "*Digna condicio*: betrothals in the Roman upper class," *EMC/CV* n.s. 3: 419–51.

(1991a) *Roman Marriage*: '*Iusti Coniuges*' *from the Time of Cicero to the Time of Ulpian*. Oxford.

(1991b) "Ideals and practicalities in matchmaking in Ancient Rome," in Kertzer, D. I. and Saller, R. P., eds., 91–108.

(1991c) "Divorce Roman style: how easy and frequent was it?," in Rawson, B. M., ed., 31–46.

(1995) "Social status and social legislation," in *Cambridge Ancient History* X. 2nd edn.

Tripp-Reimer, T. and Wilson, S. (1991) "Cross-cultural perspectives on fatherhood," in Bozett, F. W. and Hanson, S. M. H., eds., *Fatherhood and Families in Cultural Context*, 1–27. New York.

Veyne, P. (1978) "La famille et l'amour sous le haut empire romain," *Annales, ESC* 33: 35–63.

ed. (1987) *A History of Private Life: From Pagan Rome to Byzantium*. Cambridge, Mass.

Voci, P. (1963–67) *Diritto ereditario romano*. 2nd edn. Milan.

(1970) "La responsabilità dei contutori e degli amministratori cittadini," *Iura* 21: 71–154.

(1980) "Storia della *patria potestas* da Augusto a Diocleziano," *Iura* 31: 37–100.

Volterra, E. (1948) "Quelques observations sur le mariage des *filiifamilias*," *RIDA* 1: 213–42.

Wagenvoort, H. (1980) *Pietas: Selected Studies in Roman Religion*. Leiden.

Wall, R., Robin, J. and Laslett, P., eds. (1983) *Family Forms in Historic Europe*. Cambridge.

Wallace-Hadrill, A. (1988) "The social structure of the Roman house," *PBSR* 56: 43–97.

(1991) "Houses and household: sampling Pompeii and Herculaneum," in Rawson, B. M., ed., 191–227.

Watson, A. (1961) "*Captivitas* and *matrimonium*," *TvR* 29: 243–59.

(1967) *The Law of Persons in the Later Roman Republic*. Oxford.

(1971a) *The Law of Succession in the Later Roman Republic*. Oxford.

(1971b) *Roman Private Law around 200 BC*. Edinburgh.

(1975) *Rome of the XII Tables: Persons and Property*. Princeton.

(1987) *Roman Slave Law*. Baltimore.

Weaver, P. R. C. (1972) *Familia Caesaris*. Cambridge.

(1991) "Children of freedmen (and freedwomen)," in Rawson, B. M., ed., 166–90.

Wenger, L. (1924) "Hausgewalt und Staatsgewalt im römischen Altertum," *Miscellanea F. Ehrle*. 2: 1–55. Rome.

Wiedemann, T. (1989) *Adults and Children in the Roman Empire*. London.

Wiseman, T. P. (1971) *New Men in the Roman Senate, 139 BC–14 AD*. Oxford.

(1985) *Catullus and his World*. Cambridge.

Wolf, A. P. and Huang, Chieh-shan (1980) *Marriage and Adoption in China, 1845–1945.* Stanford.

Wolf, M. (1970) "Child training and the Chinese family," in Freedman, M., ed., *Family and Kinship in Chinese Society,* 37–62. Stanford.

Wolff, H. J. (1933) "Zur Stellung der Frau im klassischen römischen Dotalrecht," *ZSS rom.* 53: 297–371.

Wrightson, K. and Levine, D. (1979) *Poverty and Piety in an English Village.* London.

Wrigley, E. A. (1969) *Population and History.* New York.

Wrigley, E. A. and Schofield, R. S. (1981) *The Population History of England 1541–1871.* Cambridge, Mass.

Yadin, Y. (1989) *The Documents from the Bar Kokhba Period in the Cave of Letters: Greek Papyri.* Ed. N. Lewis. Judean Desert Studies II. Jerusalem.

Zulueta, F. de (1953) *The Institutes of Gaius, pt. II, Commentary.* Oxford.

Index of subjects and proper names

Cambridge Studies in Population, Economy and Society in Past Time

Titles available in paperback are marked with an asterisk